Media Composer® Fundamentals II

Avid Technology, Inc.

ISBN eBook: 978-1-943446-25-4

ISBN: 978-1-943446-24-7

eBook Part Number: 9511-65981-00

Part Number: 9320-70052-00 - July 2016

This book includes material that was developed in part by the Avid Technical Publications department and the Avid Training department.

Acknowledgments

Avid Education would like to recognize the following contributors for the development of this book:

Bryan Castle, Jr., Nicole Kemper, Ben Hershleder, Christine Tilden, Frank Cook, and Karleen McAllester.

We would also like to recognize the immeasurable contributions of the worldwide community of Avid Certified Instructors for their ongoing suggestions and comments, based on their experience in the classroom and their professional expertise, which have resulted in the continued improvement of Avid's curriculum.

About the Media

Avid Education would like to thank our partners for generously providing the media, music and sound effects used in this course.

EditStock

In proud partnership with Avid, EditStock.com provided much of the footage in this course. Schools have the option to upgrade their footage packages, gaining the following features:

- Un-watermarked footage.
- Usage rights for student demo reels.
- Additional footage for every project.
- Lined scripts and music.
- Higher resolutions such as ProRes and RED.

EditStock, footage worth Editing.

PremiumBeat.com

PremiumBeat.com is a curated royalty-free music website that provides high quality tracks and sound effects for use in new and traditional media projects. Our library is sourced from the world's leading producers with exclusive, pre-cleared music. This allows for a smooth licensing experience on popular video sharing sites like YouTube and Vimeo.

With thousands of handpicked tracks in more than 30 styles, PremiumBeat music is ideal for online videos, mobile apps, television, radio, feature films and other professional applications. Be sure to also check out the PremiumBeat blog for the latest news and tutorials on production and post-production.

Hollywood Camera Work

Filmmakers working to solve the problems that no one else was solving. Our courses and software come from decades of intense work on cracking the code of filmmaking and storytelling, and making maps that actually lead somewhere.

http://www.hollywoodcamerawork.com/

Pond5

Explore the world's largest collection of royalty-free video and more.

https://www.pond5.com

Table of Contents

.

Introduction

Welcome to Media Composer Fundamentals II and the Avid Learning Series. Whether you are interested in self-study or would like to pursue formal certification through an Avid Learning Partner, this book provides the first step toward developing your core skills and introduces you to the power of Media Composer software. In addition, Media Composer Fundamentals II is the second course of study for those pursuing Media Composer User certification.

The material in this book deepens the skills taught in Fundamentals I and will introduce you to more advanced techniques in editing, media management, effects, and delivery. Media Composer Fundamentals II will teach you what you need to know to be successful with Media Composer at a higher level.

Using This Book

This book has been designed to familiarize you with the practices and processes you will use to complete a Media Composer project. Lessons and exercises focus on a phase of the editing process, and will take you from syncing dailies, through editing and revision, and finally into sound mixing, effects, and title creation. You will learn all the tools required to successfully deliver a project from beginning to end.

Using the Course Material

The MC110 course media can be downloaded from EditStock.com (see "Downloading Media" below). Once the media is downloaded, you will then need to follow the "Installation Instructions" to place the media files in the correct locations on your system.

Downloading Media

If you have taken the MC101 class and already created an EditStock.com/Avid account, login to your account. Your instructor will provide you with the access code for your MC110 media.

If this is your first Media Composer class and you do not have an EditStock.com account, follow the link below for instructions on how to create an Editstock.com/Avid account, enter an access code (provided by your instructor), and ultimately download the media

Go to http://editstock.com/avidsupport for instructions.

Installation Instructions

You will download three zip files. Unzip the files and you should see three folders called "MC110_1," "MC110_2," and "MC110_3" respectively. These folders contain the project files and media required to complete the exercises in this book.

These need to be installed on your system. Please follow the instructions (below) exactly or you may not have access to all the project files and media associated with this course.

In each folder you will find sub folders containing the following:

- **MC110_1:**

  - **Course Materials**

    - Project Files

      - MC110_TN PARKOUR

      - MC110_EFFECTS

        These project folders will be used to complete the exercises in the book. Copy them to the following location:

        - Windows: Library\Public Documents\Shared Avid Projects\

        - Mac: Users\Shared\AvidMediaComposer\Shared Avid Projects\

    - Supplemental Media

      This folder contains additional media that will be needed to complete several project exercises. Store these on your computer's hard drive or external hard drive until they are needed. DO NOT put them in the "Avid MediaFiles" folder.

  - **Avid MediaFiles**

    Place this folder on the root level of your computer's hard drive or the external hard drive you are working off of. This folder contains the project media.

- MC110_2

  - <u>111</u>

    This folder contains project media. Place it in the "MXF" folder located in the "Avid MediaFiles" folder on your computer's hard drive or the external hard drive you are working off of.

- MC110_3

  - <u>112</u>

    This folder contains project media. Place it in the "MXF" folder located in the "Avid MediaFiles" folder on your computer's hard drive or the external hard drive you are working off of.

 Do not rename or move the Avid MediaFiles folder located on the media drive. Media Composer uses the folder names to locate the media files.

Prerequisites

This course is designed for those who have completed the Media Composer Fundamentals I coursework whether they are new to professional video editing or are experienced professional editors who are still becoming familiar with Media Composer software. Although this book is not aimed at teaching the theory behind film and television editing, the content of this course does provide some background on the craft of editing, making it appropriate for students or people new to the art. At the same time, its primary focus is on how the advanced tools in Media Composer work, making it a perfect course to further the skill set of seasoned professionals.

System Requirements

This book assumes that you have a system configuration suitable to run Media Composer software. To verify the most recent system requirements, visit www.avid.com/media-composer/specifications.

Storage Requirements for the Class

The storage requirements for the course are approximately 15 GB. You will need a small amount of additional storage space for title media, render files, and so on.

Becoming Avid Certified

Avid certification is a tangible, industry-recognized credential that can help you advance your career and provide measurable benefits to your employer. When you're Avid certified, you not only help to accelerate and validate your professional development, but you can also improve your productivity and project success. Avid offers programs supporting certification in dedicated focus areas including Media Composer, Sibelius, Pro Tools, Worksurface Operation, and Live Sound. To become certified in Media Composer, you must enroll in a program at an Avid Learning Partner, where you can complete additional Media Composer coursework if needed and take your certification exam. To locate an Avid Learning Partner, visit www.avid.com/education.

Media Composer Certification

Avid offers two levels of Media Composer certification:

- Avid Media Composer User Certification

- Avid Media Composer Professional Certification

User Certification

The Avid Media Composer Certified User Exam is the first of two certification exams that allow you to become Avid certified. The two combined certifications offer an established and recognized goal for both academic users and industry professionals. The Avid Media Composer User Certification requires that you display a firm grasp of the core skills, workflows, and concepts of non-linear editing on the Media Composer system.

Courses/books associated with User certification include the following:

- **Media Composer Fundamentals I (MC101)**

- **Media Composer Fundamentals II (MC110)**

These User courses can be complemented with MC239 Color Grading with Media Composer and Symphony.

Professional Certification

The Avid Media Composer Professional Certification prepares editors to competently operate a Media Composer system in a professional production environment. Professional certification requires a more advanced understanding of Media Composer, including advanced tools and workflows involved in creating professional programs.

Courses/books associated with Professional certification include the following:

- **Media Composer Professional Editing I (MC201)**

- **Media Composer Professional Editing II (MC210)**

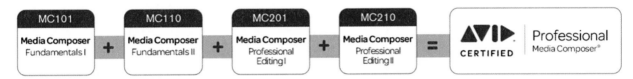

These Professional courses can be complemented with MC239 Color Grading with Media Composer and Symphony.

For more information about Avid's certification programs, please visit
www.avid.com/en/education/certification.

Avid Certified. Real skills, proven.

Avid Certification helps professionals attain and demonstrate the skills and credentials they need to increase their value, competency, and efficiency in the highly competitive media industry.

Avid certification programs cover the broad range of Avid products, as well as other professional roles, including Avid Certified Instructor, Avid Certified Support Representative, and Avid Certified Administrator.

If you want to learn more about Avid training, please check out our official online resource by going to www.avid.com/education. There you will find information about our training partners, specifics on the various certification options available, and detailed course descriptions for each course offered through our programs.

Fundamentals and Beyond

Working effectively on any editing system requires familiarity with certain technical concepts. These concepts form the foundation of everything that happens in an editing system. In this lesson, we will discuss certain primer topics related to media codecs. Understanding them will enable you to make informed decisions throughout the project—from production and acquisition to editing, finishing, output, and delivery.

The first part of this lesson is a technical primer, really. This lesson will provide you with enough information to deepen your understanding of many of the concepts taught in this book. It should also help you recognize topics with which you're unfamiliar and that merit deeper study if you are planning on a career in TV, film, or video production.

Media Used: No media used

Duration: 60 minutes

GOALS

- Review fundamental concepts of non-linear editing
- Review key functions and workflow considerations of Media Composer
- Understand the basic video editing workflow
- Learn the terminology of larger-than-HD formats
- Familiarize yourself with the new 2K/4K/UHD codecs
- Create HD and 4K projects
- Create a custom format project
- Save a custom format preset
- Learn standard industry conventions for setting up a project

Fundamental Concepts

It is assumed that as a student of this course, you have already taken the course, MC101: Media Composer Fundamentals I. Depending on how long ago that was, or how much you have worked with Media Composer since, those concepts may be fresh in your mind or they may be a bit dusty. To ensure that you are ready to move forward, let's start the course by reviewing some of the basic concepts of editing, and the basic process of starting a project on Media Composer.

Non-linear, Non-destructive Editing

Media Composer is a non-linear editing system (NLE), like any video editing application you have on your computer, tablet or phone today. This simply means that you can edit the clips into the sequence in any order you want. (The term "non-linear" was coined to contrast computer-based editing with linear, tape-based editing systems of the time.)

Like any professional NLE, editing in Media Composer is also non-destructive, meaning when you cut out a piece of a clip, the system doesn't delete the unwanted frames. You can go back to the clip later, see it again in its entirety and even reuse it numerous times in the sequence. This is possible because when you edit clips in Media Composer, you are not editing the media files themselves, but rather working with metadata that links to the media files.

Project and Media Files

Media Composer's project files can be stored in one of two preset locations, or any other custom location. You can pick the location using the PRIVATE, SHARED and EXTERNAL radio buttons and/or BROWSE FOLDER button in the Select Project window, as seen in Figure 1.1.

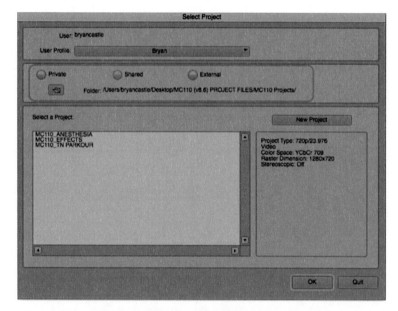

Figure 1.1
Use the Private, Shared or External buttons, and/or the Browse Folder button to designate the location to save a project.

- ■ **Private:** Saved in the documents folder (e.g. My Documents) of the logged-in OS user.

- ■ **Shared:** Saved in the Shared Documents folder, accessible to all OS users.

- ■ **External:** A custom location, saved wherever the user designates.

- ■ **Browse Folder:** This button is used to navigate to the custom location of/for a project.

The Avid project itself is a collection of independent files, rather than a single large file. You can see a sample project folder in Figure 1.2.

▼ ◻ MC110_TN PARKOUR	Folder	--
🔹 STUDENT_LESSON SEQUENCES.avb	Avid Bin File	906 KB
🔹 TNPARKOUR_EXERCISE SEQUENCES.avb	Avid Bin File	7 KB
🔹 TNPARKOUR_FOOTAGE.avb	Avid Bin File	327 KB
🔹 TNPARKOUR_GRFX.avb	Avid Bin File	5 KB
🔹 TNPARKOUR_MOTION FX.avb	Avid Bin File	5 KB
🔹 TNPARKOUR_MUSIC.avb	Avid Bin File	13 KB
🔹 TNPARKOUR_SELECTS.avb	Avid Bin File	137 KB
🔹 TNPARKOUR_SFX.avb	Avid Bin File	5 KB
📄 MC110_TN PARKOUR Settings.avs	Avid Preferences File	29 KB
📱 MC110_TN PARKOUR.avp	Avid Project File	7 KB
▶ ◻ SearchData	Folder	--
▶ ◻ Statistics	Folder	--
▶ ◻ WaveformCache	Folder	--
◉ MC110_TN PARKOUR Settings.xml	XML document	221 KB

Figure 1.2 A Media Composer "project" is folder holding a collection of project-related files.

The project files are very small because they store metadata only, no media.

This structure is different from many other applications on the market today, and offers some nice advantages. First of all, the bin is an individual file unto itself. Since the bin is the file that stores all clip and sequence information, and it is so small, one editor can send a bin to another through email, chat, etc., as a means to collaborate on a project or scene.

The media is stored separate from the project files and, for best performance, should reside on a separate hard drive. Media Composer organizes all its media at the top level ("root level") of any drive it uses, placing it in a predictable folder structure:

■   HARD DRIVE\AVID MEDIAFILES\MXF\1

This is a very specific location and naming convention. If this folder placement or naming differs in any way, Media Composer will not see it. The result would be that all media would be "Offline."

The Media Composer Interface

The Media Composer interface, as shown in Figure 1.3, has four key components: the PROJECT WINDOW, COMPOSER WINDOW, TIMELINE WINDOW, and BINS.

The PROJECT WINDOW is the central hub of your project. Its buttons, or tabs, across the top change what's visible in the display pane, including BINS, SETTINGS, EFFECTS PALETTE, and FORMAT, plus the informational panes of USAGE and INFO. If you close this window, you will save and exit the project.

The SETTINGS tab houses all customizable settings in one convenient location. Open a setting by double-clicking its name.

You can customize the colors and certain behaviors of the interface by opening and modifying the INTERFACE SETTING. You can change the size of the text in the various windows of the interface by selecting the window – e.g. a bin – and then selecting WINDOWS MENU > SET FONT.

Figure 1.3 The four main components of the interface in Source/Record editing mode.

As you work, you will open any number of other tools that are useful for the task at hand. Tool windows can be tabbed together to save space, as can Bin windows. The arrangements of tool windows are saved as WORKSPACES, which can be created, accessed, saved and updated through the Windows menu.

 With the release of Media Composer v8.5, Avid updated the menus in Media Composer to make them more intuitive and easier to use. If this is your first time working on Media Composer 8.5+, be aware that some items have moved.

Learning the Basic Workflow

Media Composer is used to cut such a wide variety of programming throughout the global industry that it is impossible to say there is a single, "standard" workflow. That said, the following is a rough outline of a common workflow to move your project through the stages from first launch to final delivery. (It also happens to outline this course; hence the lesson numbers in parenthesis.)

A common workflow for completing a project is:

1.   Create the Project files (L1)

2.   Input Media (L2)

3.   Prepare the footage and bins for editing (L3)

4.   Edit and re-edit your scene(s) for story structure (L4-L5)

5.   Trim the scene(s) to improve the pacing and timing (L6)

6.   Mix the audio as you go, and again at the end, which is known as "audio sweetening" (L7)

7.   Add titles and effects to solve problems, create magic or add eye-candy (L8-L14)

8.   Export the finished masterpiece (L15)

9.   Clean up by managing and deleting project media (L16)

Going Beyond HD

We are living in the future! With 4K cameras becoming commonplace, working in high-resolution formats is no longer the exclusive realm of high-budget productions. Many of us today even have phones capable of shooting 4K video. And with UHD TV sets and distribution becoming common, the days of 4K as an acquisition-only format are also behind us.

Figure 1.4 The progression of video TV resolutions.

There tends to be some confusion among consumers about video resolutions, particularly as it relates to their TVs. As video professionals, let's be sure we are clear on the terminology:

Table 1.1: Video Resolution Terminology

Name		Description	Raster Size (in pixels)
High Resolution		Often describes anything larger than FHD (Full HD)	> 1920x1080
Full	HD	The full-specification HD raster	1920x1080
2K	DCI	The 1.85:1 presentation variant of 2K	1998x1080
4K	DCI	Full Digital Cinema raster	2048x1080
4K	UHD	Broadcast variation of 4K, 4x larger than FHD	3840x2160
4K	Flat	The 1.85:1 presentation variant of 4K	3996x2160
4K	DCI	Full Digital Cinema raster	4096x2160
8K	UHD	Experimental UHD format; 4x larger than 4K UHD	7680x4320

Some of the confusion in terminology as we move beyond HD comes from the fact that we used to talk about vertical resolution, i.e. 480p, 720, 1080p, but with >HD rasters we are more commonly referring to horizontal resolution. At 1920x1080, Full HD (FHD) is close to the 2K spec of 2048 pixels, but no one calls it "2K HD."

Consumers and professionals alike seem to have settled on the term "4K" instead of "UHD," according to Google Trends, so we will use the term "4K" to refer to all variants of the 4K raster. (Reference: http://tinyurl.com/4K-vs-UHD)

Working in 4K

Working with 4K footage brings its own challenges when it comes to storage, playback and image processing. The 4K UHD raster has 4 times the number of pixels – that is, 4x the amount of information – as FHD. The files are dramatically bigger, and require more powerful computer systems, faster drives and drive connections to play, copy or move the files around. This is reflected in the minimum system requirements for Media Composer, as shown in Figure 1.5.

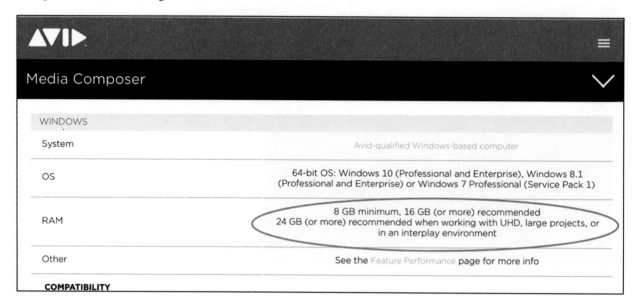

Figure 1.5. Working in 4K demands more system resources, so recommended system specs are higher.

   Avid employs a rapid development and release cycle for Media Composer to keep pace with ever-changing technology. System requirements may change with a new release.
Get the latest system specs at: www.avid.com/media-composer/specifications

Working with Avid Codecs

You may be familiar with the Avid codecs in the DNxHD family. These codecs have helped set the standard for HD quality at relatively low data rates. DNxHD codecs are named by their data rate. A few examples:

Table 1.2: Avid DNxHD Codecs

Codec	Datarate	Description
DNxHD 36	36 mbits/sec	"Offline" codec, for creative editorial
DNxHD 145	145 mbits/sec	Standard HD broadcast quality codec
DNxHD 175	175 mbits/sec	High-quality broadcast codec
DNxHD 220X	220 mbits/sec, 10-bit	Cinema quality, 10-bit finishing codec

Get the DNxHD white paper for the full story on DNxHD codecs, including detailed info on quality tests, sub-sample patterns, 3rd-party licensees and more: http://www.avid.com/~/media/avid/files/whitepaper-pdf/dnxhd.pdf?la=en

By their very name, DNx*HD* codecs are designed for just that – HD. When you move to working in 4K, the available codec family will change too.

Avid recently introduced a new family of resolution independent codecs for use in high-resolution projects – DNx*HR*. (HR stands for High Resolution.)

This new Avid UHD/2k/4k codec saves storage space and gives optimized performance for smoother playback and faster effects processing – just like its HD cousins. You can create DNxHR media through capture, import, export, transcode, or render. Other products, like Davinci Resolve, will also accept and create media in this new format.

Table 1.3: DNxHR Independent Codecs

Codec	Compression	Data Rate
DNxHR LB (low bandwidth)	22:1	39-383 Mbps
DNxHR SQ (standard quality)	7:1	123-1233 Mbps
DNxHR HQ (high quality)	4.5:1	186-1866 Mbps
DNxHR HQX (high quality 10-bit)	5.5:1	186-1866 Mbps
DNxHR 444 (cinema quality)	4.5:1	373-3730 Mbps

You may notice there is tremendous variation in the data rate (Mbps) for each codec. This is due to the fact that the codec is resolution independent, and the frame size can vary from 2k through UltraHD to 4k for each codec. DNxHR codecs also supports *proxy resolutions* which can further reduce the size of a file to 1/4 - 1/16.

Talking about codecs can be dry, geeky stuff. Few people get excited talking about data rates. But the big takeaway is this: Like the DNxHD codecs before them, the DNxHR codecs give you a way to edit 4K footage on a desktop or laptop computer without the need for a Raid system costing thousands of dollars. And *that* is something to get excited about!

Creating a New Project

Despite the fact that everything is new, nothing has really changed. The project raster sizes may be larger, and the letters on your codecs may be different, but the basic workflow of mounting and editing a project remain largely unchanged, whether working in SD, HD or UHD.

To create a 4K project:

1.   Launch Media Composer

2.   In the Select Project window, choose the location to save your project.

3.   Click the **NEW PROJECT BUTTON** on the right.

     The New Project window opens.

4. Name the project.

    Once you have named a project, it is not easily possible to change it, and is not recommended. The project name should represent the project itself, without including a version number (e.g. title of your movie, TV show title + episode number, etc.). The various versions of your production will take place within the project itself. This is more than a good-housekeeping recommendation.

5. In the New Project window, click the **FORMAT MENU**, and choose the format and frame rate for your project, as shown in Figure 1.6.

    Frame rate is still king! You can change the raster dimensions and color space of the project after the fact, but not the frame rate.

6. Click **OK** to close the window and create the project files.

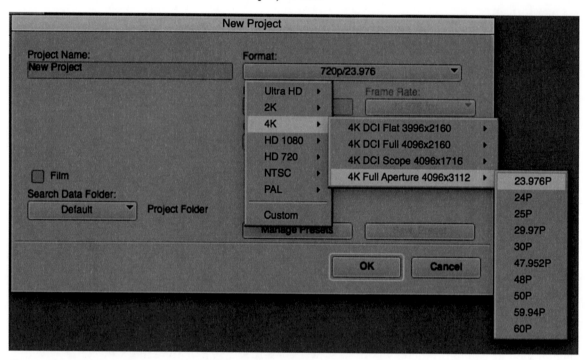

Figure 1.6 Creating a 4K project follows the same process as an HD one.

Creating Custom Projects

In addition to creating projects that are larger than FHD, Media Composer allows you to create a project with a custom raster dimension. Media today is everywhere, with new distribution formats popping up all the time. For an example, do you need to create a video to play natively on the Apple iWatch, for example? Create a custom project at 320x390 pixels.

To create a custom project:

1. Launch Media Composer

2. In the Select Project window, choose the location to save your project.

3. Click the **NEW PROJECT BUTTON** on the right.

    The New Project window opens.

4. Name the **PROJECT**.

5. In the New Project window, select the FORMAT MENU > CUSTOM.

6. Enter the RASTER DIMENSIONS and choose a FRAME RATE from the drop-down menu, as shown in Figure 1.7.

 The raster dimensions must be an even number (divisible by 2).

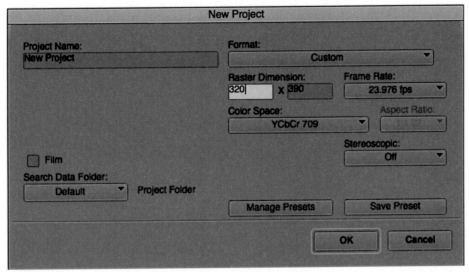

Figure 1.7 On a custom project, you define the raster dimensions.

7. (Optional) Click the SAVE PRESET BUTTON, type a name for the Preset in the dialog, and then click OK.

The Custom Preset name will then appear in the Format menu > My Presets category, as shown in Figure 1.8.

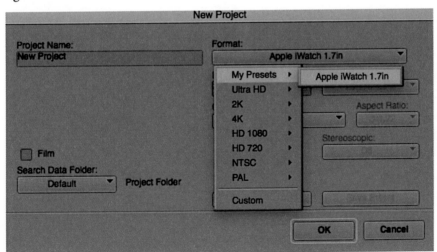

Figure 1.8 Saved presets appear in the Format menu.

8. Click OK to close the window and create the project files.

 The smallest frame size for a custom project is 256 pixels (W) x 120 pixels (H). The maximum size is 8192 x 8192 pixels. All dimensions must be divisible by 2.

Managing Presets

In the New Project window there is a button labeled Manage Presets. Click the button, and the Preset Manager window opens, shown in Figure 1.9. The window displays a list of any presets you have saved. Each entry can be edited by double-clicking on the value.

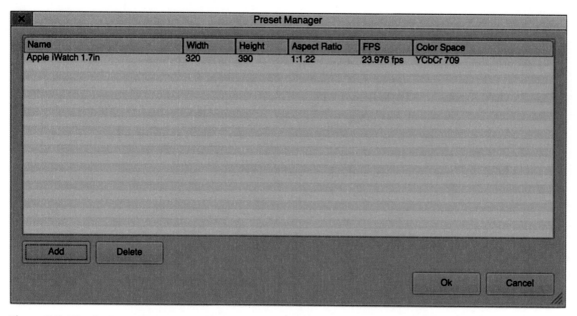

Name	Width	Height	Aspect Ratio	FPS	Color Space
Apple iWatch 1.7in	320	390	1:1.22	23.976 fps	YCbCr 709

Figure 1.9 Use the Preset Manager to add, remove, and modify your custom project formats.

- To modify an existing entry, double-click on the value to open the text field; type the new value and press Enter.

- To add a new preset, click the Add button to add an entry to the list, and then modify each of the values. This type of entry can be useful for creating a batch of presets.

- To delete a preset, select the entry in the list and click the Delete button.

If you start working with presets for custom projects, no doubt you will need to open this up at some point. Whether you create new presets for a project with multiple deliverables, you want to delete unused presets, or you simply made a mistake in creating one and need to correct it, using the Preset Manager window is simple and straight-forward.

Setting up a Project

Bin Naming Conventions

Working by yourself, how you choose to setup your bins for editing is entirely up to you. In the professional world, that decision is often made by someone else. On a TV show, the workflow is often defined by the Post Production Supervisor, and every editor on the show is expected to follow it. For many shows, multiple editors' work on every episode, and the bins must be set up in a way that everyone understands. If a scene needs to be passed from one editor to another, or an editor is out sick and another takes over, this consistency in naming conventions ensures that there is no confusion, which would cause a critical error and an undesirable delay.

On a feature film, it is the senior editor who defines their preferred method for laying out the bins. It is fairly standard to create a bin for at least every scene, and the clips are named with the standard convention of scene/setup/take.

It is recommended that you, too, create a project organization and naming scheme that remains as consistent as possible over time. This will not only be incredibly helpful while editing, but also when you return to a project after many weeks or months, and/or providing clear communication to another editor should they be required to work on the project.

Beyond Media Composer: Managing the Post Workflow

Creating and using a standardized Master Project folder for all your projects can help you manage the project efficiently. Many studios and post houses have their own proprietary workflow. In the screenshot, you can see a sample Master Project folder for a post house in Salt Lake City, Utah, generously provided to our Avid Learning Partner, the Utah Valley University.

Name	
▼ 📁 01_Documents	✓
▶ 📁 01_Scripts	✓
▶ 📁 02_Finance_Receipts	✓
▶ 📁 03_Intellectual Property	✓
▶ 📁 04_Transcription_CC	✓
▶ 📁 05_Branding Guides	✓
▶ 📁 06_Script Breakdowns	✓
▼ 📁 02_Project Files	✓
▼ 📁 03_AMA Footage	✓
▶ 📁 RAW_CAPTURED	✓
▶ 📁 TRANSCODED_MEDIA	✓
▶ 📁 04_Graphics	✓
▼ 📁 05_Sound	✓
▶ 📁 00_Final Audio Mix	✓
▶ 📁 01_ProTools Session	✓
▼ 📁 02_Languages	✓
▶ 📁 03_Sound Design SFX	✓
▶ 📁 04_Voice Over	✓
▶ 📁 05_OMF Files	✓
▶ 📁 06_Production Audio	✓
▶ 📁 07_SoundTrack Pro Sends	✓
▶ 📁 06_Music	✓
▶ 📁 07_Reviews	✓
▶ 📁 08_DVD Projects	✓
▶ 📁 09_Misc	✓
▶ 📁 10_Final Deliverables	✓
▶ 📁 Avid MediaFiles	✓

Figure 1.10 Sample Master Project folder.

Exercise Break: Exercise 1.1
Pause here to practice what you've learned.

Starting a Project

In this exercise, you will go through the steps to create and setup a project you will use in future exercises. If you have been working with Media Composer consistently since you took the MC101 course, this will be easy. If it has been a while since you have used Media Composer, this will be worthwhile review.

Media Used: No media used

Duration: 20 minutes

GOALS

- Create a new project
- Create project bins according to industry standards

Exercise 1.1: Creating and Setting Up a Project

In this exercise, you will create a new project according to a set of specifications, begin organizing your project by creating the appropriate bins, and add additional bins provided to your project folder.

1. Begin by launching Avid Media Composer.

2. Create a new project using the Select Project dialog box. Click the **NEW PROJECT BUTTON** on the right-hand side and set up your project with the following specs:

    Video resolution: **UHD 23.976P**

    FPS: **23.976**

    We won't be working in this format, but for exercise purposes, let's create it as a 4K project first.

3. Name your project **MC110_ANESTHESIA**.

    We will use this project in upcoming exercises that reference the short film, Anesthesia.

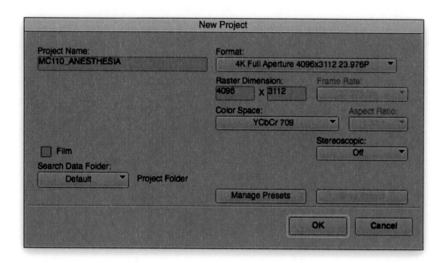

Figure 1.11..New Project window selecting a 4K project.

4. Click **OK** to create the project, and then open it.

5. Create new bins by using the key command **CTRL + N** (Windows) or **COMMAND + N** (Mac) and label them as follows:

    *   ANESTHESIA_EXERCISE SEQUENCES

    *   ANESTHESIA_INGEST

    *   ANESTHESIA_SELECTS

    *   ANESTHESIA_MUSIC

    *   ANESTHESIA_SFX

    *   ANESTHESIA_GFX

    *   ANESTHESIA_OUTPUT

Bins should be clearly labeled and assets organized so that projects can be passed from Assistant Editor to Editor or between several editors without confusion. We will continue to use these bins as we move forward with our lessons.

6. Let's finish prepping your new project by adding some bins to your project folder, provided to you by your instructor. To do this, we must leave our project for a moment and go to your computer's desktop.

    Sharing bins is a common practice among Avid editors and allows for more quick and efficient collaborating. The ability to do this is one of the advantages of Avid's workflow.

7. If you have not already done so, obtain the folder **CLASS BINS** from your instructor and copy to your hard drive.

8. Next, open your **MC110_ANESTHESIA** project folder.

    Take a moment to observe its contents:

Name		Size	Kind
ANESTHESIA_EXERCISE SEQUENCES.avb	⊘	5 KB	Avid Bin File
ANESTHESIA_GFX.avb	⊘	5 KB	Avid Bin File
ANESTHESIA_INGEST.avb	⊘	5 KB	Avid Bin File
ANESTHESIA_MUSIC.avb	⊘	5 KB	Avid Bin File
ANESTHESIA_OUTPUT.avb	⊘	5 KB	Avid Bin File
ANESTHESIA_SELECTS.avb	⊘	5 KB	Avid Bin File
ANESTHESIA_SFX.avb	⊘	5 KB	Avid Bin File
MC110_ANESTHESIA Bin.avb	⊘	5 KB	Avid Bin File
MC110_ANESTHESIA Settings.avs	⊘	30 KB	Avid Preferences File
MC110_ANESTHESIA Settings.xml	⊘	224 KB	XML document
MC110_ANESTHESIA.avp	⊘	10 KB	Avid Project File
▶ SearchData	⊘	--	Folder
▶ Statistics	⊘	--	Folder
▶ WaveformCache	⊘	--	Folder

Figure 1.12 The contents of the "MC110 _ANESTHIA" project folder.

A file labeled "MC110_ANESTHESIA.avp" is your project file. It is like the blueprint for your project.

Files labeled "MC110_ANESTHESIA Settings.avs" and "MC110_ANESTHESIA Settings.xml" contains your project's settings.

Files with the extension .avb are the bins you just created earlier in the exercise.

9. Now, let's add some bins you will need for future exercises. Open the **CLASS BINS** folder you received from your instructor. Inside you will see the following bins:

    ● ANESTHESIA_DAILIES.avb

    ● ANESTHESIA_FX TEMPLATES.avb

    ● ANESTHESIA_PRODUCTION AUDIO.avb

    ● ANESTHESIA_RAW VIDEO.avb

    ● STUDENT_LESSON SEQUENCES.avb

▼ 🗀 MC110_CLASS BINS	●	May 25, 2016, 12:57 PM	--	Folder
🎬 ANESTHESIA_DAILIES.avb		May 25, 2016, 12:56 PM	171 KB	Avid Bin File
🎬 ANESTHESIA_FX TEMPLATES.avb		May 25, 2016, 11:52 AM	8 KB	Avid Bin File
🎬 ANESTHESIA_P...TION AUDIO.avb		May 25, 2016, 12:57 PM	69 KB	Avid Bin File
🎬 ANESTHESIA_RAW VIDEO.avb		May 25, 2016, 12:57 PM	79 KB	Avid Bin File
🎬 STUDENT_LESS...EQUENCES.avb		May 25, 2016, 11:52 AM	226 KB	Avid Bin File

Figure 1.13.. The bins added to the "MC110_CLASS BINS" folder.

10. Select ALL BINS and COPY them to your project folder.

    Now, go back to your project in Avid and look in your Project window. All of the bins you just copied should now be in your project. If they have not appeared, select the Project Window > File menu > Save. The new files should appear in your Project Window as shown in Figure 1.14 below.

11. Open the **ANESTHESIA_DAILIES** bin.

12. Select a clip and load it into your Source monitor, and play it through.

    The clips in this bin reference media contained in the "Avid MediaFiles" folder on your hard drive.

    The dailies for this project are actually natively at 720p 23.976. Rather than unnecessarily scale them to 4K while we work, let's change the project to the native resolution of the clips.

13. In the Project Window, click the **FORMAT BUTTON** to display the master project format settings.

14. Select the **PRESETS MENU > HD 720 > 720P/23.976**, as shown in Figure 1.14.

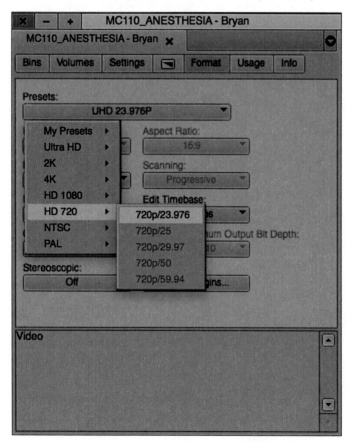

Figure 1.14 Selecting from the Presets menu: HD 720 > 720p/23.976.

Notice that you can easily switch between projects of the same frame rate. Remember, frame rate is king! As you will see in a future lesson, changing the Format tab controls other media creation options, both for input and output.

Now that your project has been set up, you are ready to begin cutting the film Anesthesia. We will continue to use this project, building an edit using the traditional workflow, in the coming lessons.

15. Conclude your lesson by making a back-up copy of your project. Remember: when backing-up, you must back up the entire project folder, not just the file inside.

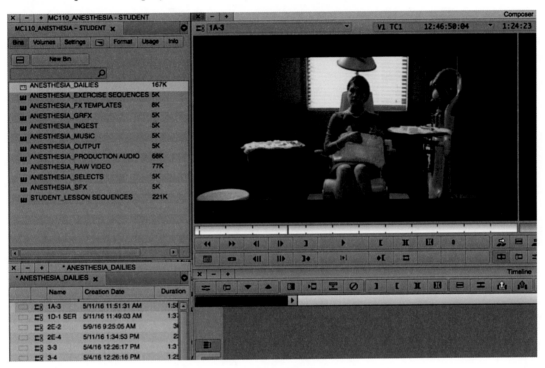

Figure 1.15 The new files should appear in your Project Window.

Inputting Media

It could almost go without saying that you have to input media into your project before you can edit it. You are probably familiar with the basic steps to import or link media files to your project. In this lesson, you will review the basics and learn additional tools and techniques for inputting particular file types.

Media: Anesthesia

Duration: 60 minutes

GOALS

- Use the Source Browser to locate camera files
- Link to camera files
- Import music files
- Organize the project media into bins
- Add notes and keywords to master clips
- Adjust the volume of video and audio clips

Ways to Input Video and Audio Clips

There are several ways to get media into your Media Composer project:

- **Tape Capture:** This allows you to record the video signal over a baseband connection from video tape, satellite, or a live camera feed. For most users, this is now uncommon.

- **Import:** Importing inputs a media file by copying the media to a predefined location and converts it to Avid native media at the same time.

- **Link:** Linking connects a media file to the project in Media Composer. It does not move or copy the media file. Media Composer will read the file from its current location and in its current format.

Media Composer v8.6 introduced a new input tool called the Source Browser, which combines the controls for linking and importing into a single window, which we will cover momentarily.

 This course assumes that you are working with all file-based media. To learn more about using Tape Capture, refer to the Media Composer Help.

A quick word about organization before we get started. Regardless of the method you use to bring media into the project, it is standard practice in the industry to initially organize it by placing the clips from each source into a new bin. By "source," we are referring to each tape, camera card, folder directory, etc. If the clips are organized into bins that match the source, it becomes very easy to relink or re-import if the need arises.

In the next lesson, we'll show you how to copy the clips into multiple bins so you can reorganize them according to whatever system you (or the editor you are assisting) may want.

Using the Source Browser

Virtually, all cameras today, professional and consumer alike, record video and audio files to memory cards instead of tape-based media. The Source Browser is designed to give you an easy way to browse for the media files, review them, and then bring selected files into your project.

To open the Source Browser, do one of the following:

■ Select File > Input > Source Browser.

■ Right-click in an open bin, and then select Input > Source Browser.

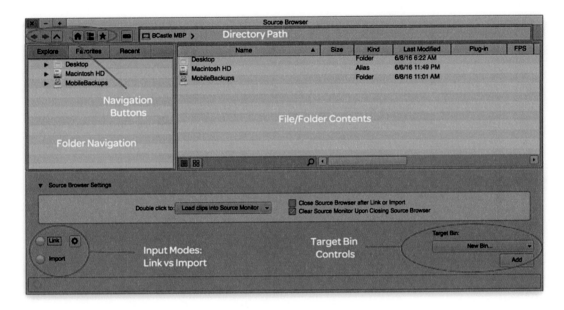

Figure 2.1 Use the Source Browser to link and import clips to your project.

The Source Browser is set up like a standard OS window, so it is intuitive and easy to use.

The pane on the left displays your computer's folders, and the large pane to the right lists the files inside each folder. Across the top there are navigation buttons – Back, Forward, and Go to Parent Folder – and the current directory path. Along the bottom is a collapsible Settings pane. You can resize the panes by dragging the divider lines between them.

The folder tree has three tabs:

■ **Explore:** Shows all your system folders.

■ **Favorites:** Lists shortcuts to the folders you've tagged as favorite.

■ **Recent:** Lists the folders you've used in previous sessions.

Marking a Favorite Folder

If there are folders you will use frequently for a project, like a folder full of stock music and sound effects or the folder for this class, you can save time by marking it as a favorite.

To mark a folder as a Favorite:

1. Navigate to the folder, and select it in the directory tree.

2. Click the **STAR BUTTON** at the top of the Source Browser.

    A star appears to the left of the folder in the directory tree, indicating that it is marked as a favorite. (See Figure 2.2) The folder now also appears in the Favorites pane, making it an easy find the next time.

3. To remove a folder from the Favorites list, simply click the **STAR** next to the folder in the directory tree.

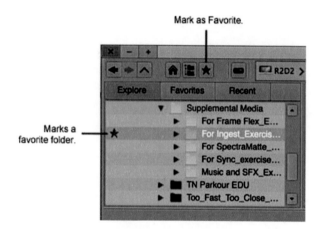

Figure 2.2   Use the Star button to mark a folder as a favorite.

Browsing Your Media Files

Seeing your files in a list is fine, but it is more meaningful to be able to watch the video clips. Most cameras name files with a meaningless code. The code ensures that each file name is unique, but doesn't tell you which is a close-up, or a wide shot, or which take was a blooper vs. a good take. (Each time a scene is recorded it is called a *take*, as in "Scene 2, Take 3… Action!")

The Source Browser also lets you play the media files before deciding if you want to add them to the project. You can view and play them as thumbnail images, or load them into the Source monitor for more careful viewing.

To view clips in Frame View:

1. Click the **SWITCH TO FRAME VIEW** button, shown in Figure 2.3.

2. (Optional) Drag the slider to adjust the size of the thumbnails.

3. Click on the file to select it.

    a. Move the mouse over the selected thumbnail to scrub through the video frames.

    b. Press the Spacebar to play the clip.

To load a file into the Source monitor:

■ Double-click the file. (With default settings.)

■ Drag the file to the Source monitor.

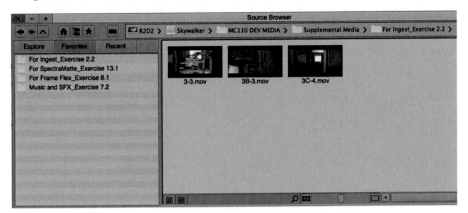

Figure 2.3 Set the Source Browser to Frame View to view your video clips.

Linking Clips to Your Project

Once you decide which clips to use, add them to your project so they appear in a bin. Placing the clips in a bin saves them as part of the project.

You can do this either one-by-one or as a group – for example, all the files in a folder, or on a camera card. You can even choose to do it through the process of editing them into your sequence. Media Composer offers the flexibility to input them however it works best for you at the moment.

To add a group of clips to a bin:

1. Select the clip(s) in the Source Browser. To select a group, do one of the following:

   • Click the first clip, then Shift+click the last one you want to select. All clips in between are selected.

   • Ctrl+click (Windows) or Command+click (Mac) each file you want.

2. Click the ADD BUTTON; or drag the selected clips to an open bin.

   The clips will appear in the bin with the linked master clip icon, as seen in Figure 2.4.

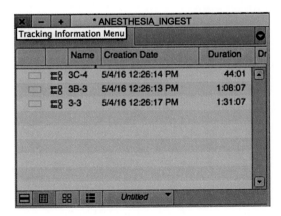

Figure 2.4 Linked master clips in the bin are saved with the project.

Understanding Media Linking

When you input media files into your project, a link is created between the *master clip* in the bin and the *media file,* which contains the actual images and sounds that you see and hear in the video. A master clip is a tiny bit of metadata – that is, info about the media – including the information the system needs to identify and link to the media file. The master clip information is stored in the bin file; meanwhile the media file is stored on the hard drive or memory card. If Media Composer ever cannot find the media file, the master clip will appear as "Media Offline."

Broadly speaking, Media Composer uses two types of media files: *Camera Native* and *Avid Native.*

Camera Native is just that, the original audio and video files created by the camera. You can input, play and edit most camera native file types in Media Composer using plug-ins, called *AMA plug-ins.* When you input camera native clips, Media Composer creates a link to the original file in its current location and reads it from there using the plug-in to decompress the file. You manage camera native files yourself through the Mac Finder, or Windows Explorer, by copying, moving or deleting the files directly. If you move, rename or delete the files in the OS, you will need to relink them inside Media Composer. (Fun Fact: *AMA* stands for Avid Media Access.)

If you are working with a camera that's new on the market, or just new to you, it may be necessary to download an additional AMA plug-in before Media Composer will be able to read the camera files.

To download additional AMA plug-ins, click the Marketplace menu > AMA Plug-ins.

Avid Native media is the media created by Media Composer when you Import, Consolidate (copy), or Transcode (convert) camera native files. Avid Native media is always created in the MXF format and is stored in a very specific location. Media Composer generally performs better and faster when you use Avid Native media. It also saves you the hassle of needing to keep track of all your own media files in the OS. You will learn more about how to manage Avid Native media later in this lesson.

Editing from the Source Browser

As mentioned, another way to commit clips to your project is to edit them to a sequence directly from the Source Browser. This enables you to use the Source Browser like a bin, accessing any media file on your system for immediate editing. Many productions can benefit from the added efficiency of editing directly from the Source Browser, including breaking news, same-day wedding or event videos, or even a quick assembly of a scene on-set.

With default settings, seen in Figure 2.5, double-clicking a clip in the Source Browser will load the clip into the Source monitor. If you then edit the clip into a sequence, Media Composer will assign the clip to the Target Bin.

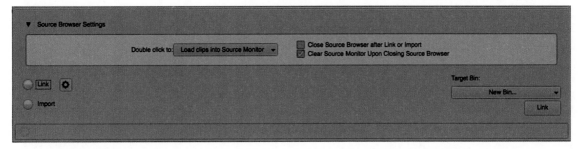

Figure 2.5 With default settings, double-clicking a clip loads it for review and editing.

To edit a clip from the Source Browser:

1. Double-click the clip in the Source Browser to load it into the Composer window.

2. Play and mark the clip as usual.

3. Edit the clip into the sequence, using your preferred editing method.

    When you do, Media Composer adds the linked master clip to the Target Bin, as designated in the Source Browser settings. The clip that appears in the bin is the full clip, not just the portion edited into a sequence.

    This function will allow you to edit directly from the original camera card. Although possible, this is not recommended. Camera cards generally lack the input/output speed required for editing. Plus, there is inherent risk when working with the only copy of a media file. Always back up your original "camera negatives" to a hard drive for editing.

Importing Media Files

Importing is a great way to input your media when you are getting started.

Importing is more time consuming than linking because it copies the media to Avid's standard media storage location, instead of just linking to the existing media files.

There are two big advantages to importing your footage:

■ All your media files will be safely in Avid's managed media directory

■ Overall system performance is better with Avid native media

Since you will be creating new media files, and investing sometime in the process, it is best to double-check your Import settings before you perform the Import.

There are settings to set before Import:

- **Import settings:** These control how Media Composer does or does not modify the image on import.

- **Media Creation settings:** These control the size, resolution, and format of the resulting media file.

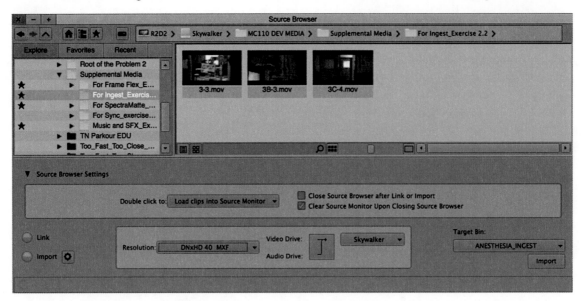

Figure 2.6 Set the Source Browser to Import Mode and set the format for the new media files using the Media Creation controls that appear.

Modifying Your Import Settings

To setup for Import using the Source Browser:

1. Click the IMPORT button in the bottom left corner of the Source Browser Settings pane.

   The Source Browser changes to Import mode and a new group of Media Creation controls appear in the Settings pane, as shown in Figure. 2.6

2. Click the GEAR ICON next to the Import button.

   The Import Settings dialog box opens, as shown in Figure 2.7.

 The Import settings can also be opened directly from the Settings pane of the Project Window.

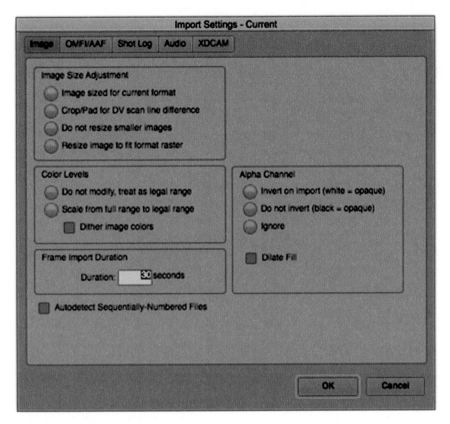

Figure 2.7 The default Import settings.

The default settings work well for video and audio files of the same format as the project. If importing still images, you may wish to modify the Image settings.

3. To import still images or graphic files and maintain their current aspect ratio, select RESIZE IMAGE TO FIT FORMAT RASTER in the Image Size Adjustment section.

    This keeps your images from being distorted on import.

4. If importing graphics with any transparency information, such as a TV station logo, select INVERT ON IMPORT in the Alpha Channel section.

5. Click OK to close the Import Settings dialog box.

6. Click the RESOLUTION drop-down menu and select the desired video resolution—for example, DNxHD 36 OR PROResES MXF.

 The Resolution settings are a subset of the Media Creation settings. To open the full Media Creation settings, select File > Media > Media Creation.

7. Select the DRIVE on which to save the new media files.

8. Click OK.
    You are now ready to import.

9. Using the Source Browser to import is the same as using it for linking –select the clips you want, and then click the ADD BUTTON, or drag them from the Source Browser to the bin.

Input Clips with Drag-and-Drop

Looking for a shortcut? You can skip the Source Browser and drag files directly from the OS to a bin. Media Composer will import them based on the current Import and Media Creation settings. The default behavior is to import them, but you can use a modifier key to link the clips instead.

To import clips:

- Drag the clips from the OS window to an open bin.

To link to clips:

- Hold the Alt key (Windows) or Option key (Mac) and then drag the clips from the OS window to an open bin.

If you plan to import clips using drag-and-drop, it is best to check your Input settings first, since the clips will be imported using the current settings.

Importing Sequential Image Files

"Moving pictures" are, as you know, just a sequence of still images played back quickly. The human brain combines and interprets them a single continuous movement rather than discrete images. In certain situations, it is preferable to record those images as individual image files, rather than a single video file. This is often done with motion graphics, stop-motion animation, and high-end visual effects. A more common way you may encounter image sequences is with timelapse images.

There has been an explosion in timelapse video in recent years. Timelapse video is created by taking a series of pictures over a long duration with a consistent interval of time between them. When those images are played back at the rate of video, one image for each frame, time is accelerated. Tiny changes and movements that would be imperceptible in real-time become clear, even fluid. Clouds morph and flow. Flowers can be seen growing, opening, turning to the sun. Magic.

Cameras and smartphones with built-in timelapse features – from iPhones to GoPro's to DSLRs – have made this art form accessible to the masses. Add to that the development of sophisticated motion-control units for camera sliders, and photographers and videographers are finding ever-increasing ways to wow us with dynamic camera moves over timelapse images.

 Out of touch with timelapse? Check out the Slow-Mo & Timelapse channel on Vimeo.com: https://vimeo.com/channels/1341

This resurgence in timelapse video has renewed the value of an old import feature of Media Composer – AutoDetect Sequentially Numbered Files – visible in the Import settings, shown in Figure 2.8. Originally designed for film scans and animation image sequences, it is equally useful for creating beautiful timelapse video clips right inside Media Composer.

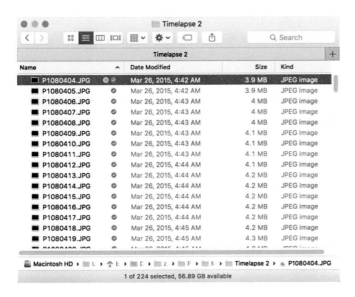

Figure 2.8
Enable AutoDetect Sequentially Numbered
files to create a timelapse video from a folder
full of stills.

By enabling Autodetect Sequentially Numbered Files, you not only queue up Media Composer for a batch import of multiple files, you enable a special bit of code that bundles them together into a video clip, and turns each still image into a single frame of video.

One additional consideration when creating a timelapse video is whether you want the video to only play full-screen, or if you want the ability to pan and zoom over the image. If you even want the option of zooming in on the image, the key is to create a high-resolution timelapse video clip, one that a good bit larger than the raster of the current project. For HD, this means creating a UHD clip. For UHD/4K, we recommend going to 6K or 8K. In a subsequent lesson, you will learn how to create the pan-and-zoom style moves, but for now, let's make sure you import it properly.

To create a high-resolution timelapse clip:

1. Click the **FORMAT TAB** of the Project window, and change the format to a format larger than HD (UHD, 4K, etc.).

    Alternatively, you could create a custom project to use for this purpose, using the native dimensions of the images, and then open the project.

2. Select **FILE > MEDIA > MEDIA CREATION SETTINGS** and then click the **IMPORT TAB**.

3. Set the **RESOLUTION** to DNxHR SQ or better.

4. Find and open the **IMPORT SETTINGS**.

5. Select the following Import Settings:

    a. Resize image to **FIT FORMAT RASTER**

    b. Scale from **RGB TO LEGAL**

    c. **AUTODETECT SEQUENTIALLY NUMBERED FILES.**

6. Select **FILE > INPUT > IMPORT** and navigate to the folder containing the Image sequence.

7. Select the first image – the one with the lowest number – and then click **OK**.

    The result of the import will be a single master clip in the bin. Each frame represents an image file in the folder.

8. If the project was previously set to an HD format (720p or 1080i/p), return to the Format tab and set the format back to HD.

   When you load and play the clip, you will find that the default setting scales the clip so you can see the full image in the HD raster.

  In Lesson 8, you will learn to use the FrameFlex controls to create dynamic pan-and-zoom style moves over this clip.

  Exercise Break: Exercise 2.1
Pause here to practice what you've learned.

Copying and Converting Linked Media

Prior to Media Composer v8.6, it was necessary to convert all linked media to Avid Native media prior to export. Although this is no longer the case, it is still advantageous to convert linked media to Avid Native media for best performance and worry-free media management. Many professional editors do this as a standard step in their workflow just after linking to the media. This is done using the Consolidate/Transcode tool.

- Consolidate *copies* the media files without re-encoding the media.

- Transcode *converts* the media.

Both Consolidate and Transcode can be used with linked media, and both functions create new Avid Native media files, which are saved in Avid's managed media directory: *drive*\Avid MediaFiles\MXF\1, 2, 3, etc. Of the two, Consolidate is faster, but only works on Avid-native codec. Transcode can convert any linked file.

Don't worry if you are unsure of the format or codec used on the file you plan to consolidate. Go ahead and try Consolidate. If it is a codec that is not native to the system, Media Composer will display an alert message and advise you to transcode instead, as shown in Figure 2.9.

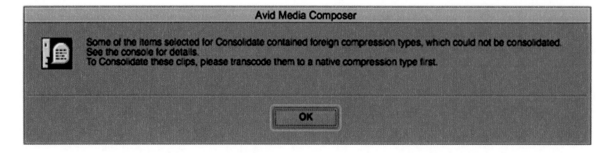

Figure 2.9 Media Composer will tell you if it is unable to Consolidate and that you need to Transcode instead.

  Consolidate/Transcode is also an important media management tool that allows you to copy or convert your project media for other purposes.

Using Consolidate

The Consolidate/Transcode tool can be used for a variety of media management tasks, and the various workflow options can get a bit complex. For our purposes of consolidating Linked clips, it is very simple.

To consolidate linked clips or sequences:

1. Open a BIN and select the master clips or sequence whose media files you want to consolidate.

2. Choose CLIP > CONSOLIDATE/TRANSCODE.

    The Consolidate/Transcode dialog box opens.

3. Select the CONSOLIDATE option button in the upper-left corner, as shown in Figure 2.10.

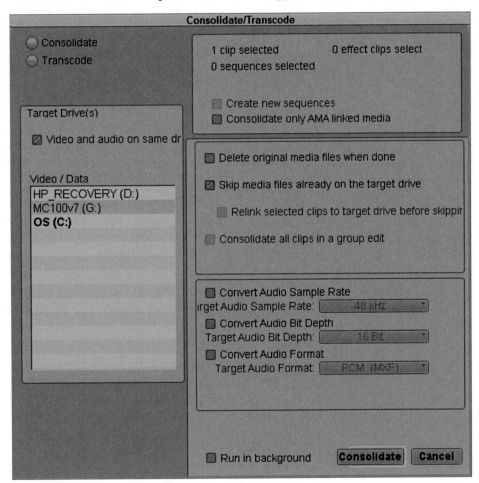

Figure 2.10 Choose Consolidate or Transcode using the option button in the top-left corner.

4. In the left column, click the check mark for "Video and audio on same drive," and then select the name of the TARGET DRIVE.

    This determines the destination for your consolidated media.

5. Select the following options for handling the media:

    - Consolidate only AMA linked media

    - Skip media files already on the target drive

6.   Optionally, convert the audio by choosing any of the AUDIO CONVERSION options.

7.   Click CONSOLIDATE.

    When you consolidate subclips or sequences, new master clips are created with a new duration, based on that of the subclip or the segment in the sequence.

If you did not choose to delete the original media files when finished – which Media Composer will not do with linked media anyway – you will have two sets of media files for the clips in your bin. To ensure that you can differentiate the copies, Media Composer will create a duplicate set of master clips. When you click Consolidate, Media Composer will ask you to choose which set of the original media files to link to. (See Figure 2.11.) The master clips pointing to the other drive are given an .old or .new extension.

Figure 2.11 Choose which drive to link your master clips to, and by extension how you want the "other" clips labeled.

This is a question of which copy you want Media Composer to be looking at for those media files. If you choose to link the original master clips to the new media files, the others are called "old." If you choose to keep the original master clips linked to the original media files, the others are called "new."

For consolidating linked media, it is recommended that you select the option:

■   Relink Master clips to media on the target drive.

This way, your clips and sequences will keep the same name, and your original camera native media files will be changed to *.old.*

Background Processing

Consolidate and Transcode can both be run as background processes. A small check box at the bottom of the Consolidate/Transcode dialog box enables you to specify that the job should run in the background, as shown in Figure 2.12. This lets you continue editing while the media is being copied or converted.

Figure 2.12 To be able to continue working while a Consolidate or Transcode job runs in the
background, select Run in background.

As a background process, it will take longer to copy or convert the files. If you continue editing, the system will allocate its resources to editing tasks first; anything left over goes to background processes. The advantage is that your editing experience is not degraded as a result.

It is recommended that you have a minimum of 16 GB ram to use this feature, so it is disabled by default. If you have less, it may not work properly.

When using background processing, the master clips (metadata only) are created immediately, and are offline until the media process has finished. Then they are automatically relinked to the new media files.

Using Transcode

While the Transcode and Consolidate processes have some similarities, transcoding is really designed for converting the media.

Perhaps the most common need you will have for transcoding is to convert linked media to native Avid MXF for better performance, such as with H.264-encoded QuickTime movies from a DSLR. For this, simply choose the target resolution and drive. If those clips are already edited into a sequence, you can efficiently convert only the linked media in the sequence by enabling the "Transcode only linked media" check box, as shown in Figure 2.13.

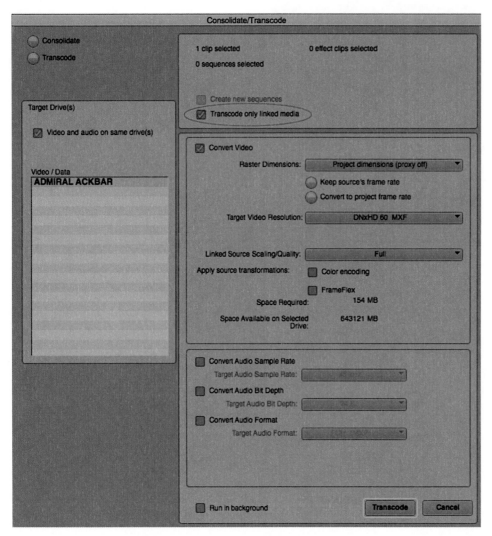

Figure 2.13 If converting a sequence, you can restrict the operation to convert only the AMA media by enabling the Transcode Only AMA Linked Media check box.

By transcoding, you can convert clips in your project to any resolution available in the project as well as convert the frame rate of the clips to match the project. In fact, if a sequence has clips with varying frame rates, you will be forced to transcode this mixed-rate material before you export. (Media players like QuickTime cannot handle changes in frame rate part-way through the video.) You can do this by clicking the button, "Convert to project frame rate," also shown in Figure 2.13.

All the format options available to you are listed under the drop-down menu, Target Video Resolution. These options will change, however, based on the current Project Format settings in the Project window. Change the Project Format settings and the options available in Transcode will change.

To transcode clips:

1. Decide on the TARGET RESOLUTION.

2. If your desired target format is different from the current project format, choose the TARGET FORMAT in the FORMAT tab of the Project window. For HD projects also choose a RASTER TYPE setting.

3. In a bin, select the CLIPS or SEQUENCE that you want to transcode.

4. Choose CLIP > CONSOLIDATE/TRANSCODE.

5. Select TRANSCODE in the upper-left corner.

6. Choose video and/or audio TARGET DRIVES.

    This determines the destination for your transcoded media.

7. Optionally, choose TRANSCODE ONLY LINKED MEDIA to restrict which clips are converted.

8. Click the TARGET VIDEO RESOLUTION pop-up menu and select a VIDEO RESOLUTION.

9. Optionally, choose CONVERT TO PROJECT FRAME RATE.

10. Choose the appropriate AUDIO CONVERSION options for the target media.

11. Click the TRANSCODE button in the lower-right corner.

    When the transcode is finished, new master clips will appear in the bin, named .transcoded.n.

 The drive whose name is bold is the drive with the most available space. It may or may not be the drive you want to use. This is true in all dialog boxes in Media Composer that show a list of drives.

 Exercise Break: Exercise 2.2 and 2.3
Pause here to practice what you've learned.

Review/Discussion Questions

1. From which menu can you open the Source Browser?

2. In the Source Browser, how can you mark a folder as a Favorite?

3. How can you remove a folder from the Favorites list in the Source Browser?

4. Name two settings that affect how files are imported to Media Composer.

5. Which setting will resize a large photograph during import to avoid distorting it?

    a. Resize Image to Fit Format Raster

    b. Crop/Pad for DV Scan Line Difference

    c. Do Not Resize Smaller Images

    d. Image Sized for Current Format

6. Describe the process to input an image sequence as a video clip.

7. Which function will copy a media file, without recompressing it?

    a. Consolidate

    b. Transcode

8. Which function will convert a media file, modifying its codec and/or frame rate?

    a. Consolidate

    b. Transcode

9. Name three reasons you might want to consolidate or transcode linked media to Avid Native media.

10. What is indicated by the bold name on one of your drives listed in Consolidate/Transcode?

Input

In this exercise, we will create a New Project and input some audio and video media to the project. Then, you will begin the process of reviewing the clips and preparing them for editing.

Media Used: Anesthesia

Duration: 45 minutes

GOALS

- Launch Media Composer
- Use the Source Browser to input media files
- Review raw footage
- Add keywords and comments to the master clips
- Save the project

Exercise 2.1: Linking to Media Files

In this exercise, we are going to practice one method of inputting footage into our project by linking to media files from the film, "Anesthesia."

Media Used: Anesthesia

Duration: 15 minutes

1. Begin by opening the **MC110_ANESTHESIA** project.

2. Open the **ANESTHESIA_INGEST** bin you created in the previous lesson.

    This is where we will store our linked media clips.

3. Choose FILE > INPUT > SOURCE BROWSER or right-click in the bin and choose INPUT > SOURCE BROWSER and navigate to the SUPPLEMENTAL MEDIA folder on your hard drive. Select the media files contained in the folder labeled FOR INGEST_EXERCISE 2.2 and click LINK in the bottom right corner of the Source Browser.

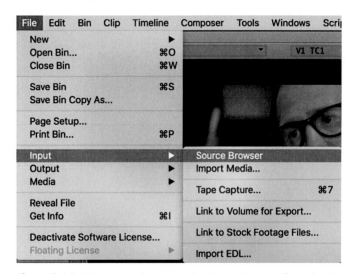

Figure 2.14 Selecting and opening the Source Browser from the File menu.

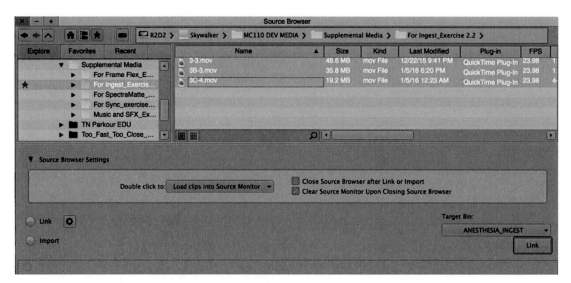

Figure 2.15 The Source Browser window.

The media files will now appear in your "ANESTHESIA_INGEST" bin.

4. Load the files into the Source monitor and observe that they are immediately available for playback and editing.

Exercise 2.2: Transcoding Linked Media Files

In this exercise, we are going to pick up where we left off in the previous exercise and transcode one of our linked media clips.

Media Used: Anesthesia

Duration: 15 minutes

For this exercise, we will continue to use the **MC110_ANESTHESIA** project.

1. If it is not already open, you will need to open the **ANESTHESIA_INGEST** bin to access the media files we ingested in the previous exercise.

    These files were ingested by linking the media, allowing the editor immediate access, but sometimes, due to playback issues or media management strategy, it is necessary to work with media files that have been transcoded from their original format. We can do that transcoding directly in the bin.

2. Start by selecting the clip labeled **3-3** in your **ANESTHESIA_INGEST** bin. Choose **CLIP > CONSOLIDATE/TRANSCODE** or right-click on the **3-3** clip and choose **CONSOLIDATE/TRANSCODE**.

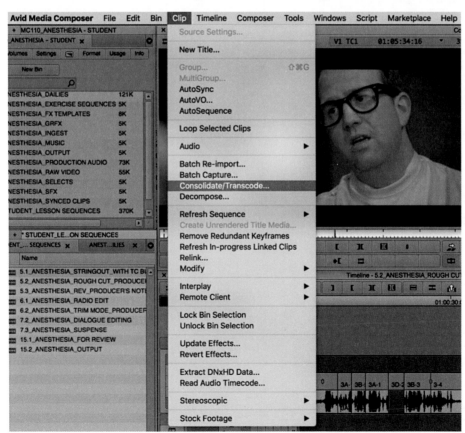

Figure 2.16 Selecting the Consolidate/Transcode option from the Clip menu.

3. In the CONSOLIDATE/TRANSCODE dialog box, select the option TRANSCODE and choose your media drive from the list of Target Drives.

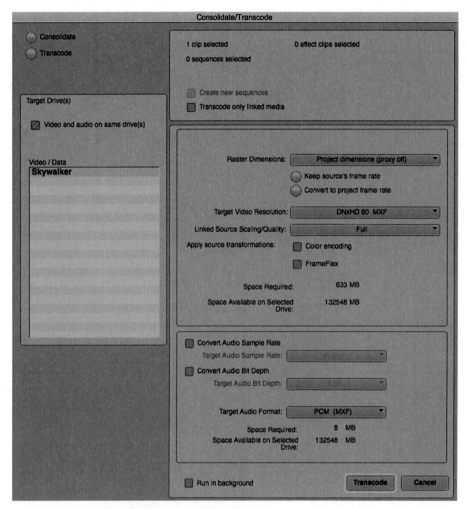

Figure 2.17   The Consolidate/Transcode dialog box.

From here, you have several more options on the left-hand side of the Consolidate/Transcode dialog box. For the purposes of this exercise, leave the default options as is.

4. You can choose to wait on the transcode or select RUN IN BACKGROUND to continue working as the transcode processes.

5. When you are satisfied with your selections, click TRANSCODE.

The "3-3" clip will now transcode from its original format to the Avid DNxHD codec without altering the original media file. A new clip called "3-3.new" will appear in your bin. This clip will reference the transcoded media located in your "Avid MediaFiles" folder.

6. Once the transcode is finished, load the clip **3-3** into the Source monitor and observe that the clip plays back normally.

7. Create a new bin called **ANESTHESIA_TRANSCODED** and move your transcoded clip into this bin.

Exercise 2.3: Transcoding a Sequence

Sometimes we have begun editing a sequence with linked media clips and discover later that we need to transcode the clips we used in the sequence. We can do this without needing to rebuild our edit.

In this lesson, we used Consolidate/Transcode to convert one of our linked media files from its native format to the Avid DNxHD codec. In this exercise, we will practice transcoding media that has already been edited into a sequence.

Media Used: Anesthesia

Duration: 15 minutes

For this exercise, we will continue to use the **MC110_ANESTHESIA** project.

1. If it is not already open, you will need to open the **ANESTHESIA_INGEST** bin to access the media files we ingested in a previous exercise.

2. Next, open the **ANESTHESIA_EXERCISE SEQUENCES** bin. Create a new sequence called **ANESTHESIA_TRANSCODE**.

3. One by one, load the clips **3B-3** and **3C-4** into the Source monitor.

4. Create a few short clips by marking **IN** and **OUT** Marks in the footage and drag the clips into the **ANESTHESIA_TRANSCODE** in the Timeline.

   Do not be concerned with trying to edit a scene. We just need at least three clips in the Timeline in any order.

5. Select the **ANESTHESIA_TRANSCODE** sequence in the **ANESTHESIA_EXERCISE SEQUENCES** bin.

6. Choose CLIP > CONSOLIDATE/TRANSCODE or right-click on the **ANESTHESIA_TRANSCODE** sequence in the bin and choose CONSOLIDATE/TRANSCODE.

7. In the CONSOLIDATE/TRANSCODE dialog box, select the option TRANSCODE and choose your media drive from the list of Target Drives.

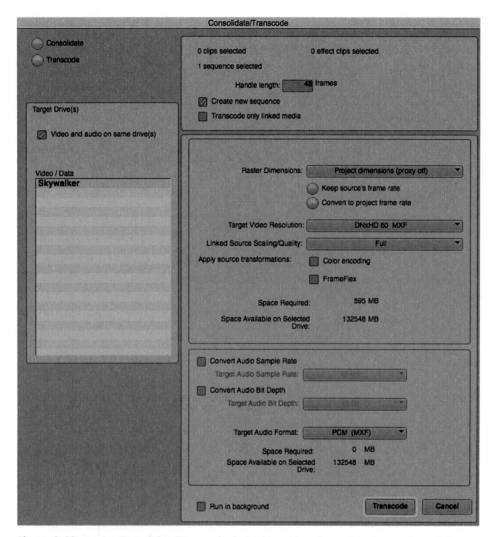

Figure 2.18 In the Consolidate/Transcode dialog box, select the option Transcode and choose your media drive from the list of Target Drives.

8. At this point, you can wait on the transcode or select **RUN IN BACKGROUND** to continue working as the transcode processes.

9. When you are satisfied with your selections, click **TRANSCODE**.

   The clips used in the "ANESTHESIA_TRANSCODE" sequence will now transcode from their original format to the Avid DNxHD codec without altering the original media file.

   When the transcode is complete, you will see the transcoded clips, labeled with the extension "new," appear in your "ANESTHESIA_EXERCISE SEQUENCES" bin.

   You will also see that a new sequence has been created, called "ANESTHESIA_TRANSCODE.Transcoded." When this new sequence is loaded, your project will reference the transcoded media located in your "Avid MediaFiles" folder.

10. Play through the **ANESTHESIA_TRANSCODE.TRANSCODED** sequence and observe that it plays back correctly.

11. Move your transcoded sequence and clips into the **ANESTHESIA_TRANSCODED** bin.

12. Conclude the lesson by saving your work.

Preparing Dailies

The task of organizing a project is ongoing. At the beginning of a project, there is much to be done to organize the material being ingested and to prepare it for edit. But it does not end when the edit begins. You will continue to use the tools and techniques taught in this lesson throughout the edit process. They are of particular importance to assistant editors.

Media Used: Anesthesia

Duration: 60 minutes

GOALS

- Change the information displayed in a bin
- Save custom bin views
- Create custom metadata fields
- Add custom information to bins
- Sort items in a bin
- Copy clips to multiple bins
- Use bins and assets from other projects
- Subclip selected shots
- Synchronize picture and sound from separate sources
- Create stringout sequences

Prepping for the Edit

One responsibility of an assistant editor is to prepare the *dailies* -- that is, raw footage -- for the editor to begin editing the scenes. Common tasks associated with preparing the dailies for editing include:

- Adding additional metadata to clips, including keywords, comments, etc.

- Copying clips into multiple bins

- Subclipping selects

- Synchronizing separate audio and video clips

Not working with an assistant? Well, that means you'll be doing it yourself! Approach your material first as the assistant, then as the editor. Take time to prep the material before beginning to cut it. By doing so, you will be more familiar with the footage and have it better organized when you do begin to edit, allowing you to focus on the creative storytelling. The time spend organizing your material will pay dividends during the edit

Adding Information to Dailies

An assistant editor spends much of his or her time focused on metadata—that is, information about the media. This information is used to organize and track the clips and sequences throughout post-production. Media Composer has robust tools to make this an efficient process.

Working with Text View

When material is first ingested into the project, one of the first tasks is to organize it. This involves correctly naming and tagging those assets for easy tracking. This type of data entry is best done in Text view.

Changing Bin Views

Recall that you can display a bin in three views: Text, Frame, and Script. Each view is useful for different situations, as shown in Table 3.1.

Table 3.1: Bins Views and their Uses

Bin View	Useful For
Text view	Data entry and tracking
	Grouping shots by statistical info
	Media management
Frame view	Visually recognizing clips
	Visually grouping shots
	Storyboarding sequences of shots
Script view	Logging footage
	Adding comments

To change the bin view:

■ Click the TEXT VIEW, FRAME VIEW, or SCRIPT VIEW button to display the corresponding view. (See Figure 3.1.)

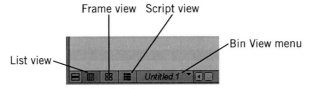

Figure 3.1 The Bin View buttons and Bin View menu.

The Frame and Script views were described in detail in Lesson 1, "Starting a Project." This lesson will focus on Text view.

Text View

Text view displays clip and sequence names along with additional information about those assets—a.k.a. **metadata**. Metadata literally means "data about data." It's a technical term that's tossed about quite a bit these days, but in this context it really just means "information about your video." It includes the information that is embedded with the video—timecode, format, etc.—as well as any information you add to it.

Looking at bin items in Text view is much like looking at files in Windows Explorer's Details view or in the List view of the Mac Finder, and it works in much the same way. You can change the columns displayed, rearrange them, and sort them alphanumerically. As such, Text view makes it easy to manage large numbers of items. If you sort a column, such as a Tape ID or Tracks column, any items that have the same information in that field will line up in a block within the bin list, as shown in Figure 3.2.

Name	Tracks	Start	End	Duration	Mark IN
FK-1A_wild	A1-4			2:23	
FK-1G	A1-4	01:06:19:00	01:09:07:00	2:48:00	
FK-1C_1	A4			2:08:15	
FK-1K	A4			1:47:03	
FK-1_2	A4			2:30:08	
FK-1G_4	A4			2:34:08	
FK-1B_x	A4			30:10	
FK-1E_7	A4			2:36:20	
FK-1J_2	A4			2:52:10	
FK-1J_1	A4			2:29:17	
FK-1B_2	A4			1:07:06	
FK-1D_2	A4			1:48:23	
FK-1E_2_x	A4			11:00	
FK-1C_2	A4			1:47:04	
FK-1J_2_x	A4			35:00	
FK-1C_1_A.sync.01	V1 A4	22:40:47:06	22:42:53:16	2:06:10	
FK-1K_3_A.sync.01	V1 A4	01:45:06:14	01:46:53:16	1:47:02	
FK-1_2_A.sync.01	V1 A4	18:41:11:03	18:43:41:11	2:30:08	
FK-1G_4_A.sync.01	V1 A4	01:15:02:22	01:17:37:05	2:34:07	
FK-1B_x.sync.01	V1 A4	19:05:15:09	19:05:45:19	30:10	
FK-1E_7_A.sync.01	V1 A4	23:56:00:16	23:58:37:12	2:36:20	
FK-1J_2_B.sync.01	V1 A4	01:32:49:16	01:35:42:00	2:52:08	
FK-1J_1_A.sync.01	V1 A4	01:29:47:19	01:32:17:11	2:29:16	
FK-1B_2_A.sync.01	V1 A4	20:27:54:15	20:29:01:21	1:07:06	
FK-1D_2_A.sync.01	V1 A4	23:22:43:21	23:24:30:23	1:47:02	

The Deal_Selects

Figure 3.2 Bin items sorted by tracks.

This is useful in many ways, both for editorial purposes and for media management. But we are getting ahead of ourselves. First you need to learn to add and remove columns from your bin, and how to add the custom info that you will often want to use as criteria for sorting.

Adding and Removing Bin Columns

You can choose to display a wide range of information in a bin, each in its own column. A new bin displays the most commonly referenced information, but there will be times that you want to see other info.

To display other clip data:

1. Click the BIN VIEW menu. (This will initially display "Untitled.")

2. Select the desired preset BIN VIEW. Choose among the following options:

    -   **Custom:** In this view, the only heading provided is the clip name. You can customize the view by displaying or hiding statistical column headings and by creating new columns.

    -   **Capture:** This view contains a set of headings that are useful when capturing footage from tape. These include Start and End Timecode, Duration, Tape, Tracks, Resolution, Offline, and Drive.

    -   **Film:** Use this view when working with 24 fps material. Information such as camroll and pull-in frame is displayed with this selection.

    -   **Format:** This option displays the video formats, resolutions, and projects for the bin's contents.

    -   **Media Tool:** This option duplicates the headings currently saved in the Media tool.

    -   **Statistics:** In this view the standard statistical column headings are derived from information established during capturing.

To add statistical headings to your current view:

1. Choose BIN > CHOOSE COLUMNS. Alternatively, right-click on one of the column headings and select CHOOSE COLUMNS from the menu that appears.

    A Bin Column Selection dialog box appears, displaying all the available headings. The ones already displayed in your bin appear highlighted.

2. To add a heading, click on the HEADING name in the list to select it.

3. To remove a heading that is already selected, click on the HEADING name in the list to deselect it.

4. Click OK.

 To quickly clear the entire list of columns in the Bin Column Selection dialog box, click the All/None button twice. This is perfect for when you only want to see a couple columns of info.

 You can also remove a column by right-clicking on the heading and choosing Hide Column.

Any new columns of info typically appear to the right of existing ones. You may need to scroll horizontally to see the added info. Following is a list of useful bin columns:

- **Color:** This column displays a color tile for each bin item. It's used to color-code bin items.

- **Drive:** This column displays the drive containing the media files for the master clip.

- **Duration:** This column displays the total duration of each bin item.

- **Format:** This column displays the raster dimension and frame rate of the clips and sequences.

- **Offline:** This column displays track names for any media files offline.

- **Tracks:** This column displays all tracks used by this media object, such as a clip or sequence.

- **Video:** This column displays the clip video format (resolution, color space, and field motion type).

 For a full list of the information displayed in each bin column, see the article "Bin Column Headings" in the Media Composer Help.

Arranging Bin Column Headings

You can rearrange columns in Text view any time by dragging the headings to the right or left. Arrange the columns with the most important information to the left, closer to the name, and those with the information that you need to reference less frequently further to the right. That way, you don't have to scroll horizontally to see the important info.

Adding Custom Information to a Bin

In addition to the standard headings that can be displayed in Text view; you can add your own custom column headings to hold text information about clips and sequences, like adding labels or keywords. Tagging the footage with this added information has both short-term and long-term value, as you will see.

To add custom information in custom columns:

1. Display the BIN in Text view.

2. Right-click any one of the headings and select ADD CUSTOM COLUMN.

3. Type a NAME (for example, SHOT TYPE) for the new column heading and press ENTER (Windows) or RETURN (Mac).

   The pointer moves to the data box beside the first clip in the bin.

4. Type the information you wish to add, such as MS (for medium shot), and press ENTER (Windows) or RETURN (Mac) to move to the next line.

5. Create additional COLUMNS and enter INFORMATION as needed.

6. If necessary, open the bin's FAST menu and choose ALIGN COLUMNS or press CTRL+T (Windows) or COMMAND+T (Mac) to straighten out the columns.

 Column headings can only display up to 14 characters, including spaces.

The following are suggestions for custom columns to track useful info:

- **Quality:** This would contain asterisks for good (*), better (**), and best (***) quality.

- **Good:** This would contain the value Yes or No.

- **Circled Take:** This would contain the value Yes or No.

- **Description:** This would describe the content of the shot.

- **Location:** This would indicate the location at which the shot was recorded. This might be a production set or location.

- **Shot Type:** This would contain an abbreviation to identify each clip's shot size, such as WS for wide shot, MS for medium shot, CU for close-up, and so on.

- **Keywords:** This would include searchable keywords to identify b-roll, stock footage, music, and sound effects.

- **Dialogue:** This would include the first few words of each dialogue clip.

- **Rights Released?:** This would contain the value Yes, No, Pending, or Denied.

- **Episode:** This would identify the number of the show episode.

- **Genre:** This would identify the type of music or sound effect.

 Circled take is a film-production term. In film production, the takes that a director deems good are circled on the lined script by the script supervisor. The circled takes are tracked all the way through the editing process.

Entering Data

After your columns are created, you can begin entering data.

To enter data in a custom column:

1. Click within the CUSTOM COLUMN, on the row for the item for which you wish to enter data.

    The empty text field appears, ready for you to type. (See Figure 3.3.)

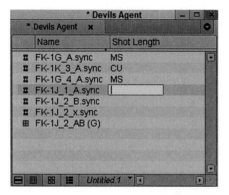

Figure 3.3 The bin in "data entry" mode.

2. Type the WORD(S) or VALUE.

3. Press ENTER on the numeric keypad to exit data-entry mode.

There are a number of data-entry shortcuts to learn to make this process as efficient as possible. Table 3.2 identifies. If you are working as an assistant (or hope to), it will be a good idea to learn these!

Table 3.2: Modifying Text View Bin

To	Do This
Repeat information from another cell in the same column. (This modification applies only to custom columns.)	Hold down the Alt (Windows) or Option (Mac) key and click on the cell in which you want the text to appear. A pop-up menu of the items already entered in that column appears. Select the correct text from the menu.
Change a column heading after pressing Return or Enter. This modification applies only to custom columns.	Hold down the Alt (Windows) or Option (Mac) key and click the heading. The heading text is highlighted. Type the new text for the heading.
Delete a custom column.	Click the column heading and press the Delete key. Note that you can delete only custom columns. You cannot delete statistical columns, only hide them.
Hide a column.	Click the column heading and press the Delete key. If you apply this to a custom column, a dialog box appears from which you can choose between deleting and hiding the column
Show a previously hidden column.	Choose Bin > Headings and select the previously hidden column.

Sorting the Bin

There is inherent value in having the information you added displayed with the clip. But, that value is increased when you leverage custom information to further organize your bins, whether it is to change how the information is displayed in an individual bin or to organize it across multiple bins.

One of the quickest ways to reorganize your project assets to be more efficient is to change how they are displayed in the bin. You can do this by sorting a bin column by the bin contents. Ask yourself, do you want to see everything in the bin, just reordered? If so, sort. Or, do you want to see just a selected few? Then, sift.

- Sorting arranges bin items in alphanumeric order (numbers first) based on the information in the column you choose to sort. All bin items are still displayed.

- Filtering changes which items are visible in the bin based on certain criteria you define. Only the items that meet the criteria are displayed; all others are filtered out.

  Sorting a column in a bin is simple and intuitive.

To sort clips in ascending order:

- In Text view, right-click the HEADING of the column that you want to sort and choose SORT ON COLUMN, ASCENDING, as shown in Figure 3.4.

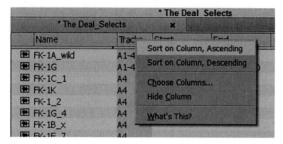

Figure 3.4 Sort a bin column by right-clicking on the column heading and choosing a sort option from the menu that appears.

To sort clips in descending order:

- In Text view, right-click the HEADING of the column that you want to sort and choose SORT ON COLUMN, DESCENDING.

In addition, there are several shortcuts built into the system:

- You can double-click a column heading to sort the column. Double-clicking again reverses the sort order.

- You can choose Bin > Sort or Ctrl+E (Windows) and Command+E (Mac)

- To reapply the last sort, choose Bin > Sort Again with no column selected.

  This is especially useful after new clips are added to a sorted bin.

  Sorting a column arranges the entries in order. If there are redundant entries in a given field, such as Shot Length, then the bin items will conveniently line up in blocks, as shown in Figure 3.5.

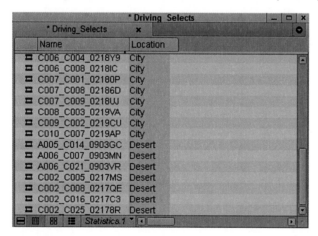

Figure 3.5 Sorting custom columns with redundant info will organize the clips into blocks.

Which column you sort depends on your needs at the moment. When initially organizing the material in a new project, sorting a column into groups gives you the perfect setup to copy those clips to another bin. Easy examples for this include columns marked Good, Circled Take, Location, or Rights Released. Later, you may sort clips into blocks for media-management purposes. For example, you could sort the Drive column to verify that all the media is on your raided media drives or the ISIS partition versus a portable drive. If not, you may need to copy those files.

Media Management is covered in Lesson 11, "Technical Fundamentals."

Sorting Multiple Columns

You can also select and sort multiple columns in a bin at once. The left-most selected column is the primary criterion for the sorting operation. You can rearrange the columns in the bin by dragging a column heading to the right or left to establish which column is primary. For example, if you want to arrange your clips according to Start Timecode Within Quality, arrange the columns as shown in Figure 3.6.

Name	Quality	Start	End	Duration	Tracks
FK-1_2	**			2:30:08	A4
FK-1_2_A	*	18:41:11:03	18:43:41:11	2:30:08	V1 E
FK-1_2_A.sync.01	***	18:41:11:03	18:43:41:11	2:30:08	V1 A
FK-1A_wild	*			2:23	A1-4
FK-1B_2	**			1:07:06	A4
FK-1B_2_A	**	20:27:54:15	20:29:01:21	1:07:06	V1 E
FK-1B_2_A.sync.01	**	20:27:54:15	20:29:01:21	1:07:06	V1 A
FK-1B_x	***			30:10	A4
FK-1B_x	*	19:05:15:09	19:05:45:19	30:10	V1 E
FK-1B_x.sync.01	*	19:05:15:09	19:05:45:19	30:10	V1 A
FK-1C_1	**			2:08:15	A4
FK-1C_1_A	**	22:40:47:06	22:42:53:16	2:06:10	V1 E
FK-1C_1_A.sync.01	***	22:40:47:06	22:42:53:16	2:06:10	V1 A
FK-1C_1_AB	*	22:40:47:06	22:42:41:09	2:08:15	V1 A
FK-1C_1_B	*	22:40:32:18	22:42:41:09	2:08:15	V1 E
FK-1C_2	***			1:47:04	A4

Figure 3.6 The Quality and Start columns are arranged to perform a dual sort, with Quality taking priority.

When sorting the Name column, you can manipulate the sort order. For example, you can keep your most recent sequence at the top of the bin by adding a special character to the beginning of the name—an exclamation point or currency sign works well. Likewise, you can keep your old sequences at the bottom of the bin by preceding their names with the character Z.

Printing a Bin

You can print whatever is displayed in the bin by choosing File > Print Bin. If your computer is connected to a printer, you can print a hard copy. If not, both Windows and Mac computers also allow you to "print" into a PDF file, either as a built-in feature of the operating system or through a bundled add-on application. This is useful when collaborating with others in the post-production process. For example, you might sort the bin to display only those music clips marked for use and then print the bin for the producer for purchasing of the rights.

Filtering the Bin

At the bottom of each bin window is a Search field, indicated in Figure 3.7.

The Search field acts as a filter. As you type, Media Composer immediately begins to filter the items in the bin using the value typed into the Search field. (Minimum value of two characters is required.) The results are based on the information currently displayed in any column.

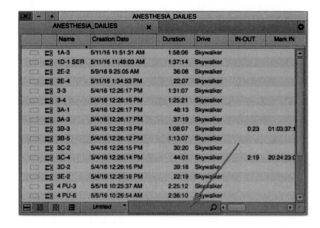

Figure 3.7   The Search field acts as a filter, limiting what is displayed.

To filter the bin using the Search field:

1. Optionally, right-click at the top of a column, select **CHOOSE COLUMNS,** and modify the columns displayed to expand or limit the information being searched.

2. Click in the **SEARCH FIELD** and type a **WORD** or **VALUE.**

    It is important to consider which columns are displayed in the bin, since this determines the information Media Composer is using to show the results.

    If, for example, you type "pu" to find some pick-up shots, the bin would filter to show you the clips with "pu" in the Name, as expected. But, if the letters "pu" appear together in the info of any other column – in a comment that mentions a "focus pull," for example – that clip would also be displayed, as shown in Figure 3.8.

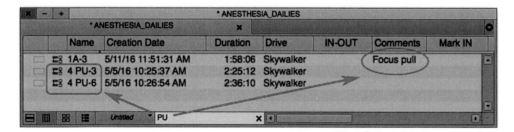

Figure 3.8 The Search field filters the information in all visible columns.

 If you change the columns displayed after the bin has been filtered, you will need to re-run the search by typing in the Search field again.

Saving Bin Views

Adding statistical columns in Text view or creating columns in custom views creates different bin views that can be saved.

 Save the default Timeline view before you make any adjustments and name it Default.

To save a bin view:

1. Click on the **BIN VIEW** menu (the default setting is Untitled).

2. Choose **SAVE AS**.

    The View Name dialog box shown in Figure 3.9 opens.

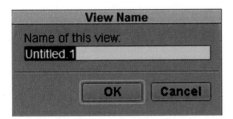

Figure 3.9 Name your bin view.

3. Type a **NAME** in the Name of This View field.

4. Click **OK**.

 Custom columns appear at the bottom of the list in the Bin Column Selection window.

Suggestions for Custom Bin Views

-   **Offline:** This view could display only the Offline and Tracks columns.

-   **Marks:** This view could display Mark IN and Mark OUT columns.

-   **Lock:** This view could display only the Lock column, to enable you to see which of your clips are locked.

-   **Tape:** This view could display only the Tape column (or both the Tape and Start columns).

Creating Subclips

Subclipping is used to divide portions of one clip into shorter clips, called subclips.

Creating subclips is a great way to manage footage. Subclips can be used for any number of reasons – to isolate important sound bites from an interview, pull good cutaway shots, separate clean room tone, or to separate individual takes (if the director resets for another take without stopping the camera), and more. The subclips can then be organized independently of the master clips. Some functions, such as AutoSync (covered shortly), create subclips automatically.

When you create a subclip, you are not creating new media, nor changing the original master clip. The subclip links to the same media file as the master clip. The original master clip used to create a subclip remains intact. In fact, a subclip edited into a sequence can be trimmed out to reveal more material from the original master clip.

 Subclips created in a film project cannot be trimmed out. This is a protective feature for traditional film workflows in which a telecine tape containing multiple film reels is captured as a single master clip, and subclips are then used to define each reel. Havoc would ensue if you could trim a subclip into the next reel.

To create a subclip:

1. Load and play a **MASTER CLIP** in the Source monitor.

2. Mark an **IN POINT** where you would like the subclip to begin and an **OUT POINT** where you would like it to end.

3. To confirm the marks, click the **PLAY IN TO OUT** button or press the **6** key.

4. Enable/disable video or audio tracks.

5. Drag the **CLIP ICON** from the Source monitor's **CLIP NAME** menu and drop it anywhere in the bin. (The mouse cursor becomes a hand over the subclip icon.) Alternatively, click and drag directly from the Source monitor to the destination bin.

    The subclip appears in the bin with an icon that is a small version of the master clip icon. It is labeled "**clipname.Sub.n**", where *n* is the number of subclips you have created from that clip. (See Figure 3.10.)

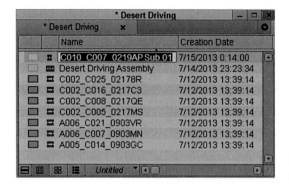

Figure 3.10
A newly created subclip in the bin; ready for renaming.

6. Name the SUBCLIP.

When creating subclip names, it's just as important to follow a good naming scheme as when creating clip names. This will help you keep track of your footage and make the subclip easy to locate when needed.

 You can map the Make Subclip button from the Command Palette (Edit tab) to a key on the keyboard. Keyboard mapping is covered in the "Media Composer Fundamentals I" (MC101) course. When using the Make Subclip button, the subclip goes into the most recently active bin and is highlighted.

Cloning Clips to Multiple Bins

As you organize the footage, it may be useful to have a clip appear in multiple bins. For example, you may want a clip in a bin with all the other material on the camera card, in a bin with all the other clips of that character, and in a bin for the scene it is from.

This simple example illustrates an important point. To keep the editing process flowing freely and efficiently, it is best to have a clip in multiple bins, one for each of the different ways you might go looking for it. At a minimum, assistant editors of scripted features will organize the footage with one copy of the master clip in the "Dailies" bin and another in the Scene bin. On reality TV shows, clips are often copied numerous times, again keeping a copy in the Capture bin but also putting copies into bins by character, location, episode, and more.

To clone a master clip:

1. Open the BIN containing the master clip to copy as well as the BIN in which you wish to place the copy.

2. ALT-DRAG (Windows) or OPTION-DRAG (Mac) the MASTER CLIP to the new bin.

    The copy appears in the new bin with the same name as the original.

    When you copy a clip from bin to bin, you are more accurately creating a clone—another instance of the same item with all its metadata. All changes made to the clip in one bin will appear on the cloned version in the other bin and vice versa. If you color-code the clip in one bin, for example, the copy in the other bin will also be color coded; comments added to one show up on the other, etc. This gives you confidence that you are always looking at the most up-to-date information, no matter where you see a copy of the clip. It also saves you the hassle of trying to track and manage those changes yourself.

 Creating a copy of the clip does not copy the media. The same media is referenced by all copies.

There may be times that you do, in fact, wish to have a separate copy of an item that you can rename, add separate comments to, or otherwise modify *without* having those changes ripple back to the original. For that, you will *duplicate* the clip instead of cloning it.

To duplicate a master clip (or other item in the bin):

1. Click the item's ICON in the bin to select it.

2. Choose EDIT > DUPLICATE. Alternatively, press CTRL+D (Windows) or COMMAND+D (Mac).

    The duplicated clip will appear in the bin. It will have the same name as the clip, with the added suffix ".Copy.01". Each additional dupe will receive the next sequential number. The system also highlights the name automatically, ready for you to change it.

Opening a Bin from Another Project

Sometimes you will want access to material from another project, but you will not want to permanently bring the material into the current project. For example, you might have a separate "library" project with bins of stock footage, sound effects, or other commonly used material.

To open a bin from another project:

1.   With the Project window active and no bins selected, choose FILE > OPEN BIN. Alternatively, press CTRL+O (Windows) or COMMAND+O (Mac).

     The Select a Bin dialog box appears.

2.   Navigate to the bin you want to open, click on the BIN and click OPEN.

     If you do not see the name of the bin you are looking for, look in other project folders.

     The bin opens in your project and an Other Bins folder appears in the Project window in italics. (See Figure 3.11.) The bin is listed inside this folder, with the originating project in the column to the right of the bin name. Remember, you are simply borrowing this bin from the other project.

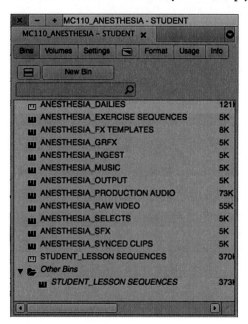

Figure 3.11 Bins opened from other projects appear in the Other Bins folder.

Although you are only borrowing this bin, it is important to note that any changes you make to it are permanent. For example, if you delete an object from this bin while you are borrowing it, that object will also be missing from the bin when it is opened again in its original project. Likewise, if you change any information about the items in the bin, those changes are also permanently saved with the bin when you close it.

If you want the contents of this bin to reside in this project, duplicate the clips to a bin in the current project. Here, it is preferable to *duplicate* the clip because it gives you the freedom to work with that clip however you need, without causing unwanted changes to the original in the library. An example would be changing the clip's assigned color, or the clip's name.

To remove borrowed bins from the Project window:

1.   Select the BINS to remove from the Other Bins folder.

2.   Press the DELETE or BACKSPACE key.

> The borrowed bin does not go to the Trash folder. It disappears from this Project window but still resides in its original project. It is important to note that removing the borrowed bin from the project does not delete the bin file or any of its information.

 Using the File > Open Bin command is discouraged in an Interplay environment. Instead, all assets from all projects can be accessed through the Interplay window, thereby eliminating the need.

AutoSyncing Picture and Sound

Video has most commonly contained both picture and sound, and editors would ingest them simultaneously. However, with the proliferation of video production on DSLR and digital cinema cameras, it is increasingly common for audio to be recorded to a separate device and therefore ingested separately.

The technique of recording audio separately to a field recorder is referred to as **double-system sound** one "system" for picture, another for sound. Double-system sound recording is how film has been produced for a very long time. At the time of this publication, DSLRs are known for high-quality imaging capabilities and low-quality audio recording. Double-system sound recording overcomes this limitation while at the same time offering certain production benefits, including the freedom to place microphones in the optimal recording location regardless of camera location.

To efficiently edit with separate audio and video sources, you need to synchronize the two and combine them into a single item. Media Composer features the ability to automatically synchronize picture and sound, called AutoSync. After you ingest the audio and video files, you use the AutoSync feature to sync picture and sound or multiple tracks of sound.

You can use any of these methods to sync the clips.

■   **Film TC/Sound TC:** With this method, the system syncs the film to the sound timecode.

■   **IN points:** Here, you mark an IN point near the beginning of each picture clip and its corresponding audio clip to indicate the point at which the clips should be synchronized.

■   **OUT points:** Here, you mark an OUT point near the end of each picture clip and its corresponding audio clip to indicate the point at which the clips should be synchronized.

■   **Source Timecode:** With this method, the system syncs each picture clip with an audio clip that has common source timecode.

■   **Auxiliary TC1–TC5, TC 24, Aux TC 24:** With this method, the system syncs each picture clip with the audio clip that has the same timecode in the same auxiliary timecode column. For example, you might use this for syncing BWF files (first copying the Start column to the TC1 column) to picture. Aux TC 24 represents the video timecode of an HD downconvert to SD video.

■   **Waveform Analysis:** This method syncs the clips by matching the patterns of the audio waveforms.

Provided that the video footage has a reasonable level of pickup in the scratch audio recorded by the camera, syncing by waveforms is the fastest and most accurate. If no audio is present, or is too different than the field audio productions, then syncing is commonly done using IN points or OUT points.

 If you are AutoSyncing clips of differing durations, the longer clip is truncated to the duration of the shorter clip.

To AutoSync clips:

1.   (Optional) Copy the clips to be synched to a new bin for sync'ing.

2.   Depending on which AutoSync method you plan to use, do one of the following:

   a.   If you're using timecode to synchronize the clips, be sure the timecode matches on each clip. Then select all the clips you want to sync.

   - **Film TC/Sound TC:** The film timecode and sound timecode must match.

   - **Source Timecode:** Each picture clip and its matching audio clip must have common overlapping source timecode.

   - **Auxiliary TC1–TC5, TC 24, Aux TC 24:** Each picture clip and its matching audio clip must have the same timecode logged in the same auxiliary timecode column.

   b.   If you're using IN or OUT points to sync the clips, do one of the following. Then select the pair of clips to be synced.

   - **IN points:** Use the Mark IN button to mark a sync point near the start of both clips.

   - **OUT points:** Use the Mark OUT button to mark a sync point near the end of both clips.

   For video clips, the sync point is usually the first frame where the slate is fully closed. For audio clips, the sync point is usually the first frame that you hear the clap of the slate.

3.   Choose CLIP > AUTOSYNC.

   A dialog box appears.

4.   Choose the METHOD you want to use to sync the selected clips.

5.   Click OK.

   The system creates a synced subclip in the source bin, named after the video master clip. Edit your sequence using these clips.

Technique: How to Find a Good Sync Point

If you're establishing sync points with IN and OUT marks, then setting the mark to a slate clap should be easy. It's easiest when a slate is properly used and recorded, but even if someone just walks onto the set and claps his or her hands where the camera and microphone can record it well, that is better than nothing.

To mark the clap in the video, make sure you mark the exact frame where the clapper touches the top of the board. Step through the footage using the Step 1 Frame keys. These are the 3 and 4 keys, by default, as well as the left arrow and right arrow.

To find the audio cue, play or drag through the footage with Caps Lock enabled for Digital Audio Scrub. Alternatively, try to spot it on the waveform and just click to move the playhead over it. Once the position indicator is close, again use the Step 1 Frame keys. As you step through, you will hear the audio associated with each "frame" you advance. Step through until you hear the clap loudly. You may have to go back and forth a couple times to be sure you are on it.

If no clap—either human or mechanical—was recorded, then look for an impact action with a distinct sound, such as a cup hitting the table, a door closing, etc.

If syncing talking heads, here are some tips that can help:

- Sync using the beginning of a sentence or the first word after a pause.

- Words that begin with a consonant with distinctive mouth movement, such as *t-*, *th-*, or *f-*, or an explosive consonant, like *p-* or *b-*, are your best bet.

- Words that begin with softer consonants like *m-* and *n-,* are less precise but can still be used under the right circumstances (and when there is no better option). For slow talkers, you may have better success syncing the frame where the mouth opens and the sound changes to the vowel.

- Words that begin with vowels are very difficult to use as a sync point and should be avoided.

- Always check the synced subclip(s) to ensure that sync is correct before moving on. If it isn't, select the subclip(s) in the bin and press Delete. Then adjust the marks and sync again.

Grouping Clips

Grouping creates a separate group clip out of a single set of master clips, from the start (or IN) point to the end (or OUT) point of the longest clip. The Group function allows you to sync clips based on common source timecode, auxiliary timecode, or marks placed in the footage.

Grouping master clips from different cameras is a step commonly associated with editing a multicamera production, such as concert footage. It is also common in film productions that utilize an A and B camera.

If the project used multiple cameras, it is common practice for the assistant editor to group the different camera angles into a group clip after AutoSyncing. This gives the editor the convenience of being able to load a single item from the bin and have simultaneous access to both camera angles, and the freedom to switch between them on the fly.

Media Composer v8.5 added the ability to group by waveform analysis, a sophisticated process of matching the waveforms. Rather than a simple match, Media Composer examines the entire waveform for similarities in peaks and valleys, regardless of amplitude. This dramatically increases its usefulness, since the audio recorded by different devices in different locations on set (or at an event) will naturally pickup different audio patterns. There are limitations, including the most obvious one being that each clip must have audio. If grouping by waveforms is unsuccessful, you will need to group by another method.

Given the speed and ease-of-use of grouping by waveforms, many editors are choosing to group audio and video clips instead of using AutoSync. Similarly, if grouping by waveforms doesn't work to sync the audio and video, you can use AutoSync as described previously.

To group clips:

1. (Optional) If grouping by marks, load each CLIP and then mark an IN POINT at the sync point near the start of each clip or an OUT POINT at the sync point near the end of each clip.

    Ideally, during production, a slate will have been recorded at the head (or tail) of each roll of film or tape, which you use for marking IN (or OUT) points.

    If the shoot didn't use a slate, use any single, discrete visual or aural event recorded by all cameras simultaneously.

2. In the bin, select the CLIPS you want to group together.

3. (Optional) Sort the clips—for example, by name within start timecode. In this case, the Start column would be to the left of the Name column.

    The order of clips in the bin determines the order in which the clips are displayed when grouped together and displayed in the Source monitor. Thus, it is a good idea to develop a good, consistent clip-naming scheme.

    If grouping A and B cameras, it is common to have the A camera be the first in the group.

4. Choose BIN > GROUP CLIPS. Alternatively, press CTRL+SHIFT+G (Windows) or COMMAND+SHIFT+G (Mac).

    The Group Clips dialog box appears, as shown in Figure 3.12.

Figure 3.12 The Group Clips dialog box.

5. Select an OPTION. The choices are as follows:

    • **Film TC/Sound TC:** Choose this option to sync based on matching film and sound timecode recorded in the field.

    • **Inpoints** or **Outpoints:** Choose this option to sync according to IN or OUT points set in each clip.

    • **Source Timecode:** Choose this option to sync based on matching timecode.

    • **Auxiliary TC1–TC5:** Choose this option to sync based on auxiliary TC.

    • **Waveform Analysis:** Choose this option to sync clips by aligning the audio waveforms in the clips.

6. Click OK.

    A group clip appears in the bin with the name of the first clip in the group followed by a .Grp.n file extension.

7. Optionally, rename the GROUP CLIP—e.g. CLIPNAME_A/B.

8. Load the GROUP CLIP into the Source monitor.

9. Create a SEQUENCE from the group clip(s).

10. In the Source or Record monitor, use the UP ARROW and DOWN ARROW keys to switch between angles while you edit.

 The master clips must have matching timecode in the same column to AutoSync using any of the timecode options.

 Exercise Break: Exercise 3.1 and 3.2
Pause here to practice what you've learned.

Review/Discussion Questions

1. Why might you need to sync audio and video master clips?

2. List the steps to sync audio and video master clips. What is the result of this process?

3. What is a group clip? What is the advantage of working with group clips?

4. How do you display the start timecode of your clips?

5. How do you add a custom column to a bin in Text view?

6. What is the shortcut to view a pop-up menu containing previously entered values in a custom column?

7. What is the difference between duplicating a clip and cloning a clip?

8. You need to track rights releases for each man-on-the-street interview in a documentary. How could you do that in the bin?

9. You have audio and video master clips that do not have a common timecode reference. Is it possible to sync these clips? If so, how?

Lesson 3 Keyboard Shortcuts

Key	Shortcut
Return or Enter	Moves the active text entry field down one row in the column
Shift+Return	Moves upward
Tab	Moves to the next column
Shift+Tab	Moves to the next column on the left
Alt-click the target cell (Windows)/ Option-click the target cell (Mac)	Repeats information from another cell in the same custom column
Alt-click the heading (Windows)/ Option-click the heading (Mac)	Changes a custom column heading
Ctrl+Shift+N (Windows)/ Command+Shift+N (Mac)	Creates a new sequence
Ctrl+O (Windows)/Command+O (Mac)	Opens a bin
Ctrl+Shift+G (Windows)/ Command+Shift+G (Mac)	Groups clips
Ctrl+D (Windows)/Command+D (Mac)	Duplicates
Alt-drag (Windows)/Option-drag (Mac)	Clones a clip from one bin to another

Prepare a Project for Editing

Media Used: Anesthesia

Duration: 60 minutes

GOALS

- Create and save custom bin views
- Add custom information to clips
- Sort and sift items in a bin
- Copy clips to multiple bins
- Use bins and assets from other projects
- Synchronize picture and sound from separate sources
- Create assembly sequences

Exercise 3.1: Syncing Audio to Video by Waveform

Before an editor begins editing footage, it is common that they will need to sync the video footage with the audio files that were recorded separately on set. This must be done even if the audio was recorded by the camera because audio recorded using a boom microphone and a recording device is superior to in-camera audio.

In the following exercises we will use two techniques for syncing audio. First, we will sync using the in-camera audio waveforms as a reference. Then we will sync by using the traditional method of using both the slate in the video and the audio spike in the production audio as our guide.

Media Used: Anesthesia

Duration: 30 minutes

For this exercise, we will use the **MC110_ANESTHESIA** project.

1. Create a new bin. Name it **ANESTHESIA_SYNCED CLIPS**.

    This is where you will put your new clips containing synced picture and sound.

2. First, open the bin **ANESTHESIA_RAW VIDEO**.

    This bin contains the video that needs synced.

    Let's start by syncing using audio waveforms. This is a quick technique for syncing audio when the video footage contains "scratch audio" from the camera.

3. Take a moment to observe the way the clips are named. They are labeled according to a common technique in film and video – Scene, Shot, Take#.

    For example, the first shot (1A-3) is Scene 1, Shot A, Take #3, as shown in Figure 3.13. Audio files will be named with the same convention and this should make it easy for you to determine which video clips and audio clips go together just by looking at the clip names in the bin. This information corresponds with the information on the slate at the beginning of each video clip.

		Name	Creation Date	Duration	Drive
☐	⊟	1A-3_NO AUDIO	5/23/16 10:45:39 AM	1:58:06	Skyw:
☐	⊟	3-3_NO AUDIO	5/23/16 10:45:39 AM	1:31:07	Skyw:
☐	⊟	3-4_NO AUDIO	5/23/16 10:45:40 AM	1:25:21	Skyw:
☐	⊟	3A-1_NO AUDIO	5/23/16 10:45:40 AM	48:13	Skyw:
☐	⊟	3A-3_NO AUDIO	5/23/16 10:45:40 AM	37:19	Skyw:
☐	⊟	3B-3_scratch audio	5/23/16 10:44:41 AM	1:08:07	Skyw:
☐	⊟	3B-5_scratch audio	5/23/16 10:44:41 AM	1:13:07	Skyw:
☐	⊟	4PU-3_scratch audio	5/23/16 10:44:41 AM	2:26:00	Skyw:
☐	⊟	4PU-6_scratch audio	5/23/16 10:44:41 AM	2:36:10	Skyw:
☐	⊟	8D-1SER_scratch audio	5/23/16 10:44:41 AM	1:37:14	Skyw:

Figure 3.13 A bin showing clips named by Scene, Shot and Take.

4. Select all the clips in the **ANESTHESIA_RAW VIDEO** bin that are labeled _SCRATCH AUDIO. ALT-DRAG (Windows) or OPTION-drag (Mac) them into the **ANESTHESIA_SYNCED CLIPS** bin.

    This will create cloned files of the clips in **ANESTHESIA_RAW VIDEO** in the new bin.

5. Next, open the bin **ANESTHESIA_PRODUCTION AUDIO**.

    This bin contains the audio that needs to be synced with the video.

6. Select all the clips in the **ANESTHESIA_PRODUCTION AUDIO** bin. ALT-drag (Windows) or OPTION-DRAG (Mac) them into the **ANESTHESIA_SYNCED CLIPS** bin.

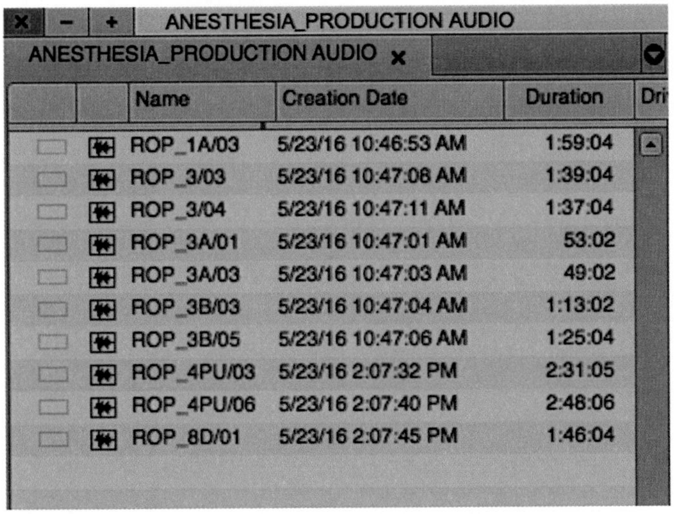

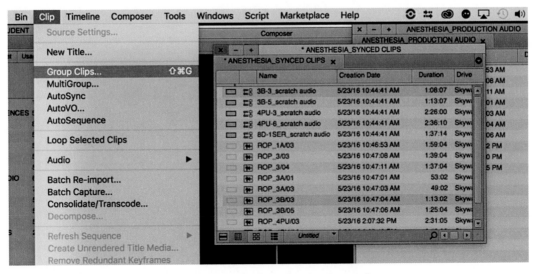

Figure 3.14 Selecting all clips in the "ANESTHESIA_PRODUCTION AUDIO" bin.

7. In the **ANESTHESIA_SYNCED CLIPS** bin, right-click the NAME column and choose SORT ON COLUMN, ASCENDING.

    This will sort all of the clips in order in the bin using the scene number.

8. To sync the audio and video clips by waveform, select two video and audio clips that match –for example, **3B-3_SCRATCH AUDIO** and **ROP_3B/03**, and choose CLIP >GROUP CLIPS or click CTRL+SHIFT+G (Windows) or COMMAND+SHIFT+G (Mac).

Figure 3.15 Grouping clips by syncing the audio and video clips by waveform.

9.   In the GROUP CLIPS window that pops up, choose WAVEFORM ANALYSIS.

Figure 3.16   Select Waveform Analysis in the Group Clips dialog.

Avid will now analyze the in-camera audio from the video clip and use it as a reference to sync the audio to the video. It will replace the audio from the video clip "3B-3_scratch audio" with the audio clip "ROP_3B/03."

A new grouped clip will be created in the bin with this icon.

Figure 3.17   Group clip icon.

10.   Rename the new grouped clip **3B-3_SYNCED**, and then load the clip into the Source monitor to verify that the audio is replaced and has been correctly synchronized with the picture.

If everything looks and sounds good, continue to the next step. If not, delete the sync'd subclip and sync the master clips again using IN or OUT marks.

		Name	Creation Date	Duration	D
	⊞	3B-3_synced	5/27/16 1:07:41 PM	1:13:02	
		3B-3_scratch audio	5/23/16 10:44:41 AM	1:08:07	
		3B-5_scratch audio	5/23/16 10:44:41 AM	1:13:07	
		4PU-3_scratch audio	5/23/16 10:44:41 AM	2:26:00	
		4PU-6_scratch audio	5/23/16 10:44:41 AM	2:36:10	
		8D-1SER_scratch audio	5/23/16 10:44:41 AM	1:37:14	
		ROP_1A/03	5/23/16 10:46:53 AM	1:59:04	
		ROP_3/03	5/23/16 10:47:08 AM	1:39:04	
		ROP_3/04	5/23/16 10:47:11 AM	1:37:04	
		ROP_3A/01	5/23/16 10:47:01 AM	53:02	
		ROP_3A/03	5/23/16 10:47:03 AM	49:02	
		ROP_3B/03	5/23/16 10:47:04 AM	1:13:02	
		ROP_3B/05	5/23/16 10:47:06 AM	1:25:04	

ANESTHESIA_SYNCED CLIPS   Untitled

Figure 3.18   Renaming the new group clip "3B-3_synced" and then load the clip into the Source monitor.

11. Continue syncing all the video clips labeled **_SCRATCH AUDIO** with their corresponding video clips.

12. Scrub through a few of the clips when you are finished to make sure everything was synced correctly.

13. Lastly, delete the clones of the original video clips, leaving only the synced clips and the cloned production audio files in the **ANESTHESIA_SYNCED CLIPS** bin. Do this by selecting the clones labeled **_SCRATCH AUDIO** and pressing **DELETE**. In the Delete dialog box, check the box that says **DELETE MASTER CLIPS**.

    This will delete them from the **ANESTHESIA_SYNCED CLIPS** bin, but not from the original bin they came from.

Figure 3.19 The Delete dialog box.

Exercise 3.2: Syncing Clips with Marks

In the last exercise, we synchronized audio and video clips using waveform analysis. In this exercise, we will use the more traditional method of syncing using the slate as visual cue and the audio spike as a reference in the audio file. We will mark an IN at each point and use those marks to synchronize our clips.

Media Used: Anesthesia

Duration: 30 minutes

1. First, open the **ANESTHESIA_SYNCED CLIPS** bin.

    The cloned audio clips you need to sync should already be in the bin (we moved them over in Exercise 3.1).

2. Open the bin **ANESTHESIA_RAW VIDEO**.

    This bin contains the remaining video that needs synced.

3. Select all the clips in the **ANESTHESIA_RAW VIDEO** bin that are labeled **_NO AUDIO**, and then hold down **ALT** (Windows) or **OPTION** (Mac) and drag them into the **ANESTHESIA_SYNCED CLIPS** bin.

    This will create cloned files of the clips in **ANESTHESIA_RAW VIDEO** in the new bin.

4. In the **ANESTHESIA_SYNCED CLIPS**, right-click the **NAME** column and choose **SORT ON COLUMN, ASCENDING** to sort all of the clips in order in the bin using the scene number.

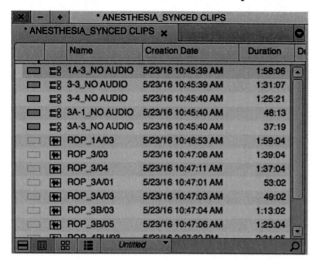

Figure 3.20   Sorting the Name column in ascending order.

5. Load the video clip **1A-3_NO AUDIO** into the Source monitor and scrub through the video until you find the part where the Assistant Cameraperson claps the slate.

6. Mark an **IN** at the point where the slate is completely closed and the sticks of the clapper touch, as seen in Figure 3.7.

This is your sync point in the video.

Figure 3.21   An IN mark at the sync point in the video.

7. Load the audio clip **ROP_1A/03** into the Source monitor.

8. Click the **TOGGLE SOURCE/RECORD BUTTON** in the bottom left of the Timeline.

    The Toggle Source/Record button will turn green and your Source clip will now appear in the Timeline.

   Figure 3.22 The Toggle Source/Record button is black when displaying the sequence (left), green when displaying the source tracks (right).

9. Open your Track Control panel and turn on your audio waveform display for A1.

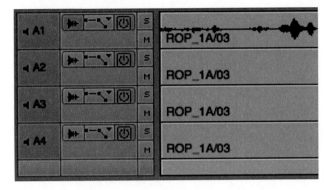

Figure 3.23 Track Control panel with waveforms on.

10. Place your position indicator at the point where the clapper from the slate causes a spike in the audio. Mark an **IN** at this point.

    This is your sync point in the audio. It is important to be precise. Even if the audio is only a single frame out of sync with the video, the viewer will notice something is off.

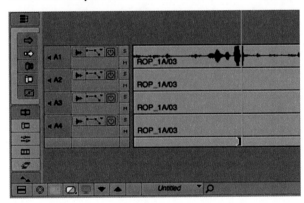

Figure 3.24 The sync point in the audio.

11. Once you have marked your sync points in the video and audio clips, select both clips in the **ANESTHESIA_SYNCED CLIPS** bin.

12. Choose **CLIP > AUTOSYNC**. In the Sync Selection window that pops up, choose **INPOINTS**.

A new subclip will be created in the **ANESTHESIA_SYNCED CLIPS** with the new audio replacing the in-camera audio in the original video clip.

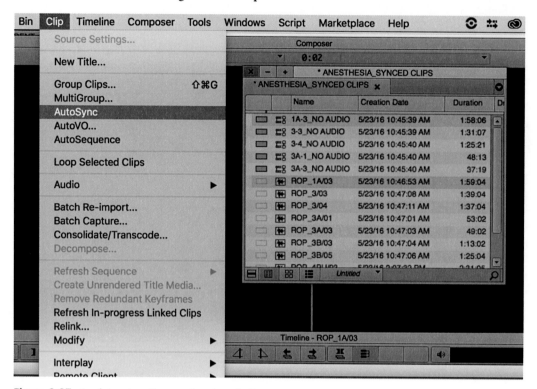

Figure 3.25 Applying AutoSync to the selected clips.

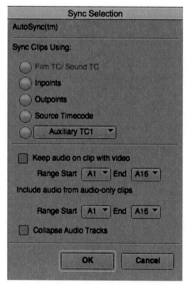

Figure 3.26 Selecting Inpoints from the Sync Selection dialog.

13. Rename the new subclip **1A-3_SYNCED**. Load the clip into the Source monitor to verify that the audio is replaced and has been correctly synchronized with the picture.

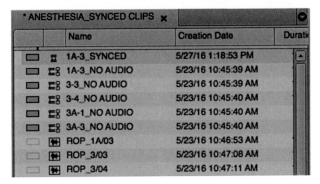

Figure 3.27 Selecting the newly renamed subclip to load in the Source monitor.

14. If everything looks and sounds good, continue syncing all the video clips labeled **_NO AUDIO** with their corresponding video clips.

15. Scrub through a few of the clips when you are finished to make sure everything was synced correctly.

16. Lastly, delete the clones of the original video clips and audio, leaving only the synced clips in the **ANESTHESIA_SYNCED CLIPS** bin. Do this by selecting the clones labeled and pressing **DELETE**. In the Delete window, check the box that says **DELETE MASTER CLIPS**.

    This will delete them from the **ANESTHESIA_SYNCED CLIPS** bin, but not from the original bin they came from.

 Figure 3.28 The Delete dialog box.

17. When you are done, be sure to return the Timeline back to Record mode, but clicking the **TOGGLE SOURCE/RECORD BUTTON** in the bottom left of the Timeline.

    The Toggle Source/Record button will return to black.

 Figure 3.29 Source/Record button.

This same tool can be used to sync audio and video using UT marks instead of IN marks.

Quick Editing Tools

In the MC101 course, you learned the fundamental editing tools of Splice-In, Overwrite, Lift and Extract and traditional three-point editing. While these are still the best tools for carefully crafting a scene, there are many other editing tools available, and in this lesson you will learn different tools and techniques to quickly assemble and cut down a sequence. In addition, we will look at how to customize your keyboard to further improve your editing speed.

Media Used: TN Parkour and Anesthesia

Duration: 60 minutes

GOALS

- Edit from the bin
- Create a stringout sequence of dailies
- Storyboard a montage sequence
- Quickly cut down sequence material with Top and Tail
- Use Extend to roll edit points or create a Split Edit
- Annotate the sequence with Markers
- Remap your keyboard

Editing from the Bin

The traditional workflow of loading clips individually into the Source monitor before cutting them to the sequence is familiar. There are several ways that Media Composer will allow you to skip the Source monitor and edit directly from a bin to the sequence. We are going to look at two methods – editing from List view to create a stringout sequence; and editing from Frame view, also called Storyboard editing.

Creating a Stringout Sequence

A stringout is a compilation of the master clips or subclips laid out in order in the sequence as they appear in the bin. Because Media Composer also allows you to use sequences as source material, which we'll cover in the next lesson, a stringout enables the editor to scrub through all the clips quickly by loading the one sequence into the Source monitor instead of each clip individually.

In many post-production facilities, it is a common task for the assistant editor when they are setting up the project to create a stringout of each Dailies bin or Scene bin with all takes. This is also a great technique for news editors editing footage shot on file-based cameras. Using stringouts can save a lot of time.

You can control the order the clips appear in the sequence simply by sorting them in the bin. If you are working as an assistant, ask the editor what his or her preference is.

To create a stringout sequence:

1. Open the BIN containing the clips.

2. (Optional) Sort the bin by the column that you wish to use to determine the order of clips in the sequence—that is, by name, scene/take, quality rating, start timecode, etc.

3. (Optional) If you want to include the full clips in the stringout, press Ctrl+A (Windows) or Command+A (Mac) to select all the clips in the bin, and then click the Clear Marks button (the G key, by default).

4. If the clips include IN or OUT marks, only the marked region will be included in the stringout.

5. Click the TEXT VIEW BUTTON in the bin.

6. Press CTRL+SHIFT+N (Windows) or COMMAND+SHIFT+N (Mac) to create a new sequence in the same bin.

7. Select the clips for the new sequence by doing one of the following:

    a. Press Ctrl+A (Windows) or Command+A (Mac) to select all the clips.

    b. Ctrl-click (Windows) or Command-click (Mac) to select individual master clips.

    c. Shift-click the first and last clip to select a group.

8. Drag the clips to the Timeline.

Which is Which?

Industry terms vary depending on the specific segment of the industry in which you work. The term stringout, as used here, is a common term in broadcast news and many types of TV production. It is used to describe a series of selected shots laid out in a sequence. In film circles, this type of sequence is also referred to as a KEM reel, named after the flatbed film editing machine. Typically a KEM reel contains all related items, i.e. all of Mary's close-ups in a scene or setup, all the wide shots from a scene or setup, all the inserts, etc.

On the other hand, our use of the term *stringout* should not be confused with an *assembly edit*, which is the first, very rough construction of the scene according to the script. An assembly is often put together by the lead assistant to save time for the editor. In some circles, *stringout* and *assembly edit* may be used interchangeably.

Adding Timecode Burn-in to Stringouts

Depending on the intended purpose for the stringout sequence, you may be expected to add a timecode burn-in over the sequence to display source timecode.

A timecode overlay is often added to dailies so that the producer and director can make notes about their favorite takes. Often scenes are patched together from several takes and timecoded notes can be very helpful in determining what pieces to use.

As you may remember from the MC101 course, Media Composer will allow you to apply video effects to Filler. In this case, you can use this technique to easily apply a Timecode Burn-in Effect (found in the Generator category) to the entire stringout, and then customizing it to display clip name and source TC.

Exercise 4.1 will give you an opportunity to practice this technique using a pre-built effect template.

 Exercise Break: Exercise 4.1
Pause here to practice what you've learned.

Storyboard Editing

Storyboarding is a powerful method used to pre-visualize scenes or entire films. In Media Composer, you can use the storyboard technique to visualize and quickly assemble scenes. This works especially well for montages or scenes that have little dialogue, such as action sequences or news packages, which will have a reporter or anchor speaking over them.

Working with the bin in Frame view, you can arrange items in the bin in the order you want them to appear in the sequence, as shown in Figure 4.1. Then, you simply select the clips and drag them to the Timeline window. Media Composer splices them into the sequence in the order they were arranged in the bin, left to right, top to bottom.

 Remember, to change the visible headframe in Frame view, you can use the Frame Advance keys (1,2,3, and 4 keys by default) or J-K-L.

To perform a storyboard edit:

1. Place the bin in FRAME VIEW.

2. (Optional) Play and mark the portion of each clip you want to use. Marks are not visible in the bin. Note: Marks can only be placed while the clip is playing.

3. Arrange the clips in your bin in rows in the desired order, left-to-right and top-to-bottom. If you need to make more room available in your bin, reduce the size of the clips by pressing Ctrl+K (Windows) or Command+K (Mac).

4. Select the TIMELINE > NEW > SEQUENCE or press CTRL+SHIFT+N (Windows) or COMMAND+SHIFT+N (Mac) to create a new sequence.

5. In the bin, select the clips by dragging a lasso around them, or Shift-click the first and last clip in the series.

6. Drag the clips to the Timeline window.

   Using this approach, you are beginning to explore the true possibilities of non-linear editing. The potential disadvantage to storyboard editing, however, is that unless you take the time to carefully mark each clip before storyboarding them, the resulting sequence will be very long and practically unwatchable. If you do take the time, you lose much of the speed and efficiency promised by storyboarding the sequence. But, don't throw the baby out with the bathwater and abandon the technique!

   Instead, this workflow calls for a reductive approach to editing the sequence. You have thrown the raw material into the sequence in the rough order that you want it to appear; now you just need to quickly cut away the excess. The key to doing this efficiently is a pair of one-step functions called Top and Tail.

Cutting Down a Sequence with Top and Tail

The Top and Tail commands enable you to perform quick edits to segments in the Timeline. Using the position indicator to determine the location of the edit, you can quickly remove the part of the segment before the position indicator, or after it, with a single keystroke.

 Top and Tail do not appear on the Media Composer interface or keyboard by default. You need to map them to the keyboard or interface for use.

Use the Top button to extract footage from the start of the clip up to the position indicator, as illustrated in Figure 4.1. It's the equivalent of pressing the T-R-X keys: Mark Clip, Mark OUT, and Extract.

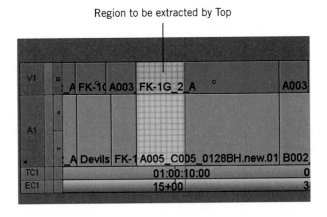

Figure 4.1
Top extracts the first portion of the segment, before the position indicator.

Use the Tail button to extract footage from the position indicator to the end of the clip, as illustrated in Figure 4.2. It's the equivalent of pressing the T-E-X keys: Mark Clip, Mark IN, and Extract.

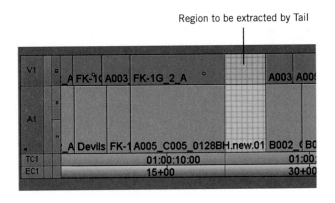

Figure 4.2
Tail extracts the later portion of a segment, after the position indicator.

To extract footage using the Top and Tail commands:

1. In the Timeline, select the TRACKS you want to edit and deselect all other tracks.

2. Park the POSITION INDICATOR where you want to perform an edit.

3. To extract, press the key to which you mapped the Top button.

   This extracts the footage from the start of the segment to the position indicator.

4. Alternatively, press the key to which you mapped the Tail button.

   This extracts the footage from the position indicator to the end of the segment.

Tips for Using Top and Tail

Top and Tail is most frequently used at the very rough cut stage, when all cuts are straight, and there aren't many other tracks in the sequence. This tool came over from Newscutter years ago. It's especially useful for news editors since they often have to very quickly create packages. Using Splice, Top/Tail, and Extend (which also came from Newscutter) allows them to work very fast. It's also a great tool when cutting down animatic (for shot timing).

There are two things to keep in mind when using Top and Tail: track activation and sync. As you know by now, sync is an important consideration when working with sync sound. Because Top and Tail remove material by extracting it, there is the possibility that using them could cause you to break sync. There are a few ways to safeguard against this.

To avoid breaking sync with Top and Tail:

■   Enable SYNC LOCKS on tracks that must stay in sync.

     Media Composer will keep all tracks in sync by removing the same amount of material from all sync-locked tracks, even if only one of the tracks was selected for editing.

    Enable Sync Locks to avoid breaking sync with Top and Tail.

Top and Tail references the active tracks and removes everything up to the next **common** edit point—e.g., a straight cut—on all active tracks. For this reason, Top and Tail are often used most frequently early in the process of rough cutting a sequence, when it is composed primarily of straight cuts.

In Figures 4.1 and 4.2, the segment has straight cuts on either side, so Top or Tail would remove the material from just that segment. But if there were split edits or if other tracks with different edit points were active, the system would cut everything up to the next straight cut across all tracks. In some cases, that may be the end of sequence! So, you can either remove the split edit before performing Top or Tail, or skip that and have Media Composer reference the next edit point on any active track instead.

For example, Figure 4.3 shows a more complicated sequence. If you use Tail on the V1 and A1 segments as shown, by default, the edit would remove much more material because there is no straight cut until further down the sequence. Using a modifier, Media Composer will remove only the frames up to the edit point on V1 as illustrated. Plus, because all tracks are active, it would remove the filler frames from V3, V2, and A2, and keep all downstream material in sync.

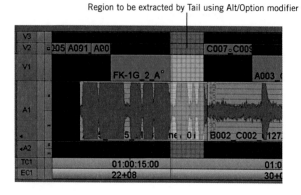

Figure 4.3
Adding the Alt or Option modifier limits Top and Tail to the next edit point on any track.

To reference the next edit point on any active track:

■ Hold the **ALT** (Windows) or **OPTION** (Mac) key and press the **TOP** or **TAIL** key.

Media Composer will extract frames up to the next edit point on any active track, which solves the problem of the edit above.

Exercise Break: Exercise 4.2
Pause here to practice what you've learned.

Using the Extend Function

Extend is a function that allows you to roll edit points without going into Trim mode. The result of using Extend is identical to using a dual-roller trim. If used on just audio or video, Extend allows you to very quickly create split edits (L-cuts and J-cuts) using marks in the Timeline to define the edit point. Extend is found under the Record monitor by default, as shown in Figure 4.4.

Because Extend functions like a dual-roller trim, there is no chance that you can break sync using it.

Using Extend fits nicely as a final tool in the "quick edit" workflow we have been discussing, following Storyboard edit and Top/Tail. Like Top/Tail, edits with Extend are made based on the location of the position indicator. However, you decide which transition – the preceding or following – will be extended by adding an IN or an OUT before clicking Extend.

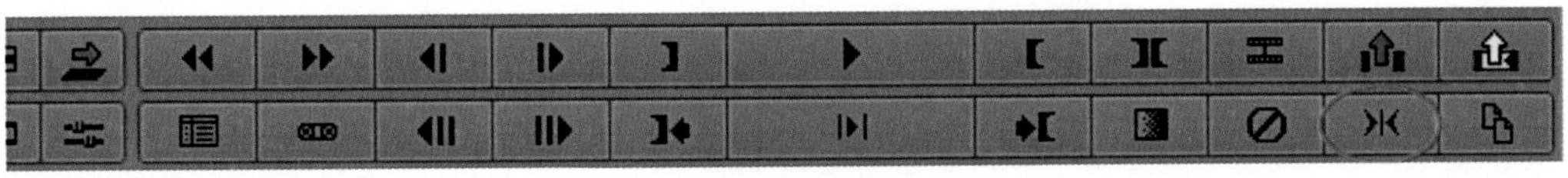

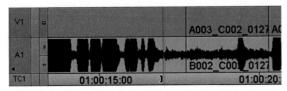

Figure 4.4 Extend is found under the Record monitor.

To roll an edit using Extend:

1. Play the **SEQUENCE** that you want to adjust and decide where you want the edit to begin or end.

2. If you want to cut to the following segment moved earlier, park the position indicator where you want to make the edit, and mark an **IN POINT**. Conversely, if you want the preceding segment to end at that location, mark an **OUT POINT**.

    In the example shown in Figure 4.5, the edit point will be extended to the IN mark.

Figure 4.5 The IN mark will cause both the V and A segment to be extended earlier in the sequence since both tracks are enabled.

In the example shown in Figure 4.6, the preceding edit point will be extended to the OUT mark.

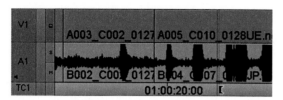

Figure 4.6 The OUT mark will cause both the V and A segment to be extended later in the sequence since both tracks are enabled.

3. (Optional) To create a split edit, turn off the TRACK button(s) for either audio or video, depending on whether you want to extend the video over the audio or the audio under the video.

4. Click the EXTEND button to trim the edit back to the IN or forward to the OUT.

5. Press the **G** key to clear the marks before moving on.

Extend can be used just as efficiently to remove split edits in the sequence. There are various reasons why you would want to remove a split edit. For example, you may want to relocate a shot, but the split edits on either side aren't the same and doing so would break sync. In this case, you might want to quickly remove the split first, segment-drag the clip, and then add the split back. Or, as you saw with Top and Tail, you may want to remove a split edit to make the use of those easier or to clean up any fragments left behind.

Figure 4.7 illustrates the setup to remove a split edit. Reference this image as you read the steps that follow.

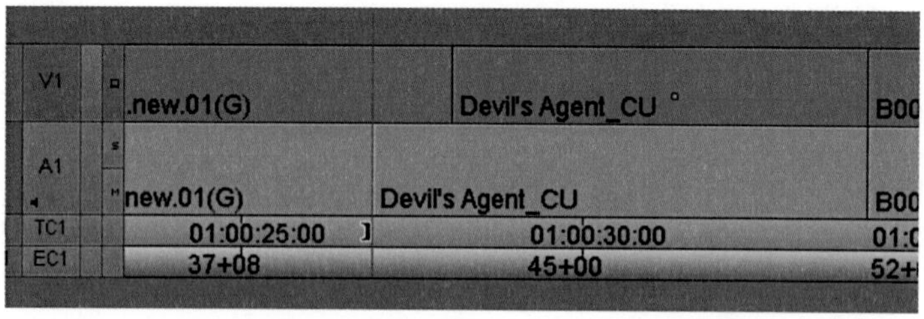

Figure 4.7 The Timeline is set up to remove the split edit by extending the video segment of "Devil's Agent_CU."

To remove a split edit:

1. Snap the POSITION INDICATOR to the edit point you want to turn into a straight cut.

2. Select the TRACK you want to extend and deselect all other tracks.

3. Mark an **IN** or an **OUT**, based on the direction of the edit.

4. Press the EXTEND key.

Comparison: Trim vs. Extend

You can create split edits using either Trim mode or Extend edit. The choice of which one to use is largely a matter of personal preference. Here are some nuances of each that may be helpful to consider as you develop your editing habits.

- Extend can be used on the fly while playing in the Timeline, without entering Trim mode. Dual-roller trim requires you to enter Trim mode.

- Trim mode offers specialized tools, including the ability to see the incoming and outgoing frame simultaneously. Extend does not.

- Extend can be easier if you are confident and precise in your decision. If you need to experiment with the position of the edit point, Trim will be easier to use.

Using Markers

Markers are like electronic stamps that enable you to find and identify specific frames during editing. Markers can be added to any kind of clip or to the sequence. A comment can be added to each marker, making markers like sticky notes for editors. While you can add markers to clips or sequences, editors find many more uses for them in sequences than in clips. You can add markers to your sequence at any time during the editing process.

Common uses for markers include the following:

- Marking the location of good bites in an interview

- Providing the correct spelling for titles

- Identifying shots that will be added later

- Marking the location to add music cues or sound effects

- Including notes for a producer, colorist, audio mixer, or graphic artist

- Identifying remaining tasks (when all your markers are gone, you have made all necessary changes to an edit)

 Media Composer also has spanned markers, used to mark a region of the sequence or clip rather than a single frame. Spanned markers are designed for use with the broadcast file delivery standard AS-11. Spanned markers and AS-11 are both covered in detail in the course *MC201: Media Composer Professional Editing I.*

To add a marker:

1. Open a CLIP or SEQUENCE.

2. Cue the POSITION INDICATOR to the frame and select the TRACK where you want to add the marker. You can even add markers to the TC1 track or in filler.

3. Click the ADD MARKER button in the Tool Palette, shown in Figure 4.8.

    An oval appears at the bottom of the frame in the monitor, in the position bar under the active monitor, and if you have added the marker to the sequence, on the highest active track in the Timeline.

    The Marker dialog box opens (see Figure 4.9.)

Marker button   Marker in position bar

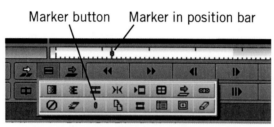

Figure 4.8
Click the Marker button in the Tool Palette, and a marker appears under the position indicator.

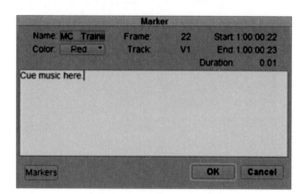

Figure 4.9 The Marker dialog box.

4. Type your COMMENT.

5. Optionally, open the COLOR menu and select a different color.

6. Click OK.

    The colored marker appears in the position track of the monitor and in the Timeline, and the first line of the information appears at the bottom of the Composer window, as shown in Figure 4.10.

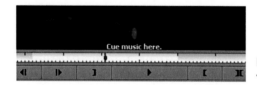

Figure 4.10
The Marker icon and comment in the Composer window.

 If a marker exists within the segment of a source clip you edit to the Timeline, the marker will follow the segment and be visible in the Timeline as well. This can be changed in the Composer Settings.

Some cameras, such as Sony XDCAM cameras, allow you to apply "essence marks" in-camera or through logging software. These marks will appear on the master clip in Media Composer as markers.

Using the Markers Tool

The Markers tool, shown in Figure 4.11, is designed to show you all the markers present on the sequence or source clip. Its display corresponds to the active monitor in the Composer window.

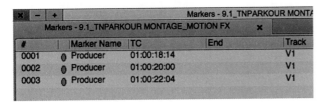

Figure 4.11 The Markers tool.

To open the Markers tool:

■   Choose TOOLS > MARKERS.

All additional functionality of the Markers tool is accessed through the Fast menu in the bottom-left corner of the window or from the right-click menu. Both menus contain the same options, shown in Figure 4.12, which includes options to sort the columns, show the image of each marked frame, and even import and export the markers (as text or XML).

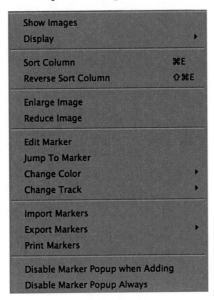

Figure 4.12 The Fast menu options available in the Markers tool.

Adding Markers On the Fly

You may want to play your sequence and add markers on the fly. For example, you might do this to note where you want to add sound effects, music strings, cutaways, and so on.

To add markers on the fly:

1.   Map one or more marker buttons (found in the More tab in the Command Palette) to keys.

2.   Play the CLIP or SEQUENCE, pressing the marker keys at any time.

     When you stop play, all markers appear.

3.   To view the list of markers you created, choose TOOLS > MARKERS.

4.   To annotate the marker, type your comment into the COMMENT field of the Markers tool.

Removing Markers

You can remove markers one at a time by deleting them in the Timeline. You can also delete markers from the Markers window.

To remove a marker:

1.   Go to the FRAME that contains the marker.

2.   Press the DELETE key on the keyboard.

     The marker is removed.

To remove several markers from the Markers tool:

1.   Choose TOOLS > MARKERS to open the list of markers.

2.   CTRL-CLICK (Windows) or COMMAND-CLICK (Mac) the MARKERS you want to delete.

3.   Press DELETE.

     The markers disappear.

   Exercise Break: Exercise 4.3
Pause here to practice what you've learned.

Mapping Buttons and Menus

The functions covered earlier in this lesson – Top, Tail, and Extend – are a few examples of useful functions that you may wish to map to your keyboard to increase your speed and efficiency in editing. In this section, you will learn to map both buttons and menu items to the keyboard.

Mapping User-Selectable Buttons

The Command Palette, shown in Figure 4.13, provides a central location for all user-selectable buttons. It presents them in groups by category: Move, Play, Edit, Trim, FX, 3D, CC (color correction), MCam (multicam), Tracks, Smart Tools, Other, More, and Workspaces.

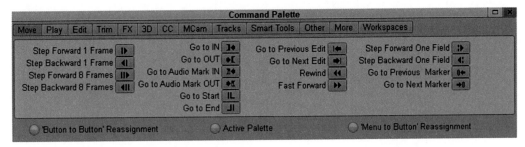

Figure 4.13 The Command Palette enables you to remap buttons on the interface and keyboard.

The radio buttons across the bottom determine the mode of the Command Palette:

- **Button to Button Reassignment:** This allows you to remap buttons by dragging them from the Command Palette to the interface or to the open keyboard setting. When active, you can also drag the buttons in any of the tool bars of the interface to rearrange them.

- **Active Palette:** This enables the Command Palette to function as an editing tool. When set to Active Palette, clicking a button in the Command Palette will perform the function.

- **Menu to Button Reassignment:** This allows you to map menu commands for which there is no preset button to the keyboard or interface—for example, Export.

When Button to Button Reassignment or Menu to Button Reassignment is active, none of the buttons on the interface will work. It is similar to when you rearrange the apps on an iPhone or iPad: if the apps are jiggling, you can rearrange them, but not open them. Media Composer icons don't jiggle, but the principle is the same.

Remapping Buttons

Remapping buttons is the most common way to customize the interface and keyboard.

To remap buttons or keys using the Command Palette:

1. If you want to map a button to the keyboard, open the KEYBOARD settings from the Settings pane of the Project window.

2. Choose TOOLS > COMMAND PALETTE.

    The Command Palette appears.

3. Click the BUTTON TO BUTTON REASSIGNMENT button if it's not selected.

4. Click the TAB for the category that contains your user-selectable button.

5. Click and drag the BUTTON from the Command Palette to the Keyboard Palette or to a location on a row of buttons—for example, under a monitor or in the Tool Palette.

    If you press the Shift key down as you drag the button to the Keyboard Palette, you can map to Shift+[key].

6. Close the Command Palette when finished.

Table 4.1 includes useful buttons covered in this course but not found by default on the keyboard (or in some cases the interface).

Table 4.1   Suggested Buttons to Map to Your Keyboard

Category	Button(s)
Move	Rewind Fast Forward
Edit	Add Edit Top Tail Select Left/Right/IN–OUT
FX	Effects Mode Remove Effect
Smart Tools	Transition Manipulation Keyframe
Other	Find Bin Match Frame Toggle Source/Record in Timeline
More	Bin Text View Bin Frame View Bin Script View Add Marker (color of choice)
Workspaces	Source/Record Editing Audio Editing Effects Editing

Mapping Menu Items

Mapping menu items is a great convenience, especially for those menu items you use regularly. It allows you to execute the function without reaching for the mouse (or at least without having to find it in a menu list).

To map menu commands:

1. If you want to map a menu item to the keyboard, open the KEYBOARD settings from the Project window.

2. Choose TOOLS > COMMAND PALETTE.

    The Command Palette appears.

3. Click the MENU TO BUTTON REASSIGNMENT button.

4. Click a BUTTON on the keyboard, in the interface or the Tool Palette.

    The pointer icon changes to a small white menu when it's over the keyboard. In addition, the selected button remains highlighted, indicating that it is ready to be mapped. (See Figure 4.14.)

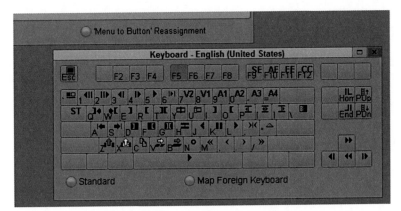

Figure 4.14 For Menu-to-Button reassignment, click the button on the keyboard first to highlight it, and then select the menu item.

5. Choose a COMMAND from a menu.

    The initials for the command appear on the button.

Table 4.2 includes menu items covered in this course that have no preset button or default keyboard shortcut. You may consider mapping some of these to your keyboard.

Table 4.2   Suggested Menu Items to Map to Your Keyboard*

Menu	Command
File	Source Browser
Bin	Fill Window or Fill Sorted (for use with Bin Frame view)
	AutoSync
Clip	Consolidate/Transcode
	Relink
Timeline	Audio Mixdown
	Video Mixdown
Tools	Audio Mixer
	Audio EQ
	Audio Suite
	Clipboard Monitor
	Markers (tool)
	Media Tool
	Title Tool Application
Windows	Set Font

*Some features listed are covered later in the course.

Keyboard-Mapping Strategies

Most editors tend to have their own unique keyboard mapping. Some are just a slight modification of the system defaults, while others have the keys so completely rearranged that if you sat in their edit bay, you may have a hard time even performing the basic functions of marking a clip and making a simple edit. As with other topics we have discussed, there is no right or wrong way *per se*. For editors who first learned their trade on another NLE, working on Media Composer's default keyboard may feel awkward. Remapping the keyboard to place similar functions in the same location as other applications can be a good way to ease the transition.

In general, when deciding how to map your keyboard, there are two main approaches:

- Map keys into functional groups.

- Map functions based on a letter mnemonic.

The default Media Composer keyboard map includes both, but tends to follow the first approach. For example, on the left side of the keyboard, the functions for marking and editing a clip are grouped together. As an example of a mnemonic association, the I and O keys are mapped to Mark IN and Mark OUT. Whichever way you choose to map your keyboard; above all it should be quick to use and easy to remember. If not, change it.

Before changing the keyboard, however, take a moment to study the default mapping. The commands for playing, shuttling through, marking, and editing footage are clustered around the "home" position of each hand (assuming the index finger of each hand sits on the F and J keys, respectively).

Figure 4.15 and Figure 4.16 illustrate the default arrangement of commands for each hand on the U.S. keyboard. There will obviously be times when you will "drive" with one hand on the mouse and one on the keyboard, but if you develop the habit now of using both hands on the keyboard, you'll find that when you need to go fast, it will serve you well. (Note: International keyboard mappings differ slightly, but the principle still applies.)

Figure 4.15 The left-hand functions.

Do you use the mouse with your left hand? No problem! Simply remap the keyboard to be the mirror image of the default, giving you the same convenience.

The right-hand functions (see Figure 4.16) are more diverse. They include J-K-L shuttle, redundant I/O, trim keys, and edit/trim mode keys. During the assembly stage, the right hand plays a supporting role of offering redundant I/O keys just above J-K-L. Many editors prefer to shuttle and mark with the right hand and then edit with the left. Perhaps most importantly, the right-hand keys include track activation keys for V1, V2, A1, A2, A3, and A4.

Figure 4.16 The right-hand functions.

Throughout the rest of this course, practice using the keyboard as much as possible. Especially in the exercises, challenge yourself to release the mouse whenever possible.

Interested in seeing how other editors map their keyboard? Check out the Keyboard Exchange web page: http://hershleder.com/content/keyboard-exchange-get-ideas-other-editors-mapping.

Copying and Updating User Settings

If you work on multiple Avid systems, even moving between the classroom and your home system, you will likely want to copy your settings from one system to another.

Copying User Settings Between Avid Workstations

To move your user settings between edit workstations of the same platform, it is best to use the Export and Import functions. To export or import user settings, click the User Profile pop-up menu and choose one of the following:

- **Export User Profile:** This exports all of your user settings into a folder for easy transport.

- **Import User Profile:** This opens a browse dialog box used to direct the system to a previously exported user profile.

Updating User Profiles

The Update User Profile command updates your Settings list when you upgrade to a new version of your Avid editing system. For example, if you are upgrading to a version that contains the Send To option from a version without that option, choosing the Update User Profile command adds the Send To setting.

To update user profiles:

1. Click the SETTINGS tab in the Project window.

2. Click the USER PROFILE pop-up menu and select UPDATE USER PROFILES.

   Any options that have been added to the upgraded version of the application now appear in the Settings list.

Exercise Break: Exercise 4.4
Pause here to practice what you've learned.

Review/Discussion Questions

1. If editing a group of clips to the sequence from the bin in Text view, what controls the order the clips will appear in the sequence?

2. If editing a group of clips to the sequence from the bin in Frame view, what controls the order the clips will appear in the sequence?

3. Which function is related to Top or Tail?

   a. Splice-In

   b. Overwrite

   c. Lift

   d. Extract

   e. Extend

4. How is Extend similar to Trim? Most specifically, what type of trim?

5. Name three uses of markers.

6. Which two windows must be open to change the keyboard settings?

Lesson 4 Keyboard Shortcuts

Key	Shortcut
Alt-drag (Windows)/Option-drag (Mac)	Creates a sub-sequence by dragging the image from the Record monitor to the bin
Alt+Find Bin (Windows)/Option+Find Bin (Mac)	Finds the bin for the segment under the position indicator on the upper most active track
Shift+I*	Top
Shift+O*	Tail
N*	Match Frame
Shift+B*	Find Bin
Semicolon (;)*	Extend

*Not a system default.

Quick Editing Techniques

In this exercise, you will practice the new quick-edit techniques covered in the lesson.

Media Used: TN Parkour and Anesthesia

Duration: 2 hours 20 minutes

GOALS

- Edit from the bin
- Use Top and Tail to extract sequence material
- Use Extend to roll edit points
- Remap your keyboard settings

Exercise 4.1: Creating a Stringout for Review

In the previous exercise, we synced the audio and video footage for the short film, "Anesthesia." In this exercise, we will quickly create a sequence of all the synced footage for the director and producer to review. We will start by sorting the clips in order by name and then drag them all to the Timeline at once.

Media Used: Anesthesia

Duration: 20 minutes

For this exercise, we will use the **MC110_ANESTHESIA** project.

1. Begin by opening the bin, **ANESTHESIA_DAILIES**.

2. In TEXT VIEW, right-click the NAME column and choose SORT ON COLUMN, ASCENDING.

    This will sort all of the clips in order in the bin using the scene number.

	Name	Creation Date	Duration	Dri
	1A-3	5/11/16 11:51:31 AM	1:58:06	
	1D-1 SER	5/11/16 11:49:03 AM	1:37:14	
	2E-2	5/9/16 9:25:05 AM	36:08	
	2E-4	5/11/16 1:34:53 PM	22:07	
	3-3	5/4/16 12:26:17 PM	1:31:07	
	3-4	5/4/16 12:26:16 PM	1:25:21	
	3A-1	5/4/16 12:26:17 PM	48:13	
	3A-3	5/4/16 12:26:17 PM	37:19	
	3B-3	5/4/16 12:26:13 PM	1:08:07	
	3B-5	5/4/16 12:26:12 PM	1:13:07	
	3C-2	5/4/16 12:26:15 PM	30:20	
	3C-4	5/4/16 12:26:14 PM	44:01	
	3D-2	5/4/16 12:26:16 PM	39:18	
	3E-2	5/4/16 12:26:16 PM	22:19	
	4 PU-3	5/5/16 10:25:37 AM	2:25:12	
	4 PU-6	5/5/16 10:26:54 AM	2:36:10	
	4B-1	5/12/16 12:33:53 PM	2:04:22	
	4B-2	5/12/16 12:33:54 PM	2:03:16	
	4C-1	5/12/16 12:36:54 PM	1:24:21	
	4C-2	5/12/16 12:36:54 PM	1:30:15	

Figure 4.17 Clips sorted by scene number.

3. Select all clips in the bin using CTRL+A (Windows) or COMMAND+A (Mac) and press the G KEY to clear all IN or OUT marks.

4. In your **ANESTHESIA_EXERCISE SEQUENCES** bin, create a new sequence called **ANESTHESIA_STRINGOUT**.

5. In your **ANESTHESIA_DAILIES** bin, select all the clips using CTRL+A (Windows) or COMMAND+A (Mac) and DRAG them into the Timeline.

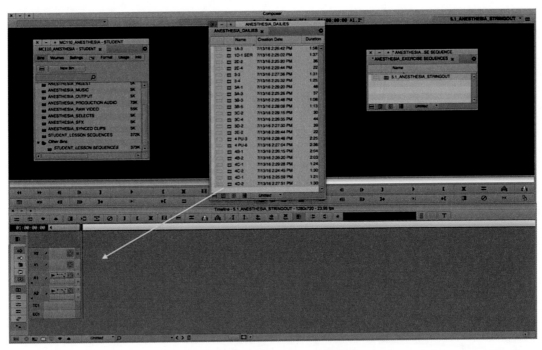

Figure 4.18 Selecting all the clips in the "ANESTHESIA_DAILIES" bin and dragging them to the Timeline.

6. Scrub through the sequence to verify that all of your synced dailies are in the sequence **ANESTHESIA_STRINGOUT** in the same order that they were in your bin.

    You now have a stringout of the footage you can export and send to the director and/or producer of the film to review and reference during the editing process.

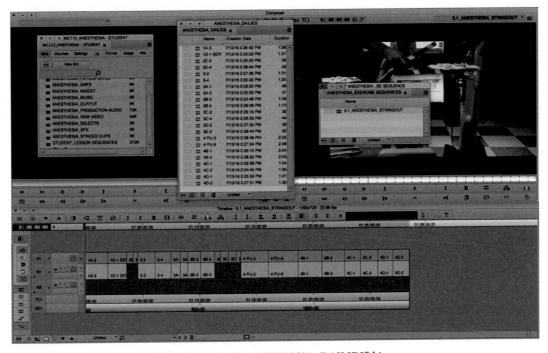

Figure 4.19 A stringout of all the clips in the "ANESTHESIA_DAILIES" bin.

7. Press **CTRL+D** (Windows) or **COMMAND+D** (Mac) to duplicate this sequence and name the duplicate sequence **ANESTHESIA_STRINGOUT_WITH TC BURN**.

8. Press **CTRL+Y** (Windows) or **COMMAND+Y** (Mac) or choose **TIMELINE > NEW VIDEO TRACK** to create a second video track above V1 in your sequence.

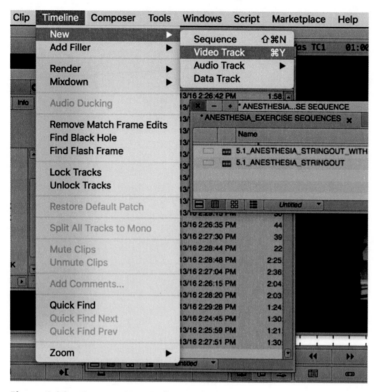

Figure 4.20 Choosing New Video Track to create a second video track above V1 in your sequence.

9. Open the bin **ANESTHESIA_FX TEMPLATES** and select **TIMECODE BURN IN_DAILIES**.

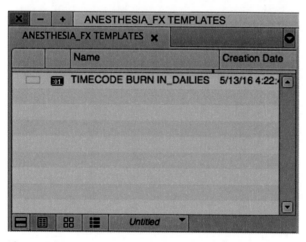

Figure 4.21 The "ANESTHESIA_FX TEMPLATES" bin with the "TIMECODE BURN IN_DAILIES" clip.

10. Drag this effect to the V2 track in your Timeline.

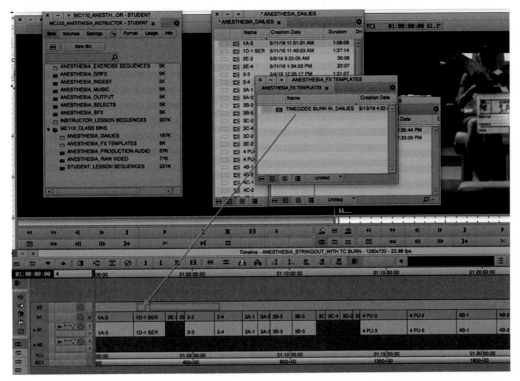

Figure 4.22 Drag the "TIMECODE BURN IN_DAILIES" clip to the Timeline.

You will now see a timecode overlay that will provide the timecode for your sequence
ANESTHESIA_STRINGOUT_WITH TC BURN on the left side of the screen and the name of the
source video clip on the right side of the screen.

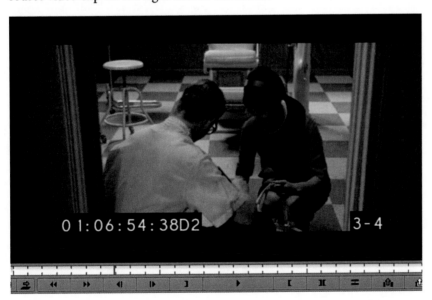

Figure 4.23 A timecode overlay displayed on the left side with the name of the source video clip on the right side.

 You can find the "TIMECODE BURN-IN" effect under the Effects tab in your Project window by selecting
the "GENERATOR" category. You can customize the size, color, or position of the time code overlay in
the Effect Editor.

Exercise 4.2: Tennessee Parkour Montage

In this exercise we will subclip selects from the Tennessee Parkour footage and use a storyboard editing technique to create an exciting montage set to music.

Media Used: Tennessee Parkour

Duration: 1 hour

1. Begin by opening the project **MC110_TN PARKOUR** in Media Composer.

2. Open the bin **TNPARKOUR_EXERCISE SEQUENCES**, and create a new sequence called **TNPARKOUR_MONTAGE**.

3. Open the bin **TNPARKOUR_MUSIC**, and load the track **40_SHORT_5-AM_0035.WAV** into the Source monitor.

   Let's start by laying in our music track.

4. Mark an **IN** point at the beginning of the music track using the **I** KEY.

5. Make sure the YELLOW SPLICE-IN ARROW is enabled in the SMART TOOL and that the **A1** and **A2** audio tracks are enabled in the Timeline.

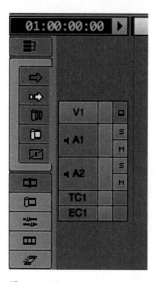

Figure 4.24 Enable the Yellow Splice-In arrow and select A1 and A2 audio tracks.

6. Drag your audio track from the Source monitor to the Timeline.

    You have now spliced your audio track into the **TNPARKOUR_MONTAGE** sequence.

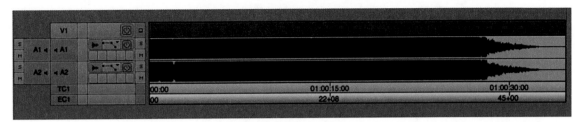

Figure 4.25 The audio track spliced into the "TNPARKOUR_MONTAGE" sequence in the Timeline.

7. Listen to the entire audio track (it is about 30 seconds).

    This will give you an idea of the rhythm and feel of your montage. Is it slow and contemplative? Quick and upbeat?

    Let's take a look at the footage we have to work with.

8. Open the bin **TNPARKOUR_FOOTAGE**. Scrub through a few of the clips and get a feel for what you would like to use in your montage.

9. Using **CTRL+N** (Windows) or **COMMAND+N** (Mac) create a new bin. Label the bin **TNPARKOUR_SELECTS**.

    Now that you've had a look at some of the footage, let's make subclips of your "selects."

10. Load a clip from the **TNPARKOUR_FOOTAGE** bin into the Source monitor and Mark an **IN** and an **OUT** around the parts of the clip you would like to use.

Figure 4.26 A Mark IN and OUT applied to a clip in the Source monitor.

11. To create a subclip, grab the CLIP ICON in the upper-left corner of the Source monitor and DRAG it to the **TNPARKOUR_SELECTS** bin.

Figure 4.27   Click and grab the Clip icon in the upper-left corner of the Source monitor and drag it to the "TNPARKOUR_SELECTS" bin to create a subclip.

You have now created a subclip of just the footage contained within the IN and OUT points you marked in the original clip. You still have access to material from the source clip that extends past the IN and OUT points you marked. This is known as "handles."

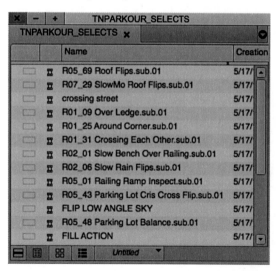

Figure 4.28   Subclips you've created displayed in the "TNPARKOUR_SELECTS" bin.

12. Continue pulling subclips into your **TNPARKOUR_SELECTS** bin.

Remember, your music track is only about 30 seconds, so about twenty subclips should give you a lot to work with for your montage.

Now that you have made your selects, it's time to decide in what order to edit them into your montage. For this, you will use a storyboard.

13. To **STORYBOARD** your shots, change your **TNPARKOUR_SELECTS** bin view from Text view to **FRAME VIEW.**

    You will now see thumbnails representing your selects, starting with the first frame.

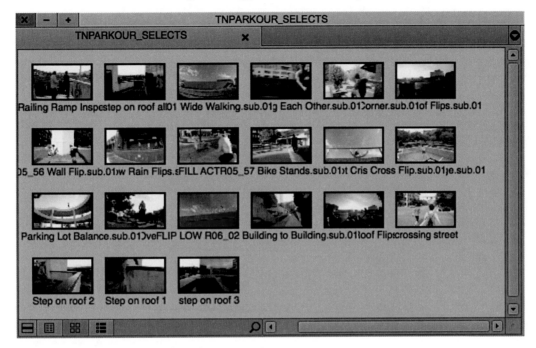

Figure 4.29 Storyboard view of our shots.

14. (Optional) Adjust the size and displayed headframe of the thumbnail images.

    Remember, you can play these thumbnails by selecting them and pressing the Spacebar or using J-K-L. You can make the thumbnails larger by clicking Ctrl+L (Windows) or Command+L (Mac). Ctrl+K (Windows) or Command+K (Mac) will make the thumbnails smaller.

15. Arrange the thumbnails in a line in the order that you would like them to appear in the Timeline.

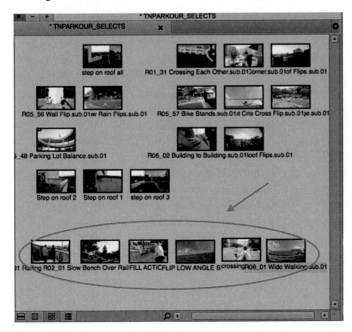

Figure 4.30 Thumbnails of the clips you arranged in a line as to the order they will appear in the Timeline.

Once you are happy with the order of the shots in your bin, you will need to get them into the Timeline. We want to OVERWRITE our clips into the Timeline so we don't disturb the audio track we have already placed in the Timeline.

16. Begin by turning OFF the **A1** and **A2** tracks and ENABLING the **V1** track.

17. Turn OFF the YELLOW SPLICE-IN arrow and enable the RED OVERWRITE arrow in the SMART TOOL.

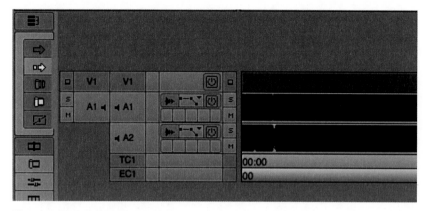

Figure 4.31 The Timeline with A1 and A2 tracks turned off and the V1 track enabled. Red Overwrite enabled.

18. Still in FRAME VIEW, click and drag a lasso around your storyboard in the **TNPARKOUR_SELECTS** bin to select all the clips and then DRAG them into the Timeline.

Your clips will now be added to the **TNPARKOUR_MONTAGE** sequence in the order in which they appear in your storyboard.

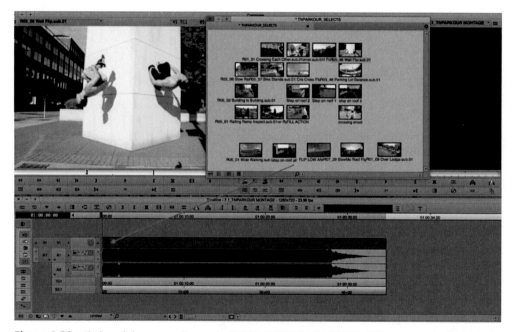

Figure 4.32 Click and drag your clips to the "TNPARKOUR_MONTAGE" sequence in the Timeline.

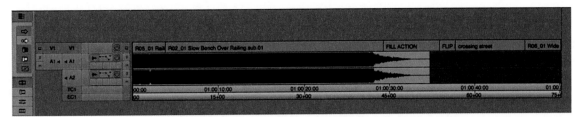

Figure 4.33 The clips you set up in a storyboard displayed in the correct order in the Timeline.

19. Play through the **TNPARKOUR_MONTAGE** sequence.

    You will no doubt find that the clips are too long and do not quite fit with the music. We will make some quick edits and adjustments using Top and Tail and Extend in the next exercise.

Exercise 4.3: Improving a Montage with Split Edits

In this exercise, we will use Markers to review our initial edit of the TN Parkour Montage and make quick adjustments to our edit using Top and Tail and Extend.

First, you will use some Markers to make notes to ourselves about what changes we would like to make. These notes might include "beat shift in music here," and "speed up cutting here," or "swap X shot with Y shot."

Media Used: Tennessee Parkour

Duration: 45 minutes

For this exercise, we will continue to use the **MC110_TN PARKOUR** project.

1. Click **CTRL + 3** (Windows) or **COMMAND + 3** (Mac) or choose **TOOLS > COMMAND PALETTE** to open the Command Palette.

2. Select **ACTIVE PALETTE** in the bottom of the **COMMAND PALETTE** window to use the buttons in the Command Palette.

    We will use the Marker buttons from the Active Palette. If you prefer, you can map them to your keyboard or interface and use them from there.

Figure 4.34 Opening the Command Palette from the Tools menu.

3. Navigate to the MORE TAB in the Command Palette to locate the Markers.

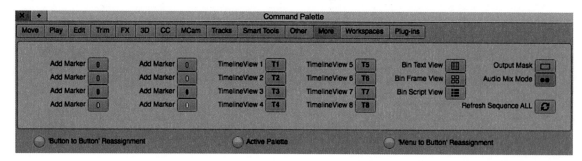

Figure 4.35 The More tab in the Command Palette displays the Add Marker buttons.

4. Park the position indicator in the Timeline where you would like to leave yourself a note and click the ADD MARKER BUTTON.

Figure 4.36 Marker button.

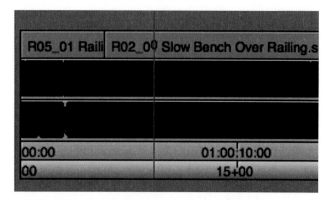

Figure 4.37 Marker button displayed in the Timeline under the position indicator.

The Marker Dialog box will appear when you place a Marker in the Timeline. You can add notes and change the color of the Markers in the Marker Dialog box.

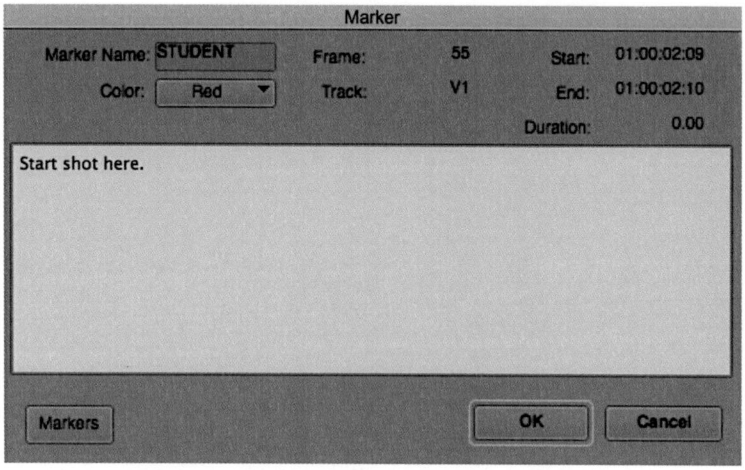

Figure 4.38 Enter a note and select a marker color in the Marker dialog.

5. To pull up a list of your Markers and notes, choose **TOOLS >MARKERS**.

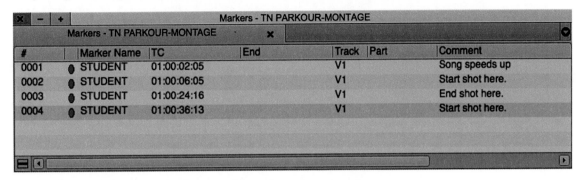
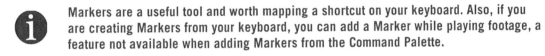

Figure 4.39 Markers window displaying markers and notes you created.

 Markers are a useful tool and worth mapping a shortcut on your keyboard. Also, if you are creating Markers from your keyboard, you can add a Marker while playing footage, a feature not available when adding Markers from the Command Palette.

6. You can move quickly from one Marker to the next in the Timeline by using the **GO TO NEXT MARKER** and **GO TO PREVIOUS MARKER** buttons located in the Command Palette.

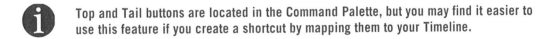

Figure 4.40 Go to Next Marker button and Go to Previous Marker button.

You can find these buttons under the "Move" tab in the Command Palette.

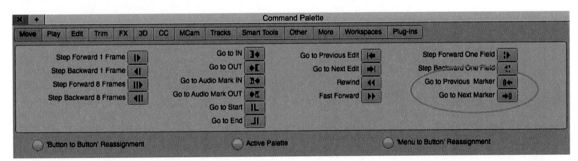

Figure 4.41 Go to Previous Marker/Go to Next Marker buttons located under the Move tab in the Command Palette.

7. Once you have decided where to make your changes, use the **TOP**, **TAIL**, and **EXTEND BUTTONS** to make quick edits in the Timeline.

Top and Tail buttons are located in the Command Palette, but you may find it easier to use this feature if you create a shortcut by mapping them to your Timeline.

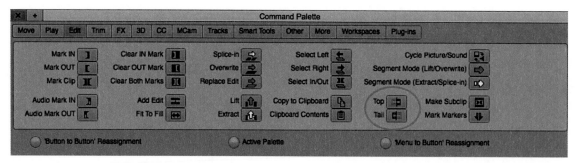

Figure 4.42 Top and Tail buttons located under the Edit tab in the Command Palette.

8. To trim the head of a shot, park the position indicator at the part of the clip in the Timeline where you would like the new edit point to begin and select the TOP BUTTON.

Figure 4.43 Top button.

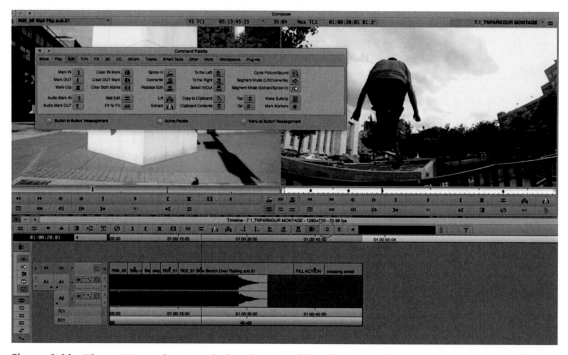

Figure 4.44.. The position indicator parked at the part of the clip in the Timeline where you would like the shot to begin and the Top button selected.

This will trim the shot from the beginning of the segment to the position indicator.

9. To trim the tail of the shot, park the position indicator at the part of the clip in the Timeline where you would like the shot to end and select the TAIL BUTTON.

Figure 4.45 Tail button.

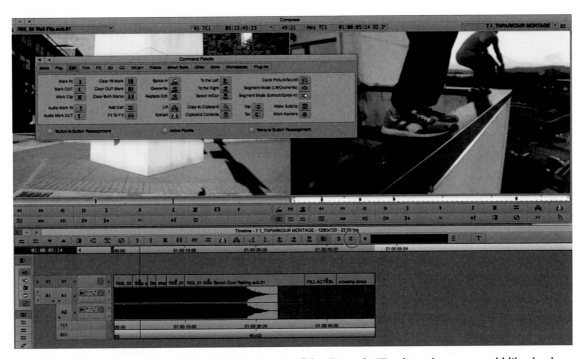

Figure 4.46 The position indicator parked at the part of the clip in the Timeline where you would like the shot to end and the Tail button selected.

This will trim the shot from position indicator to the current end of the segment.

10. If you would like the edit point of a shot to start earlier than it does, Mark an **IN** at that point on the Timeline and click the **EXTEND BUTTON**.

Figure 4.47 Extend button.

Figure 4.48 Marking an IN point in the Timeline and selecting the Extend button.

11. If you would like the edit point of a shot to end later than it does, Mark an **OUT** at that point in the Timeline and click the **EXTEND BUTTON**.

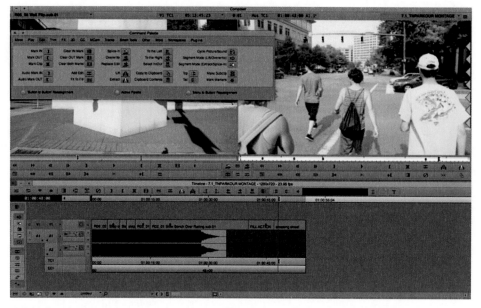

Figure 4.49 Marking an OUT point in the Timeline and selecting the Extend button.

Remember, Extend allows you to adjust the end point of one shot and the beginning of the next shot without going into Trim mode.

Figure 4.50 Extend button on the bottom row of the Record monitor.

12. You can also use the **SMART TOOL** to swap shots around or delete shots from the Timeline.

Keep in mind that when the yellow Splice-In/Extract arrow is used to select the segment, clips will be moved around in the Timeline, but that when the red Overwrite/Lift arrow is selected, clips will be overwritten or leave a gap when removed.

13. Conclude the lesson by saving your work.

Exercise 4.4: Map the Keyboard of a New User

Create a user profile and map the keyboard with useful functions for faster editing.

Media Used: No Media Required

Duration: 15 minutes

1. Open the **SETTINGS** tab in the Project window.

2. (Optional) Create and name a new **USER PROFILE** for yourself, if you don't already have one.

    Next, you will need to open the Keyboard Setting and the Command Palette.

3. With the Settings pane active, press the **K KEY** to jump to the **KEYBOARD SETTING** and then press the **ENTER KEY** to open it.

4. Select the **TOOLS MENU > COMMAND PALETTE**.

5. (Optional) If you are working on a Macintosh system and want to use the Function keys for Media Composer functions, you must first enable the system setting.

    Choose **SYSTEM PREFERENCES > KEYBOARD > KEYBOARD TAB**, and select the box next to "Use all F1, F2, etc. keys as standard function keys," as shown in Figure 4.51.

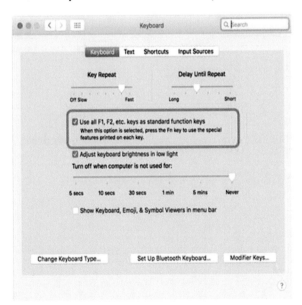

Figure 4.51 On a Mac, select "Use all F1, F2, etc. keys as standard function keys" to use the function keys.

6.   Map the following commands to the key suggested:

- Smart Tool Toggle: Tab key

- Link Selection: Shift+Tab key

- Toggle Source/Record: Esc key

- Toggle Source/Record in Timeline: Tilde key

- Track Control Panel (from Timeline Fast menu): Shift+Tilde key

- Match Frame: N key

- Find Bin: Shift+N key

- Add Edit: H key

- Top: Shift+I key

- Tail: Shift+O key

- Extend: Semicolon key

- Fast Forward: Shift+Up Arrow key

- Rewind: Shift+Down Arrow key

- Source/Record Editing workspace: F9 key

- Audio Editing workspace: F10 key

- Effects workspace: F11 key

- Color Correction workspace: F12 key

7.   Export the USER setting to the desktop.

8.   If you have a removable flash drive, copy your USER setting from the desktop to your flash drive.

Cutting and Recutting a Scene

Editing is a process of revision. For many editors, finishing a sequence is just the beginning of the review-recut-repeat process. As review notes and requests from the director, producer, or client come back, the "perfectly trimmed" sequence needs to be broken down, modified, and rebuilt. In this lesson, you will learn the tools and techniques for doing that efficiently.

Media Used: Anesthesia

Duration: 75 minutes

GOALS

- Review basic edit tools
- Learn to use scratch sequences
- Copy material between sequences
- Use sequences as source material
- Create sub-sequences
- Use Match Frame and Find Bin
- Use the Find tool to search across bins
- Use track-based segment tools

Review of Basic Edit Tools

In MC101: Media Composer Fundamentals I, you learned the basics of three-point editing using Splice-In, Overwrite, Lift and Extract, the button icons for which are shown in Figure 5.1. Using these should become second nature to you, so it is worth taking a moment to review these functions briefly before we go on.

Splice-In		Inserts new material into the sequence at the designated edit point. All existing material to the right of the edit point – that is, all downstream material – is moved farther to the right, which is later in time.
Overwrite		Replaces existing material in the sequence with the new material being added. No other material in the sequence is moved.
Lift		Removes the material marked between the IN/OUT marks in the sequence and leaves a gap of filler. No other material in the sequence is moved.
Extract		Removes the material marked between the IN/OUT marks in the sequence and closes the gap by moving all downstream material upstream (to the left).

Figure 5.1 Splice-In, Overwrite, Lift and Extract buttons.

Key points to remember:

1. To make an edit, Source tracks must be patched to Record (sequence) tracks.

2. All four edit functions affect material on all active tracks, regardless of patching. Use track selection to control which tracks are affected by your edits. This is key especially for maintaining sync.

Understanding Three-Point Editing

When adding material to the sequence, every edit requires three points: two points to mark a duration and one point to mark the location. The most common way to define an edit, then, is with three marks, which is called *three-point editing*. When drag-and-drop editing, you define the portion of the source clip to use with IN and OUT marks, then dictate the third point by where you release the clip after dragging it to the Timeline. Traditional three-point editing, however, uses a third mark with Splice-In or Overwrite.

Let's look at the various ways you can use three-point editing and some other variations in setting IN and OUT marks:

- **Source priority:** With source priority three-point editing, you mark an IN point and an OUT point in the source clip and mark an IN point or an OUT point (but not both) in the Timeline. If you mark an IN point in the Timeline, the first frame of the source segment (a.k.a. the head) will be positioned at the location of the IN mark when the edit is made. In other words, the sequence IN mark defines where the clip will start. If you mark an OUT point in the Timeline, the last frame of the source segment (a.k.a. the tail) will be positioned at the OUT mark when the edit is made. In other words, the sequence OUT mark defines where the clip will end.

If you mark an IN point in the Timeline, you can use Splice-In or Overwrite. If you mark an OUT point in the Timeline, you can only use Overwrite.

■ **Sequence priority:** With sequence priority three-point editing, you mark an IN point and an OUT point in the Timeline, and mark an IN point or an OUT point (but not both) in the Source monitor (location). This method gives priority to the amount of material (duration) needed to fill a space in the sequence. You define where that duration will begin or end in the source material (location) by using an IN mark or an OUT mark, respectively. This edit is typically performed using Overwrite to replace the content marked in the Timeline. When you use an OUT mark only (no IN mark) in either the source clip or the Timeline, the system will automatically determine the start frame of the source clip. This is referred to as backtiming the shot. (See Figure 5.2.)

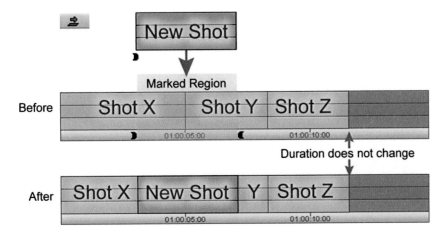

Figure 5.2 A "sequence priority" three-point edit.

The following table, Table 5.1, is a helpful summary of the possible combinations of IN and OUT marks in the Source and Record monitors.

Table 5.1: Possible Combinations of IN and OUT Marks

Source monitor	Record monitor/Sequence	Behavior
] [	]	Source material between the IN-OUT marks is placed in the sequence with the first source frame at the sequence's IN mark.
] [	[	Source material between IN-OUT is placed in the sequence with the last source frame at the sequence's OUT mark.
]	] [	The frame at the IN mark of the Source is placed at the location of the IN mark in the sequence. The duration marked with the sequence's IN-OUT will be filled with available source material. If there is not enough available source material to fill the duration marked in the sequence, then a dialog window will display Insufficient Source.
[	] [	The frame at the OUT mark of the Source is placed at the location of the OUT mark in the sequence. The duration marked with the sequence's IN-OUT will be filled with available source material. If there is not enough available source material to fill the duration marked in the sequence, then a dialog window will display Insufficient Source.

In Media Composer, you can also define your edits with more or less than three marks, with varying results.

- **No marks:** If you don't add IN and OUT marks to the source clip or the Timeline, the system will use the portion of the source clip from the blue position indicator to the end of the clip, splicing or overwriting at the location of the position indicator in the Timeline. In other words, the blue position indicator in the sequence acts as the IN mark.

- **IN marks only:** If you add IN marks in both the source clip and the Timeline, the system will use the portion of the source clip extending from the IN mark to the end of the source clip, splicing or overwriting at the location of the IN point in the Timeline.

- **Four marks:** Suppose you apply IN and OUT marks to both the source clip and the Timeline. In that case, the Source OUT is ignored and the Timeline marks define the duration of the edit to be made as illustrated in the table above.

Maintaining Sync

Maintaining the sync relationship between picture and sound is a basic requirement of editing. Like any "yellow" function, Splice-In ripples downstream material in the sequence and therefore can break sync. To maintain sync between picture and sound, you must edit tracks of synced audio and video equally.

Figure 5.3 illustrates a fairly common situation. You want to splice-in an MOS (no audio) shot to V1, but there is sync sound on A1 further down the Timeline. How can you make the edit without breaking sync? Simple: Enable the A1 record tracks when you make the edit.

Because you've enabled A1, your edits will affect those tracks equally. Because there is no source audio to put into A1, Media Composer simply fills the space with filler.

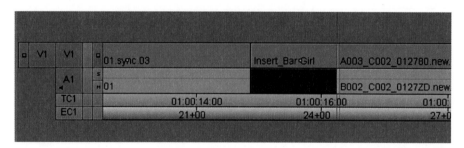

Figure 5.3 Use track selection to automatically edit in filler, thereby maintaining sync.

  Tracks matter! Always glance at your track selection before you perform an edit.

Concept: Understanding Filler

Filler refers to the empty space in the Timeline. The term is derived from the blank celluloid used to keep film in sync whenever there was a gap in the film during the edit process. Thinking of it as filler rather than empty space is more accurate. In Media Composer, you can manipulate filler in the same ways you edit video or audio segments. You can add edits to it, trim it, apply effects to it, and more. This is different from any other NLE on the market, and provides some real advantages, specifically with trimming and in working with effects.

So, what about Sync Locks? Couldn't you have performed the edit shown in Figure 5.11 with Sync Locks and arrived at the same result? Sure. But it is a best practice to use Sync Locks only as a safety net—to edit as if they weren't there. As you edit, you may intentionally disable them to perform a particular edit and then forget to turn them back on right away. If you have good habits of track selection, you'll have fewer problems. This is equally true for both cutting as well as trimming.

Using Lift and Extract

Lift

Lift removes material from the Timeline, leaving filler in its place. It is represented by a red up arrow (see Figure 5.4).

    Figure 5.4 Lift button.

Lift is used if you want to maintain the rhythm of a sequence or the synchronization of the picture and audio tracks. This action is the inverse of overwriting; both lifting and overwriting maintain the integrity and duration of the sequence. You are already familiar with performing a lift. When you deleted a segment using the Lift/Overwrite segment tool, the system was performing a lift.

To lift material from the Timeline:

1. Mark an **IN** point and an **OUT** point at the start and end of the material to be removed.

2. Select the desired record **TRACKS**.

3. Press **Z** or click the **LIFT** button in the Timeline.

    You can use the Mark Clip button (or press the T key) to quickly select a whole clip for removal. Based on the record tracks you have selected and the location of the blue position indicator, the Mark Clip function automatically finds the IN and OUT of a clip(s) in the sequence.

Extract

Extracting removes material from the Timeline and closes the gap left by its removal. In other applications, this is often referred to as a "ripple delete." This action is the inverse of splicing; both extracting and splicing affect the length of the sequence. When you deleted segments from sequences using the yellow Extract/Splice-In Segment tool, you performed an extract. It is represented by a yellow up arrow (see Figure 5.5), and if you look closely at the icon, you'll see a small, gray arrowhead pointing to the left, indicating that downstream material will move upstream (to the left) when the extract is performed.

    Figure 5.5 Extract button.

To extract material from the Timeline:

1. Mark an **IN** point and an **OUT** point at the start and end of the material to be removed.

2. Select the desired record **TRACKS**.

3. Press **X** or click the **EXTRACT** button in the Timeline.

Technique: Compressing Time with Jump Cuts

As you move past the elementary stages of editing, you should start to think outside the box of existing segments in your sequence. Lift and Extract have the advantage of allowing you to mark a custom IN and OUT area in the Timeline, and therefore do not limit you to removing only existing segments.

One technique is to use Extract to cut down a lengthy shot into a series of jump cuts. There is nothing subtle about this technique, which works great for high-energy spots, sports promo montages, etc. No doubt you have seen this effect before. It is often created with a subject moving toward the camera—i.e., an athlete running, a snowboarder flying through the air, or a car driving down a long road, etc. Each jump cut moves the subject significantly closer to the viewer. (See Figure 5.6.)

Figure 5.6 Use Extract to create dynamic jump cuts.

This same technique can be used in sequences with less energy. Images of a slow process can be fascinating when sped up with jump cuts and dissolves, whether it is actual time-lapse footage or just a long video recording. Examples might include a sunrise, a POV shot of driving between locales, a lockdown shot of someone making something, or even chocolate melting. Regardless of the footage, the technique is the same. Drop a long segment into the sequence, then mark and extract multiple sections from within it.

Selecting Multiple Segments

There will be times when you want to move (or remove) multiple segments in the Timeline. Using segment mode (the red and yellow arrows in the Smart Tool), you can select multiple segments at once. There are several ways to do this, as you might expect. No doubt you will use each method at a different time.

Let's go through each method.

To select multiple segments:

■ While pressing the **SHIFT** key, click on each **SEGMENT**.

   Each segment is highlighted to indicate it is selected. This is useful for selecting a few segments, whether they are contiguous or not.

To lasso segments:

1. Starting in the gray space above the top video track, click and drag the POINTER down and to the right. This creates a lasso. Alternatively, hold down the Alt (Windows) or Option (Mac) key to allow lassoing directly in the Timeline.

2. Continue dragging to draw the LASSO around the SEGMENTS you want to select. The lasso must completely encompass a segment to select it.

3. Release the MOUSE button to select the segments.

   All segments completely inside the lasso will be highlighted when you release. This is useful for selecting a contiguous group on adjacent tracks.

 The direction in which you draw the lasso is important. Moving from left to right, as described here, selects the segments. Moving from right to left sets up a slip trim on the segments. Slip trim is covered in Lesson 7, "Trimming Dialogue."

Finally, you can select a group of segments by track using dedicated buttons in the Timeline rather than the Smart Tool. These are shown in Table 5.2.

Table 5.2: Buttons for Selecting Segments

Button	Name	Description
	Select Left	Selects the segments under the position indicator and all segments to the left on active tracks.
	Select Right	Selects the segments under the position indicator and all segments to the right on active tracks.
	Select In/Out	Selects all segments between the IN and OUT marks on active tracks.

To select segments by track:

1. Select the TRACKS containing segments you want to move.

2. Optionally, add IN and OUT marks to define a region of the sequence.

3. Click the SELECT LEFT, SELECT RIGHT, or SELECT IN/OUT button to make your selection.

   The segments are selected in the same way as if you had selected them with the Smart Tool. You can now move or delete all those segments.

Technique: Give Yourself Space to Work

A useful application of the track-based Segment tools is to give you space to work in the middle of a sequence. For example, suppose you have the rough cut of a sequence mostly complete, but you find that you need to do some additional editing in the middle. Depending on the sequence, it may be easier to simply open some space to revise that portion of the edit and then rejoin the sequence.

Here's how you could do that:

1. Park the position indicator where you want to open the gap and select the specific tracks, as shown in Figure 5.7.

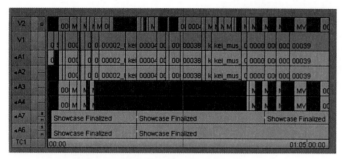

Figure 5.7 Park the position indicator as needed.

2. Click the Select Right button. As shown in Figure 5.8, the segments are selected.

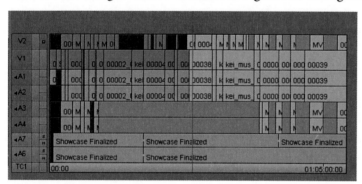

Figure 5.8 Select the segments.

3. With the red Lift/Overwrite arrow button selected in the Smart Tool, drag the segments to the right. (See Figure 5.9.)

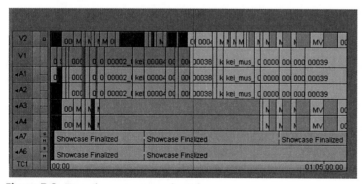

Figure 5.9 Drag the segments to the right.

4. After performing additional edits in the gap, rejoin the sequence by parking the position indicator at the beginning of the group to move.

5. While pressing Alt (Windows) or Option (Mac), click the Select Right button. This selects the segments of material but does not select the filler between. (See Figure 5.10.)

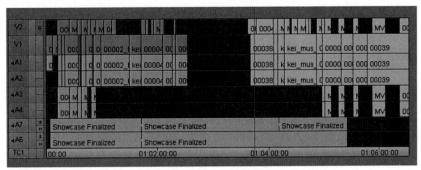

Figure 5.10 The segments are selected, but not the filler.

6. While pressing Ctrl (Windows) or Command (Mac) to snap, drag the group back into place.

 Filler can also be excluded from the Segment Mode tool selection in the Timeline Settings > Edit tab > uncheck Select Filler with Segment Tools.

 Exercise Break: Exercise 5.1
Pause here to practice what you've learned.

Alternate Ways to Use Sequences

One of the constraints that novice editors struggle against when it comes time to approaching larger projects is trying to do everything in one sequence. Cutting multiple scenes, replacing shots, adding new material, trimming, etc. all become more complicated when you are worried about adversely affecting the "good parts" of a sequence. This is an unnecessary frustration, which stems from thinking about "the project sequence" as a singular item.

Professional editors will tell you that typically there are many sequences for any given project. You have already started to see this start to play out. In your coursework so far, you have duplicated sequences to get new versions. You have also created stringout sequences of ingested material and selects. This section is a focused study in the various ways that you can create and, more importantly, utilize multiple sequences in the editing process.

During the creative process, there are times when you may want to experiment with a scene or a small portion of a scene—maybe an action sequence or a tricky portion of a dialogue scene. Rather than trying to experiment within the confines of a larger program sequence, it can be helpful to put that material into a new sequence.

Don't be afraid to create and use many sequences. The sequence is your canvas. Starting a new one is like grabbing a blank sheet of paper to sketch out a new idea. To keep things organized, follow these tips:

- Keep your sequences in dedicated sequence bins.

- Name every sequence.

- Use a consistent naming convention that includes version numbers or a date/time.

- Avoid definitive labels, such as "final." Things inevitably change.

- Use the Comments field in Text or Script view to briefly note what is unique, changed, or being attempted with that sequence. You will not remember next week what the difference was between v.13 and v.15 without a note like, "recut fight, skipped chair breaking over back, cut straight from hand fighting to villain pulling out his knife."

Of course, for a scratch sequence to be a real benefit there has to be an easy way to use material from one sequence in another. As you might expect, there are several ways to do so.

Loading Sequences into the Source Monitor

As we've alluded to already, Media Composer allows you to load a sequence into the Source monitor to use as source material. This is especially useful for editing from stringout sequences, or for incorporating a scene that you "sketched out" in a scratch sequence into the larger program sequence.

To load the sequence into the Source monitor:

- Drag the SEQUENCE icon from the bin to the Source monitor.

    Once the sequence is loaded into the Source monitor, you can use the playback, marking, and editing controls to edit in the same way that you would a master clip or subclip. The sequence icon in the Source monitor, and possibly the number of source track selectors, is your confirmation that you are looking at the sequence. (See Figure 5.11.)

Figure 5.11   The sequence icon in the Source monitor's Clip Name menu confirms that you are working off a sequence—perfect for cutting from assembly sequences.

The Toggle Source/Record in Timeline button is especially useful when editing from a sequence in the Source monitor.

Creating Sub-Sequences

Creating a sub-sequence from the Record monitor breaks up the sequence into shorter sections and turns each of these sections into a discrete sequence. Creating a sub-sequence is like duplicating only a portion of the sequence instead of the whole thing.

This technique is useful when you want to store parts of a sequence in your bin for future use. For example, you can use a sub-sequence to isolate the program opener and closer that will be used on multiple episodes, to pull individual scenes from one version of the program to use in another version, etc. It can also be useful for separating out a problematic portion of the scene so that you can experiment with it, free from the concerns of messing up the "real" sequence.

To create a sub-sequence:

1. Load the SEQUENCE into the Record monitor and mark an IN at the start of the section that you want to sub-sequence.

2. Mark an OUT where you want to end the sub-sequence.

3. Select the RECORD TRACKS that you want to be in the sub-sequence.

4. To create the sub-sequence, drag the SEQUENCE icon above the Record monitor to the bin. Alternatively, Alt-drag (Windows) or Option-drag (Mac) the PICTURE from the Record monitor to the destination bin.

5. When you release the mouse button, the marked frames are saved as a new sequence.

    This new sequence has the name of the original sequence followed by Sub.n, where **n** is the number of times the sequence has been sub-sequenced to that bin. (See Figure 5.12.)

6. Name the SUB-SEQUENCE.

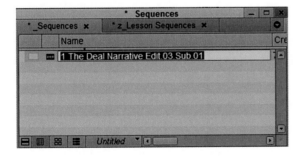

Figure 5.12
A newly created sub-sequence, ready for renaming.

 To save clipboard contents, drag the icon from the Clipboard monitor to a bin instead of from the Record monitor. Clipboard contents are saved as a sub-sequence.

Creating a Sequence from a Selection

Media Composer v8.6 introduces a new feature that provides using selected segments (rather than marking IN/OUT) in a current sequence to quickly create a new one.

To create a new sequence from a Segment Mode selection:

1. Select the SEGMENTS IN THE TIMELINE you wish to include in the new sequence.

    You can do this by lassoing them, enabling one of the Segment Mode tools and then Shift-clicking, or using one of the options Select Left, Select Right or Select In-Out.

2. Right-click in the Timeline and choose CREATE SEQUENCE BASED ON SELECTION.

3. (Optional) If more than one bin is open, the Select a Bin dialog box will appear. Select the bin to save the new sequence, and click OK.

    The new sequence will appear in the bin with the same name as the original sequence, with the suffix ".Copy.01".

    Creating a subsequence can be especially useful to experiment with different edits on a particular part of the scene or program. You can perform your edits directly on the sub-sequence, duplicating as needed to create additional versions. When you are ready to reincorporate the new-and-improved section back into the larger film, just load it into the Source monitor.

 A sub-sequence does not maintain a link to the original sequence from which it came. Changes to the original sequence do not appear in the sub-sequences created from it or vice-versa.

This approach to using sequences is really rooted in a film paradigm, like many things in Media Composer. Imagine a film editor cutting celluloid film. The film editor would not constantly fight to manage the entire film sequence as he or she cuts individual scenes or trimmed a segment from the middle of a scene in the middle of the reel. That would be madness. Instead, the film editor would cut individual scenes that are assembled into a completed whole at the end. Using multiple sequences that are then recombined into a cohesive whole is the same approach, adapted to the digital age. Aside from the computer magic of being able to have unlimited copies of the clips, it is really the same process.

Finding Alternative Shots

When you get to the point in the edit process that you are working to revise a scene or sequence, you are often faced with questions like the following:

- What else was in that shot?

- Are there alternate takes for that line?

- Wasn't there another angle on that?

- Is there more coverage for this scene?

The two functions that can help answer those questions quickly are Match Frame and Find Bin. They are indispensable to professional editors. They are used so frequently that they are typically mapped to the keyboard.

Match Frame

As shown in Figure 5.13, the Match Frame button has the same icon as a master clip, which makes sense. Match Frame locates the frame currently displayed in the Record monitor by loading its source clip into the Source monitor, locating the frame with the blue position indicator, and selecting the track. The source clip is loaded into the Source monitor, and an IN point is marked at that location.

Figure 5.13 Match Frame button.

If you want to view earlier or later source footage from a clip in the sequence, just park the position indicator near the beginning or the end of the segment and then use Match Frame. You can quickly see in the Source monitor what else the master clip contains.

To find the original master clip for a segment in the sequence:

1. Move to the **FRAME** in your sequence that you want to match.

2. Select the **TRACK** in the Track Control panel that you want to match and deselect higher tracks. (Match Frame only responds to the upper-most selected track.)

3. Click the **FAST** menu in the Composer window; then click the **MATCH FRAME** button in the Tool Palette, as shown in Figure 5.14.

Figure 5.14
The Match Frame button is found in the Composer window's Tool Palette.

 It's faster to right-click on a track selector and choose Match Frame Track. This does not require the track selectors to be set before the operation. Faster still, put Match Frame on your keyboard! See "Mapping Buttons and Menus" in the previous lesson.

You may notice that Match Frame is mapped by default under the Source monitor. Match Frame also works in the Source monitor to go from a subclip or group clip back to the original master clip.

Find Bin

Because you invested the time at the beginning of your project to organize the footage into topical bins (one that contains only sunset shots, one that contains just aerial view shots, and another that contains only under water shots, etc.), you can now use Find Bin to find alternative shots. With a clip or sequence loaded into a monitor, you can click the Find Bin button (see Figure 5.15) to find the original bin in which it is stored. Media Composer finds the bin, opens it, and highlights the clip or sequence within the bin. This works for sequences and source clips alike.

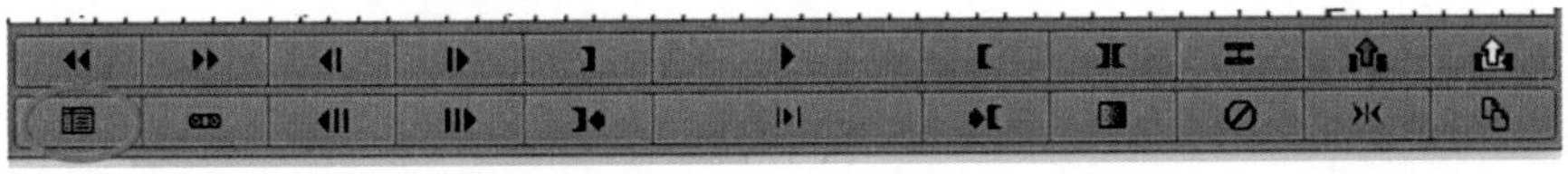

Figure 5.15 The Find Bin button, under the Record monitor, will find the bin for the entire sequence. Another is in the same location under the Source monitor to find the bin for the source clip.

To find the bin for the clip or sequence currently in the Composer window:

1. (Optional) Load a CLIP into the Source monitor using Match Frame.

2. Click the FIND BIN button in the toolbar under the Composer window.

    The bin is opened and the item highlighted.

    If you click the Find Bin button under the Source monitor, it will find the source clip; if you click the one under Record, it will find the sequence.

To find the bin of the clip currently under the position indicator:

1. Place the POSITION INDICATOR on the clip within the sequence.

2. (Optional) Select the TRACKS.

    The system will find the clip on the upper-most active track.

3. ALT-CLICK (Windows) or OPTION-CLICK (Mac) the FIND BIN button.

    The system opens the bin and highlights the clip.

The Find Tool

Media Composer has a Find feature that you can use to search for items in any bin. The difference between this and the Search feature found in the bins or Timeline is that the Find tool searches across all metadata in the project, regardless of which bin, clip, or sequence contains the info. It makes finding the clip you're looking for very easy, even if you don't know which bin the clip is in, you can find it quickly.

To open the Find window:

■ Press CTRL+F (Windows) or COMMAND+F (Mac). Alternatively, select EDIT > FIND.

    The Find window opens, as shown in Figure 5.16.

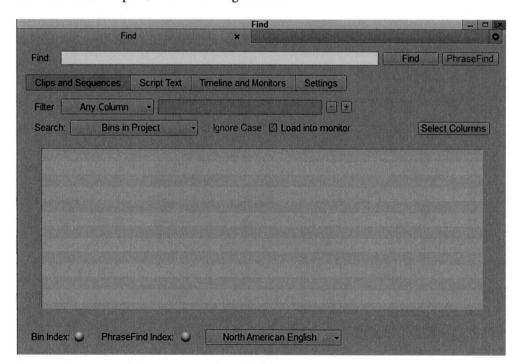

Figure 5.16 You use the Find window to search for text in any bin.

The tab at the top of the window, labeled Find, can be combined with other tool tabs, such as the Project window or Markers tool. Simply drag the tab to the other window and release it.

The Find window has three tabs:

- **Clips and Sequences:** Use this tab to search text in bin columns. For example, any metadata tags you added to bin items in Lesson 3, "Preparing Dailies," could be found using this option.

- **Script Text:** Use this tab to search the text of scripts imported into the project. It's useful for finding specific lines of dialogue.

- **Timeline and Monitors:** Use this tab to search text displayed on segments in the Timeline or in the Composer monitors. This includes clip names, markers, local comments, and any additional text displayed on the segments. To display additional information to the clip name, click the Timeline Fast menu and choose Clip Text.

- **Markers:** Use this tab to search the text contained in markers on any item in the bins.

Within each of the tabs, you have additional options in the drop-down menus to refine the search. The result of your search will also differ based on what options you select.

Searching Across Multiple Bins

You can search across multiple bins. For example, you could use the default selections to search any column in the bins in the project. The results will be displayed as a list in the Find window, as shown in Figure 5.17.

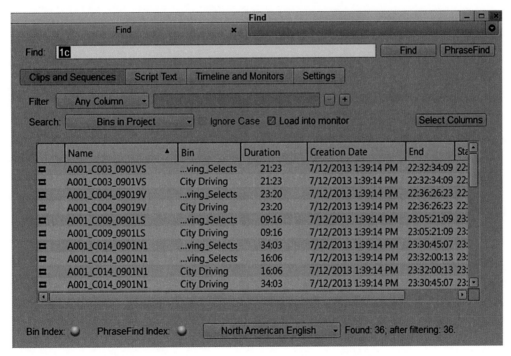

Figure 5.17 Searching for clips and sequences in any bin results in a list of assets.

From the results list, you can reveal the file in its original bin and/or load it into the Source monitor.

To reveal the item in the bin:

■   Double-click the ITEM in the list

If the Load into Monitor check box is selected, double-clicking will simultaneously load the item into the Source monitor (sequences included).

Searching in a Specific Location

If you use the Find tool to search in a specific location, such as the current sequence in the Timeline and monitors (see Figure 5.18), you are not given a list of search results. Instead, the system highlights the results one by one, revealing the next result by advancing the playhead to its location.

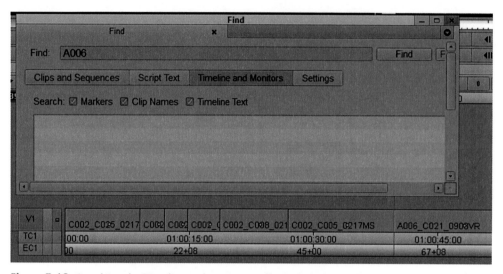

Figure 5.18 Searching the Timeline and monitors will reveal results one by one.

If searching in the current bin, the first result will be highlighted in the bin. If searching in the Timeline and monitors, the blue position indicator will jump to the location of the first search result.

To advance to the next result:

■   Press CTRL+G (Windows) or COMMAND+G (Mac).

When the search has reached the last instance of the search term in the Timeline, it will circle back to the beginning of the Timeline and continue scanning from there.

Detailed explanations of each of the options in this window are found in the Media Composer Help article, "Searching for a Clip or Sequence with Text Find."

Essential Tools

The following tools are indispensible when working in the sequence to edit and re-edit a scene.

Fast Forward and Rewind

Fast Forward and Rewind are found in the toolbar of each Composer window. They have the common icons, as shown in Figure 5.19.

Rewind

Fast Forward

Figure 5.19 Rewind and Fast Forward buttons.

Fast Forward and Rewind function a bit differently in Media Composer. Rather than playing at high speed as you might expect, like J-K-L, these buttons jump the position indicator through the edit points. By default, they respond to the active tracks, stopping only at common edit points. When working with a large complex sequence, this default behavior gives you precise control over where the position indicator will stop. Many editors, however, would prefer to not have to think about their track selection and simply have the position indicator stop at every edit point on any track.

To momentarily make FF/RW disregard the active track selectors, and stop at every cut point on every track, press and hold Alt (Windows) or Option (Mac).

To set FF/RW to stop at every edit point:

1. Right-click on the **COMPOSER** window and choose **COMPOSER SETTINGS**.

    The Composer Settings–Current dialog box opens. (See Figure 5.20.)

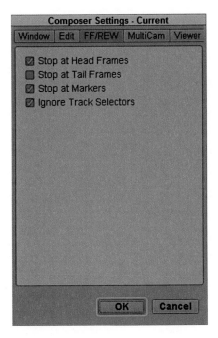

Figure 5.20 The Composer Settings—Current dialog box.

2. Click the **FF/REW** tab.

3. Click the Ignore Track Selectors check box to select it.

4. Click **OK**.

 Fast Forward and Rewind are not on the keyboard by default but many editors like them there. Two popular places to map them are the Up/Down arrow keys or the A and S keys (replacing Go to Next/Go to Previous Edit).

Displaying and Navigating by Timecode Values

Above the Source and Record monitors is a one- or two-line info display that shows data, typically timecode, about the source of the frame currently displayed in the monitor. These data fields can display the clip name, duration, timecode, and/or film tracking data in a broad range of views. If you like, you can display two rows of data.

To change the number of rows displayed:

1. Right-click on the Composer window and select Composer Settings.

2. In the Window tab, select your preference:

    - Always Display One Row of Data

    - Always Display Two Rows of Data

    - Flow Data Dynamically

    Great, now that you're set up, let's look at the various information and displays available.

To adjust the Timecode display:

1. Click the first (or second) Row of the timecode display.

    A menu appears. As shown in Figure 5.21, it has three sections.

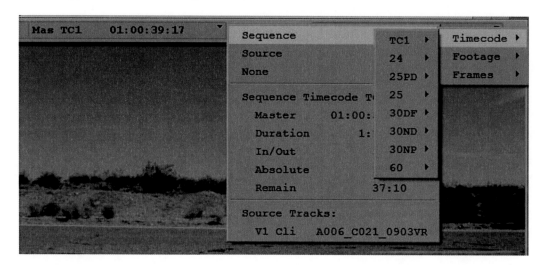

Figure 5.21 The drop-down menus in the Composer hold a wealth of information.

2. Make a selection from one of the three sections:

- Choose a timecode type from the first section
- Choose from the second section for data about the clip (Source monitor display) or sequence (Record monitor display)
- Choose from the third section for data about the source clip

Let's look at the three sections more closely:

- **Section 1:** This section enables you to tell the system how you want to display information in sections 2 and 3: as timecode, clip names, or frames. In most cases, you want to display timecode, and will use this section if timecode is not displayed.

- **Section 2:** This section gives you information about the clip loaded in the Source monitor (Source monitor display) or the sequence loaded in the Timeline (Record monitor display). The timecodes are as follows:

  - **Master (M):** This displays the location of the position indicator on the sequence's Timecode track (known as Master timecode). This matches the green timecode display in the top-left corner of the Timeline window.

  - **Duration (D):** This displays the duration of the entire clip or sequence.

  - **In/Out (IO):** This displays the marked IN to OUT duration.

  - **Absolute (Ab):** This displays the time from the head (00:00) to the position indicator (known as absolute timecode).

  - **Remain (R):** This displays the time remaining from the position indicator to the end of the sequence.

- **Section 3:** This section lists information for each track of the clip in the Source monitor (Source monitor display) or where your position indicator is parked in the Timeline (Record monitor display).

Many editors keep Master timecode on the top row (to take advantage of a couple navigation features to be discussed in a moment), and use the second row for whatever info they need at the moment. (Personally, I tend to keep duration in the second row, letting me see with a glance the total duration of the sequence as I edit.)

To change a display to timecode (TC1), navigate the menu as shown in Figure 5.22. After you release the mouse, the source V1 track will be displayed as timecode (TC1) in the Timecode display and in the third section of the menu.

Jumping to a Specific Timecode

After loading a clip or sequence into a monitor, you can go to a specific frame by typing its video timecode. You can also move forward or backward from your position by entering a frame offset.

To find a specific frame using timecode:

1. Load a CLIP or SEQUENCE into a monitor.

2. Click the MONITOR in which to search. (The active monitor has the brighter position bar.)

3. Verify that the proper timecode is displayed in the monitor:

    • For source clips, make sure the Source Video (V1) timecode is displayed.

    • For sequences, make sure the Mas (TC1) timecode is displayed.

    • When two rows of data are displayed, the upper display must show the timecode in order for these features to work properly.

4. Enter the TIMECODE using the numeric keypad, typing the hours, minutes, seconds, and frames, omitting leading zeros. For example, to enter 01:23:02:00, type `1230200`.

    As you start typing, an entry field opens in the middle of the monitor, showing the numbers you type. (The system inserts the colons.)

 If working on a laptop or keyboard with no numeric keypad, rapidly press twice on the Ctrl (Windows) or Control (Mac) key to open the entry field, then enter the number using the numbers at the top of the keyboard.

5. Press ENTER on the numeric keypad. The position indicator locates the specified timecode, if it exists.

    The system beeps if it can't find the specified timecode number in the clip or sequence. Check the top row of the Timecode display and make sure the appropriate timecode is shown.

There are a couple nice, built-in shortcuts, too.

■ If you are looking for a timecode that starts at the same hour as the current timecode, just type the last digits. For example, if you happen to be currently parked at timecode 1:05:12:13 and you type 50423, the system finds the frame at 1:05:04:23.

■ If you type a period (.), the system will add 00. For example, to search for 01:21:00:00, you could type 121. (Note the extra period.)

Check the Timecode Display

The monitor's timecode display determines the way the system references the numbers you type into the monitor. If you use a two-line timecode display, the top line is the reference timecode. For example, if you want to reference the V1 (video) timecode of a clip, you must select V1 in the top line of the timecode display. If you instead display I/O timecode, the system won't be able to find a frame using the preceding method.

Typing a Frame Offset

You can also use Media Composer's frame offset feature to move the position indicator from its current frame forward (or backward) a specified number of frames. This procedure is similar to the method for adding and removing frames using the numeric keypad in Trim mode, covered in the previous lesson.

To type a frame offset with a clip or sequence loaded in a monitor:

1. Make sure the monitor with the clip or sequence is active.

2. Using the numeric keypad, press the PLUS SIGN (+) key before typing the number to move forward or the MINUS SIGN (−) key before the number to move backward from the current position.

 If working on a laptop or keyboard with no numeric keypad, rapidly press twice the Ctrl (Windows) or Control (Mac) key and then press the minus sign (−) key Shift+Plus sign (+) (Windows)/Shift+Plus sign (+) (Mac) or before entering the number.

3. Enter the number of frames for the offset by doing one of the following:

    *   Type a number between 1–99.

    *   Enter a number of 100 or more to move forward or backward a specified number of seconds and frames.

    *   With Caps Lock off, add a lower case "f" for a number greater than 99 to have the number recognized as a frame count as opposed to seconds and frames. For example, typing +200 results in moving forward two seconds (2:00), while typing +200f results in moving forward 200.

4. Press ENTER.

5. Optionally, press ENTER again. The system will repeat the last entry.

    You can also use this method to mark a duration. When going forward or backward, enter one less frame than desired. This is because an OUT mark includes the final frame. For example, if you want to mark three seconds, mark an IN, type 229 (NTSC) or 224 (PAL) for the frame offset, and mark an OUT. Or, if you don't want to do the mental math, simply enter the duration you want and then step back one frame before setting the OUT mark.

 Exercise Break: Exercise 5.2 and 5.3
Pause here to practice what you've learned.

Review/Discussion Questions

1. How many edit points are required to define an edit when adding a shot to the sequence?

    a. 0

    b. 1

    c. 2

    d. 3

    e. 4

2. True or False: Media Composer will not allow you to make an edit with no marks.

3. How can Filler help maintain sync?

4. True or False: To load a sequence into the Source monitor, you should double-click the icon in the bin.

5. What is a sub-sequence? What can it be used for?

6. Which function loads the source clip for a segment in the sequence into the Source monitor?

    a.   b.   c.   d.   e.

7. What does Find Bin do?

8. What is the difference between Find, Find Bin and Match Frame?

9. What is the difference between using Find and the Search field in the bin?

10. What value would you type to advance the position indicator 2 seconds?

11. How do you type to jump the position indicator to a specific timecode?

12. What is the difference between Fast Forward/Rewind and J-K-L?

Lesson 5 Keyboard Shortcuts

Key	Shortcut
Alt-drag (Windows)/Option-drag (Mac)	Creates a sub-sequence by dragging the image from the Record monitor to the bin
Alt+Find Bin (Windows)/Option+Find Bin (Mac)	Finds the bin for the segment under the position indicator
Shift+I*	Top
Shift+O*	Tail
N*	Match Frame
Shift+B*	Find Bin
Semicolon (;)*	Extend

*Not a system default.

Alternative Editing Techniques

In previous exercises, you completed a fine-cut narrative scene and a separate montage. In this exercise, you will combine those, and integrate the requested changes from your (fictitious) producer. It is a challenge, but using the tools and techniques in this lesson, you have the knowledge you need to get it done.

Media Used: Anesthesia

Duration: 3 hours 15 minutes

GOALS

- Rough cut a dialogue scene
- Copy material between sequences
- Use sequences as source material
- Create sub-sequences
- Use Match Frame and Find Bin
- Use Top and Tail to extract sequence material
- Use Extend to shift edit points

Exercise 5.1: Crafting a Dialogue Scene

In this exercise we will revisit the basic tools Extract/Splice-In and Lift/Overwrite to put together a rough cut of a scene from the short film Anesthesia. We will also focus on sharpening our skills using keyboard shortcuts.

Media Used: Anesthesia

Duration: 1 hour 15 minutes

The director and producer of the film Anesthesia have reviewed the timecoded stringout and sent back a list of notes based on their favorite takes. Using these notes and the script for the scene as your guide, you will navigate to the preferred takes in the stringout and splice shots into the Timeline that will serve as your rough cut of the scene.

For this exercise, we will use the **MC110_ANESTHESIA** project.

1. Begin by opening the bin **STUDENT_LESSON SEQUENCES**.

2. Select the sequence **5.1_ANESTHESIA_STRINGOUT_WITH TC BURN** and drag the sequence into the Source monitor.

    You will now be able to use the Producer's notes to navigate to certain shots in the sequence and Splice or Overwrite the footage from the Source monitor directly into the Timeline.

3. Create a new sequence in the bin **ANESTHESIA_EXERCISE SEQUENCES** and call it **ANESTHESIA_ROUGH CUT**.

4. Make sure the **TRACKING INFORMATION MENU** in the Source monitor is set to **SEQUENCE >TIMECODE >TC1 > MAS** so that we can use the Producer's notes to navigate by timecode.

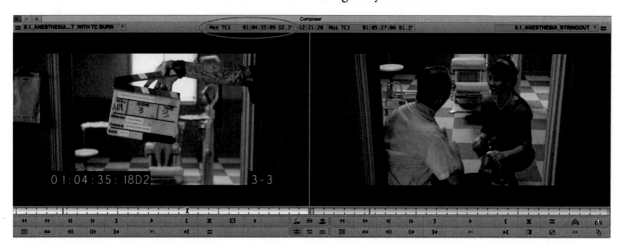

Figure 5.22 The Source monitor set to Mas TC1 from the Tracking Information menu.

5. Read through the Producer's notes. Select the Source monitor and type in the timecode referred to in the notes to navigate to the specific shot in the sequence **ANESTHESIA_STRINGOUT** the Producer wants you to use.

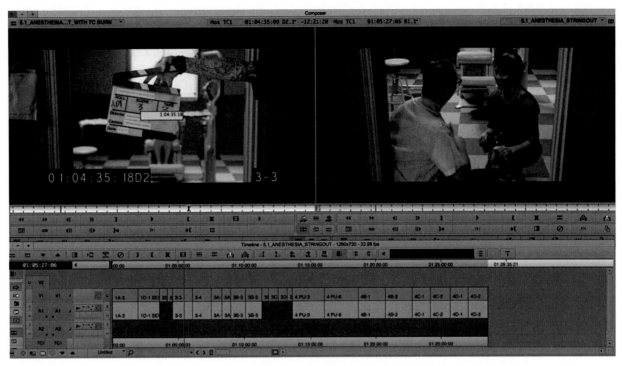

Figure 5.23 The typed in the timecode referred to in the Producer's notes brings you to that timecode in the sequence.

Producer's Notes:

01:06:08:10 – Let's use this take as the opening where she walks to the door way and runs into the dentist

01:06:08:10 – Let's use this take also for "You could say that" till Mary and the dentist begin walking back to the chair

01:07:34:06 – Best take for Mary's close-u"

01:09:04 – Best for dentist "Look who's keeping the tooth fairy busy"

01:10:06:18 – Best for dentist "You're not running out on me, are you?"

01:12:36:10 – good insert of photo

01:16:36:15 – great expression from Mary as she turns to camera, let's use this to get us into the bit in the chair

01:22:51:16 – best for Mary's close-up in chair

01:27:05:00 – best for Dentist close-up

01:20:56:12 – best coverage of Sue

01:16:57:00 – use for Dentist introducing Mary to Sue

6. Now it's time to get creative! Read through the script and using the takes the Producer has requested, put together a rough edit of "Anesthesia."

   Be sure that only the V1 and A1 tracks are activated in the Timeline. You don't need to add the timecode effect from your stringout into your **ANESTHESIA_ROUGH CUT** sequence.

7. Mark an **IN** points using the **I** KEY and mark an **OUT** points using the **O** KEY.

8. Add shots to the sequence **ANESTHESIA_ROUGH CUT** in the Timeline as you build your edit.

   Try to practice using the keyboard to make your edits as much as possible. This will allow you to move faster.

9. When you have finished editing your rough cut, be sure to save your work.

                                                                2.

```
BACK IN THE ROOM --

That's all Mary needs. She gathers her things and heads for
the door.

Just as she's about to exit -- DR. CLAYTON APPEARS!

Mary startles. Drops her purse. Contents scatter.

Dr. Clayton (33) is mild. Unassuming. He has a slightly
receding hairline and an easy smile. Stitched on his tunic:
"Dr. Clayton, DDS."

Mary squats. Gathers her things. Clayton helps.

                    DR. CLAYTON
               You're not running out on me are
               you?

                         MARY
               Sorry. I was just...

Clayton grins. Crouches down to help.

                    DR. CLAYTON
               No problemo. Happens all the time.

He picks up Mary's wallet. There's a photo inside --

BOBBY (6). Hugh smile. Missing a few teeth.

                    DR. CLAYTON (CONT'D)
               Looks like someone's keeping the
               tooth fairy busy?

                         MARY
               Yeah, you could say that.

Clayton nods. He helps Mary back to the chair. She
reluctantly takes a seat. Holds her purse close.

Clayton notes her anxiety. Takes a seat.

                    DR. CLAYTON
               Listen Mary, I know coming to the
               dentist can be scary, but I want to
               assure you, we're not monsters.

                         SUE (O.S.)
               Speak for yourself.

SUE (20's), Clayton's perky assistant, enters with a
mischievous grin. She pushes a covered cart.
```

Exercise 5.2: Cutting a New Opening for Anesthesia

In the previous exercise, we used basic editing tools to put together a rough cut of the short film, Anesthesia. In this exercise, we will continue to refine our edit by using Match Frame and Find Bin to swap out shots as requested in our Producer's notes, and we'll add an extended opening by creating a Subseqeunce.

Media Used: Anesthesia

Duration: 1 hour

For this exercise, we will continue to use the **MC110_ANESTHESIA** project.

1. Begin by opening the bin **STUDENT_LESSON SEQUENCES** and load the sequence **5.2_ANESTHESIA_ROUGH CUT_PRODUCER'S NOTES**.

    You will notice that the Producer has used markers to provide you with notes regarding the changes that need to be made to the rough cut. Before we make any changes, we want to preserve the last version of our edit with Producer's notes.

Figure 5.24 Markers are used to provide you with notes regarding changes that need to be made to the rough cut.

2. DUPLICATE the sequence **5.2_ANESTHESIA_ROUGH CUT_PRODUCER'S NOTES** and name the duplicate **ANESTHESIA_REVISED**.

3.   Choose **TOOLS > MARKERS** to open the Marker tool.

Now you will be able to see all of the Producer's notes. Read through each of the notes so you can see what changes need to be made.

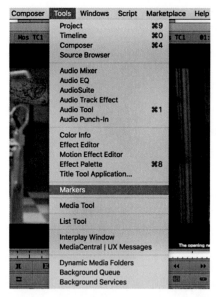

Figure 5.25 Choosing the Markers tool from the Tools menu.

4.   In the **MARKER WINDOW**, click on the **TC COLUMN HEADER** to select the column. Then right-click and choose **SORT COLUMN** or press **CTRL + E** (Windows) or **COMMAND + E** (Mac).

This will sort the Producer's notes by timecode, so you can move through and make the changes sequentially.

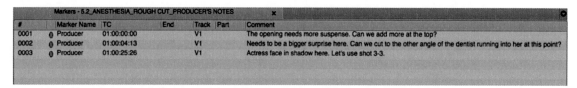

Figure 5.26 The Markers window displaying the Timecode (TC) column sorted.

5.   Enable the sync locks for V1 and A1 so that your audio and video will remain in sync as you edit.

6.   Read the first two notes from the producer:

a.   "The opening needs more suspense. Can we add more at the top?"

b.   "Needs to be a bigger surprise here. Can we cut to the other angle of the dentist running into her at this point?"

It sounds like we need to do a pretty dramatic recutting of the opening. Let's start by creating a subsequence of our current opening and recutting that opening in the subsequence. Once we are happy with our revised opening, we can add it back to the **ANESTHESIA_REVISED** sequence.

7.   To create a **SUBSEQUENCE**, go to the start of the **ANESTHESIA_REVISED** and mark an **IN** point using the **I KEY**.

8. Select the RECORD MONITOR and type in the timecode **01:0010:04** and press ENTER.

   This will take you up to the point where Mary crouches down to pick up the fallen contents of her purse.

9. In the RECORD MONITOR, mark an OUT point using the O KEY.

10. Using your mouse, grab the SEQUENCE ICON in the top right corner of the Source monitor and DRAG IT into your ANESTHESIA_EXERCISE SEQUENCES bin.

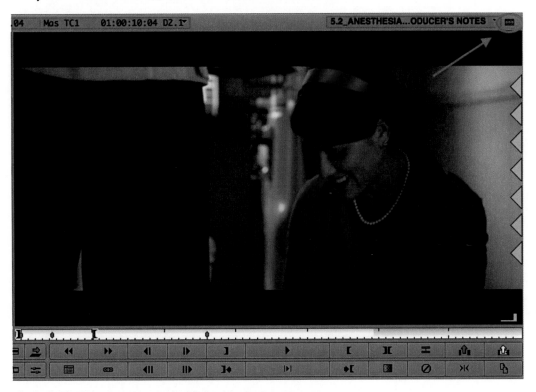

Figure 5.27 The Sequence icon highlighted in the Source monitor.

This will create a subsequence of the clips you marked between your IN and OUT points in the ANESTHESIA_REVISED sequence.

11. RENAME your subsequence ANESTHESIA_NEW OPENING and load it into the Timeline by double clicking on it.

   The Producer has provided a list of favorite takes for the new opening below:

   • 2E-2

   • 3-4

   • 3A-1

   • 3B-5

   • 3C-4

12. To locate these takes, park the position indicator on the shot **3-4** in the Timeline and using the FAST MENU between the Source and Record monitors, click the MATCH FRAME button.

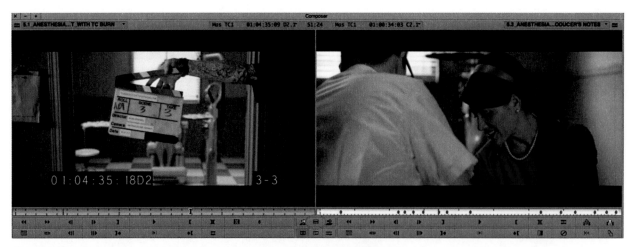

Figure 5.28 The Fast menu located in between the Record and Source monitors.

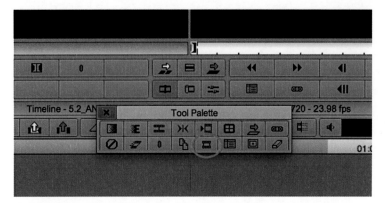

Figure 5.29 The Fast menu button highlighted in the Tool Palette.

This will load the clip **3-4** into the Source monitor.

Figure 5.30 Clip "3-4" loaded into the Source monitor.

13. Next, click the FIND BIN BUTTON.

    This will take you to the bin where all of your synced clips are located.

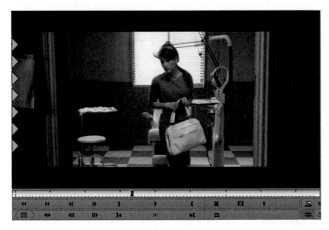

Figure 5.31 The Find Bin button under the Record monitor highlighted.

Figure 5.32 After selecting Find Bin, the system takes you to the bin where all of your synced clips are located.

14. Using the Producer's favorite takes, begin building a new, more suspenseful opening in the **ANESTHESIA_NEW OPENING** sequence.

    Try adding a moment at the beginning where Mary notices the flickering X-rays on the wall before she gets up to leave the room. Experiment with the different angles from which she approaches the doorway and how cutting to a new angle creates suspense by extending the action. Explore at what point does cutting from shot **3-4** to **3B-5** create the biggest surprise when Mary runs into the Dentist.

15. When you are satisfied with your new cut, DRAG the sequence **ANESTHESIA_NEW OPENING** from the **ANESTHESIA_EXERCISE SEQUENCES** bin into the Source monitor.

16. Load the sequence **ANESTHESIA_REVISED** into the Timeline and CLEAR your previous MARKS using the **G** KEY.

17. Mark an **IN** point at the beginning of the **ANESTHESIA_REVISED** sequence in your Timeline and an IN point in your **ANESTHESIA_NEW OPENING** in the Source monitor.

18. Make sure your **V1** and **A1** tracks are ENABLED and SPLICE your new opening into the **ANESTHESIA_REVISED** sequence by hitting the **V KEY**.

    You have now spliced your new opening into the beginning of the **ANESTHESIA_REVISED** sequence.

19. Check to make sure your new opening is intact.

    If you are missing any part of it, or if you get an error message that you have "Insufficient source material," press Ctrl + Z (Windows) or Command + Z (Mac) to undo and make sure there are no OUT points marked in your Source or Record monitors. Repeat step 16.

    If everything looks good, proceed to step 20 to remove the old opening.

20. Select the RECORD MONITOR, enter the timecode **01:0027:13**, and press ENTER. This will take you to the beginning frame of your old opening. Mark an **IN** point using the **I KEY**.

21. Next, select the RECORD MONITOR, enter the timecode **01:00:37:16**, and hit ENTER. This will take you to the last frame of your old opening. Mark an **OUT** point using the **O KEY**.

Figure 5.33 An IN and OUT mark set at the specified timecode locations.

22. EXTRACT the old opening using the **X KEY**.

    The clips from the old opening will be removed from the Timeline without leaving a gap in the sequence.

23. Check your re-edit of the opening to make sure you are happy with it and that it flows into the next shot in the sequence.

    At this point in the process, you would show your new cut to the Producer and wait for the next round of notes!

Exercise 5.3: Second Revision of Anesthesia

In the previous exercise, we used a subsequence to create a new opening for the short film, Anesthesia. Nice work! The Producer liked the new opening and would like to move on with the next round of changes.

In this exercise, we will continue to sharpen our skills with Match Frame, Find Bin, and the basic editing tools Extract/Splice and Lift/Overwrite to revise our edit of Anesthesia using keyboard shortcuts.

Media Used: Anesthesia

Duration: 1 hour

For this exercise, we will use the **MC110_ANESTHESIA** project.

1. Begin by opening the bin **STUDENT_LESSON SEQUENCES** and load the sequence **5.3_ANESTHESIA_REV_PRODUCER'S NOTES**.

    The Producer has again used Markers in the sequence to communicate notes about the changes that need to be made.

2. Duplicate the sequence **5.3_ANESTHESIA_REV_PRODUCER'S NOTES**, and name the duplicate **ANESTHESIA_REVISED 2**.

    Before we make any changes, we want to preserve the last version of our edit with Producer's notes.

3. Choose **TOOLS > MARKERS** to open the Marker tool.

    Now you will be able to see all of the Producer's notes.

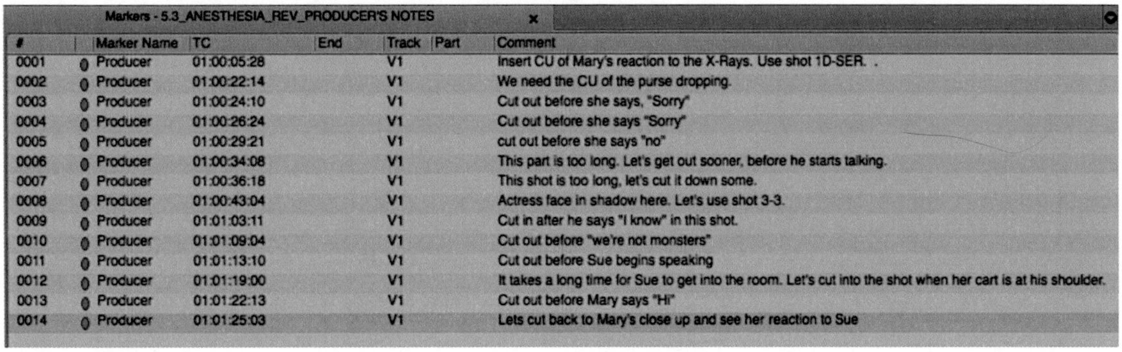

#		Marker Name	TC	End	Track	Part	Comment
0001	◊	Producer	01:00:05:28		V1		Insert CU of Mary's reaction to the X-Rays. Use shot 1D-SER. .
0002	◊	Producer	01:00:22:14		V1		We need the CU of the purse dropping.
0003	◊	Producer	01:00:24:10		V1		Cut out before she says, "Sorry"
0004	◊	Producer	01:00:26:24		V1		Cut out before she says "Sorry"
0005	◊	Producer	01:00:29:21		V1		cut out before she says "no"
0006	◊	Producer	01:00:34:08		V1		This part is too long. Let's get out sooner, before he starts talking.
0007	◊	Producer	01:00:36:18		V1		This shot is too long, let's cut it down some.
0008	◊	Producer	01:00:43:04		V1		Actress face in shadow here. Let's use shot 3-3.
0009	◊	Producer	01:01:03:11		V1		Cut in after he says "I know" in this shot.
0010	◊	Producer	01:01:09:04		V1		Cut out before "we're not monsters"
0011	◊	Producer	01:01:13:10		V1		Cut out before Sue begins speaking
0012	◊	Producer	01:01:19:00		V1		It takes a long time for Sue to get into the room. Let's cut into the shot when her cart is at his shoulder.
0013	◊	Producer	01:01:22:13		V1		Cut out before Mary says "Hi"
0014	◊	Producer	01:01:25:03		V1		Lets cut back to Mary's close up and see her reaction to Sue

Figure 5.34 The Marker window displaying the set markers and Producer's notes.

4. Read through each of the notes so you can see what changes need to be made.

5. In the Marker window, click on the **TC COLUMN** header to select the column. Then right-click and choose **SORT COLUMN** or press **CTRL + E** (Windows) or **COMMAND + E** (Mac).

    This will sort the Producer's notes by timecode, so you can move through and make the changes sequentially.

6. Enable SYNC LOCKS for **V1** and **A1** so that your audio and video will remain in sync as you edit.

As you move through executing the changes, experiment with what types of editing tools are best suited for each task. For example:

- While a Splice edit might work best for Edit note #1, an Overwrite edit can be used to add a cutaway on V2 of the bag mentioned in Edit note #2.

- Use Match Frame to see what other parts of Mary's close-up would best suit Edit note #14.

- Use the FF and RW buttons to move quickly from edit point to edit point.

 You can increase your speed and efficiency as an editor by mapping the FF and RW buttons to your keyboard using your Keyboard Settings in the Project window and your Command Palette Tool.

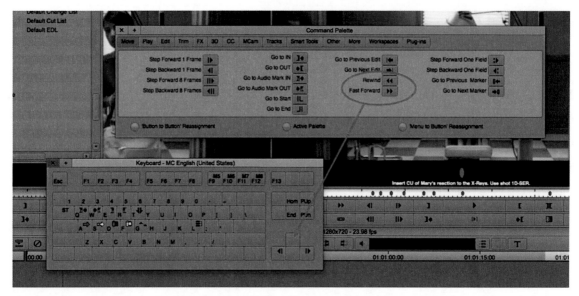

Figure 5.35 Map the Rewind (RW) and Fast Forward (FF) buttons from the Command Palette to your Keyboard Settings.

As shots are swapped out and cut down, the edit begins to take shape. Do not get too hung up on getting the pacing perfect just yet. We will refine our pacing to a greater degree in Lesson 6: "Pacing Your Scene with Trim".

7. Conclude the lesson by saving your work.

Trimming Dialogue Scenes

Now that you have created the rough cut, watch it through. You can start to see where it drags, where you want to add emphasis, and how you want to build the rhythm of shots. This lesson covers techniques for refining the rough cut dialogue scene with trim. It is here, trimming dialogue scenes, that the value of using Media Composer's trim tools can really be seen.

Media Used: Anesthesia

Duration: 60 minutes

GOALS

- Understand the Trim mode
- Control the pacing of the edit using Ripple trims
- Create L- and J-cuts for a seamless edit
- Perform dynamic trimming on the fly
- Identify and correct audio problems at the edit point
- Maintain sync and repair broken sync
- Use Slip and Slide trims to adjust the content or placement of segments

Understanding Trim

Trimming remains one of the most powerful tools in editing. Simply put, it is the process of adding and removing frames to refine the edit. In Media Composer, Trim is also an edit mode with special functions. Media Composer's Trim tools are the best in the industry, known for their precision, fluidity, and intuitive operation.

Trimming is where the real work of editing is done. By adding or removing frames in just the right places, you can energize a dull conversation, increase (or decrease) the apparent tension between characters, extend a poignant moment for maximum impact, and more. Trimming undoubtedly enables you to move from a good to a great sequence.

There are certain commonalities to cutting dialogue regardless of genre. Whether it is a scene of actors performing scripted dialogue, or the "dialogue" of documentary interviews, as an editor you are concerned with the following:

- Pacing a scene for the right emotional impact

- Keeping everything in sync

When trimming sync sound, you obviously need to keep everything in sync. And, you need to keep the audio edits clean. There shouldn't be any clicks, pops, or partial words at an edit point. This is relatively easy to accomplish within Media Composer, but many editors also work with audio post professionals who perform final sweetening of the audio with more sophisticated software, such as Avid Pro Tools. The pacing of the scene is the harder part.

Pacing

Yellow Ripple Trim lets you adjust the pacing. This is done in two ways:

- **A-side (outgoing shot)** – This trim adjusts the timing as you leave a shot and move on to the next, adjusting how long you want to stay focused on that shot before cutting to the next. In the context of cutting a dialogue scene, this typically refers to how quickly you cut away from an actor after he or she finishes speaking.

- **B-side Incoming shot)** – This trim adjusts the timing of the shot you cut to. This often refers to how long it takes an actor to start speaking after you cut to him or her.

As a general rule, dialogue scenes are cut tight, meaning there are very few additional frames beyond where the character speaks. Dialogue scenes can slow down a film if not kept tight. A shot shouldn't hold on to an actor any longer than is necessary to deliver the line or to react. You never want to show the actor waiting to act or "letting down" from the performance. Trimming away the extra frames will increase the pace of the scene and can help to avoid boring the audience.

On the other hand, if there is reason for the pause, hold the shot. Allowing a pause in the scene can be a powerful technique. Pauses refocus the attention of the viewer.

Have you ever heard a song on the radio where the music stops unexpectedly for a beat or two? It catches your attention. The break in the predictable rhythm of the beat—the silence—refocuses your attention. It is just as true in film as it is in music. When you allow (or create) a pause, you refocus the attention of the viewer. If you use this at a key moment in the scene or the overall story, it can be very powerful!

The natural question in the mind of the viewer at that moment is what happened? Most of us know from experience what it is like to be in a tense conversation. That pregnant pause or awkward silence between when one person says something and the other responds is telling of the emotion. But it's not just the pause that creates the tension; it is the actors' body language. As an editor, you may even be able to create that too, by manipulating when and where the audience sees a certain reaction.

    Tension in a scene is often most evident in the pauses left in the dialogue.

Let's look at an example from "Anesthesia." In this scene, the dentist, Dr. Clayton, tries to ease Mary's fears:

Clayton nods. He helps Mary back to the chair. She reluctantly takes a seat. Holds her purse close.

Clayton notes her anxiety. Takes a seat.

DR. CLAYTON
Listen Mary, I know coming to the dentist has gotta

be frightening, but I assure you, we're not monsters.

We could cut the scene in a very, straightforward way- with Dr. Clayton speaking to Mary in close-up as one continuous sentence like it is written. Or we could reimagine the pacing of the scene, by cutting it like this:

Clayton notes her anxiety. Takes a seat.

DR. CLAYTON
Listen Mary, I know coming to the dentist has gotta

be frightening, but I assure you-

Pause. Mary looks back at him.

DR. CLAYTON

We're not monsters.

By adding the pause here, we're not only increasing the tension and the anticipation surrounding what Dr. Clayton is going to say, we are also drawing attention to the statement itself. The audience begins to wonder: Is he a monster?

Which way is the right way? Whichever best communicates the emotion of the scene within the greater arch of the story, and ultimately, most accurately portrays the vision of the director.

Now, lest I leave you with the impression that controlling the pace of the scene is about inserting these big dramatic pauses all over the place, it's not. You control the pace by extending or reducing the time between lines, at every edit point. In terms of the overall rhythm, the difference can often be felt with just a few frames at every edit point.

Eliminating Dialogue

Another consideration in cutting a dialogue scene is, ironically, what words or lines can be left out without sacrificing any of the story. A scene that runs too long, even if it is well-paced, can slow the film down. This is just as true in a documentary as in a narrative film. Generally, there are two ways you can safely cut lines.

 Speed up a scene by cutting out unnecessary lines.

Scripts are meant to be read, but movies are meant to be watched. Often, lines are written into the script that becomes redundant to the actor's body language when played out. A physical response can easily replace a line like, "Okay, sure."

Frequently, you can also find throwaway lines in a script that do nothing to further the story. The line may add color to a conversation or to a character's personality, but the key story points of the scene can stand without the line. These may be removed in the interest of time. (Of course, a balance must be maintained so as not to strip too much away from the texture of the character.) An example of this from our scene is the line, "…the devil is in the details."

The "Radio Edit" Technique

A popular approach to cutting a dialogue scene is known as the "radio edit." The idea is that when working on the pacing of a scene, you focus on the pacing of the audio, as if cutting it for radio. You've nailed the pacing if you can turn off the video, listen only to the audio, and have the scene play well. Then you turn your attention to the video edits.

To perform a radio edit:

1. (Optional) Turn OFF the VIDEO MONITOR on track V1.

    This will force you to listen and avoid the visual distraction.

2. Enter TRIM MODE at the cut point (transition) between the two shots you want to trim.

3. Enable RIPPLE TRIM.

4. Select all tracks to maintain sync.

5. Ripple trim the entire sequence to perfect the pacing of the dialogue.

6. Enable the video monitor.

7. Use dual-roller trim on V1 to create split edits.

    This will be discussed later in this lesson.

    No doubt as you ripple trim to adjust the pace and timing, you will create some awkward visual transitions—mismatched action, an absent or interrupted reaction shot, etc. Fix them using split edits and/or cutaway shots. The key is that this work is done **only on the video track**. (After all, you just perfected the audio pacing. Don't change that now.)

Exploring Trim Mode

You are familiar with trim mode already, but let's review some of the key features. Refer to Figure 6.1.

- **Trim Mode toggle:** This activates and deactivates Trim mode. It is mapped to the U key by default.

- **A-side monitor:** The left Trim monitor shows the last frame of the outgoing shot.

- **B-side Monitor:** The right Trim monitor shows the first frame of the incoming shot.

- **Pre-roll/post-roll durations:** These display the amount of time before and after the edit point included in the playback loop. By default, the duration is 2.5 seconds before and after the cut point, which totals a five-second loop. You can change this by typing in different values.

- **Trim buttons:** The trim buttons (circled in Figure 6.1) enable you to trim one frame or 1/3 second in either direction. In a 30 fps project, 1/3 second = 10 frames; in a 24 fps project, 1/3 second = 8 frames.

- **Trim counters:** These indicate the number of frames that have been trimmed on each side of the edit (A-side and B-side). Negative numbers mean you've trimmed to the left, while positive numbers indicate you've trimmed to the right.

- **Play Loop button:** This plays a loop around the edit point and provide a single monitor. It allows for focused attention on the edit point you are trimming at the moment. All locations of the standard Play button automatically become Play Loop when in Trim mode. Examples are the space bar, the 5 key and the tilde key.

- **Trim Rollers:** Indicate the location and side of the edit point(s) being trimmed, as well as the type of trim to be performed – ripple trim, overwrite trim, or roll trim.

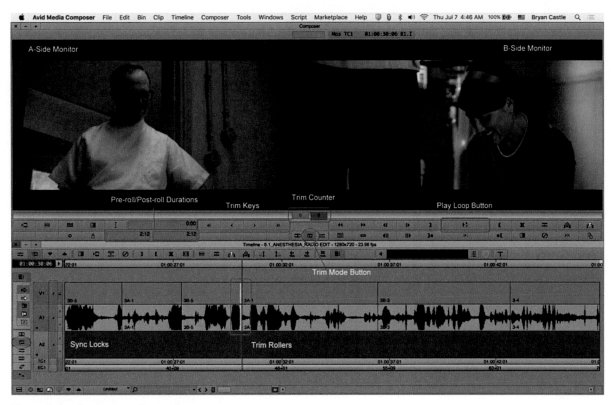

Figure 6.1 The Trim mode interface.

Entering and Exiting Trim Mode

There are several different ways to enter and exit Trim mode. The first method is to use the Trim Mode button, shown in Figure 6.2. The Trim Mode button is found at the bottom-center of the Composer window, in the Timeline Palette (under the Smart Tool), and on the U key of the keyboard.

 Figure 6.2 Trim Mode button.

To enter Trim mode using the Trim Mode button:

- Click the **TRIM MODE** button on the interface in the Timeline Palette or between the Source and Record monitors.

- Press the **U** key on the keyboard.

Media Composer will enter Trim mode, the position indicator will jump to the nearest edit point, and trim rollers will appear on all selected tracks. By default, the system selects both the outgoing and incoming material for the transitions on the selected tracks. After you enter Trim mode, if necessary, select or deselect Record Track buttons.

You can also enter Trim mode by lassoing an edit point in the Timeline, as shown in Figure 6.3. The advantage of this method is that by lassoing, you are simultaneously selecting the tracks you wish to trim. Media Composer will activate the tracks for any transitions you lasso and deactivate all other tracks.

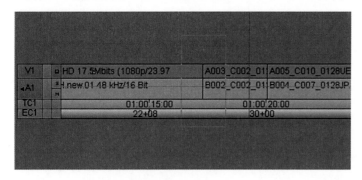

Figure 6.3
Lasso the edit points you wish to trim.

To lasso transitions in the Timeline:

1. Position the **CURSOR** above the top track displayed in the Timeline.

2. Click and drag a **LASSO** around a transition (on one or more tracks).

    The position indicator snaps to the lassoed transition.

 You can start a lasso in the middle of the tracks by holding the Alt (Windows) or Option (Mac) key when you click and drag.

To use the Go to Previous/Go to Next Edit buttons:

The Go to Previous/Go to Next Edit is useful not only for entering Trim mode, but also for moving between edit points. Mapped by default on the A and S keys (see Figure 6.4), Go to Previous Edit (A) and Go to Next Edit (S) behave identically to FF/RW, discussed earlier in Lesson 5.

Just as with FF/RW, the function is looking for common edit points on the tracks that are selected. Also, as with FF/RW, you are able to hold the Alt (Windows)/Option (Mac) key to make them ignore the Track Selectors in order to have them stop at every cut on every track. Unlike FF/RW, however, there is no setting that controls their behavior.

 Go to Previous Edit

Go to Next Edit   **Figure 6.4** Go to Previous Edit and Go to Next Edit buttons.

These functions allow you to very quickly move between edit points when trimming.

 If you'd like to Go to Previous/Go to Next Edit and always ignore the Track Selectors so that they respond to every edit point on every track: In the Command Palette, in the tab labeled as "Other," you'll see a button in the lower left that says "Add Option Key" (Mac) or "Add Alt Key" (Windows). Use Button to Button Reassignment to add that to the Go to Previous/Go to Next Edit button. When added, you'll see a very small dot added to the key to indicate that it has been applied.

There are several ways to exit Trim mode.

To exit Trim mode and return to Source/Record mode:

- Press the U key to toggle off Trim mode.

- Press the Esc key.

- Click anywhere in the Timecode (TC1) track or the Timeline ruler. The position indicator is positioned where you click in the TC1 track.

- Click the Source/record button to take you back to that mode.

- Click the Effect Mode button to put you into Effect mode at that cut point (transition).

 It is efficient to click in the TC track or Ruler trim you just made so you can exit Trim mode and immediately play back the sequence.

Trimming with the Keyboard

The Smart Tool is well-suited for rough trimming, performed quickly by dragging. But to really master the art of trimming, you will need to master the intuitive trim functions of Media Composer. These are all performed via the keyboard. Let's begin by learning to perform the different single-roller trims using the keyboard.

To perform a single-roller trim:

1. Enter TRIM mode.

2. Select the SIDE you wish to trim doing one of the following:

   • Pressing the key to select the side of the transition you wish to trim (see Figure 6.5).

   A-Side   Dual Roller   B-Side
   Trim   Trim   Trim

   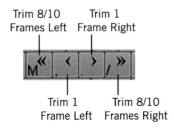 **Figure 6.5** Select which side of the edit you want to trim using these keys.

   • Clicking in the monitor of the outgoing (A-side) or incoming (B-side) frame.

   The Trim mode rollers in the Timeline move to the corresponding side to be trimmed and the corresponding Trim box (in the Trim window) is highlighted.

3. Optionally, change the MODE of the single-roller trim using the keyboard shortcuts:

   • Pressing Shift+D enables Ripple Trim

   • Pressing Shift+F enables Overwrite Trim

4. Use the TRIM buttons on the keyboard to add or remove frames from the selected material at the selected transition. (See Figure 6.6.)

   Trim 8/10   Trim 1
   Frames Left Frame Right

   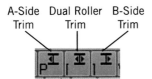 **Figure 6.6** Use the trim keys to trim precisely. The frame rate of your project determines whether you will trim 8 or 10 frames. 30fps projects will be 10 and 24fps will be 8.

   Trim 1   Trim 8/10
   Frame Left Frames Right

5. Use any of the PLAY shortcuts (which become Play Loop when in Trim mode) to play the trim loop (for example, the space bar or the 5 key).

   The system plays the number of outgoing and incoming frames currently set in the Preroll and Postroll boxes in the Trim mode window.

6. To stop, use any of the PLAY shortcuts again.

7. Trim FRAMES and play the LOOP until you are satisfied with the trim.

 In Trim mode, the Play function converts to Play Loop.

Adding and Removing Frames When Trimming

Use any of the following methods involving the numeric keypad to trim by adding frames to one side of the selected transition and/or removing them from the other:

■ Type a plus sign (+) and the number of frames (from 1–99) when you want to move the Trim Roller(s) to the right. Press Enter to execute the trim.

■ Type a minus sign (–) and the number of frames (from 1–99) you want to move the Trim Roller(s) to the left. Press Enter to execute the trim duration.

■ Type a number larger than 99 to enter a timecode. For example, to enter 1 second and 2 frames, type 102. Or, with Caps Lock off, type an f after values greater than 99 to enter it as a frame count. For example, to enter 200 frames, type 200f and press Enter.

Note that the plus (+) and minus (–) keys refer only to the *direction* of the trim. They do not necessarily indicate that frames will be added or removed. Think plus (+) to move a transition later, and think minus (–) to move a transition earlier.

Table 6.1 shows the equivalent methods for moving backward and forward on the clip's source timecode as you trim. The actions in the left column move an edit to earlier in the Timeline; the actions in the right column move an edit later in the Timeline.

Table 6.1: Trimming Earlier and Later in a Sequence

Moving Earlier in Time	Moving Later in Time
Negative (–) numbers	Positive (+) numbers
Drag trim roller(s) back	Drag trim roller(s) forward
Moves the edit point earlier in the source timecode	Moves the edit point later in the source timecode

Scrubbing Audio While Trimming

Digital Audio Scrub allows you to hear the digital audio samples when the position indicator moves over each frame. Some editors like to have the audio reference as they move through the sequence; others find the staccato sounds distracting.

To use Digital Audio Scrub while trimming:

■ Press the Caps Lock key to toggle on Digital Audio Scrub.
Trim the edit using the Trim buttons or drag the trim rollers.

 If you are listening for a critical audio cue, such as the beginning or end of a word, you may find it easier to solo the track.

Analyzing Audio at the Cut Point

Many audio edits in a rough cut need to be cleaned up. Crossfades (added with the Quick Transition button) can help smooth out certain pops, but if the problem is a partial word or the clicking of the talent's mouth as they begin to speak, a crossfade probably isn't going to fix it. Instead, you need to trim away a frame or two from the audio.

"Okay, easy enough," you say. But which side of the edit needs to be trimmed? Sometimes, answering that question is difficult. You can play the transition over and over and still not be sure on which side the audio pop exists. The solution is to analyze the audio by playing just the incoming or outgoing side.

To analyze audio on one side of the edit:

1. In Trim mode, click the **PLAY LOOP** button.

   The transition will loop.

2. Press the **Q** (GO TO IN) key to play the outgoing side of the transition only. To play the incoming side, press the **W** (GO TO OUT) key. Pressing either key a second time will play back both sides again.

   The Play Loop button changes to indicate whether you are playing to from IN or to OUT.

Monitoring Audio in Dual-Roller Trim

Much of the time that you are trimming dialogue, you will use Ripple trim, but there are times when dual-roller trim fits the bill. As you know, dual-roller trimming allows you to monitor the image on both sides of the transition simultaneously. But, you only want to listen to one side. So, which side will it be?

The green bar below the Trim counters indicates the side you are monitoring when you perform the trim. Before performing the trim, choose whether you want to hear the outgoing audio (A side) or incoming audio (B side).

Figure 6.7 The green bar indicates which side of the transition is heard during the trim.

To monitor incoming or outgoing audio in dual-roller trim:

- Before you dual-roller trim, move your **CURSOR** over either the outgoing or incoming image in the monitor. Do not click on the picture; just place your cursor over it.

  You can still move your cursor into the Timeline, just be careful not to accidentally move the cursor over the other monitor, changing the monitoring. The side you monitor does not affect which side you trim.

 If you are working with an external client monitor connected through a breakout box, you will see that the green bar also controls which image appears on the client monitor while trimming.

Trimming On the Fly

Trimming on the fly involves performing a trim while you play the sequence. In Trim mode, the standard play buttons change. With the exception of J-K-L, all play buttons will play a loop around the edit point. You can use keyboard shortcuts to trim without stopping the looped playback. The system will adjust the edit and restart the playback loop. This allows you to make several adjustments very quickly and dynamically, being able to see an immediate comparison every time it loops. Let's look at the various on-the-fly Trim functions, including J-K-L.

J-K-L Trimming

By now, you should be familiar with the J-K-L shuttle controls. As you know, the advantage of using J-K-L is the ability to play at variable speeds. When used in Trim mode, these controls allow you to actually perform the trim while you watch the footage.

This method is powerful because it can play your incoming or outgoing material beyond the edit point, allowing you to see your source material. You can use this technique to trim long sections of clips quickly—for example, trimming in additional interview material while you watch it in real time or faster than real time. Even more important to fine-tuning dialogue, though, is that J-K-L allows you to trim in **slow motion**.

To use J-K-L Trim:

1. Enter TRIM mode.

2. Place ROLLERS at the appropriate points.

3. If you want to trim back from the edit, press the **J** key alone or the **J+K** combination.

4. At the desired frame, release the KEYS to stop playback and perform the trim.

5. If you want to trim forward from the current edit, press the **L** key alone or the **K+L** combination. At the desired frame, release the keys to stop playback and perform the trim.

    The system tracks the overall number of frames you have trimmed from either side in the outgoing and incoming trim boxes.

6. If you are not sure which way you want to trim, press the **J** key to back up a little; then press the **L** key to take you forward again. Press the **K** key to choose your new edit.

 J-K-L trim will never completely trim away a shot. It will stop when one frame of the clip remains. If you trim away too much material, just reverse your direction to add more of the shot back in again.

Trimming with J-K-L keys also allows you to scrub audio as you trim. Especially in slow-motion or 1/4 speed, J-K-L trim can allow you to hear the precise point a sound begins or ends, even if it is not clearly visible in the waveforms.

The "Intuitive Edit"

There is another on-the-fly technique that allows you to make an edit by immediately jumping to a specific point in the footage. This works best when you are trimming a shot to make it shorter. It's called the intuitive edit because, while watching the playback, you may intuitively know where the edit should occur. This gives you a way to execute the edit precisely based on that intuition.

To trim during playback:

1.   Enter TRIM mode and select the outgoing side, incoming side, or both for trimming.

2.   Optionally, increase the PREROLL and POSTROLL durations.

3.   Click the PLAY LOOP button to loop playback of the selected transition.

4.   During the playback loop, press a MARK IN or OUT key on the keyboard (I, O, E, or R) to trim to the mark.

     The system trims the transition to the mark and restarts its playback loop, allowing you to review your edit and make further adjustments. Fine adjustments can be made using J-K-L or the keyboard Trim keys.

To fine-tune the edit using the keyboard Trim keys on the fly:

1.   Start the PLAYBACK LOOP.

2.   Press the keyboard equivalents for 8 OR 10 FRAMES LEFT, 1 FRAME LEFT, 1 FRAME RIGHT, and 8 OR 10 FRAMES RIGHT to trim the edit by these values during playback.

     You see the result on the next loop.

3.   Repeat as needed.

Exercise Break: Exercise 6.1
Pause here to practice what you've learned.

Creating Split Edits

One of the basic techniques to achieving a seamless, invisible edit is to simply get rid of straight cuts. If the video and audio always change at the same time, the edits may become obvious to the viewer. Not good. Instead, by having the audio and video change at different moments, called a split edit, you effectively interweave the audio and video into a cohesive whole. Split edits can also be used to solve the problem of visual mismatch.

 Split edits are also commonly referred to as L-cuts or J-cuts.

There are two keys to creating split edits:

- Use dual-roller trim.

- Disable Link Selection Toggle.

When you enter Trim mode with a keyboard shortcut, the system automatically activates dual-roller trim. Remember, dual-roller trimming affects both sides of a transition by adding frames to one shot while subtracting the same number of frames from the adjacent shot.

You can use dual-roller trims to move the transition point earlier or later in the sequence. Because both sides of the transition are equally affected, the combined duration of the two clips being trimmed does not change. Because the combined duration of these clips does not change, the trim does not affect the position of any other clips in the track.

Figure 6.8 shows what happens when you use dual-roller trim to move the edit point later in the sequence.

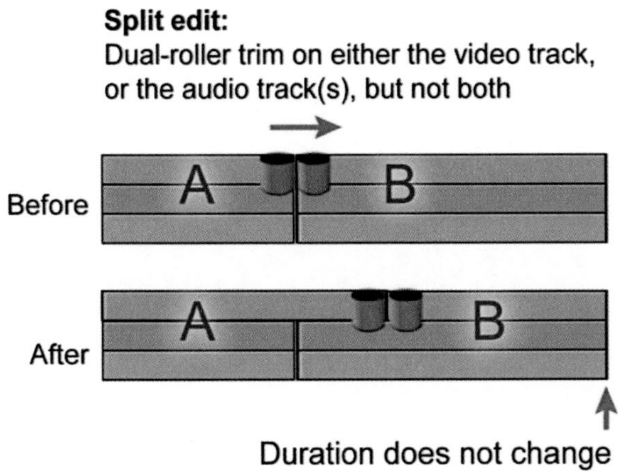

Split edit:
Dual-roller trim on either the video track, or the audio track(s), but not both

Before

After

Duration does not change

Figure 6.8
A dual-roller trim on either the video track or the audio track(s) but not both (here, on the V1 track) creates a split edit.

To perform a dual-roller trim:

1. Move the **POSITION INDICATOR** near the edit you want to trim and activate the desired tracks.

2. Enter Trim mode using a keyboard shortcut (**A**, **S**, or **U**).

    Both pink Trim mode rollers appear in the Timeline, the mouse pointer becomes a dual-roller icon, and both Trim boxes are highlighted.

3. Drag the **TRANSITION POINT** left to move the transition point earlier.

4. Drag the **TRANSITION POINT** right to move it later.

5. Press the **CTRL** (Windows) or **COMMAND** (Mac) key while dragging to snap to an IN or OUT mark, to the previous or next edit point, or to an edit point on another track. (This can also be used to remove split edits.)

As you trim, the Trim boxes display the number of frames that have been trimmed from the outgoing and incoming sides of the transition.

You can also use the Trim buttons to move or refine the position of the transition.

 You can easily remove split edits using dual-roller trim, too. Set up the dual-rollers on the cut point you wish to move and Ctrl-drag (Windows) or Command-drag (Mac) to snap it to the location of the other edit.

Trimming Split Edits

Theoretically, if you follow the radio-edit technique perfectly, you would never have to trim the audio and video in a split edit. But in the real world, there will be plenty of times that you will need to trim a split edit. For example, suppose that after a review session, it has been decided that a sequence needs to be cut down further, meaning you need to pull out a few throwaway lines. You obviously wouldn't want to start the edit process over again just because there are split edits in place, nor do you want to remove every split edit, either.

There is no problem trimming a split edit in Media Composer. Once the rollers are set up in the right place, you can use any trim function you prefer to make the edit. And, if you properly include both audio and video, everything will stay in sync just like a straight cut.

To set up trim on a split edit:

1. Enter **TRIM MODE** with rollers on one track.

2. Shift-click the other **EDIT POINTS** to add or remove Trim Rollers as needed.

Be careful when Shift-clicking to add or remove Trim Rollers at edit points making sure that all the rollers you set up are on the same side. If not, you may get unexpected results.

 Media Composer is capable of very complicated trim setups, including trimming in opposite directions simultaneously. You can learn these advanced trim techniques by taking the MC201 course, *Media Composer Professional Editing I.*

Alternatively, you can:

■   Drag a **LASSO** around the edit point on both audio and video.

This technique works well if you can draw a lasso that includes only the edit points and doesn't encompass a segment. If you include a complete segment in the lasso, you will get a different result.

Changing the Center of the Trim Playback Loop

If the distance between the video and audio edit points is significant, you may find it difficult to perform the trim because the edit point you are most interested in—audio or video—may be outside the trim loop, or you need to her the audio at the cut point rather than what is under the blue position indicator (see Figure 6.9).

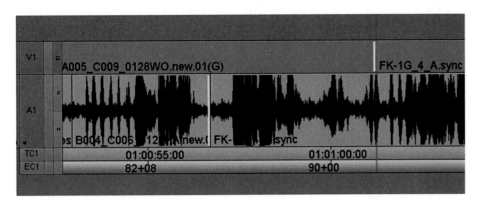

Figure 6.9
A long split edit with the position indicator on video. The audio is outside the play loop.

To move the position indicator to a different edit point:

■ Click directly on any other TRIM ROLLER.

When you click, pay close attention. Make sure that your cursor's icon matches the current roller configuration (either A-side or B-side). If it does not, you will be swapping the trim rollers to the opposite side.

The position indicator will move to the other edit point without altering the trim roller setup, as shown in Figure 6.10.

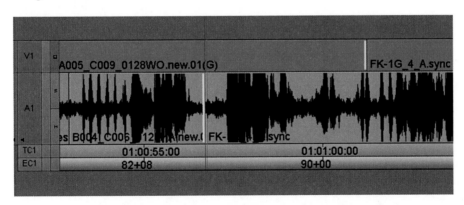

Figure 6.10 The position indicator is now centered on the more critical edit point.

 Exercise Break: Exercise 6.2
Pause here to practice what you've learned.

Maintaining Sync

Previously, you already learned the basics of maintaining sync. It is easy, in theory. Nonetheless, many new editors struggle to keep it together. This is especially true as you start to increase the number of tracks in the sequence.

There are several ways that you might break sync. Likewise, there are several easy ways to avoid breaking sync. Here's a quick review.

Common ways to break sync include the following:

- Trimming only one side of a transition, without selecting all tracks

- Extracting frames from only the video or audio track

- Splicing in only audio or video

- Moving only audio or video when in Segment mode

It follows that you can prevent breaking sync by:

- When trimming a single track, always use either dual-roller, or the Overwrite Trim, found in the Smart Tool.

- Whenever you add frames or subtract frames from an audio or video track, also add or subtract them from all the others. It is especially helpful to remember this rule when using any of the yellow tools, for example: trimming, splicing, or extracting.

- Whenever you want to add frames to or subtract frames from only one track, use Lift or Overwrite instead of Extract or Splice-In.

- Work with Sync Locks turned on.

Using Filler to Maintain Sync

You already know that you can edit in filler to maintain sync. This happens automatically when you use the Overwrite Trim tool in the Smart Tool, as shown in Figure 6.11.

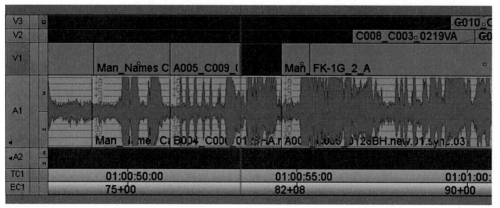

Figure 6.11 Removing frames with Overwrite Trim automatically puts filler in place of the removed frames to maintain sync.

You can also use filler to trim a track where there is no clip. To do so, simply add edit points to cut the filler in line with the edit point you need to trim. This is a great way to keep the trim setup easy while ensuring that you aren't throwing any downstream material out of sync. Figure 6.12 illustrates this technique. If you think of filler as empty space, it makes no sense. If you think of filler in the filmic way—as strips of clear material—then this makes perfect sense.

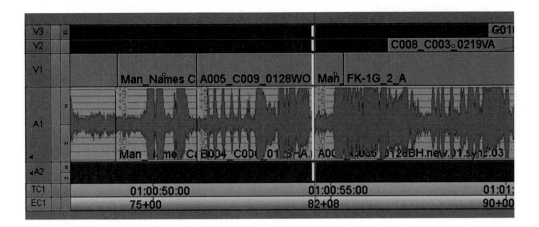

Figure 6.12 By adding edits to filler, you ensure that you're either adding or removing the same number of frames from all the tracks, which keeps everything in sync.

As your sequences grow in complexity, you will start working with multiple audio and video tracks. This technique is a great way to maintain sync.

To maintain sync on multiple tracks:

1. Move the **POSITION INDICATOR** close to the edit point you want to trim.

2. Enter **TRIM MODE**.

   The trim rollers appear on the audio and video segments on active tracks.

3. While pressing the **ALT** (Windows) or **OPTION** (Mac) key, click the **ADD EDIT** button or press the key to which you mapped it. Edit points are added to all the filler tracks at the location of the position indicator.

   If you do not hold the modifier key, edit points will be added to any active tracks.

4. Optionally, Shift-click **ROLLERS** to add or remove them from the trim setup.

Recognizing and Repairing Broken Sync

By default, the Timeline displays sync breaks whenever they occur during editing. These appear at break points as positive or negative numbers indicating the number of frames out of sync. Sync-break indicators appear only in the affected track(s). (See Figure 6.13.)

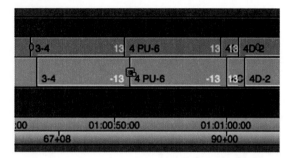

Figure 6.13 These segments are out of sync by 13 frames.

To change which tracks show sync breaks:

■ Open the TIMELINE menu, choose SYNC BREAKS, and then choose one of the following:

- **Video:** Tracks display the number of frames the video is out of sync with the audio.

- **Audio:** Tracks display the number of frames the audio is out of sync with the video.

- **Both:** Tracks display both the video and audio data.

 Sync break information is not displayed if the audio and video tracks come from different sources.

Using Trim Mode to Correct Sync

In Trim mode, you can restore sync by performing one or more single-roller trims on the out-of-sync track(s). To reverse the sync break, you trim the exact number of sync-break frames displayed in the Timeline. Dual-roller trims do not remove sync breaks.

To fix broken sync:

1. Review the areas where Sync break indicator numbers appear. Verify that they are unintentionally out of sync. Begin the resyncing process at the edit point closest to the beginning of the sequence.

    Since you'll be using the yellow Ripple trim to make the correction, your work ripples downstream, to the right.

2. Enter TRIM mode at the first transition that displays a number.

3. Select one of the TRACKS that is out of sync. If you know which one caused the issue, then select that one. If you're unsure, it can often be easiest to simply select the video.

4. Click the A SIDE MONITOR.

    You could instead choose the B side, but it's much easier to choose the A side since it's a bit easier to visualize what is happening in the Timeline.

5. Using single-roller trim, add or subtract the appropriate number of FRAMES.

    •   If the number shown in the segment is negative, you know that track is delayed by that number of frames. You will need to add to one side of the edit on one track.

    •   If the number shown in the segment is positive, it is ahead of the other track by that many frames. You will need to add frames in order of the segment (and all the other segments after it) to be pushed downstream (to the right) so that they once again align with their counterparts. If you have selected the A-side, then this means you will trim to the right.

    •   If the numbers increases, then simply trim in the opposite direction.

  Simply removing the white numbers does not mean the original edit has been restored. A sync break can be fixed while altering the original edit. To make sure that your sequence is in sync, play it and carefully review the repaired section for errors.

Slipping and Sliding Segments

In addition to the trimming you've learned so far, there is quite a bit more that Media Composer's robust trimming capabilities can accomplish. In this section, we'll discuss Slip and Slide. Let's discuss them conceptually first, then explore the mechanics of using these functions.

  You may be familiar with these functions from other NLEs. Avid's naming convention of Slip and Slide has remained consistent in other applications that have adopted these features.

Slip: Changing the Contents of a Shot

Slip and Slide are forms of dual-roller trimming, where two consecutive transitions are trimmed simultaneously. To slip a shot, the rollers are set on either end of the segment you are slipping. Like a scroll, one is rolled up as the other is rolled out. The duration of the shot does not change. What Slipping does is to change the content, allowing you to see and/or hear a different portion of the original Master clip.

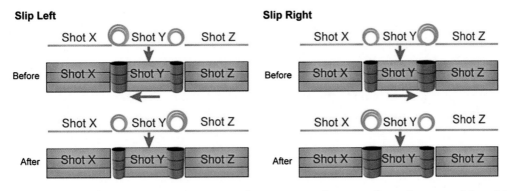

Figure 6.14 Slip lets you change the content of a segment, to show an earlier or later part of the original master clip. Slipping to the left will reveal earlier content from the Master clip, while Slipping to the right reveals later content.

Slide: Changing the Position of a Shot

To slide a shot, the rollers are set to the tail frame of the segment before the segment(s) your sliding and the head frame of the segment(s) after the shot you are sliding. These two rollers work in tandem to move the shot in either direction. The result is the position of the shot changes. Sliding is essentially a dual-roller trim, with one or more segments between the trim rollers. (See Figure 6.15.)

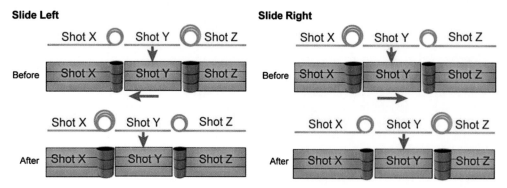

Figure 6.15 Slide lets you move a segment, but not change its content.

Slipping a Shot

You can set up a Slip trim in a number of ways.

To set up for a Slip trim on a shot:

1. In Trim mode, double-click an audio or video TRIM ROLLER on the shot you wish to slip.

2. In Trim mode, Shift-click inside the opposite end of the SEGMENT you are.

3. In Trim mode, right-click on that SEGMENT and choose SELECT SLIP TRIM from the menu that appears.

4. In Source/Record mode, drag a LASSO around the entire segment from right to left.

    The direction in which you drag the lasso is important.

 The advantage of entering Slip using the lasso is that it takes you directly into Trim mode, with the Slip set up, and changes the active track selection to include only those segments that you lassoed.

Once the Slip trim is set up, press Play, and the system will play the loop. To execute the trim, you can drag the rollers or use any of the Trim keys or shortcuts to slip the shot. All the trim methods you have learned apply here.

To slip the shot:

1. Drag the TRIM ROLLERS left to reveal an earlier portion of the shot or right to reveal a later portion of the shot.

2. Use the Trim keys: M, comma (,), period (.), and forward slash (/).

    -   Trim Left reveals an earlier portion.

    -   Trim Right reveals a later portion.

3. Use the **J-K-L** keys for multispeed play/trim.

4. Trim on the fly using the **MARK IN** and **MARK OUT** buttons.

When set up for Slip or Slide, the Composer window converts to the four-frame display, as shown in Figure 6.16. This gives you an immediate reference of how you are affecting both edit points—the one at the beginning and the one at the end—of the segment you are slipping or sliding.

Figure 6.16 The four-frame display allows you to simultaneously see both edit points you are changing.

If you trim using the Trim keys or by dragging the rollers, all four frames will update as you go. If you perform the trim on the fly, only one image will play in real time. Park your mouse pointer over the one you want to see play while you perform the trim. This is another instance where we will use monitoring to our advantage. Take note of the green light beneath the Trim Counters. As you hover your cursor back and forth over the two center images in the four image display, you'll see the green light change sides. The side with the green light will be the one that is monitored during the trim.

Sliding a Shot

The process of setting up for and executing a Slide trim is very similar to Slip trim.

To set up for a Slide trim:

1. While in Trim mode, double-click an audio or video **TRIM ROLLER** on the shot you wish to slide. This enters Slip mode. Double-click a second time to enter Slide mode.

2. Enter **TRIM MODE** at the head of the segment you want to slide.

3. Right-click on that **SEGMENT**. From the menu that appears, choose **SELECT SLIDE TRIM**.

4. While in Source/Record mode, hold the **SHIFT+ALT** (Windows) or **SHIFT+OPTION** (Mac) keys and drag a **LASSO** from right to left around the material you want to slide.

The lasso method here has the same benefits as those described for Slip trim—namely, that it takes you directly into Trim mode with the slide already set up with the correctly enabled tracks. In addition, you can use this method to slide multiple clips. This is useful, for example, if you need to change the position of a group of clips in the sequence—imagine a montage of cutaway shots in a travel show, for instance—but not change their relationship to each other.

Once the Slide trim is set up, all methods of trimming can be used.

To slide the shot:

1.   Drag the TRIM ROLLERS left to move the shot earlier in the sequence or right to move the shot later in the sequence.

2.   Use the Trim keys: M, comma (,), period (.), and forward slash (/).

     -   Trim Left moves the shot earlier in the sequence.
     -   Trim Right moves the shot later in the sequence.

3.   Use the **J-K-L** keys for multispeed play/trim.

4.   Trim on the fly. While the playback is looping, press the **IN** or **OUT** mark on the keyboard.

Sliding Versus Segment Editing

Sliding a clip is similar in many ways to moving a clip in Segment mode, but there are important differences between the two functions.

-   Nudging or dragging clips with the Segment mode Lift/Overwrite leaves a gap or filler in the sequence. Slide will not leave a gap.

-   Segment mode Extract/Splice-In inserts a clip at a new location. If the insertion point is not at an existing edit, the remaining frames of the shot are moved downstream.

-   Sliding does not allow you to skip over other clips to an entirely new location in the sequence.

-   J-K-L cannot be used with Segment mode.

Review/Discussion Questions

1.   Name two ways to enter Trim mode without using the Smart Tool.

2.   Name the keys on the keyboard associated with choosing the A side, B side, or dual-roller trim.

3.   Which keys trim left or right, either 8 or 10 frames at a time?

4.   What can be done in Trim mode when using J-K-L?

5.   What function is associated with the Play button when in Trim mode?

6.   If you hear a pop in the audio at an edit point, but can't tell which side contains the problem, what can you do to find out?

7.   What is a split edit? What is the benefit of creating split edits in the sequence?

8.   What is the process of creating a split edit?

9.   What is the radio-edit technique?

10. How can you ensure that you maintain sync while using Ripple Trim?

11. Describe the process to restore broken sync.

12. How can you use filler to maintain sync when trimming with multiple tracks of audio or video?

Lesson 6 Keyboard Shortcuts

Key	Shortcut
U	Toggles Trim mode
Esc	Exits Trim mode
P	Selects A-side trim
Close Bracket (])	Selects B-side trim
Open Bracket ([)	Selects dual-roller trim
M	Trims 8 or 10 Frames Left
Comma (,)	Trims 1 Frame Left
Period (.)	Trims 1 Frame Right
Forward Slash (/)	Trims 8 or 10 Frames Right
A	Go to Previous Edit
S	Go to Next Edit
Caps Lock	Toggles Digital Audio Scrub
J-K-L	Plays and trim simultaneously in Trim mode
I or O	Trims on the fly, during a playback loop while in Trim mode
Q	Plays only the A side, during a playback loop while in Trim mode
W	Plays only the B side, during a playback loop while in Trim mode

Trim the Dialogue Scene

Media Used: Anesthesia

Duration: 1 hour 45 minutes

GOALS

- Use the keyboard to trim a dialogue scene
- Perform dynamic trimming on the fly
- Control the pacing of the edit using Ripple Trim
- Create split edits with dual-roller trim
- Overwrite cutaway shots
- Identify and correct audio problems at the edit point
- Maintain sync and repair broken sync

Exercise 6.1: Performing a Radio Edit

In this exercise, we use the "Radio Edit" technique to refine the editing of a dialogue scene from the film, Anesthesia.

Media Used: Anesthesia

Duration: 45 minutes

For this exercise, we will use the **MC110_ANESTHESIA** project.

1. Once you have loaded your project, begin by opening the bin **STUDENT_LESSON SEQUENCES**.

2. Duplicate the sequence **6.1_ANESTHESIA_RADIO EDIT** and move the duplicate into the **ANESTHESIA_EXERCISE SEQUENCES** bin.

3. Load the duplicate **6.1_ANESTHESIA_RADIO EDIT**.

4. Play through the sequence to get a feel for what can be improved or refined in the pacing.

    You will notice many instances when dialogue is duplicated from one shot to the next.

5. Turn off the Video monitor by clicking the button in the Track panel.

    This will allow you to use your ear to fine tune the dialogue without being distracted by the video.

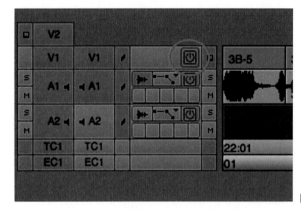

Figure 6.17 Video monitor in the Track panel.

The only value in leaving the video monitor turned on is that it's another chance to see the expressions of the actors. As you trim down the dialogue for pacing, you may be removing some good reactions shots. Don't change the radio edit because of a reaction, but take mental note of it (or add a marker nearby). You can create a split edit later to reveal it again.

6. Enable all tracks.

7. Enter Trim mode by hitting the **U** KEY.

8. Make sure the red Overwrite trim is disabled. Overwrite trim is not recommended for this technique.

9. **PLAY** the first transition using the **SPACEBAR** KEY.

10. Using the **YELLOW RIPPLE TRIM** tool, add or removes frames from each side of the edit using your ear to tune into duplicate lines, overlapping dialogue, and the predicable rhythm of a normal conversation.

11. Pressing the **P** KEY will select the **A** SIDE of the trim.

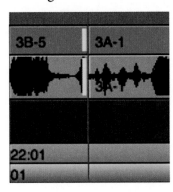

Figure 6.18 Selecting the A side of the trim.

12. Pressing the **RIGHT BRACKET OR]** KEY will select the B side of the trim.

13. Pressing the **LEFT BRACKET OR [** KEY will take you into Double Roller Trim.

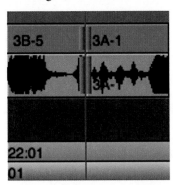

Figure 6.19 Double Roller Trim.

14. Practice using the trim keys to trim using the keyboard.

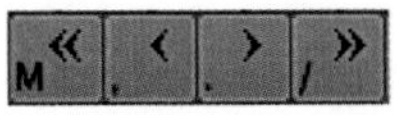

Figure 6.20 Trim keys.

15. Once you are satisfied with the way the first transition sounds, continue moving through the sequence and fixing each transition.

    • Use the "S" key to move to the next edit transition while in Trim mode.

    • Use the "A" key to move to the previous edit transition while in Trim mode.

16. When you are satisfied with the entire edit, turn the Video Monitor back on and watch the entire sequence.

    You will find you came a long way in fixing the problems! A few adjustments will likely be necessary taking visual cues and actor performances into account now that you can see the video again.

    We will explore Trim mode in greater depth in the next exercise.

Exercise 6.2: Creating Split Edits

In this exercise, we will use Trim mode to tackle producer revisions and refine your edit of the film "Anesthesia."

Media Used: Anesthesia

Duration: 1 hour

For this exercise, we will continue to use the **MC110_ANESTHESIA** project.

1. Begin by opening the bin **STUDENT_LESSON SEQUENCES**.

2. Duplicate the sequence **6.2_ANESTHESIA_TRIM MODE_PRODUCER'S NOTES** and rename the sequence **6.2_ANESTHESIA_REV 3**.

3. Move the sequence **6.2_ANESTHESIA_REV 3** into the **ANESTHESIA_EXERCISE SEQUENCES** bin.

4. Load the sequence **6.2_ANESTHESIA_REV 3**.

   The Producer has left you markers regarding the next round of changes.

5. Open the Markers window by choosing TOOLS > MARKERS, and go through each marker and read the notes.

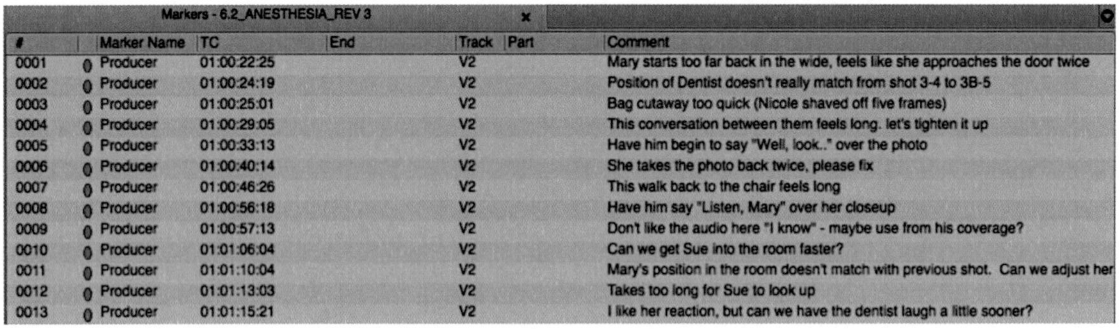

#		Marker Name	TC	End	Track	Part	Comment
0001	●	Producer	01:00:22:25		V2		Mary starts too far back in the wide, feels like she approaches the door twice
0002	●	Producer	01:00:24:19		V2		Position of Dentist doesn't really match from shot 3-4 to 3B-5
0003	●	Producer	01:00:25:01		V2		Bag cutaway too quick (Nicole shaved off five frames)
0004	●	Producer	01:00:29:05		V2		This conversation between them feels long. let's tighten it up
0005	●	Producer	01:00:33:13		V2		Have him begin to say "Well, look.." over the photo
0006	●	Producer	01:00:40:14		V2		She takes the photo back twice, please fix
0007	●	Producer	01:00:46:26		V2		This walk back to the chair feels long
0008	●	Producer	01:00:56:18		V2		Have him say "Listen, Mary" over her closeup
0009	●	Producer	01:00:57:13		V2		Don't like the audio here "I know" - maybe use from his coverage?
0010	●	Producer	01:01:06:04		V2		Can we get Sue into the room faster?
0011	●	Producer	01:01:10:04		V2		Mary's position in the room doesn't match with previous shot. Can we adjust her
0012	●	Producer	01:01:13:03		V2		Takes too long for Sue to look up
0013	●	Producer	01:01:15:21		V2		I like her reaction, but can we have the dentist laugh a little sooner?

Figure 6.21 Marker window displaying markers and Producer's notes.

We are at the point in the edit when changes will require fine-tuning. The best way to fine tune your edit by a few frames here or there is to use the tools of Trim mode to make your changes.

Start with the first note.

6.   The Producer feels like the approach to the doorway Mary is making in shot "3C-4" and the wide shot that follows ("3-4") don't match up. In a case like this, where you have an action beginning in one shot that carries into the next shot (this is known as "matching action") it is common that the editor will need to use trim mode to refine the edit points between the two shots by adjusting a few frames on either side. This creates action that flows seamlessly from one shot into the next.

7.   Using the **U** KEY, open this transition in Trim mode.

8.   Begin by removing some frames from the B side (shot "3-4") using the YELLOW RIPPLE TRIM tool, and play through the transition using the SPACEBAR.

9.   Try to avoid using your mouse and instead use the trim keys to trim the shot.

 Figure 6.22 Trim keys.

Figure 6.23 Removing some frames from the B side (shot "3-4").

10. Make adjustments to the A side that will create a seamless transition between the action in shot **3C-4** and the completion of the action in shot **3-4**.

     You can move between the A side and B side in Ripple trim using the "P" and Right Bracket ( ]) keys. The Left Bracket " [" key will allow you to shift the edit points of both shots using Double Roller trim.

11. When you are satisfied with the way the action flows from one shot to the next, move on to the next note.

     There are several more notes in this exercise where the matching action needs to be adjusted. Any time the positioning of a character varies greatly from shot to shot or an action appears to happen twice, this technique will help you solve the problem.

12. In the MARKERS WINDOW, double-click marker **#0003**.

     The Producer thinks the cutaway to the bag dropping happens too quickly.

13. Using the RED OVERWRITE TRIM, add frames until the cutaway feels like it is up too long and then begin removing frames one at a time until the amount of screen time feels right.

14. Use the SPACEBAR to play through the transition to check your work.

    The bag should be up long enough that the audience will have to process what they are seeing, but not up so long that it distracts from the interaction between Mary and the Dentist.

15. In the MARKERS WINDOW, double-click marker **#0006**.

    The Producer would like the Dentist's dialogue to begin over the photo of the boy.

    In this instance, we can use Trim mode to create a split edit in which the audio from the B shot begins under the video from the A shot.

    You will begin by removing the portion of the Dentist's dialogue up to "Well, look who's keeping the.." from the B side.

16. In Trim mode, setup for a Ripple trim on tracks **V1** and **A2** on the **B-SIDE**, and then use **J-K-L** to remove the several frames.

17. Disable the V1 track so you will only be trimming the audio.

18. Turn off sync lock so it will not interfere with your trim.

19. In Trim mode, use the DOUBLE ROLLER TRIM tool to trim the audio from the B side backwards so that it overlaps with the shot on the A side.

Figure 6.24 Use the Double Roller trim tool to trim the audio from the B.

 Remember, do not use Ripple trim to perform split edits. It will cause your video to go out of sync.

20. Adjust the timing of the split edit until you are satisfied.

    You can jump back into Ripple Trim to adjust the amount of the A shot that proceeds the split edit or the amount of video we see in the B shot that follows the split edit.

    When using the Ripple Trim to adjust the split edit, be sure to enable the V1 and A1 track to avoid causing sync issues.

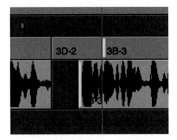

Figure 6.25 When using Ripple Trim to adjust the split edit, enable the V1 and A1 track to avoid causing sync issues.

You can use the split edit technique to adjust the pacing in other places in the scene as well. Split edits can tighten the pacing of a dialogue scene and create the illusion of connected conversation that flows between characters.

Let's go over one last note together.

21. Double-click marker **#0013** in the MARKERS WINDOW.

The Producer likes the placement of the shots, but would like the timing of the Dentist's laugh to happen sooner.

22. Open the shot **4C-2** by selecting it in Trim and then double-clicking on it while in Trim mode.

This will allow you to use adjust the clip with Slip.

23. Disable the V1 track so that we are only slipping the audio track.

24. Make sure sync lock is turned off.

25. Slip the Dentist's audio so that the duration and placement of the shots won't change, but that the timing of the Dentist's laugh will.

Figure 6.26 Slip the Dentist's audio so that the duration won't change, but the timing of the Dentist's laugh will.

Numbers will appear in the Timeline to make you aware that you are slipping the shot out of sync. This is OK because we are not concerned with keeping dialogue in sync in this case.

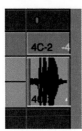

Figure 6.27 Numbers appear in the Timeline to show that the shot is out of sync.

Experiment with the timing of the laugh and observe how it changes how we perceive Mary's reaction.

26. Use the SPACEBAR to play through your edit until you are satisfied with the new placement of the Dentist's laugh.

27. Now go back through the markers and tackle any changes you may have passed over.

28. When you are finished, conclude the lesson by saving your work.

Mixing Sequence Audio

It's commonly believed that 50 percent of your audience's experience will come from audio, so your understanding of audio mixing, and when, how, and why you should use audio signal processing plug-ins can make or break your program.

In the previous course, MC101, you learned to make simple adjustments in clip gain to individual segments in the Timeline. In this lesson, you will learn techniques to efficiently mix the overall sequence, plus learn to address specific audio problems or challenges using Audio EQ and audio keyframes.

Media Used: Anesthesia and TN Parkour

Duration: 60 minutes

GOALS

- Learn an efficient audio mix workflow
- Use the Audio Tool to monitor and measure audio levels
- Adjust the output volume of the sequence
- Configure and use the Audio Mixer to adjust sequence audio
- Adjust pan values
- Use the Audio EQ tool to enhance dialogue and reduce unwanted sounds
- Create audio keyframes to solve problems and enhance the overall mix

Mixing Audio Efficiently

The goal of audio mixing is twofold: to set a consistent audio level for the program and to balance the audio elements to focus the viewer's attention on the correct audio sources or elements.

The sample projects included in this course are real-world projects. As such, there are inconsistencies in the audio levels of the raw production audio. This is common, especially in documentary films, due to the nature of recording in an uncontrolled production environment. But no production audio will be perfect. To keep these inconsistencies from distracting the viewer, the audio levels need to be balanced from shot to shot. As you add audio elements to your program—for instance, music or sound effects—you need to mix the relative audio levels between these different elements and the dialogue. In addition, EQ (equalization) and audio effects are used to blend and shape the sounds into a cohesive soundscape. The entire mix process is commonly referred to as "audio sweetening."

Like everything in editing, there are certain techniques to learn that will help you mix your program audio efficiently. It starts with an efficient workflow. The key to mixing audio efficiently is to make multiple passes, fixing one aspect of the audio with each pass. Like many workflow recommendations, there are no hard and fast rules to this, but the following is a good way to start.

Stages of audio mixing:

1. Use clip gain and audio crossfades to create smooth audio edits and achieve consistent and appropriate audio levels on all segments

2. Apply audio keyframes to fine-tune levels and create dynamic volume changes.

3. Use equalization and audio keyframing to solve specific issues and enhance the overall mix.

Collaborating with a Sound Mixer

Most professional editors in broadcast and film work with sound mixers. You should do the same every chance you can. A good mixer can do wonders for your project! Most sound mixers in the post-production world work on Avid Pro Tools, the industry-standard DAW (digital audio workstation) for audio post-production, which features unparalleled integration with Media Composer.

You can learn more about the workflow for sending your rough mix to Pro Tools in the MC201 course, Media Composer Professional Editing I.

Setting Up for Audio Mixing

When preparing to mix audio in a focused way, it is best to rearrange the Media Composer interface to make the process as efficient as possible. One of Media Composer's prebuilt workspaces is the Audio Mixing workspace. By default, it will open the Audio Mixer tool and rearrange the windows slightly. It is recommended that you customize this for your needs. Figure 7.1 illustrates how you might customize the workspace. The use of workspaces is covered in detail in the MC101: Media Composer Fundamentals I course.

Figure 7.1 The Audio Mixing workspace.

Using the Audio Mixer

The Audio Mixer is the primary tool for adjusting volume levels and pan values in a sequence.

To open the Audio Mixer, do one of the following:

■ Choose Tools > Audio Mixer.

■ Choose Workspace > Audio Mixing.

QuickView of the Audio Mixer

Look at Figure 7.2 to identify the following controls in the Audio Mixer before moving on:

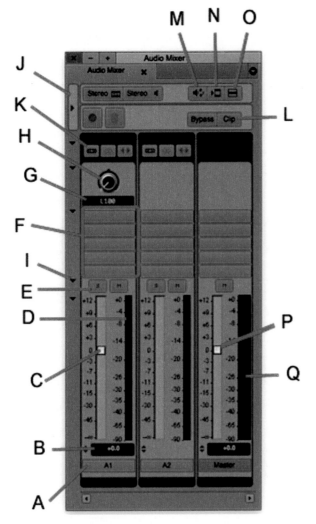

- **Track selector (A):** Enable/disable track selector.

- **Volume Level display (B):** Displays the precise decibel value of the fader adjustment.

- **Volume Level slider (C):** Changes the level of clip gain or volume, based on the Audio Mixer mode.

- **Track level meter (D):** Indicates the level of the audio signal for that track. This changes as adjustments are made.

- **Solo/Mute buttons (E):** Solo or mute the track. Same as the buttons in the Timeline.

- **Effect Insert buttons (F):** Insert positions for track based effects (currently AAX format) plug-ins. Clicking the button opens the Audio Track Effect tool.

- **Pan value indicator (G):** Displays the current pan value.

- **Pan knob (H):** Adjusts the L–R pan in a stereo mix. Operates like a value shuttle (drag up to raise value, drag down to lower it).

Figure 7.2 The Audio Mixer tool.

- **Disclosure Triangles (I):** Toggle the disclosure triangle to show / hide the corresponding control groups in the Audio Mixer; i.e. Track Effect buttons, Pan Knobs, etc.

- **Track Sidebar Button (J):** Toggles a sidebar panel used to control which tracks are displayed in the Audio Mixer as well as Group controls to group tracks into multiple groups.

- **Gang/Group buttons (K):** Groups together tracks for simultaneous adjustment. Each track with the Group button active is added to the group.

- **Audio Mixer Mode button (L):** Cycles the Audio Mixer through its three modes: Clip, Auto, and Live. (More on these shortly.)

- **Audio Loop button (M):** Plays the marked region of the Timeline in a loop.

- **Render button (N):** Used to render non–real-time audio effects for playback.

- **Fast menu button (O):** Opens the Fast menu for the Audio Mixer.

- **Master Volume Slider (P):** Raises or lowers the output volume (the sum of all the individual tracks).

- **Master Volume Meters (Q):** Displays the combined mix (sum) of all the individual tracks. This is the same information displayed in the Audio Tool.

Customizing the Audio Mixer Display

When all controls in the Audio Mixer are displayed, it can take up quite a bit of screen real estate. In addition to the disclosure triangles, you can choose to hide a few controls by changing the Audio Mixer display settings.

To hide controls in the Audio Mixer:

1. Right-click in the **AUDIO MIXER** and choose **DISPLAY OPTIONS**.

2. Deselect any **CONTROLS** you wish to hide.

3. Click **OK**.

Monitoring Audio Levels

When mixing, you need an objective reference point. The Audio Tool displays audio levels of the combined mix on digital and analog scales, as shown in Figure 7.3. Because of its size, it makes reading the precise levels of your mix easy to do.

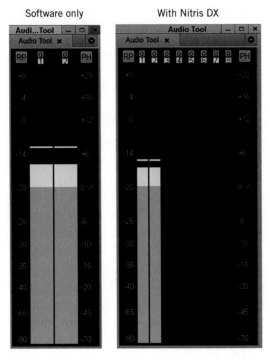

To open the Audio Tool:

- Choose **TOOLS > AUDIO TOOL**. Alternatively, press **CTRL+1** (Windows) or **COMMAND+1** (Mac).

Figure 7.3 The Audio Tool, displayed in a software-only configuration (left) and with Avid Nitris DX attached (right).

 The Audio Tool displays the number of output channels supported by your system configuration. With software only, that is two channels. With input/output hardware, that may be four or eight channels. (Audio levels displayed in the screenshots are not from the same frame.)

Generally speaking, you want the audio levels to bounce along between –26 dB and –8 dB on the digital scale. Films created for theatrical release tend to have a greater dynamic range than programming for television or streaming. (**Dynamic range** is the amount of variation between the loudest and quietest sounds.) If the audio levels are too high, you need to lower the levels in the mix. If they are too low, you need to raise them. The precise upper and lower limit is ultimately determined by the delivery specification for your specific distribution.

You will work with the Audio Tool throughout this lesson. Take a moment to review the features and functions of the Audio Tool, identified in Table 7.1.

Table 7.1: Features and Functions of the Audio Tool

Feature	Function
Reset Peak (RP) button	Resets the current maximum peak measurements and stops the playback of the internal calibration tone.
In/Out toggle buttons	Switches the meter displays for each channel between input levels from a source device and output levels to the speakers and record devices. I indicates input and O indicates output.
Peak Hold Menu (PH) button	Lets you select options for customizing the meter displays and for setting and playing back the internal calibration tone.
Digital scale to the left of the meters	Displays a fixed range of values from 0 to –90 decibels (dB), according to common digital peak meter standards.
Volume unit (VU) scale (analog) to the right of the meters	Displays a range of values that you can conform to the headroom parameters of your source audio.
Meters	Dynamically tracks audio levels for each channel as follows: • Meters show green below the target reference level (default reference level is –20 dB on the digital scale). • Meters show yellow for the normal headroom range, above the reference level to approximately –3 dB. • Meters show red for peaks approaching overload, between –3 dB and 0 (zero) dB. • Thin green lines at the bottom indicate signals below the display range.

Adjusting Level and Pan in the Audio Mixer

The Audio Mixer makes it easy to set the level and pan for a clip, sequence, or multiple clips within a sequence. Whenever it is open, the Audio Mixer is active, and can be used to make adjustments to the material in whichever monitor is active: Source or Record (Timeline).

Changes made in the Audio Mixer affect the entire clip in the Source monitor or the entire segment on which your blue position indicator is parked in the sequence. This can be especially useful when making adjustments to source material. If you know an entire clip is too loud or soft, it is more efficient to adjust the clip before editing it into the sequence, especially if you know you will edit repeatedly from the clip.

To adjust Clip Gain level:

1. Load a source CLIP into the Source monitor or move the POSITION INDICATOR over a segment in a sequence loaded into the Timeline.

2. Set the AUDIO MIXER mode to CLIP.

    Clip is the default mode, but the Audio Mixer will reopen in the mode last used.

3. Optionally, to link tracks together so they are adjusted in tandem, click the **GROUP** buttons on the desired tracks.

4. Click the **PLAY LOOP** button. The system repeatedly loops through the selected area as follows:

   • If IN and OUT marks are set, it loops over the marked area.

   • If there are no IN or OUT marks, it loops from the location of the position indicator to the end of the sequence.

5. Click the **SLIDER** for the track you want to adjust. Then do one of the following:

   • Drag the fader up or down.

   • Type a number in the Volume Level display (not available during Audio Loop Play).

   • Click a number in the legend next to the fader.

 If you adjust the level while playing, the new level will be heard on the next loop.

The adjustment in the Audio Mixer is reflected in the Timeline if Clip Gain data is enabled on the track(s). When you make your first adjustment, the light gray line turns black and moves up or down according to your adjustment. If the Timeline track is wide enough, you will see level indicators at the head of the track.

To type a number in the Volume Level display, click on the fader slider or on the Volume Level display box and then type a number (a negative number to decrease the level) on the numeric keypad. To adjust pan, click and drag the pan knob up or down. The knob will appear to rotate. Or, click the pan knob and then type a number. Positive numbers pan right, negative numbers pan left.

 To quickly reset the slider level to unity (0), Alt-click (Windows) or Option-click (Mac) the level slider. Alt-click (Windows) or Option-click (Mac) a pan knob to set the pan to MID.

Setting Pan and Level for Multiple Segments

The Global Pan and Global Level options apply the current pan or level settings to all clips on entire track(s) in a sequence. One way to speed your mixing workflow (and develop professional habits) is to segregate audio material by source or type onto designated tracks. For example, in an uncomplicated short form project, it is very common to place dialogue on A1 and A2, nat sound on A3 and A4, sound effects on A5 and A6, and music on A7 and A8. Like creating a rough cut, you can establish a rough mix by quickly setting levels globally on the tracks based on the type of audio material. For more precise control, you can also set level and pan for clips contained within marked IN and OUT points or from the beginning of a clip with an IN point to the end of the sequence.

Often, numerous segments in a sequence will need a similar adjustment, such as a series of sound-bite segments from an interview. An interview that was recorded loud will often be equally loud in all the segments. Rather than adjusting each individually, it is more efficient to make the adjustment to one and apply it to the others. Applying the adjustment from the first segment ensures that they are all consistent.

Applying the adjustment from one segment to others is done through a Fast menu command, as shown in Figure 7.4. The options in the menu change based on the presence of marks in the sequence.

Figure 7.4
The Fast menu option to apply an adjustment to other segments as it appears with IN and OUT marks set in the sequence.

To set up for the Global option:

■ Clear any **IN** and **OUT** marks from the Timeline.

Remember, pan and level will be set throughout the entire segment, not just the portion of the segment within the IN and OUT marks.

To set up for the IN-OUT option:

■ **Marked region:** Mark an IN and OUT in the sequence around segments you want to affect. Make sure the position indicator is within the IN and OUT marks and within an audio clip (not filler) on the track(s) you are adjusting.

■ **From In:** Mark an IN in the sequence. The adjustment is applied to all segments after the IN, all the way to the end of the sequence.

■ **To Out:** Mark an OUT in the sequence. The adjustment is applied to all segments before the OUT, all the way to the start of the sequence.

 The change will be applied to all active tracks. Check your track selection before choosing the Fast menu command.

To adjust the level or pan of multiple segments in the Timeline (with marks):

1. Select **TOOLS > AUDIO MIXER**.

2. Set the **MIXER** mode to Clip if it is not already.

3. Set **IN/OUT** marks around the segments to be adjusted. If no marks are present, the adjustment is applied to the entire track, if the track is selected.

4. Adjust the **CLIP GAIN** or **PAN** of one segment within the marked region.

5. Click the **TRACK SELECTION** button(s) in the Audio Mixer for the track(s) you want to modify. The adjustment will be applied to all active tracks.

6. In the Audio Mixer, click the **FAST MENU** button and choose the desired option: **SET LEVEL (OR PAN) ON TRACK–IN/OUT**.

Changing the Clip Gain Level of Master Clips in the Bin

There is also a way to adjust the clip gain for multiple segments in the bin. This is perfect for dropping the level on a bin full of music or sound-effect tracks.

To adjust the clip gain on multiple clips in the bin:

1. Select the MASTER CLIPS or SUBCLIPS to change.

2. Right-click on one of them and choose AUDIO > APPLY GAIN. Alternatively, this selection is also available on the Clip menu.

   The Apply Clip Gain dialog box opens, as shown in Figure 7.5.

   Figure 7.5
   The Apply Clip Gain dialog box is used to change the clip gain on multiple bin items.

3. Type the decibel value to which you wish to adjust the clip gain.

   For example, to lower the level of a typical music track, type –12.

4. Click OK.

Changing the Output Volume of the Sequence

If the combined output of the entire sequence plays too loudly or too softly, there are two ways to fix the problem:

■ Adjust the output monitor volume (the level you are hearing the mix through your speakers).

■ Adjust the Master fader in the Audio Mixer (the level of the audio signal being output from the system).

To decide, ask yourself this question: Am I hearing it too loudly or too quietly because of my current listening environment? Or is it because the audio signal level is really too high or too low?

In today's world, editors are often forced to edit in less-than-ideal listening environments—for example, editing on a laptop in a noisy environment without noise-isolating headphones. In this kind of situation, you most likely need to turn up the volume of the monitors. You want to be able to hear it right now, without making it a permanent change in the sequence. The opposite can be equally true. I've sat in edit bays where the monitors were louder than I thought comfortable, which makes editing unpleasant.

The best way to determine with any certainty if the sequence audio levels are too loud or soft is to look at the meters. (If the Audio Tool isn't currently open, open it again now.) Remember, the rule of thumb is to keep audio levels between –26 dB and –8 dB, as measured by the digital values on the left side of the meter. If the levels are consistently high or low, then change the Master fader level. If the audio levels are consistently within this range, change the monitor level for more comfortable listening.

Adjusting Monitor Volume

Early in the edit process, it is more common to need to adjust the monitor levels than the Master fader.

To adjust the monitor level using Nitris DX or Mojo DX:

1. Click and hold the MONITOR icon to the left side of the Timeline meters.

    A pop-up volume fader will appear, as shown in Figure 7.6.

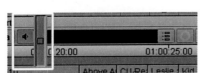

Figure 7.6
A pop-up fader under the Timeline monitor icon allows you to change the volume of the signal being output through the hardware for monitoring.

2. Without releasing the mouse button, drag the FADER to the desired level. Then release the mouse button.

    If you're running Media Composer software only, with no hardware attached, how you change the monitor volume depends on the operating system.

To adjust the monitor level using software only:

■   **Windows:** Click the monitor icon to the left side of the Timeline meters. A Windows volume slider pop-up window appears. Drag the fader to the desired level, and then click elsewhere in the Media Composer interface to close the pop-up.

■   **Mac:** Click the audio speaker icon at the top of the screen. Drag the fader to the desired level and then click anywhere on the Media Composer interface to close the pop-up.

Adjusting Sequence Volume

To adjust the volume for the whole sequence, you will use the Master fader in the Audio Mixer, shown in Figure 7.7. The Master fader changes the volume of the complete audio mix simultaneously, meaning all tracks for the entire duration of the sequence. It is always visible to the right of the other faders in the Audio Mixer and is labeled "Master" at the bottom of the fader.

Adjusting the Master fader works best if the sequence already plays at a consistent level. If not, take a few minutes to adjust the level of the segments that play loud or soft compared to the rest of the sequence. Then, if it is still necessary, adjust the sequence volume.

The real value of the Master fader is in being able to apply the Audio Track Effect plug-ins to the entire mix. The types of effects that would be applied to the Master fader are used primarily for signal monitoring and control, such as a Compressor/Limiter.

Figure 7.7
The Master fader.

To adjust the sequence volume:

1. Choose **TOOLS > AUDIO MIXER**.

2. If necessary, expand the **WINDOW** until the Master fader is visible. It will appear to the right of other faders.

3. Verify the **MIXER** mode is set to **CLIP**. If not, click the **MIXER MODE** button (see Figure 7.8) until it reads **CLIP**.

Figure 7.8 The Audio Mixer Mode button.

4. Move the **POSITION INDICATOR** to a region of the Timeline that is representative of the general mix.

5. Press the **SPACE BAR** or click the **PLAY** button on the Record monitor.

6. While the sequence plays, drag the **SLIDER** on the Master fader to raise or lower the volume. Watch the Audio Tool as you do to ensure that the level you set falls within the recommended range.

Exercise Break: Exercise 7.1
Pause here to practice what you've learned.

Audio EQ Tool

You've probably used an equalizer before if you've ever adjusted the bass or treble frequency on your stereo or car radio. Although a bit more advanced, the Audio EQ (equalization) tool in Media Composer lets you boost or cut (raise or lower) the bass, midrange, and treble frequencies of an audio clip. It also includes a number of EQ presets that make it easy to get commonly used EQ settings without a lot of fiddling.

One method of using the Audio EQ tool:

1. Select tracks that you want to EQ, and make sure all other tracks are deselected.

2. Click the **MARK CLIP** button or press **T** to set IN and OUT points around the clip.

    Marking the clip makes it possible to Loop Play after making the adjustment, or even during the process of making the adjustment.

3. To clearly hear the EQ changes you will make, click the **SOLO** buttons for the track(s) you're adjusting.

4. Select **TOOLS > AUDIO EQ**.

    The Audio EQ tool opens, as shown in Figure 7.9.

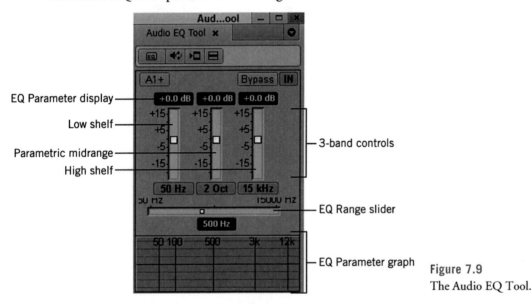

Figure 7.9
The Audio EQ Tool.

The Audio EQ tool provides three "bands" (section) of EQ. The left slider is the bass or "Low Shelf," which affects all low frequencies from 240 Hz to 50 Hz and below. The far right slider is the treble or "High Shelf," which affects all high frequencies from 6 kHz to 20 kHz and higher. The middle slider is the midrange, which affects frequencies between the low shelf and the high shelf as narrow as 1/4 octave or as wide as two octaves.

 An *octave* is a doubling of the sound frequency. From 60 Hz to 120 Hz is one octave.

To transfer the concepts of manipulating bass, midrange, and treble frequencies from the music in your car to a dialogue scene, for instance, you first need to learn where in the frequency range a particular sound exists. For example, the human voice has a frequency range of approximately 100 to 5,000 Hz, but is most noticeably affected by adjustments in the 1 to 3kHz range. Mechanical rumbles and hums—like car engines, generators, etc.—tend to sit below 500 Hz. Hisses and squeals are up around 8 kHz and above.

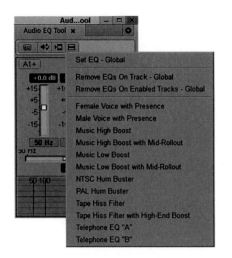

Much like the Clip Gain feature, Audio EQ is applied only to an entire segment or to multiple segments between IN and OUT points. To affect portions of a segment, you can use the Add Edit button to create smaller segments.

As shown in Figure 7.10, the Audio EQ Fast menu provides access to a number of EQ presets designed to address the most common needs in video editing.

Figure 7.10 The Audio EQ Fast menu contains useful presets

To apply an Audio EQ preset:

1. Move the POSITION INDICATOR to the target segment.

2. Optionally, mark IN and OUT around a group of clips to which you want to apply the effect simultaneously.

3. Select any TRACKS to which you want to apply the preset. Deselect all others.

4. Click the Audio EQ FAST MENU and choose the template of your choice—for example, MALE VOICE WITH PRESENCE.

   An EQ icon appears on the Timeline segment that was selected, indicating that an EQ effect is applied. (See Figure 7.11.)

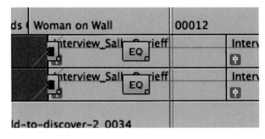

Figure 7.11
The Audio EQ effect icon appears with a green dot, indicating real-time playback.

5. Click the AUDIO LOOP PLAY button to hear the applied template.

    Depending on the frequency response (ability to reproduce the entirety of the audible frequency spectrum) of your speakers, you may or may not be able to notice audio problems or EQ adjustments. As with color grading the image, where you need a proper professional monitor to accurately make assessments and modifications, the same is true for audio.

6. Optionally, while the audio plays, click the BYPASS button to listen to the original audio. Then click BYPASS again to hear the change.

7. To apply the preset to the other segments in the marked area, open the Audio EQ FAST MENU and choose SET EQ-IN/OUT.

As a general rule, when dialogue or narration will be over a soundtrack, it's best to aim for a thinner-sounding EQ-less bass, more treble and midrange. The Female Voice with Presence and Male Voice with Presence templates create this effect. However, to fine-tune the sound, you may wish to create it manually. You can return to the EQ adjustments and set the EQ yourself. Click the Override with Default EQ button. The EQ tool returns to display the EQ parameter adjustments.

Before overriding a template, look at its frequency adjustment in the EQ graph display at the bottom of the EQ tool. Re-create the shape yourself as a starting point; then modify it to fine-tune the effect for your particular needs.

Exercise Break: Exercise 7.2
Pause here to practice what you've learned.

Technique: Building a Soundtrack

The addition of music and sound effects can take your video to another level. A rich multilayered soundtrack will bring depth to the video, immersing your viewer in the story in a way that visuals alone can never achieve. In other words, it feels like a real movie.

There are certain techniques that, even when applied at a basic level, make a big difference in the quality of the soundtrack. Learn and use these now to give your videos a professional polish.

• **Break the silence.** Our experience in the world is one of sound. It is extremely rare that there is nothing to be heard. Likewise, in your video, the audio should never completely drop out. Fill any gaps in the audio track with room tone. (Room tone is also called presence because it gives the viewer a sense of being there.) The sound recorder should be careful to record a period of "silence" on set for this purpose. (If not, you'll have to hunt for quiet places in the recording.) Overwrite that "silence" into the gaps in the audio track. Just be careful that extraneous noises don't become a rhythmic pattern when you loop the same segment of room tone in the Timeline.

• **Create a multilayered atmosphere.** Building on the room tone, add other sounds that create a sonic atmosphere. Our aural experience is one of hearing many sounds at once. If you stop right now and listen, you can probably hear numerous sounds at varying distances. To re-create this in your sequence, you need to layer multiple sounds. Don't rely on one sound effect. Media Composer gives you 64 audio tracks to play with, so use them. Stock music and sound effects companies also sell ambience tracks—such as "train station," "small café," etc.—designed to make this easier.

The quality of these can vary, but there's nothing like authentic location sounds. Here too, a good audio person can do you a huge favor by recording dedicated location audio, aside from the production takes. (Don't be afraid to ask them directly for this before production. Then, if they do, be sure to thank them and maybe get them a little "thank you" treat too.) Also look for useful incidental sounds in B-roll footage and between takes. You can use these like custom sound effects.

- **Play with the location of sounds.** Not all sounds come from right in front of us; similarly, not all the sounds in your film should come from the center of the screen. Play with the pan values for sounds, matching them to the "location" of their source in the picture. For example, suppose a truck comes down the street toward the camera and passes offscreen to the left. Keyframing the pan to start in the center and end 100% left would trick the viewers' brains into thinking that they are really hearing the truck they see onscreen.

- **Use your imagination.** What does an alien monster sound like? I don't know. And neither does your viewer. What does a truck sound like? Well, first tell me what kind of truck you mean, and then I'll tell you. Sounds from everyday objects are far more recognizable than imaginary creatures. But, even with everyday objects and scenarios, you can often mix in novel sounds without the viewer noticing.

For example, to make a storm more menacing, you might mix the sound of a snarling lion together with the howling wind. Mixed properly, you wouldn't even know it was there, but the storm would be terrifying.

- **Try doing some free association.** Play the scene, and sing, say, or otherwise make the noises that you imagine hearing. Describe them in as many ways as you can and write them down. Then, read the list and imagine all the things that make a similar noise or fit the description, even if it's outside the context of the scene. For the preceding example, the wind could have been described as howling, biting, vicious, and scary. With that kind of list, it's not hard to see how you could come up with snarling lion to mix in with the wind. Point is, don't be afraid to experiment.

Keyframing Volume and Pan Changes

Another tool at your disposal for addressing audio challenges is to make precise adjustments to volume or pan using audio keyframes.

You no doubt remember the term keyframe from your work with video effects in the MC101 course. Keyframe really is a generic term used to describe a control point that records a specific value for a parameter at a specific point in time. The system will automatically calculate the change in value over time between the keyframes. In Media Composer, the audio keyframing is done through the Volume Automation mode. This is abbreviated as "Volume" in the Timeline Control panel, while in the Audio Mixer it is referred to as "Auto."

Volume Automation allows you use keyframes to change the volume within a segment. They allow you to ramp the volume up and down, for instance, to have the music get softer when someone speaks, then return to full volume when they stop. It is also commonly used to remove clicks, pops, and "ums" from dialogue.

This technique is sometimes called audio rubberbanding. At some point in your life, you probably have used a rubberband to make a slingshot, stretching it between the fingers of one hand and pulling it with the other hand. As shown in Figure 7.12, the volume line between three keyframes is similar to the V-shape of that rubberband. The sloping line it creates is also why we use the term "ramp."

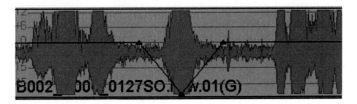

Figure 7.12 Audio rubberbanding.

Not all keyframing is done with three keyframes. On the contrary, you can have any number of keyframes to create simpler or more complex changes.

Audio keyframes are additive to the Clip Gain values set in the Audio Mixer or Timeline. When you add a keyframe, the system adds the point at the level currently set for that track. Any changes made with keyframes are relative to the Clip Gain level.

In addition to volume, Media Composer allows you to keyframe pan values in the same way. Pan, short for panoramic, is the relative left/right balance of a sound (in a stereo sound field). By adjusting pan, you can place the sound on the soundstage to coincide with the placement of its "source" on the screen. For example, if the car moves through the frame left to right, the sound effect is much more convincing if it also moves from left to right.

 When adjusting pan keyframes, the top of the track is 100% left, and the bottom of the track is 100% right.

Preparing the Timeline

Before you can manually add keyframes in the Timeline, you need to display the volume or pan data, available in the Audio Data menus, which are found within the Track Control panel or the Timeline. Volume and pan data lines and keyframes look the same, so to avoid confusion; Media Composer will display only one or the other at a time.

To prepare the tracks to manually add and manipulate keyframes:

1. Enable the **KEYFRAME** button in the Timeline Palette, as shown in Figure 7.13.

    The Keyframe button is enabled by default. If it is disabled, you cannot add, remove, or manipulate keyframes. Disabling this can be helpful when using the Smart Tool functions to avoid making keyframe changes.

2. In the Timeline, select the audio **TRACK(S)** you want to adjust.

3. If the Timeline Track Control panel is not displayed, click the small **DISCLOSURE TRIANGLE**, next to the green timecode display, to open it.

Figure 7.13 The Keyframe button.

4. Choose **VOLUME** to enable the ability to manually add keyframes. (see Figure 7.14).

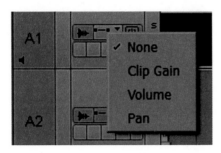

Figure 7.14 The Audio Data menu.

When no black Volume graph line appears on the track after Volume has been enabled, it relates that it is at the 0 dB value, meaning there has been no change to the Volume level. If the tracks are tall enough, a decibel graph is displayed on the track as well. Once a keyframe is added, the black Volume graph line appears. See Figure 7.15.

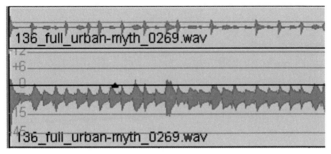

Figure 7.15 The decibel graph on a segment.

5. Optionally, press **CTRL+L** (Windows) or **COMMAND+L** (Mac) to expand the audio track(s) you will be keyframing.

 Holding the Ctrl key (Windows) or the Option key (Mac), you can click and drag the bottom of a track selector button to resize the track individually.

Audio Gain Adjustment Notification

If you apply volume keyframes on a track in your sequence and do not display any volume information, the keyframes will be hidden. To keep you aware of these hidden keyframes, Media Composer displays a little pink triangle on each clip containing keyframes, as shown in Figure 7.16.

Figure 7.16 The small pink triangle at the base of a segment
           indicates the presence of hidden volume keyframes.

Adding and Adjusting Keyframes in the Timeline

There are two ways that you can add keyframes directly in the Timeline. Like other functions in Media Composer, one uses the keyboard and relies on track activation and the position of the playhead, while the other involves the mouse. In the end, the result is the same, so use whichever is more comfortable to you.

To manually add a keyframe using the keyboard:

1. First, don't forget that Audio keyframes cannot be added manually unless "Volume" is displayed/enabled for the track (s).

2. Place the POSITION INDICATOR where you want to add the keyframe in the sequence.

3. Select the TRACK(S) where you want to add the keyframe(s).

4. Press the APOSTROPHE (') key to add a keyframe at the location of the position indicator.

    A keyframe will appear on all active tracks.

 It is easier to apply the first keyframe using the keyboard, since the keyframe line doesn't appear until the first keyframe has been added.

To add a keyframe using the mouse:

1. Holding CTRL+SHIFT (Windows) or COMMAND+SHIFT (Mac), slowly move the mouse over the center of the segment (at 0dB).

    The arrow pointer changes to a finger, pointing along with a crosshair.

2. Click where you want to create the keyframe.

    This process is easier after the first keyframe has been added, and the black graph line is visible.

    Once the keyframes are on a segment(s), there are shortcuts to make this process faster and more precise:

    • Click and drag a keyframe up or down to increase or decrease the gain at that point.

    • To snap to the volume decibel lines, hold the Ctrl key (Windows) or Command key (Mac) while dragging the keyframe up or down. The track must be enlarged to display the decibel lines.

    • After selecting one or more keyframes, press Ctrl+Shift (Windows) or Command+Shift (Mac) and then press the up and down arrow keys.

        • If adjusting volume, the keyframe moves in 1 dB increments.

        • If adjusting pan, the keyframe moves in 1 percent increments.

To adjust multiple keyframes simultaneously:

1. Shift-click the KEYFRAMES individually, or lasso to select a GROUP. When lassoing inside the Timeline, hold the Alt (Windows) or Option (Mac) key.

    Selected keyframes appear pink, as shown in Figure 7.17.

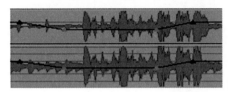

Figure 7.17 Selected keyframes become highlighted.

2. Add **IN** and **OUT** marks around the group of keyframes. Then adjust one KEYFRAME within the group.

    All keyframes on active tracks will move as a group.

When adjusting a group of keyframes, all selected keyframes maintain their relative position to each other. The only ramps to change are the ones between selected and non-selected keyframes—e.g., the ramp before the first keyframe and the one after the last keyframe in the group. Use this technique to raise or lower the volume of a keyframed section of music without having to adjust each keyframe individually. Moving keyframes horizontally, early or later within the clip, allows you to adjust the length/duration of the ramp from one keyframe to the next.

To move keyframe(s) earlier or later:

1. Select the KEYFRAME(S) you want to adjust.

    You can move non-contiguous keyframes, but you cannot move one keyframe on top of another or past another.

2. Move the MOUSE POINTER over a KEYFRAME.

    The mouse pointer changes to a hand. The keyframe does *not* have to be active (pink) to go to the next step.

3. Press and hold the **ALT** (Windows) or **OPTION** (Mac) key and drag the keyframe earlier or later.

To delete keyframe(s):

1. Select the KEYFRAME(s) to delete.

2. Press the **DELETE** or **BACKSPACE** key.

You can delete multiple keyframes by first selecting them with a lasso.

Adding and Adjusting Keyframes with a MIDI Audio Mixer

You can also add and modify keyframes using a MIDI Audio Mixer, such as the Avid Artist Mix, shown in Figure 7.18.

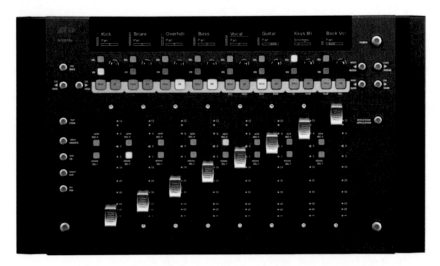

Figure 7.18 The Avid Artist Mix integrates seamlessly with Media Composer, giving you touch-sensitive faders for real-time mixing capabilities across multiple channels simultaneously.

Using a MIDI mixer allows you to adjust Volume levels by adding keyframes in real time, during playback. More information on this topic can be found in Avid Help in the section titled "Recording Volume Automation and Pan with Artist Series Controllers."

Exercise Break: Exercise 7.3
Pause here to practice what you've learned.

Audio Ducking

Media Composer 8.6 introduces a new feature called Audio Ducking that, in some scenarios, can reduce or eliminate the need for manually adding keyframes while producing very similar results in much less time.

The Audio Ducking tool automatically reduces, or "ducks", the volume of music below a certain level whenever dialogue or narration is present on designated dialogue tracks, as if it were automatically keyframing the volume on the music track. Like any automated function, it will not produce the level of customization or creativity that is possible when you mix the audio yourself, but it offers a huge savings in time for those projects that must be delivered quickly with only a simple mix. News packages, magazine-style packages, trailers, and product videos are all examples of these types of projects.

To get started using Audio Ducking:

1. With a cut sequence already loaded right-click the Timeline window and select Audio Ducking. The Audio Ducking window opens, as shown in Figure 7.19.

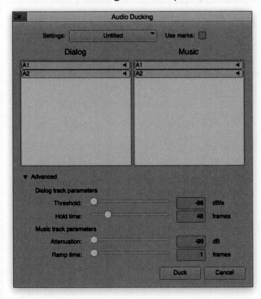

Figure 7.19 The Audio Ducking window.

2. In the left column, select the track(s) that contain dialogue (in this example, it would be A1). These tracks will not be adjusted during the Audio Ducking analysis and modification process.

3. In the right column, select the music track(s) (in this example, it would be A2). These music tracks will be reduced by the amount designated in the setting in the Advanced section.

4. Adjust the Dialog track > Threshold to approx. -25 dBfs.
   This determines the level at which Media Composer registers that there is dialogue present;

5. Adjust the Music track > Attenuation to approx. -14 dB; Ramp time to approx. 12 frames.
   Attenuation determines by how much it lowers the music; higher negative number = larger decrease. Ramp time determines how quickly or gradually the change is made; higher values = slower change.

6. Click the button labeled Duck to close the window. This will begin the analyzing and keyframing process. When it's finished, playback the sequence to hear the changes.

Review/Discussion Questions

1. From where do you open the Audio EQ window?

2. The Audio EQ tool is which of the following?

    a. A midrange band EQ

    b. A four-band EQ

    c. A three-band EQ

3. How can you change the clip gain for all segments in a track?

4. What is the Audio Tool used for?

5. Why is it important that you use the Audio Tool while mixing?

6. What is the decibel range that is recommended for most projects?

7. Which EQ control would be most effective in addressing the rumble of a truck in the background?

    a. Low Shelf

    b. Midrange Parametric

    c. High Shelf

8. In what range of frequencies will an EQ adjustment have the greatest impact on the sound of a person's voice?

    a. 100-300 Hz

    b. 500-800 Hz

    c. 800-1000 Hz

    d. 1000 – 3000 Hz

    e. 5000 – 8000 Hz

9. What Audio Mixer Mode enables manual audio keyframing?

10. Which type of adjustment is most similar to Audio Ducking?

   a. Clip Gain

   b. Pan

   c. EQ

   d. Volume Keyframing

   e. Pan Keyframing

Lesson 7 Keyboard Shortcuts

Key	Shortcut
Alt-click (Windows)/Option-click (Mac)	Resets the value of a slider or knob in any audio tool
Click the control, type the value	Enters a precise value for a control in an audio tool
Ctrl+Shift-click (Windows)/ Command+Shift-click (Mac)	Adds a keyframe by clicking at the 0dB location of a clip, or on an existing black volume graph line.
Alt-drag left/right (Windows)/ Option-drag left/right (Mac)	Drags a keyframe earlier or later in time
Ctrl-drag up/down (Windows)/ Command-drag up/down (Mac)	Snaps keyframes to decibel graph lines
Shift-click	Selects multiple keyframes
Lasso the keyframes Hold Alt (Windows)/Option (Mac) to lasso inside the Timeline	Selects multiple keyframes

Mix Your Audio

In this exercise, you will apply the tools and techniques of audio mixing together with your editing skills to refine the audio tracks in both the TN Parkour and Anesthesia projects.

Media Used: TN Parkour and Anesthesia

Duration: 2 hours 45 minutes

GOALS

- Replace music tracks
- Perform dialogue editing and mixing
- Use the Audio EQ tool to improve the clarity of dialogue

Exercise 7.1: Replace Music in TN Parkour

The Producer loved your edit of the TN Parkour Montage, but would like you to swap out the current music track "40_short_5-am_0035.wav" for a new music track, "40_full_wet-bread_0232.wav". This music track is too long for your montage, and will need to be cut down to 30 seconds before you can swap out the previous track.

In this exercise we will cut down a music track, change out the music in your TN Parkour Montage, and use the Audio Mixer to set the audio level to an industry standard.

Media Used: TN Parkour

Time: 45 minutes

For this exercise, we will use the **MC110_TN PARKOUR** project.

1.   Load the **MC110_TN PARKOUR** project if it is not already opened, and then open the **STUDENT_LESSON SEQUENCES** bin.

2.   Duplicate the sequence **7.1_TNPARKOUR MONTAGE** and rename the sequence **7.1_TNPARKOUR MONTAGE_REV**.

3.   Move the sequence **7.1_TNPARKOUR MONTAGE_REV** into the **TNPARKOUR_EXERCISE SEQUENCES** bin.

4.   Load the sequence **7.1_TNPARKOUR MONTAGE_REV** into the Timeline.

5.   Prepare to remove the existing music track by disabling the V1 track so that only the A1 and A2 tracks are active, and Mark an IN at beginning of the sequence and an OUT at the end of the sequence.

6.   Press the **Z KEY** to Lift the existing music track out of the sequence.

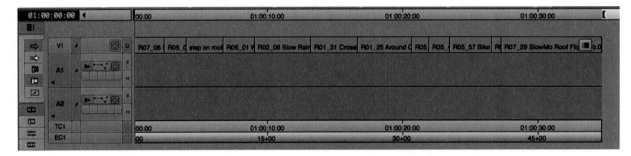

Figure 7.20..The Timeline after the existing music track is taken out of the sequence.

7.   In your **TNPARKOUR_EXERCISE SEQUENCES** bin, create a new sequence called, **7.1 TNPARKOUR NEW MUSIC**.

8.   The music track **40_FULL_WET-BREAD_0232.WAV** is too long for your 30 second montage. You will need to create a 30 second version before adding it to your **7.1_TNPARKOUR MONTAGE_REV** sequence.

9.   Open the **TNPARKOUR_MUSIC** bin and load the track labeled **40_FULL_WET-BREAD_0232.WAV** into the Source monitor.

10. Use the **TOGGLE SOURCE/RECORD BUTTON** to view the waveform from this track in the Timeline.

Figure 7.21.. Toggle Source/Record button.

11. Use the section that begins at **01:00:22:20** and ends at **01:01:34:21**. Mark **IN** and **OUT** points around this section.

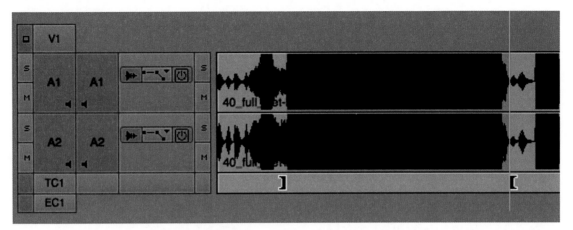

Figure 7.22 The Timeline displaying the IN and OUT at the beginning of 01:00:22:20 and at the end of 01:01:34:21.

12. Use the **TOGGLE SOURCE/RECORD BUTTON** to return the Timeline to Record display.

Figure 7.23 Toggle Source/Record button.

13. Make sure the sequence is loaded.

14. Overwrite the new music track into the **7.1 TNPARKOUR NEW MUSIC** sequence using the **B KEY**.

15. Listen to the section of the track and determine where there are repetitions in the track that can be removed to further edit your track down to the required 30 second length.

16. Mark **IN** and **OUT** points around the remaining sections of music you intend to remove and Extract them using the **X KEY**.

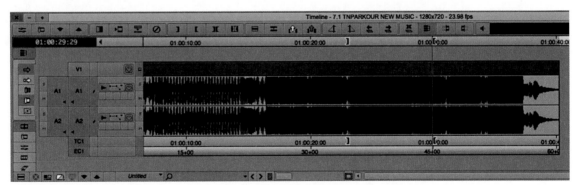

Figure 7.24 The Timeline with the remaining music section removed.

 To keep track of the duration of your sequence, go to the Tracking Information Menu above the Record monitor. Select "Duration." If you have both rows of data displayed, it is most common to have Master timecode (MAS) in the upper display and duration (DUR) in the lower. This way you can navigate the Timeline with timecode, when needed.

17. Fine tune the transitions between the cuts and get the duration to 30 seconds.

18. When you are satisfied with your edited music track, load the sequence **7.1 TNPARKOUR NEW MUSIC** by dragging it into the Source monitor.

19. Load the **7.1_TNPARKOUR MONTAGE_REV** sequence into the Timeline.

20. CLEAR the **IN** and **OUT** points in your Timeline using the **G** KEY.

21. In the Source monitor, Mark an **IN** at the beginning of **7.1 TNPARKOUR NEW MUSIC** and an **OUT** at the end.

22. OVERWRITE the new music track at the beginning of the **7.1_TNPARKOUR MONTAGE_REV** sequence using the **B** KEY.

Figure 7.25 The new music track added to the beginning of the sequence.

23. Make sure that the V1 track remains disabled so that you don't disturb the video portion of your montage.

24. Play through the entire sequence.

   You will notice the rhythm of the piece has changed. We will address this in a moment, but first let's finish smoothing out the editing and set the levels appropriately.

25. Using the **QUICK TRANSITION BUTTON**, add a **2 FRAME** cross dissolves between all the audio transitions to smooth them out.

    Remember, you can add the same transition to all the cuts simultaneously by Marking IN and OUT points around the music track and checking the box "Apply to All Transitions" in the Quick Transition dialog box.

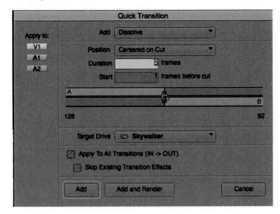

Figure 7.26 The Quick Transition dialog box.

26. Open the Audio Mixer by navigating to **TOOLS >AUDIO MIXER**.

27. In the top right of the Audio Mixer, set the Audio Mixer mode to **CLIP**.

28. Play through the sequence and observe the audio level that the music track is currently at.

    We want the audio to stay mostly within the -12db range, with levels not rising above -6db.

29. Park the position indicator at the first audio segment.

30. Group the **A1** and **A2** tracks together in the mixer by pressing the **GROUP BUTTON** on both tracks. (See Figure 7.27.)

    When tracks are grouped together, changes made to one track will also be made to the other.

Figure 7.27 The Group button in the Audio Mixer dialog.

31. Adjust the music track. You can do this by using the Volume Level Slider or by typing a value into the Volume Level Display.

32. Now that the first clip has been adjusted, keep your position indictor at that location.

33. Set the levels for all active audio tracks in the Timeline by navigating to the FAST MENU in the AUDIO MIXER and choosing SET LEVEL ON TRACK – GLOBAL. (See Figure 7.28.)

Figure 7.28 Choosing "Set Level on Track – Global" from the Audio Mixer Fast menu.

34. Play through the montage once again and check to make sure the audio levels are correct.

35. Enable your V1 track and finish out your revision by making slight adjustments to the timing of your video edit with Trim mode, and the other editing tools.

36. Be sure to disable your A1 and A2 track while making changes to your video.

Exercise 7.2: Dialogue Editing in Anesthesia

In this exercise we will use a part of the short film Anesthesia to practice some basic techniques for dialogue editing, mix to industry standard levels, and apply EQ templates using the Audio EQ Tool.

Media Used: Anesthesia

Time: 45 minutes

For this exercise, we will use the MC110_ANESTHESIA project.

1. Begin by opening the bin STUDENT_LESSON SEQUENCES.

2. Duplicate the sequence 7.3_ANESTHESIA_DIALOGUE EDITING and move the duplicate sequence into the ANESTHESIA_EXERCISE SEQUENCES bin.

3. Load the duplicate 7.3_ANESTHESIA_DIALOGUE EDITING into the Timeline.

4. Take a look at the sequence.

    You have been given a portion of the Anesthesia edit we have been working on. You will use this to practice some basic dialogue editing and mixing techniques.

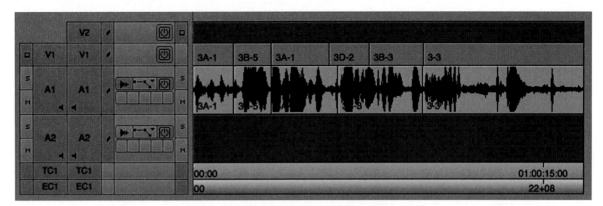

Figure 7.29 The duplicate "7.3_ANESTHESIA_DIALOGUE EDITING" sequence.

Your goal when editing dialogue is to make it sound as clear as possible, create transitions from shot to shot that sound seamless, and set the audio at consistent levels.

You will begin by separating the individual character audio onto separate tracks.

5. Using LIFT/OVERWRITE segment mode, drag the Dentist's audio from A1 to A2. Hold down CTRL+SHIFT (Windows) or COMMAND+SHIFT (Mac) as you drag the audio segments down to A2 to avoid breaking sync.

    This is a technique known as "checkerboarding." This will allow you to make changes to each character's audio separately.

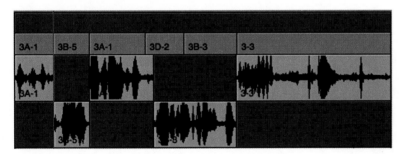

Figure 7.30 Checkerboarding in the Timeline.

6. Using the AUDIO MIXER, set the level of Mary's audio to fall mostly at **-12DB**.

This level was dictated to you in the fictitious Delivery Requirements by the equally fictitious Post Production Supervisor.

Figure 7.31 Using the Audio Mixer to set the level of Mary's audio to fall mostly at -12db.

7. Apply this level to all of Mary's dialogue from this camera set-up (3A-1) by first Marking an **IN** and **OUT** around the segments. Then click the **FAST MENU** on the mixer and choose **SET LEVEL ON TRACK – IN/OUT**. (See Figure 7.32.)

8. Make sure A2 is disabled while you are mixing A1 so that the Dentist's audio is not affected.

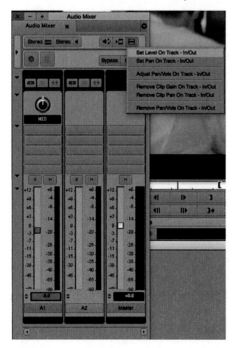

Figure 7.32 Selecting "Set Level on Track – In/Out" from the Audio Mixer Fast menu.

9. You will find that the shot of Mary from a different camera set-up will require its audio level be set separately. It is common to find slight fluctuations in sound levels and quality between different camera set-ups.

   Once Mary's audio levels are set, move on to the Dentist's audio.

10. Disable A1, enable A2 and set levels for the Dentist's audio.

11. Save time by using **SET LEVEL ON TRACK – IN/OUT** in the **FAST MENU** to apply your levels to all the Dentist's audio from camera set-up **3B**.

12. Once all the audio levels for both characters are set, open the Audio EQ Tool by navigating to **TOOLS > AUDIO EQ**.

    Starting with the Dentist on A2, you will apply an EQ (equalization) template to enhance dialogue recording.

13. Go to the **FAST MENU** in the **AUDIO EQ TOOL** and select **MALE VOICE WITH PRESENCE**.

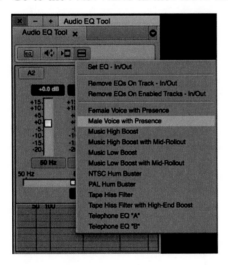

Figure 7.33 Selecting "Male Voice with Presence" from the Audio EQ Tool's Fast menu.

14. Play through the affected clip. To play through the effect on a loop, Mark an **IN** and **OUT** around the clip and hit the **PLAY LOOP BUTTON** in the Audio EQ Tool.

15. You can compare the EQ effect to the sound of the original clip by clicking the **BYPASS BUTTON**.

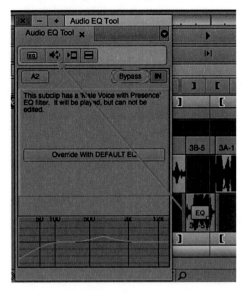

Figure 7.34 The Play Loop and the Bypass button in the Audio EQ Tool.

16. Add the same EQ filter to the rest of the Dentist's audio. Begin by clearing any marks in the Timeline. From the Fast menu in the Audio EQ Tool, select **SET EQ – IN/OUT**.

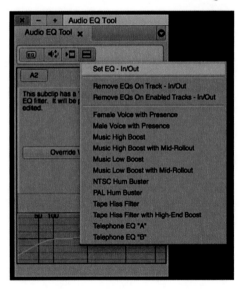

Figure 7.35 Selecting Set EQ – In/Out from the Audio EQ Tool's Fast menu.

Next, you will add an EQ template to Mary's audio.

17. Disable A2, enable A1, and park the position indicator over one of Mary's audio segments.

18. From the Audio EQ Tool's Fast menu, choose the template **FEMALE VOICE WITH PRESENCE**.

19. Add the same EQ filter to the rest of the Mary's audio by marking and **IN** and **OUT** around all of her segments on A1 and choosing **SET EQ – IN/OUT** from the **FAST MENU** in the Audio EQ Tool.

20. Try adding a different EQ template ("NTSC Hum Buster") to shot **3-3** in order to minimize the slight hum. Use Undo and Redo to go back and forth between the two templates to see which one makes the audio sound best.

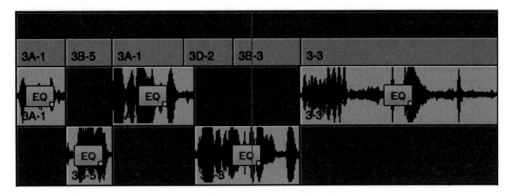

Figure 7.36 Adding a different EQ template ("NTSC Hum Buster") to shot 3-3.

21. Lastly, smooth out the audio cuts between shots by adding 2-frame cross dissolves at just the transitions that need one.

22. Next, practice adding a 2-frame crossfade to all the transitions on both tracks, all in one step. Place IN and OUT marks around the entire sequence.

23. In the QUICK TRANSITION dialog, enable the check box next to APPLY TO ALL TRANSITIONS (IN -> OUT).

24. Click the ADD BUTTON to apply all of the cross fades.

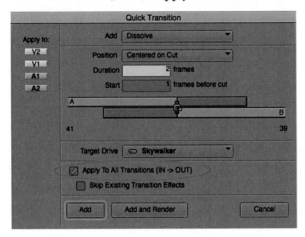

Figure 7.37 Selecting the "Apply To All Transitions (IN > OUT)" in the Quick Transition dialog.

Exercise 7.3: Adding Music and Sound Effects to Anesthesia

In this exercise we will use a part of the short film Anesthesia to practice adding some sound effects and music to the film Anesthesia. We will use the Audio Mixer Tool to set appropriate audio levels and we'll keyframe a crescendo (raise the volume gradually) in the music to heighten tension.

Media Used: Anesthesia

Time: 1 hour and 15 minutes

For this exercise, we will use the **MC110_ANESTHESIA** project.

1. Begin by opening the bin **STUDENT_LESSON SEQUENCES**.

2. Duplicate the sequence **7.3_ANESTHESIA_SUSPENSE** and move the duplicate sequence into the **ANESTHESIA_EXERCISE SEQUENCES** bin.

3. Load the duplicate **7.3_ANESTHESIA_SUSPENSE** into the Timeline.

4. Open the bin **ANESTHESIA_MUSIC** and import the music for this exercise by navigating to the following folders on your HARD DRIVE > SUPPLEMENTAL MEDIA > MUSIC AND SFX_EXERCISE 7.3 > MUSIC.

5. Open the bin **ANESTHESIA_SFX** and import the sound effects for this exercise by navigating to the following folders on your HARD DRIVE > SUPPLEMENTAL MEDIA > MUSIC AND SFX_EXERCISE 7.3 > SFX.

6. After import, select all the SFX clips (Ctrl + A (Windows) or Command + A (Mac)) and select CLIP > AUDIO > APPLY GAIN. Set the level to **-17** and click **OK**.

    This will lower the level to -17dB so that the audio will not be unpleasantly loud. This level can be changed at any time, including in the sequence.

7. Select the Timeline and go to TOOLS > MARKERS to pull up a list of notes the Producer has left you regarding the sound effects and music that need to be added.

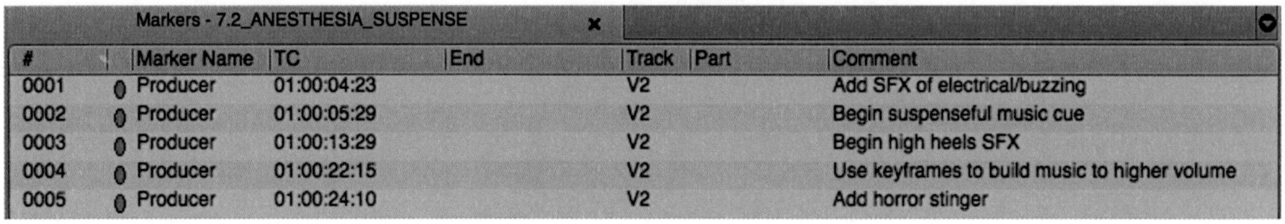

#		Marker Name	TC	End	Track	Part	Comment
0001	○	Producer	01:00:04:23		V2		Add SFX of electrical/buzzing
0002	○	Producer	01:00:05:29		V2		Begin suspenseful music cue
0003	○	Producer	01:00:13:29		V2		Begin high heels SFX
0004	○	Producer	01:00:22:15		V2		Use keyframes to build music to higher volume
0005	○	Producer	01:00:24:10		V2		Add horror stinger

Markers - 7.2_ANESTHESIA_SUSPENSE

Figure 7.38 Markers window displaying the Producers notes.

Let's start with the first note. The producer wants you to add electrical/buzzing sounds to the shot of the X-Ray coming on.

8. Listen to your options by loading the SFX labeled ELECTRICAL or BUZZING.

    Decide what might give you the right feel for a creepy or suspenseful scene.

    You may find that several SFX in combination will be needed to achieve the right effect.

9. Once you have made your choices, load an audio file into the Source monitor and use the TOGGLE SOURCE/RECORD BUTTON to view the audio waveforms and Mark IN and OUT points around the portion of the audio file you want to use.

Figure 7.39 Toggle Source/Record button.

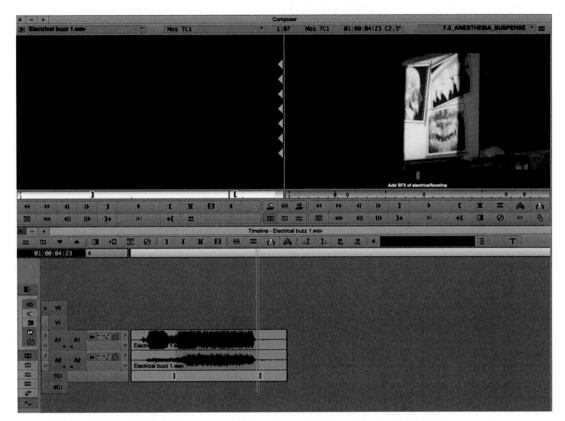

Figure 7.40 Using Audio waveforms, mark IN and OUT points around the portion of the audio file you want to use.

10. Click the TOGGLE SOURCE/RECORD BUTTON again to return the Timeline back to Record view.

Figure 7.41 Toggle Source/Record button.

11. Go to the image of the X-Ray at **01:00:04:00** to begin layering in your sound design.

12. Disable V2, V1, and A1 and then edit the SFX to the A2 track.

To keep this sequence more manageable for this exercise, we're having you edit in only one channel from the SFX. In a full editing situation, you would edit in both tracks and pan one to 100 Left and the other to 100 Right. Alternatively, you could modify the source clip into Stereo clips, and edit them onto a Stereo track.

It is best to keep the music and SFX on separate tracks to make mixing easier.

13. Add tracks **A3-A5**, for the music cue requested in NOTE **#2**.

Figure 7.42 Adding tracks A3-A5.

14. Open the bin **ANESTHESIA_MUSIC** and load the track ANESTHESIA MUSIC.WAV into the Source monitor.

15. Use the **TOGGLE SOURCE/RECORD BUTTON** to view the audio waveform and Mark an **IN** where the music starts.

Figure 7.43 Toggle Source/Record button.

16. Click the **TOGGLE SOURCE/RECORD BUTTON** again to return the Timeline to Record view.

Figure 7.44 Toggle Source/Record button.

17. In the Timeline, Mark an **IN** where you feel that the music should start and an **OUT** at the point when Mary bumps into the Dentist.

18. Overwrite the music cue onto the A4 and A5 using the **B** KEY.

19. Read NOTE **#3**: the Producer needs you to add footsteps foley to the images of Mary walking to the doorway from 01:00:13:29 to 01:0024:04.

    You have two options for footsteps. Listen to both and decide what will fit best in the scene.

20. **MUTE** tracks **A4** and **A5** so the footsteps will not be obscured by the sound of the music in the Timeline as you work.

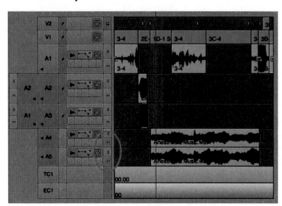

Figure 7.45 Mute tracks A4 and A5 in the Timeline.

21. Use the TOGGLE SOURCE/RECORD BUTTON again to single out individual footsteps so that the SFX will match the pace of Mary's walking.

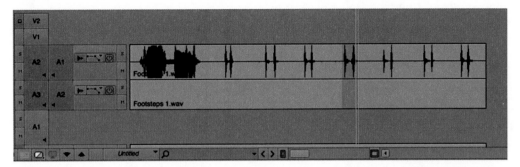

   Figure 7.46 Toggle Source/Record button.

Figure 7.47 Single out individual footsteps so that the SFX will match the pace of Mary's walking.

22. Go back and forth between Source and Record view in the Timeline to select your footsteps and Overwrite them into the Timeline, as seen in Figure 7.48.

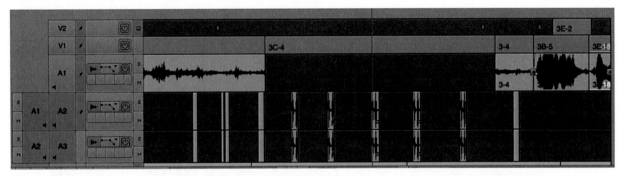

Figure 7.48 Go back and forth between Source and Record view in the Timeline to select your footsteps and Overwrite them into the Timeline.

23. Finish adding your sound design by choosing a "stinger" from the two options in the bin **ANESTHESIA_SFX**.

24. Overwrite the stinger sound effect onto A2/A3 right when the Dentist collides with Mary.

25. Use SLIDING in Trim mode to get the timing just right.

26. Trim off the end of the stinger to make it fit and use a 5 frame fade out to smooth it out.

   To get the result in Figure 7.49, in the Quick Transition dialog, use the Position menu to change the placement from "Centered on Cut" to "Ending at Cut."

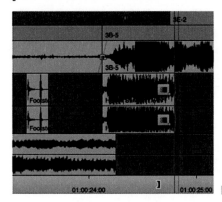

Figure 7.49 Using "Ending on Cut" from the Quick Transition dialog.

27. Now that all your music and sound effects are placed in the Timeline, play through the sequence and listen.

   You will notice that adjustments need to be made.

28. Open your **AUDIO MIXER TOOL** and go through the sequence, setting all the music and SFX to the correct levels.

   Generally, nothing should be louder than -12db.

   Make choices about which SFX should be louder than others. If everything is at the same volume, your SFX and music will compete with one another instead of working together.

Figure 7.50 Setting the correct audio levels using the Audio Mixer.

29. When you have finished setting all the proper levels, keyframe a crescendo in the music cue starting around 01:00:22:05 to heighten the tension.

Keyframing can be done when "Volume" is turned on in the Track Control Panel.

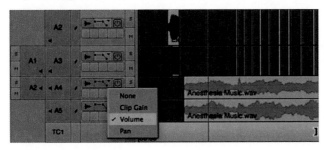

Figure 7.51..Selecting "Volume" in the Track Control panel.

30. Use the QUOTE SYMBOL KEY (") on the keyboard to add keyframes in your audio segment.

31. Keyframe a quick fade out in the music when the stinger sound effect comes in.

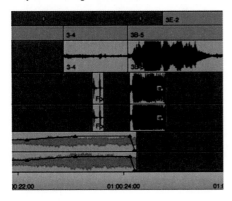

Figure 7.52 Keyframe a quick fade out in the music when the stinger sound effect comes in.

32. Finish your mix by adding 2 frame dissolves to any transition that needs them, in order to smooth them out, or remove pops, clicks, or other unwanted sounds.

33. Conclude the exercise by backing up this project's folder.

Working with High-Resolution Images

Media Composer makes it easy to work with large digital images that are 2K and up through a feature known as FrameFlex.

FrameFlex can be used to simply scale and adapt high-resolution images for display in the aspect ratio of the project. If the original high-rez image is larger than the project, FrameFlex can be used to zoom in over a portion of the photo or video and create dramatic "camera moves."

Media: MC110_EFFECTS

Duration: 80 minutes

GOALS

- Pan and zoom on high-resolution photos
- Explore the Source Settings dialog box

Understanding Pan & Zoom Effects

Pan-and-zoom effects are nothing new. Originally these were "motion control" effects created in-camera with expensive motion control rigs that allowed for precise camera moves over photographic prints, adding movement and drama to an otherwise static image. Today, of course, these are rarely created in camera. Even many "camera moves" over video are created in post, as you have no doubt done yourself. Keyframing a change in the scale value of a Resize effect, for example, creates an artificial zoom.

Any move that artificially enlarges the image greater than 100% runs the risk of degrading the quality. Sharpness can be reduced, and pixels can become visible. That's never good.

A true pan-and-zoom effect with high-resolution images, however, avoids this problem because the image itself is larger than the display raster of the project. Figure 8.1 shows the cyan colored outline of a 1920x1080 frame over a 4K clip that measures 4096x2160. As you can see, the 1080 frame covers only one-quarter of the image. Even though we are looking at a much smaller portion of the image, the source image is not being scaled up or down, meaning full quality is maintained.

Figure 8.1   A 1920 x 1080 excerpt from the 4K image retains full image
quality, even though it appears zoomed in.

 You can link to still images which appear in the bin with a default duration of 30
seconds.

Exploring the Source Settings Dialog Box

As production moves quickly from HD to 4K and beyond, managing various high-resolution images, color bit depth, and color spaces in post-production is critical to allow as much creative and quality control as possible. RAW and Log-based digital cinema cameras commonly record 2.5K, 3K, 4K, and higher images in their own unique recording formats.

Each manufacturer adds its own "special sauce" to the recording format using a combination of coded luminance values, resolution, color bit depth, and color space. Manufacturers do this with the hope that you will like their "sauce" best and choose their camera. That aside, the various RAW and Log-based recording formats require Media Composer to provide more control and flexibility when dealing with image resolution, color bit depth and color space.

When you link directly to high-resolution RAW or Log files, those files become master clips in your bin. Using the Source Settings dialog box, shown in Figure 8.2, you can manage the differences in resolutions as well as color space.

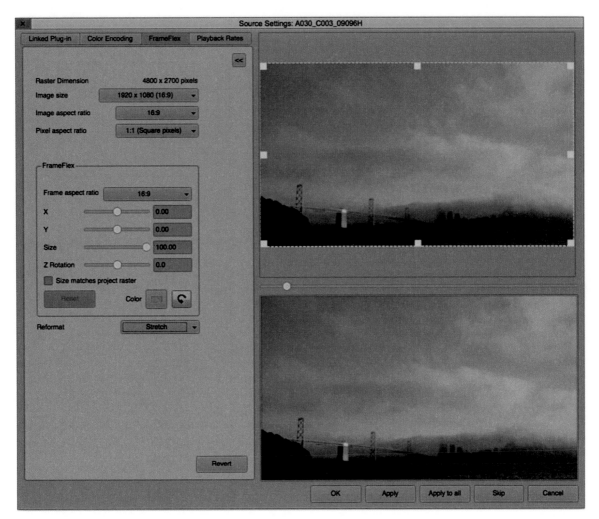

Figure 8.2 The Source Settings dialog box.

The Source Settings dialog box detects the properties of the source media based on their metadata. It allows you to quickly see the properties of the files you've linked to and make changes if necessary. You can also view any reframing applied on the image, as well as a histogram showing the distribution of colors in the image.

To access the Source Settings dialog box:

1. Select one or more linked CLIPS in the bin.

2. Right-click and choose SOURCE SETTINGS from the menu.

3. (Optional) If the image viewers are not displayed in the Source Settings dialog box, click the SHOW VIEWERS button, located in the top-right corner of the Source Settings window.

    The Source Settings dialog box includes two primary tabs. The FrameFlex tab is used to reformat high-resolution clips to fit within a smaller project raster (frame size). This is all done interactively and in a non-destructive process that can be updated at any time. The Color Encoding tab is used to manage the color conversion from the high-resolution camera's native color space to Media Composer's HD broadcast standard, called Rec. 709.

    After you have modified the framing or the color space in the Source Settings dialog box and applied them, the results are saved with the clip in the bin. When the clip is placed on the Timeline, any of these changes will be indicated as adapter effects and will display as an icon on the clip, as shown in Figure 8.3. In this instance, the "S" indicates that it has a scaling adapter which is scaling the 4K image down to fit in the HD frame.

Figure 8.3 A Source Settings–modified segment, indicated by a green dot.

 All Source Adapters are real-time effects, as indicated by the green dot.

Understanding Timeline Adapter Icons

There are other display adapters that will also be displayed in the Timeline.

Media Composer allows you to easily mix video clips with different properties – i.e. frame size, frame rate, color space, etc. Any clip that does not match the project's Format settings is automatically adapted. (Source Settings allow you to change how the system will adapt the video.) When we place one of these clips in the Timeline, the segment appears in the Timeline with a small green square on the video segment. This indicates an adapter had been applied to this segment. In previous versions, all adapters appeared as a small green dot on the segment, with no indication as to the type of adapter(s) being used.

In addition to the green dot, you now have the icon(s) which identify which adapter(s) are being used. The icon will have 1 to 3 letters on it – T, S, or C – identifying the adapter(s) in use. All three are visible in Figure 8.4.

     Figure 8.4 The three source adapter icons.

The three adapters are:

T   Temporal Adapter - Adapts the speed / rate of playback of a clip

S   Spacial Adapter - Scales the size of the image (FrameFlex)

C   Color Adapter - Adapts the colors of the image per the Source Color settings

In the Timeline, it is possible to hide or show any combination of these three adapters. From the Timeline Fast menu, choose **SHOW ADAPTERS** and select which ones you wish to see, as seen in Figure 8.5.

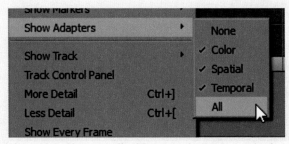

Figure 8.5 You can disable any adapters you don't want to see.

Using FrameFlex on 2K+ Clips

The FrameFlex tab in the Source Settings dialog box allows you to work in HD projects using high-res sources by extracting a 1,920 $\times$ 1,080 portion from the high-res frame. You can use the full, high-resolution image (it will be scaled down to fit within the smaller raster), or reframe a portion of it to the HD project size. Because this is a non-destructive process you can change it at any time.

The top Source viewer shows the full high-resolution image with a framing box that reflects the area to be used in Media Composer. The bottom viewer displays the framed area as it would appear within the actual project (see Figure 8.6). The slider between the two viewers moves through the clip so you can view a different frame.

Figure 8.6 A framing box outline in the Source viewer and the framed area below.

The new framing of the image will be visible when you drop the clip in the Source monitor or in the Timeline.

 If you have placed your clip in the Timeline before performing the reframing, you can refresh your Timeline. Select the sequence in the bin, then choose Clip > Refresh Sequence > Aspect Ratio and Reformatting Options.

Although you can drag the framing box to reposition and resize it directly in the Source viewer, the framing parameters in the FrameFlex box are where the dimensions of the framing box can be adjusted more precisely, as shown in Figure 8.7. The area within the framing box is what will finally be fit into the project dimensions when the clip is used in a sequence.

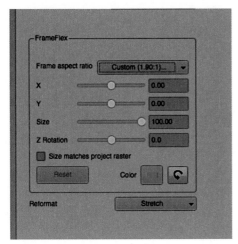

Figure 8.7 FrameFlex framing box parameters.

To maintain the project's aspect ratio and dimensions, you can select the "Size matches project raster" check box. This quickly sets the framing box to match the project's 1,920 X.1,080 dimensions. Any changes to the Frame Aspect Ratio or the size will disable the check box. The X and Y parameters control the positioning of the framing box, while the Size parameter is used to resize the box proportionately. Z

To use FrameFlex:

1. Select one or more AMA linked CLIPS in the bin and choose SOURCE SETTINGS.

2. Select the FRAMEFLEX tab.

3. Drag the video SLIDER to the frame you want to view.

4. In the FrameFlex box, adjust the FRAMING PARAMETERS to set the new dimensions.

> If you select more than one AMA-linked clip in the bin before opening the Source Settings dialog box, a Skip button allows you to view the next clip and an Apply to All button allows you to apply the current FrameFlex setting to all the selected clips.

Creating a Pan and Zoom Effect with FrameFlex

The Source Settings allow you to reframe an image, but all adjustments are applied to the entire clip. To create an animation of the FrameFlex parameters, you need to edit the clip into a sequence and then open the Effect Editor to modify its parameters, shown in Figure 8.8. Changes made here do not affect the entire clip; they modify only the segment you selected in the Timeline.

The parameter groups are similar to the ones found in the Resize effect. They include Size and Position, plus Z Rotation. Two check boxes allow you to lock the aspect ratio, or "Match Project Raster," which snaps the wireframe to the pixel dimensions of the project. The latter is especially useful to give yourself a quick visual reference of how small you can make the wireframe – or, how far in you can zoom – before you are enlarging the image and risk degrading it.

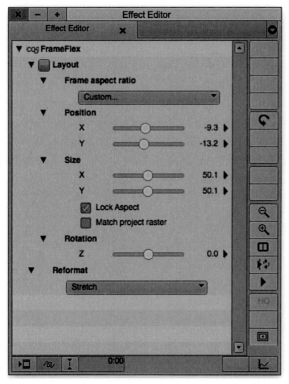

Figure 8.8 FrameFlex parameters in Effect mode include standard groups for Position, Size, and Rotation.

To create a pan-and-zoom effect with FrameFlex:

1.   Link to a high-resolution video clip or still image.

2.   Edit the linked clip into a sequence.

3.   Park the position indicator over the clip, and open the **EFFECT EDITOR**.

The Effect monitor (on the right) displays a wireframe outline for direct manipulation, and the Effect Analysis monitor (on the left) gives you a preview of the finished effect, as shown in Figure 8.9.

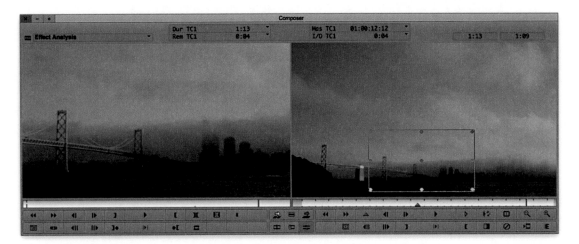

Figure 8.9 When in Effect Mode, FrameFlex is displayed with Effect Analysis (the result of your changes) on the left, while the entire source image appears on the right, in the Effect monitor.

4.   Scrub or play the clip, stopping at the point you want the animation to begin.

5.   Click the **ADD KEYFRAME BUTTON** in the Effect Preview (right) monitor.

6.   Manipulate the wireframe box to reframe the shot at this point in time, by doing the following:

  a.   Click and drag any of the control points around the wireframe to resize the frame

  b.   Click and drag inside the wireframe to reposition it over the image

7.   Move the position indicator to the point in time that you want the animation to end, and repeat steps 5-6.

8.   While still in Effect Mode, click on the Effect Analysis (left) monitor to make it the active monitor. To play a preview of the animation, click the **PLAY BUTTON** under the Effect Analysis window, or press the spacebar.

Changing the Behavior of the Animation Between Keyframes

The default method of processing the animation between keyframes (known as interpolation) is "Linear," which creates a consistent rate of change between keyframes. This can appear almost mechanical in its movement. Many times the pan-and-zoom effect looks better if there is some slowing down and acceleration between keyframes, creating an ease-in and ease-out around the keyframes. This appears more natural, more organic.

To change the keyframe interpolation:

1. Click the SHOW/HIDE KEYFRAME GRAPHS BUTTON in the bottom-right corner of the Effect Editor.

   Keyframe tracks appear to the right of the parameter sliders.

2. Right-click the master keyframe track at the top, which reads FrameFlex, and choose SPLINE from the pop-up menu, as shown in Figure 8.10.

   To restore the original animation mode, select Linear.

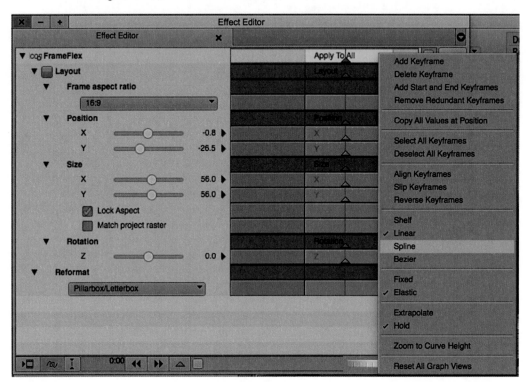

Figure 8.10 Right-click on the top-most track and select Spline to add easing around all keyframes.

  You will learn more about the four different animation modes of Shelf, Linear, Spline, and Bézier – aka, keyframe interpolation options – in upcoming lessons.

  Exercise Break: Exercise 8.1
Pause here to practice what you've learned.

Review/Discussion Questions

1. What is the name of the function used to create pan-and-zoom effects, described in this lesson?

2. How do you access the Source Settings dialog box?

3. Name two Source Settings.

4. How can you tell that a Source Setting is acting on a segment in the Timeline?

5. What is the difference between modifying FrameFlex as a Source Setting rather than in the Timeline using the Effect Editor?

6. If you reframe a shot using FrameFlex on a clip in a bin, after placing it in the sequence, how can you update the segment in the Timeline to show the change?

7. True or False: Using FrameFlex is a one-time option. Once you apply the reframing, a file is created, and you can no longer reframe the native high-resolution clip.

8. What is the name of the animation mode (keyframe interpolation) that creates an ease-in / ease-out behavior around the keyframes?

Making Corrections to Shots

In this exercise, you will use FrameFlex to resize shots and add camera movement to high resolution shots in the Timeline.

Media Used: Ah San Francisco

Duration: 45 minutes

GOALS

- Reformat clips using FrameFlex
- Use AMA Source Settings to create a look
- Pan and zoom over a still photo

Exercise 8.1: Using Frame Flex to Modify Shots in the Timeline

In this exercise, we will use Frame Flex to resize shots, and add camera movement to shots in the Timeline without any loss of quality to the image.

For this exercise, we will use the **MC110_EFFECTS** project.

1. Begin by launching Media Composer and loading the **MC110_EFFECTS** project.

2. Open the **STUDENT_LESSON SEQUENCES** bin.

3. Duplicate the sequence **8.1_AH SAN FRAN_FRAME FLEX** and drag the duplicate into the **EFFECTS_EXERCISE SEQUENCES** bin.

4. Load the duplicated **8.1_AH SAN FRAN_FRAME FLEX** sequence into the Timeline.

5. Choose **TOOLS > MARKERS** to pull up a list of notes the Producer of "Ah San Francisco" has left you regarding changes that need to be made to the shot in the **8.1_AH SAN FRAN_FRAME FLEX** sequence.

#		Marker Name	TC	End	Track	Part	Comment
0001	⊙	Producer	01:00:04:29		V1		Zoom into cars and crop by ??%
0002	⊙	Producer	01:00:08:10		V1		Zoom into cars and crop by ??%
0003	⊙	Producer	01:00:18:28		V1		Create a gentle push in here.
0004	⊙	Producer	01:00:21:01		V1		Zoom and crop to bridge, create a zoom out move and pan across the clouds

Markers - 8.1_AH SAN FRAN_FRAME FLEX

Figure 8.11 Markers window displaying the Producers notes.

Start with the first note. The Producer needs you to resize the shot by zooming in 25%.

6. To resize the shot using the Frame Flex, park your position indicator in the Timeline on the shot that needs to be resized, and pull up the Effect Editor by clicking the **EFFECT MODE BUTTON**.

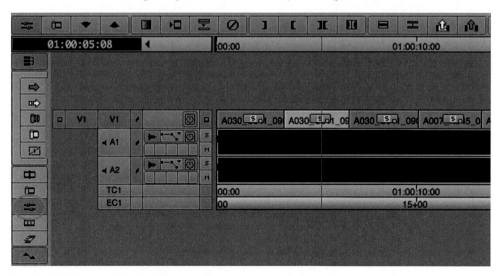

Figure 8.12 The position indicator is parked on the shot that needs to be resized.

7. Click the arrow next to Frame Flex in the Effect Editor to open your parameters.

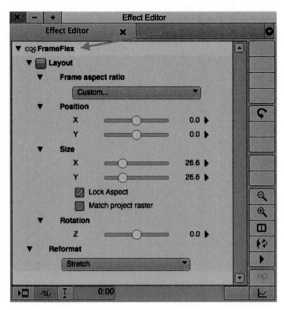

Figure 8.13 Click the arrow next to FrameFlex to display the parameters.

8. Click the **MATCH PROJECT RASTER BOX** in the Effect Editor.

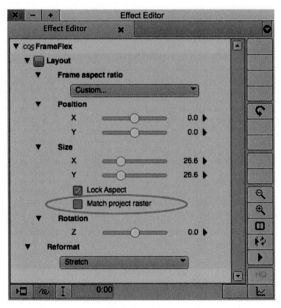

Figure 8.14 Select the "Match project raster" option.

You will now see a box appear in the Effect monitor to the right and the result of zooming into the source image on the left.

Figure 8.15   A box appears in the Effect monitor to the right and the result of zooming into the source image on the left.

The Effect monitor on the right allows you to see the portion of the native image you are working with, while the Effect Analysis monitor on the left will show you how your changes will appear.

9.   To zoom in and crop the image by 25%, click the SLIDER under SIZE and TYPE in the number **75**. Make sure the box LOCK ASPECT is checked.

You are now cropped to 75% of the original image size.

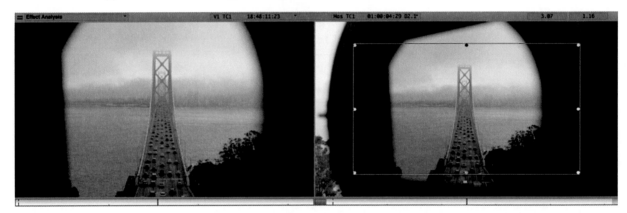

Figure 8.16   You are now cropped to 75% of the original image size.

10. Use the Position sliders to adjust to the part of the frame you want to see.

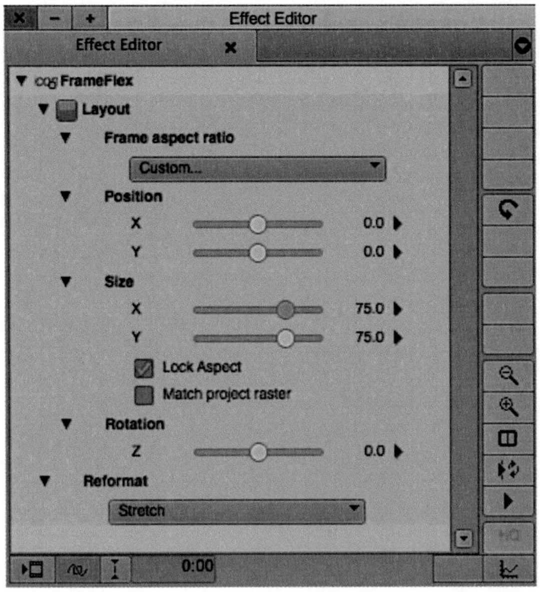

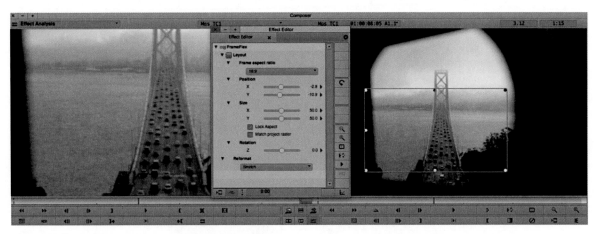

Figure 8.17 Click and drag the X and Y Position slider to adjust the part of the frame you want to see.

11. Move on to the next note and use the same technique to zoom and crop the shot by 50%.

Figure 8.18 Zooming and cropping the shot by 50%.

12. Read the third note.

The Producer needs you to add a camera move that does not already exist in the shot. You will need to use Frame Flex and keyframing to create a "gentle push" into the shot.

13. First, open the shot in the **EFFECT EDITOR**.

14. Click the **MATCH PROJECT RASTER** box in the Effect Editor.

15. Move the SLIDER in the SIZE parameter until you resize the crop to see as much of the image as possible.

    Under Size, the X and Y parameters will become set to 100.0 (100% of the original source frame).

Figure 8.19 After moving the SLIDER in the SIZE parameter you can see as much of the image as possible.

16. Next, create a keyframe at the beginning of the shot using the KEYFRAME BUTTON.

    This is the starting point of your camera move.

17. Create a second keyframe at the end of the shot.

    This is the ending point of your camera move.

Figure 8.20 Adding a keyframe at the beginning and end of the shot.

18. Activate the second keyframe by selecting it.

    You will know the keyframe is active when it is pink.

19. In the Effect Editor, select CENTER CROP from the Reformat parameter.

20. Use the SIZE parameter in the Effect Editor to set the size at **95**.

    The Producer has called for a "gentle push," so the size change is small.

21. Ensure the second keyframe is active, and then move the wireframe to the top, right corner of the image until it cannot be moved any farther.

22. Close out of the Effect Editor and play through your changes.

23. (Optional) Re-adjust the parameters of the second keyframe until you are happy with the result.

24. Now that you know how to keyframe a camera move, use what you have learned to apply a crop and keyframe a camera move to complete note #4.

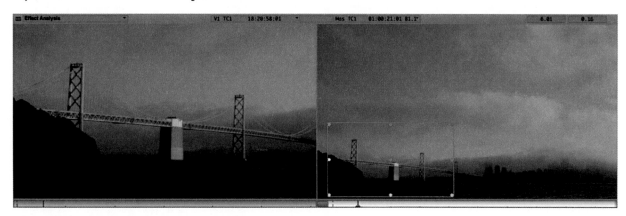

Figure 8.21 Cropping the shot using FrameFlex.

Remember:

- Make a keyframe at each point you would like the camera movement to begin.

- If you want to hold a move, copy/paste parameters from one keyframe to another.

- You can move the placement of keyframes by holding down the Alt (Windows) or Option (Mac) key, then click and drag with your mouse.

- The last keyframe is where you would like your move to end.

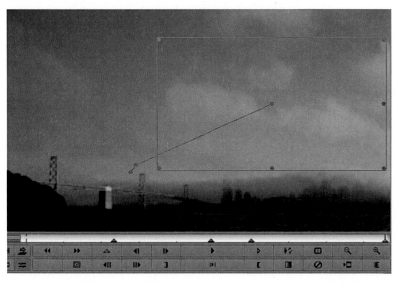

Figure 8.22 Keyframes added to your shot at each point you would like camera movement.

Creative Retiming Effects

When putting a scene together, sometimes the original timing of the shot needs to be adjusted. Media Composer includes tools for creating constant-speed motion effects, plus an advanced retiming effect called Timewarp capable of creating very high-quality speed ramping to visibly change the speed of the clip on screen.

In this lesson, you will briefly review the use of Motion Effects then go on to learn to use Timewarps to create dynamic, eye-catching effects that boost the impact of your video.

Media Used: TN Parkour

Duration: 60 minutes

GOALS

- Explore the different types of motion effects
- Review the use of Motion Effects
- Create motion effects with Fit to Fill and Trim to Fill
- Use a Timewarp preset
- Use a Timewarp as a corrective effect

Review of Freeze Frames and Motion Effects

Motion effects vary the speed at which frames from clips play. Media Composer can create three different types of motion effects:

- **Freeze frames:** Appear to stop playback, "freezing" the image on screen for a period of time. These are created using a master clip or subclip in the Source monitor and create a new clip containing only the desired frame.

- **Motion effects:** Used to speed up or slow down the action in the original video. The speed of playback is constant, albeit faster or slower than the original. These are also created using a master clip or subclip in the Source monitor.

- **Timewarp effects:** A motion effect that allows for speed ramping, where the rate of speed visibly changes. These are applied to a segment in the Timeline in the same way you have applied other segment effects, like Mask or Resize.

You learned about Freeze Frames and Motion Effects in the previous course, MC101. Before we turn our attention to Timewarp effects, let's briefly review how to create Freeze Frames and traditional Motion Effects.

Creating Freeze Frames

A Freeze Frame, of course, stops all motion in the video clip. Since playback of the sequence cannot be paused for a set period of time to freeze the image, we can create and render a new video clip that contains just the one frame we want to see.

As you may remember, to create a Freeze Frame:

1. Load the desired clip into the Source monitor.

    If the clip is already in the Timeline, park over it and use Match Frame.

2. Move the position indicator to the desired frame, then right-click on the Source monitor and choose FREEZE FRAME > [DURATION].

3. Select the DRIVE on which to store the new video file you are creating and click OK.

    The new "FF" clip appears in the bin and is automatically loaded into the Source monitor.

4. Mark the freeze frame clip and edit it to your sequence, using standard editing techniques.

In Media Composer v8.6, the default render method is Interpolation, which is preferable for most freeze frames. If you want to change the render method, do so in the menu before selecting the duration to create the Freeze Frame.

Creating Motion Effects

With traditional Motion Effects, you control the frame rate at which a clip plays, resulting in fast or slow motion. The speed is constant, with no visible change throughout the clip.

Let's review how to create a standard motion effect.

To create a Motion Effect:

1. Load the clip to be adjusted into the Source monitor.

   If the clip is already in the Timeline, do this using Match Frame.

2. Mark the portion of the clip you wish to use in the Motion Effect.

3. Choose **MOTION EFFECT** from the Composer window's **FAST** menu, shown in Figure 9.1.

Figure 9.1 Motion Effect button.

4. Choose **OPTIONS** you want in the Motion Effect dialog box, shown in Figure 9.2.

5. Click **CREATE AND RENDER**, and then select the **BIN** and **DRIVE** on which to save the new clip and media.

   A new motion effect clip is created and appears both in the bin and in the Source monitor, ready for editing.

6. Edit the clip to the Timeline.

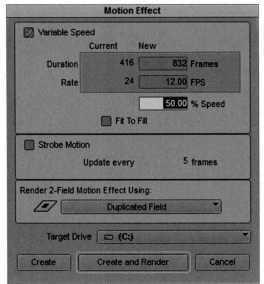

Figure 9.2 The Motion Effect dialog box.

 Exercise Break: Exercise 9.1
Pause here to practice what you've learned.

Creating Motion Effects to Fill a Duration

There are times when the duration of a motion effect will be more important than its speed. For example, you need a B-roll shot to hold slightly longer to finish a soundbite, or you want to slow a shot to add drama, but also make the start and end coincide with a music cue.

For scenarios like these, Media Composer offers two solutions:

- **Fit to Fill:** A traditional Motion Effect that uses four marks – two in Source, and two in the Timeline – to create and render a new clip that fits exactly within the marked duration in the Timeline.

- **Trim to Fill:** A Timewarp effect that enables you to adjust the speed of a clip by changing its duration in the Timeline using the trim tools.

Using Fit to Fill

Remember, Fit to Fill breaks the three-point editing convention and requires four marks, which define two separate durations. Media Composer will calculate the difference between them to create the effect.

In the MC101 course, you used the Fit to Fill option in the Motion Effect window. An easier way to use this tool is to map the Fit to Fill button to your keyboard or Source monitor. It is available in the Command Palette > Edit tab, as shown in Figure 9.3.

Figure 9.3 The Fit to Fill button appears in the Edit tab of the Command Palette.

To create a Fit to Fill motion effect:

1. Mark **IN AND OUT** in the Timeline to mark a video segment or duration in the sequence where you want the motion effect to appear.

2. Load a **CLIP** in the Source monitor.
    If it is from a clip that is already in the Timeline, park over the segment and use Match Frame.

3. Mark an **IN** and **OUT** on the clip in the Source monitor.

4. Click the **FIT TO FILL** button or press the key to which you mapped it.

5. Select the **BIN** and **DRIVE** on which to save the new clip and media, and click OK in each of the dialog windows.
    The system creates the motion effect clip and edits it into the sequence.

 Exercise Break: Exercise 9.2
Pause here to practice what you've learned.

Using Trim to Fill

As mentioned, Trim to Fill adjusts the speed of the clip as the segment is made longer or shorter, using the Trim tools. It is a standard segment affect, found in the Timewarp category of the Effect Palette, as seen in Figure 9.4.

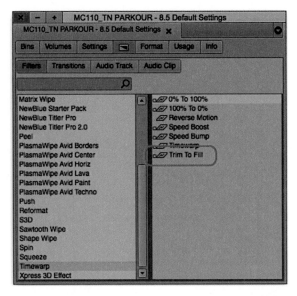

Figure 9.4 The Trim to Fill effect appears in the Timewarp category.

Trim to Fill is often used as a problem-solving effect. It is the kind of thing you reach for later in the edit process when you find you want to see all the frames in a segment (and only those specific frames), but you need it to be just a little longer or shorter and the tradeoff in changing the speed slightly doesn't matter.

You can, of course, use Trim to Fill creatively as an alternative to Fit to Fill. For example, if cutting a music video and you want to retime a shot to fit a phrase in the song or a bar in the music, you could just as easily edit a shot to the Timeline and then apply a Trim to Fill.

One advantage to using Trim to Fill instead of Fit to Fill is that it is a real-time effect, giving you the freedom to experiment with the timing of the effect without re-rendering each time.

To use Trim to Fill:

1. Open the Effect Palette and select the Timewarp category.

2. Drag the Trim to Fill effect to the segment to be adjusted.

3. Enter Trim mode and trim the clip to the desired length.

    In this case, trimming does not add or remove frames to the segment. Instead, Media Composer "stretches" or "compresses" the segment, so to speak. If it stretches it out to a longer duration, the clip plays slower. If it compresses it to a shorter duration, it plays faster. This change in speed is displayed as a percentage on the segment, in parenthesis next to the clip name, as shown in Figure 9.5.

Because no frames are added or removed from the segment you're trimming, your choice of which trim mode to use – single-roller Ripple or Overwrite, or a dual-roller trim – is based only how you want to affect the other segments affected by the edit.

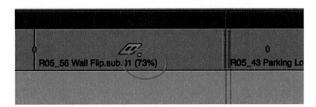

Figure 9.5 The percent change in speed is visible on the segment.

  The render method applied to Fit to Fill and Trim to Fill effects can be configured in the Settings window > Render settings. Set the default render method for all new effects by using the menus labeled "Motion Effects Render Using:," and "Timewarps Render Using:".

  Exercise Break: Exercise 9.3
Pause here to practice what you've learned.

Creating Timewarp Effects

Timewarp effects are an advanced type of motion effect. They differ from traditional motion effects in several ways:

■ Timewarp effects are applied to segments in a sequence, not to original source clips.

■ Timewarp effects do not change the duration of a segment in the Timeline. The duration is modified using standard trim techniques.

■ Timewarp effects do not have a fixed rate of speed. The speed can be varied over time. You can use keyframes to set multiple rates of speed, and the software will smoothly ramp between them. Optionally, you can specify start and end frames, and the software will calculate the rate required.

■ Timewarp effects contain additional, higher-quality render methods. These new methods add the capability to blend field data, potentially resulting in much smoother motion.

■ Timewarp effects are real-time effects. You can freely experiment with the effect and play it back immediately, rather than waiting for it to render after each change.

■ Timewarps need to be rendered if one of the following conditions is true:

• if the motion is reversed

• if the play rate exceeds 1400%

• if Bézier keyframes are used

• or, if the render type is set to FluidMotion

Timewarp Preset Effects

Media Composer ships with a number of prebuilt Timewarp effects. These are accessible via the Timewarp category in the Effect Palette. (See Figure 9.6)

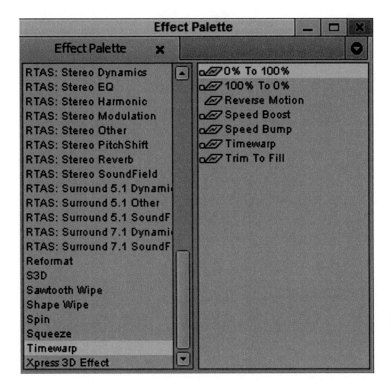

Figure 9.6 The Timewarp category in the Effect Palette contains a number of prebuilt effects.

Most of the preset effects are designed to generate variable-speed motion effects. For example, the 0% to 100% preset ramps the speed gradually between a freeze frame and the clip's native speed. The 100% to 0% preset does the opposite, gradually slowing down from the clip's native speed until stopping at a freeze frame.

An extremely useful preset is Reverse Motion. This enables you to instantly reverse the motion of a clip that you've already inserted into the Timeline. Depending on the type of work you do, this may become one of your "go-to" effects.

To apply a Timewarp preset:

1. Choose **TOOLS > EFFECT PALETTE** to open the Effect Palette.

2. Click the **TIMEWARP** category.

3. Select a **PRESET** and drag it onto a segment in the Timeline.

4. Play back the effect to view the results.

    Note: Only if you have chosen the Reverse Motion will you need to render.

5.   (Optional) Place the POSITION INDICATOR on the segment; then click the RENDER EFFECT button in the Timeline button bar.

Timewarp presets are designed to use all the frames, and only the frames, that were visible in the segment when you applied the effect. In other words, a preset will not change what's visible in the segment, only change its speed. This explains why with the Speed Bump, for example, not only slows the shot in the middle of the segment, but also speeds it up at the beginning and the end of the clip to compensate. Sometimes this is acceptable, sometimes not.

For full manual control, you will want to use the Timewarp effect itself.

Creating a Timewarp Effect

Among the preset effects, you will find the generic effect, Timewarp. Like the Resize or Mask effects, Timewarp is a "neutral" effect, and has no immediate impact on the image.

To create an effect, you must manipulate its unique parameters. The Timewarp effect has its own editing window, called the Motion Effect Editor. After you apply the Timewarp effect to a segment in the Timeline, you can open it by clicking either the Motion Effect Editor button or the Effect Mode button.

To apply and edit the Timewarp effect:

1.   Drag the TIMEWARP effect from the Effect Palette to a segment in the Timeline.

2.   Click the EFFECT MODE button or the MOTION EFFECT EDITOR BUTTON in the Timeline Palette, as shown in Figure 9.7.

The Motion Effect Editor will open, as shown in Figure 9.8.

Figure 9.7   To edit a Timewarp effect, you can click either the Effect Mode button, or the Motion Effect Editor button.

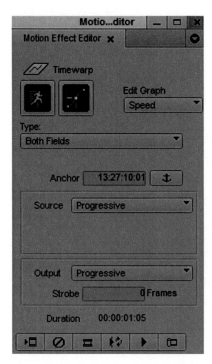

Figure 9.8 The Motion Effect Editor.

You may recognize a few of the controls immediately, based on your experience with the traditional Motion Effect dialog box. But, the real work of using the Motion Effect Editor is done via two pop-out graphs, the Speed graph and the Position graph. (We'll primarily cover the speed graph in this course.)

The Speed Graph and Position Graph icons are the large buttons visible in the top-left corner of the window. Clicking either button expands the Motion Effect Editor to reveal the actual graph, as shown in Figure 9.9.

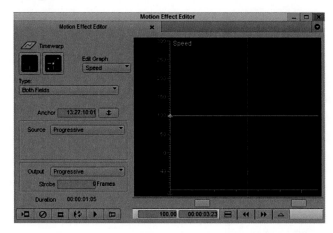

Figure 9.9 The Motion Effect Editor with the speed graph displayed.

 While you can view both the Speed and Position graphs simultaneously, you can only use one or the other to control the effect. The Edit Graph menu indicates which you are using. If you change it, the effect will reset to its default settings.

Understanding the Speed Graph

The speed graph allows you to set the speed of the Timewarp effect using keyframes. For illustrative purposes, Figure 9.10 uses the graph of the 100% to 0% Timewarp preset.

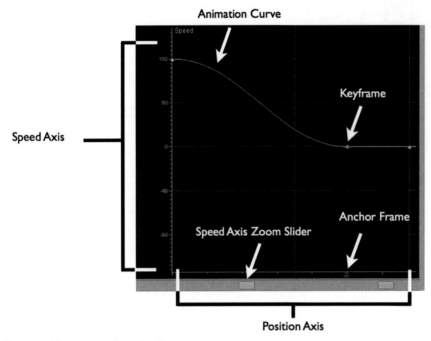

Figure 9.10 The speed graph's functions.

Features of the Speed graph include:

- **Speed axis:** Displays a range of speeds available. 100 is equal to sound speed (29.97 fps in NTSC, 25 fps in PAL). By default, the speed axis displays speeds between 300% and –100%.

- **Speed Axis Zoom slider:** Zooms in and out on the speed axis. Drag left to reveal additional rates of speed and right to show fewer rates of speed.

- **Effect position axis:** Displays position information. By default, the effect position axis displays only the duration of the effect.

- **Position Axis Zoom slider:** Zooms in and out on the effect position axis. Drag left to reveal position information beyond the effect duration and right to zoom in on the effect duration.

- **Animation curve:** Indicates the speed or change in speed created with the Timewarp effect. Drag the position indicator to see the speed at any point along the curve.

- **Keyframe:** Used to set the rate of speed at a given position.

- **Anchor frame:** Indicates the point where the source footage is anchored in the effect.

 After zooming in and out, the curve can become offset partially offscreen. To reposition the curve within the graph, hold the Alt key (Windows) or Option key (Mac) and drag the curve to the desired position.

Choosing a Render Type

The Type menu allows you to choose the render method used to create the Timewarp effect. The menu contains the same render methods you have used with standard, constant rate motion effects, plus several additional ones, as shown in Figure 9.11.

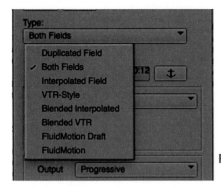

Figure 9.11 The Timewarp effect contains additional, higher-quality render types..

The motion effect icon not only indicates that the clip is a motion effect, but it also relates the render method used to generate it. This extra bit of information is extremely useful in the later stages of editing, especially if a previous editor used the wrong type of motion effect. Table 9.1 shows the different icons and what they indicate.

Table 9.1 Timewarp Effect Icons

Icon	Render Method	Icon	Render Method
	Duplicated field		Blended Interpolated
	Both fields		Blended VTR
	Interpolated field		FluidMotion Draft
	VTR-style		FluidMotion

Keyframing a Timewarp Effect

All Timewarp effects have a single keyframe at the beginning of the effect. Additional keyframes can be added, using the same basic process you have already learned: move the position indicator to the desired location and click the Add Keyframe button. Keyframes are added and manipulated in the Motion Effect Editor, and in this case, the Speed graph.

Dragging a keyframe up or down changes the rate of speed; similar to entering a value in the Motion Effect dialog box. If you work with the single keyframe that appears on the clip by default, you can speed up or slow down the clip at a constant speed. The advantage to doing it with the Timewarp versus a Motion Effect is that it is a real-time change. You can keep playing and adjusting the clip until it's perfect, without having to render.

Instead of limiting you to one rate of speed for the entire segment, in the Motion Effect Editor, you can add multiple keyframes, each with a different percentage speed value. As with any keyframe, the system will automatically calculate – or *interpolate* – the values between the keyframes. This creates a ramp in speed.

To add a Timewarp keyframe:

1. Place the **POSITION BAR** in the Motion Effect Editor on a desired frame.

2. Click the **ADD KEYFRAME** button in the lower-right region of the Timewarp Editor to add a keyframe to the current frame. (See Figure 9.12.)

Figure 9.12 Add Keyframe button.

As you drag keyframes up and down in the graph, you can see the exact value you are moving to via the green indicator at the top-left of the graph, as shown in Figure 9.13.

Figure 9.13 The speed value indicator.

Using the Anchor Frame

When you add multiple keyframes, at some point you may want to ensure that a Timewarp effect does not shift the position of a specific frame. To achieve this, you can designate a keyframe as an anchor. (See Figure 9.14.) This is especially useful when you want to sync a particular action in the effect to a cue in the music.

The anchor ensures that a given source frame will be held to a specific point in the Timeline. You can only designate one frame as the anchor.

To set the Anchor frame:

1. Apply the Timewarp effect to a segment in the sequence, and then open the **MOTION EFFECT EDITOR** to manipulate it.

2. Open the **SPEED GRAPH**.

3. Drag the position indicator in the Speed graph to the frame you want to designate as the anchor frame. Add a keyframe at that location.

4. Click the **SET ANCHOR BUTTON**, shown in Figure 9.16.

   It is important to set the Anchor frame *before* adding any other keyframes.

Figure 9.14 The Set Anchor button.

Types of Keyframe Interpolation

By default, keyframes are set to create a smooth change in speed between any two keyframes. Though this is the default type of animation method (called interpolation), there are actually four different types:

- **Linear:** Creates a direct path between two keyframe values. With the linear method, the rate of change is continuous between the two keyframes, and there is no gradual acceleration ("ease-in") or deceleration ("ease-out") from one keyframe into another. (See Figure 9.15.)

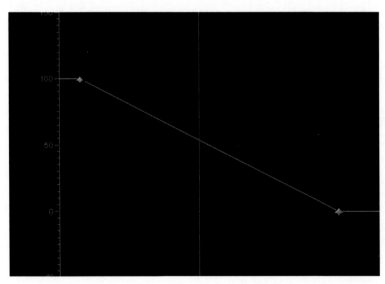

Figure 9.15 Linear keyframes.

■ **Spline:** Creates a path with a natural ease-in and ease-out at every keyframe. The amount of ease-in and ease-out is automatically calculated to create a smooth transition into and out of keyframes and cannot be adjusted. (See Figure 9.16.)

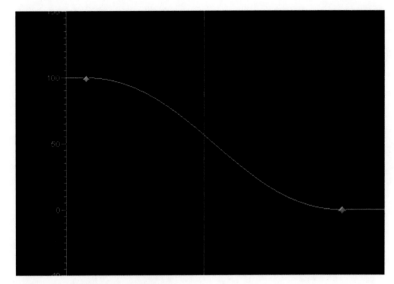

Figure 9.16 Spline keyframes.

■ **Bézier:** Creates a path with a natural ease-in and ease-out at every keyframe. Unlike spline interpolation, the shape of the animation curve can be adjusted on either side of the keyframe by manipulating the Bézier curve handles. (See Figure 9.17.) Bézier curves are not covered in this class, but you can learn more about them in the Avid Media Composer Help.

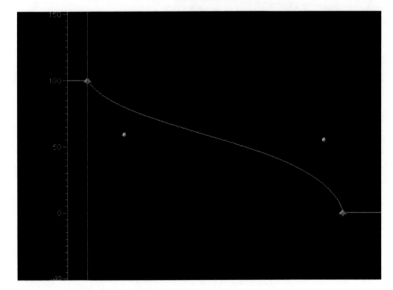

Figure 9.17 Bézier keyframes.

- **Shelf:** Holds a keyframe's value until the next keyframe. This interpolation type is used to cause the parameter to jump instantly from one value to another. (See Figure 9.18.)

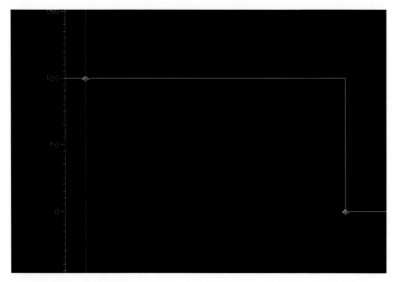

Figure 9.18 Shelf keyframes.

To change the interpolation method:

- Right-click on a KEYFRAME in the graph and select a new type from the pop-up menu.

 Hold the Alt+Shift (Windows) or Option+Shift (Mac) keys down while dragging the keyframe to move it to an earlier or later frame in the clip.

 Exercise Break: Exercise 9.4
Pause here to practice what you've learned.

Review/Discussion Questions

1. What are the three types of motion effects?

2. How are freeze frames created?

   a. They are generated from a source clip.

   b. They are applied to a clip in the sequence.

3. How are motion effects created?

   a. They are generated from a source clip.

   b. They are applied to a clip in the sequence.

4. How does creating a motion effect via the Fit to Fill command differ from creating one via the Motion Effect command?

5. How are Timewarp effects created?

   a. They are generated from a source clip.

   b. They are applied to a clip in the sequence.

6. What are the four different types of keyframe interpolations?

Creative Retiming Effects

In this exercise, you will create motion effects, freeze frames and Timewarp effects to enhance the sequences. Have fun!

Media Used: TN Parkour

Duration: 90 minutes

GOALS

- Create freeze frame effects

- Create traditional motion effects

- Use Fit to Fill and Trim to Fill

- Create a series of Timewarp effects whose motion is synchronized with anchor frames to specific locations in the Timeline

- Use different interpolation methods to create different types of motion in the effect

Exercise 9.1: Adding Motion Effects to the TN Parkour Montage

In this exercise, we will create a freeze frame and motion effects and edit them into the TN Parkour Montage we created in a previous exercise.

Media Used: TN Parkour

Duration: 30 minutes

For this exercise, we will use the **MC110_TN PARKOUR** project.

1. Once you have opened your project, begin by opening the bin **STUDENT_LESSON SEQUENCES**.

2. Duplicate the sequence **9.1_TNPARKOUR MONTAGE_MOTION FX** and move the duplicate into the **TN PARKOUR_EXERCISE SEQUENCES** bin.

3. Load the duplicate **9.1_TNPARKOUR MONTAGE_MOTION FX** into the Timeline.

   You will notice the Producer has made markers in the sequence that contains notes regarding some motion effects that need to be added to the piece.

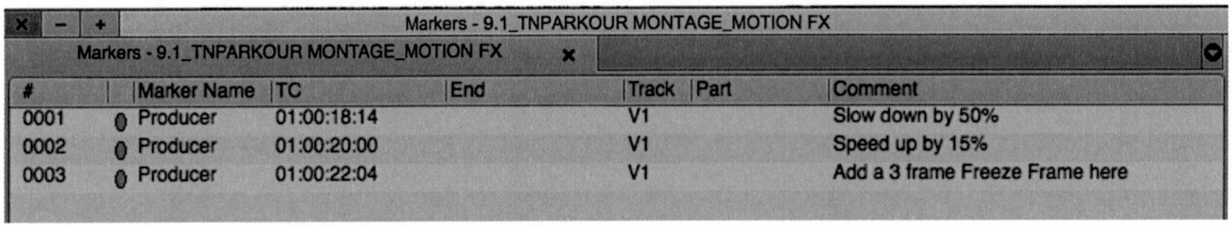

#		Marker Name	TC	End	Track	Part	Comment
0001	◍	Producer	01:00:18:14		V1		Slow down by 50%
0002	◍	Producer	01:00:20:00		V1		Speed up by 15%
0003	◍	Producer	01:00:22:04		V1		Add a 3 frame Freeze Frame here

Markers - 9.1_TNPARKOUR MONTAGE_MOTION FX

Figure 9.19 The Markers window displaying markers and the Producer's notes.

4. Go through each marker and read the notes.

   You can pull up a list of the markers by navigating to **TOOLS > MARKERS**.

5. Create a new bin and label it **TNPARKOUR_MOTION FX**.

6. Let's start with the first note, "Slow down by 50%", by parking your position indicator on the first marker.

7. Open the Fast menu located between the Source and Record monitors and click the **MATCH FRAME BUTTON**.

Figure 9.20 The Match Frame button off the Fast menu in between the Source and Record monitor.

   The subclip for "R01_25_Around Corner" will now load into the Source monitor.

8. Set a mark **IN** and **OUT** at the beginning and end of the subclip.

9. To create a new clip that is 50% slower, click the **MOTION EFFECT BUTTON**, located in the Fast menu between the Source and Record monitors.

Figure 9.21 The Motion Effect button off the Fast menu in between the Source and Record monitor.

The Motion Effect dialog box will open.

10. In the Motion Effect dialog box, choose to render **BOTH FIELDS**.

The default option is to create a motion effect that slows the clip down 50%, so you can leave that option as is.

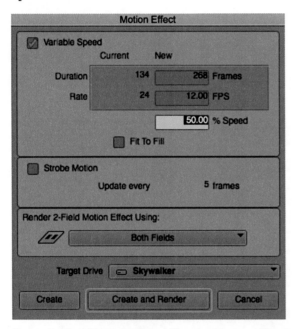

Figure 9.22 Selecting Both Fields in the Motion Effect dialog.

11. Click **CREATE AND RENDER** to create the new clip with the motion effect.

A Select window opens asking you to choose where to put this new clip.

12. Select **TNPARKOUR_MOTION FX**.

Figure 9.23 Select "TNPARKOUR_MOTION FX" from the Select dialog.

Your new clip will load automatically in the Source monitor. Because the clip is 50% slower, it will be longer than the original clip in the Timeline.

Figure 9.24 The new clip loaded into the Source monitor.

13. In the Timeline, enable only the V1 track and then select the original **R01_AROUND CORNER** and press the **T KEY**.

    This will mark IN and OUT points around the clip in the Timeline.

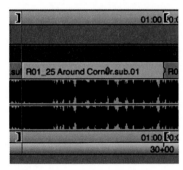

Figure 9.25 IN and OUT marks added around the clip in the Timeline using the T key.

14. In the Source monitor, mark in **IN** using the **I KEY** at the location you would like the shot to begin. **OVERWRITE** the new, slowed down clip into the Timeline using the **B KEY**.

    Make sure the V1 track is active, but that the A1 and A2 tracks are turned off so that you don't disturb your music track.

    Your new clip will now appear in the Timeline with a motion effect icon on it.

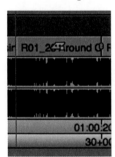

Figure 9.26 Your new clip will in the Timeline with a motion effect icon on it.

15. Play through the clip and its accompanying transitions.

    You can make adjustments to the timing of your new shot within the piece by slipping the shot directly in the Timeline.

16. Park the position indicator anywhere on the clip in the Timeline and use the Trim keys on your keyboard.

 Figure 9.27 Trim keys.

17. Repeat steps 6-13 for the next Producer's note for the shot at 01:00:20:00 to "Speed up by 15%."

18. This time, when the Motion Effect dialog appears, type **115** into **% SPEED** to speed the shot up to 115%.

19. To create the freeze frame at 01:00:22:04, park the position indicator on the marker in the Timeline.

Figure 9.28 The position indicator parked on the marker in the Timeline.

20. Open the Fast menu located between the Source and Record monitors and click the MATCH FRAME BUTTON.

    The subclip for "R05_43 Parking Lot Cris Cross Flip" will load into the Source monitor.

21. Right-click on the Source monitor and choose FREEZE FRAME >5 SECONDS.

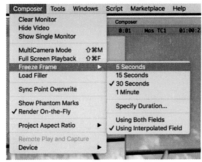

Figure 9.29 Selecting Freeze Frame > 5 Seconds from the Composer menu.

    You will then be prompted to render the effect to your media drive and to select a bin to save the freeze frame to.

22. Choose TN PARKOUR_MOTION FX.

Figure 9.30 Selecting "TN PARKOUR_MOTION FX" from the Select dialog.

Your freeze frame will be created and loaded automatically into the Source monitor.

23. In your **SOURCE MONITOR**, Mark an **IN**, using the **I** KEY. Move the position indicator ahead **2 FRAMES** and Mark an **OUT** using the **O** KEY.

24. In the **TIMELINE**, mark an **IN** at **01:00:22:04** where your marker is located.

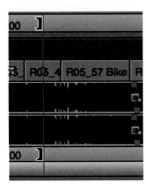

Figure 9.31 A mark IN added at 01:00:22:04 in the Timeline.

25. **SPLICE** your freeze frame into the Timeline using the **V** KEY.

    Because the Sync Locks are enabled, this will also splice filler into the music track.

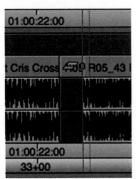

Figure 9.32 A splice used on your freeze frame in the Timeline.

26. Play through the shot and the shots that follow. They will now be shifted down by 3 frames.

27. Make any necessary adjustments to the music and to the timing of the piece using Trim mode.

Exercise 9.2: Using Fit to Fill

In this exercise, we'll use the motion effect "Fit to Fill" to lengthen or shorten shots in the Timeline as needed.

Media Used: TN Parkour

Duration: 15 minutes

For this exercise, we will continue using the **MC110_TN PARKOUR** project.

1. Begin by opening the bin **STUDENT_LESSON SEQUENCES**.

2. Duplicate the sequence **9.2_TNPARKOUR MONTAGE_FIT TO FILL** and move the duplicate into the **TN PARKOUR_EXERCISE SEQUENCES** bin.

3. Load the duplicate **9.2_TNPARKOUR MONTAGE_FIT TO FILL**.

4. Pull up the Producer's notes. Choose **TOOLS > MARKERS**.

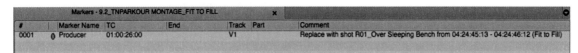

Figure 9.33 The Markers window displaying markers and the Producer's notes.

The Producer has specified a shot that needs to be replaced as well as the specific timecodes in the replacement shot for the IN and OUT marks.

5. To find the shot the Producer wants, use **CTRL + F** (Windows) or **COMMAND + F** (Mac) to open the Finder window.

6. Type **R01_16 OVER SLEEPING BENCH** and click **FIND**.

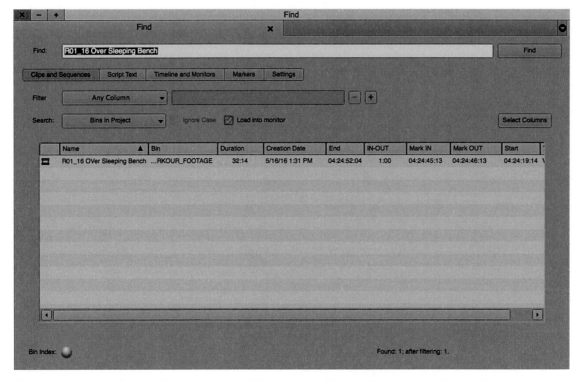

Figure 9.34 The results found from the search of "R01_16 Over Sleeping Bench" in the Find window.

7. Double-click the **R01_16 Over Sleeping Bench** clip in the Find window to load it into the Source monitor.

    The bin that contains the "R01_16 Over Sleeping Bench" clip also opens.

8. Type the timecode, specified by the Producer's notes into the Source monitor, and then mark your **IN** and **OUT** points.

Figure 9.35 The timecode specified by the Producer's notes and the mark IN and OUT points.

The shot you have been asked to replace is longer than the shot that is currently in the Timeline. If you overwrite the shot into the Timeline, you will run over the following shot. If you perform a three-point edit, you will cut off the end of the new shot.

Using Fit to Fill, you can apply a motion effect that will speed up the new shot exactly as much as is needed to fill the space required to replace the shot in the Timeline.

9. In the Timeline, enable only the V1 track and then select the clip you are replacing, **R05_69 Roof Flips.sub.01** and press the **T key** to mark an **IN** and **OUT** point around it.

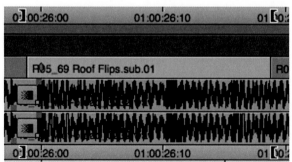

Figure 9.36 IN and OUT marks added around the clip.

10. Select the Source monitor to activate it. With the **R01_16 OVER SLEEPING BENCH** clip still loaded in the Source monitor, click the **MOTION EFFECT BUTTON** from the Fast menu between the Source and Record monitors.

Figure 9.37 The Motion Effect button off the Fast menu in between the Source and Record monitor.

The Motion Effect dialog opens.

11. In the Motion Effect dialog, check the **FIT TO FILL** box and choose to render **BOTH FIELDS**.

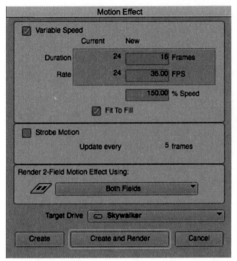

Figure 9.38 The options "Fit to Fill" and "Both Fields" selected in the Motion Effect window

12. Click **CREATE AND RENDER** to create the new clip with the motion effect.

A window opens asking you to choose where to put this new clip.

13. Select **TNPARKOUR_MOTION FX**.

    Your new clip will load automatically in the Source monitor.

Figure 9.39 The "TNPARKOUR_MOTION FX" clip loaded in the Source monitor.

14. The new clip you created is the exact number of frames as marked in the Timeline, and the position indicator is at the beginning, so overwrite the new clip, **R01_16 Over Sleeping Bench (36.00 FPS)** into the Timeline using the **B** KEY.

    Make sure only the V1 track is active, and that the A1 and A2 tracks are turned off so that you don't disturb your music track.

    Your new clip will now appear in the Timeline with a motion effect icon on it.

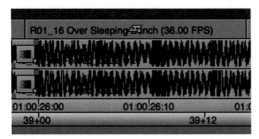

Figure 9.40 The new clip in the Timeline with a motion effect on it.

15. Play through the shot and surrounding transitions.

16. Make any adjustments to pacing as needed by using Trim mode.

Exercise 9.3: Using Trim to Fill

In this exercise, we'll utilize another motion effect tool, "Trim to Fill", that allows us to lengthen or shorten shots in the Timeline as needed.

Media Used: TN Parkour

Duration: 15 minutes

For this exercise, we will continue using the **MC110_TN PARKOUR** project.

1. Begin by opening the bin **STUDENT_LESSON SEQUENCES**.

2. Duplicate the sequence **9.3_TNPARKOUR MONTAGE_TRIM TO FILL** and move the duplicate into the **TN PARKOUR_EXERCISE SEQUENCES** bin.

3. Load the duplicate **9.3_TNPARKOUR MONTAGE_TRIM TO FILL** into the Timeline.

4. Pull up the Producer's notes. Choose **TOOLS > MARKERS**.

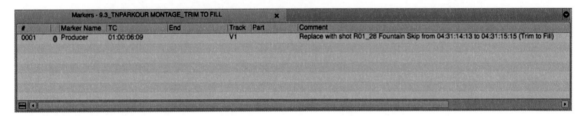

Figure 9.41 The Markers window displaying markers and the Producer's notes.

The Producer has specified a shot that needs to be replaced as well as the timecodes for the IN and OUT points in the replacement source clip.

5. To find the shot the Producer wants, use **CTRL + F** (Windows) or **COMMAND + F** (Mac) to bring up the Find window.

6.   Type **R01_28 FOUNTAIN SKIP** and click **FIND**.

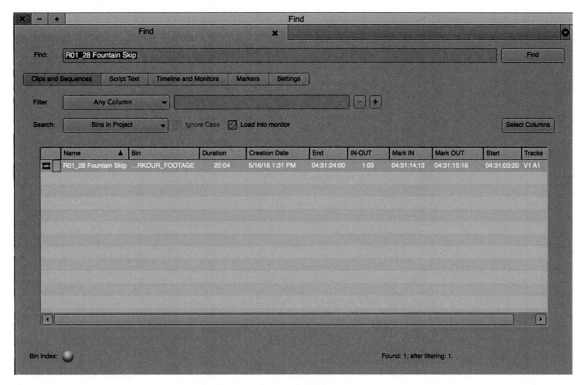

Figure 9.42 The "R01_28 Fountain Skip" clip in the Find window.

7.   Double-click the **R01_28 FOUNTAIN SKIP** clip in the Find window and it will load into the Source monitor.

8.   Type the timecode, specified by the Producer into the Source monitor and mark your **IN** and **OUT** points.

Figure 9.43 The timecode specified by the Producer's notes and the mark IN and OUT points.

9. Go to the Marker in the Timeline at the first shot that needs to be replaced and Mark an **IN** on the head frame (the very first frame) of the shot you will be replacing.

10. Overwrite the new shot into the Timeline using the **B** KEY.

   You will notice the new shot is shorter than the shot that is being replaced.

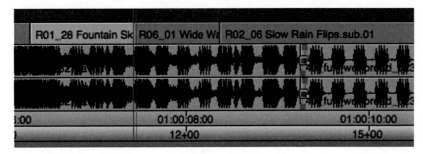

Figure 9.44 The new shot in the Timeline is shorter.

We can lengthen the new shot to fit the required space using "Trim to Fill." The speed of the shot will change relative to the amount it is being stretched or shortened. In this case, the shot will slow down.

11. To apply Trim to Fill, go to your Project window and select the **EFFECTS TAB**.

12. In the left column, select **TIMEWARP** and click the **TRIM TO FILL** effect.

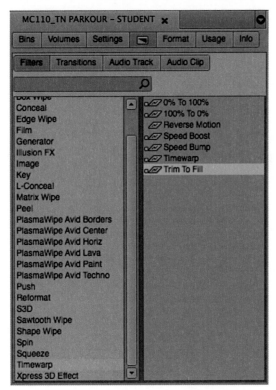

Figure 9.45 The Trim to Fill effect selected from the Effects tab.

13. DRAG the TRIM TO FILL effect onto the **R01_28 FOUNTAIN SKIP** clip in the Timeline.

    A motion effect icon will appear on the clip.

Figure 9.46 The "R01_28 Fountain Skip" clip with the Trim to Fill effect applied to it in the Timeline. A motion effect icon appears on the clip.

14. Using the DOUBLE ROLLER TRIM TOOL, DRAG the end of the **R01_28 FOUNTAIN SKIP** shot until it is the same length as the clip you are replacing.

    Media Composer has a helpful feature where the trim will automatically stop once it hits a transition.

Figure 9.47 The Double Roller Trim tool displayed in the Timeline.

The percentage by which the speed of the shot has changed will appear on the clip in the Timeline.

Figure 9.48 The percentage by which the speed of the shot has changed appears on the clip in the Timeline.

15. Play through the shot and surrounding transitions.

16. Make any adjustments to pacing as needed using Trim mode.

Exercise 9.4: Working with Timewarp Effects

In this exercise, we'll use Timewarp templates and keyframing to create a motion effect that slows down and speeds up action within the same segment.

Media Used: TN Parkour

Duration: 30 minutes

For this exercise, we will continue using the **MC110_TN PARKOUR** project.

1. Begin by opening the bin **STUDENT_LESSON SEQUENCES**.

2. Duplicate the sequence **9.4_TNPARKOUR MONTAGE_TIMEWARP** and move the duplicate into the **TN PARKOUR_EXERCISE SEQUENCES** bin.

3. Load the duplicate **9.4_TNPARKOUR MONTAGE_TIMEWARP** into the Timeline.

4. Pull up the Producer's notes. Choose **TOOLS >MARKERS**.

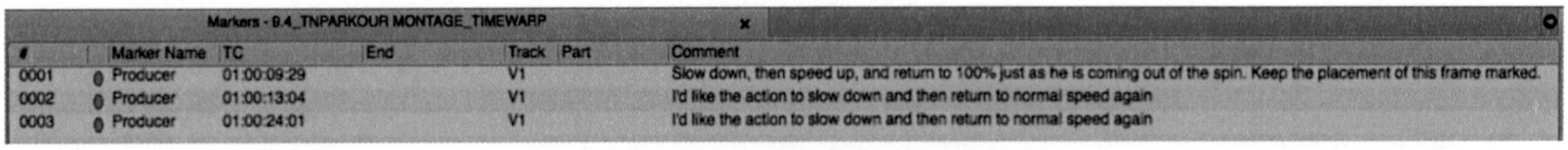

Figure 9.49 The Markers window displaying markers and the Producer's notes.

The Producer has requested that several shots in the TN Parkour Montage slow down and speed up within the same shot. This is a common technique and there are several ways to achieve this.

Let's start with the third note at 01:00:24:01.

5. In your Markers tool, double-click on **NOTE #3**.

   The position indicator will jump to that marker in your Timeline.

   The Producer would like the shot "R05_57 Bike Stands" to speed up and then slow down.

   One of the ways we can do this is to apply the Timewarp effect "Speed Boost."

6. To apply "Speed Boost," go to your Project Window and select the **EFFECTS TAB**.

7.   In the left column, select **TIMEWARP** and click the **SPEED BOOST** effect.

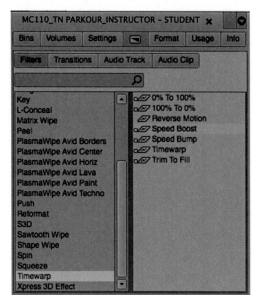

Figure 9.50 The Speed Boost effect selected from the Effects tab.

8.   **DRAG** the **SPEED BOOST** effect onto the **R05_57 BIKE STANDS** clip in the Timeline.

A motion effect icon will appear on the clip.

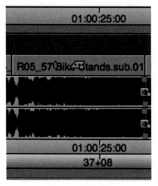

Figure 9.51 The "R05_57 Bike Stands" clip with the Speed Boost effect applied to it in the Timeline. A motion effect icon appears on the clip.

9.   Play through the effect and observe the way it changes the clip.

Let's tackle the second note next at: 01:00:13:04.

10.   Pull up the Producer's notes. Choose **TOOLS > MARKERS**.

The Producer would like the action in the shot "R01_31 Crossing Each Other" to slow down and then return to normal speed. We can use the "Timewarp" effect to keyframe the desired effect.

11.   Go to your Project Window and select the **EFFECTS TAB**.

12. In the left column, select **Timewarp** and click the **Timewarp effect**.

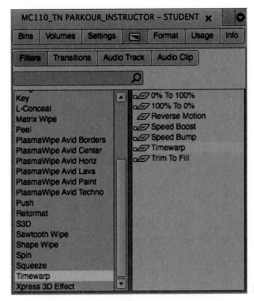

Figure 9.52 The Timewarp effect selected from the Effects tab.

13. Drag the Timewarp effect onto the **R01_31 Crossing Each Other** clip in the Timeline.

    A motion effect icon will appear on the clip.

14. In your Timeline, along the left side, just below the Smart Tool, click the **Motion Effect Editor button** to open the Motion Effect Editor.

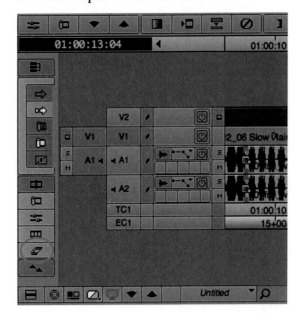

Figure 9.53 The Motion Effect Editor button in the Timeline.

15. In the Motion Effect Editor, click on the Speed Graph icon to expand the Speed Graph.

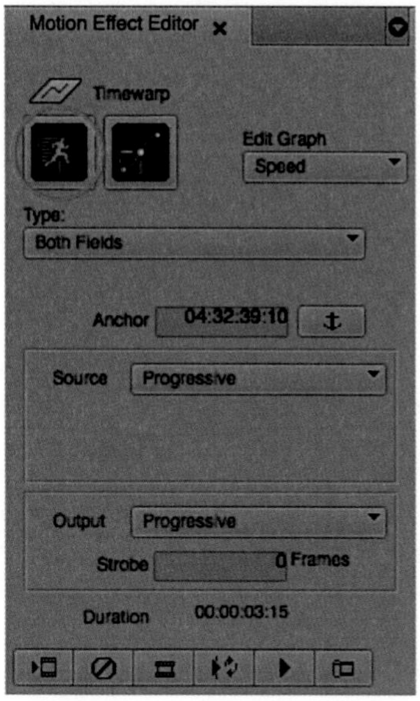

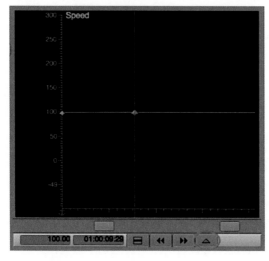

Figure 9.54 The Speed Graph icon in the Motion Effect Editor.

16. In the Speed Graph, move the position indicator to the point at which you would like the shot to be at its slowest point and add a keyframe using the **ADD KEYFRAME BUTTON**.

Figure 9.55 The Add Keyframe button in the Speed Graph.

17. Pull this keyframe down to **50** to slow the shot down by 50%.

18. Find the point at which you would like the shot to return to normal speed and add another keyframe.

19. Pull the new keyframe back up to **100** to return the speed to 100%.

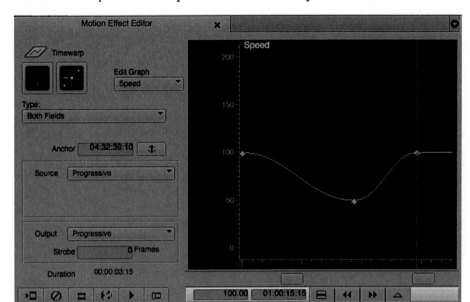

Figure 9.56 The Motion Effect Editor displaying the new keyframes with the speed dipping to 50% and then back up to 100%.

You will notice that the duration of the shot doesn't change in the Timeline, but that the content within the shot will change to accommodate your motion effect.

20. You can make adjustments to the content of the shot by adjusting the position of your keyframe.

   Keyframes can be shifted to the left or right by holding down Alt (Windows) or Option (Mac) and clicking and dragging the keyframe with your mouse.

21. Pull up the Marker tool to read the final Producer's note. Choose **TOOLS > MARKERS**.

   This note is more specific. The Producer would like the shot at 01:00:09:29 (R02_06 Slow Rain Flips) to slow down, speed up, and return to 100% speed just as the young man is coming out of his turn. They have placed the marker on the exact frame that they want to remain in its current location in the Timeline.

   You observed in the last shot that as we create keyframes and change the speed of the shot that the content within the shot changes. We can hold the requested frame in place by applying a Timewarp effect and setting an Anchor Frame, at the location specified, before we keyframe the effect.

22. Repeat Steps 10-14 to apply the Timewarp effect to the **R02_06 SLOW RAIN FLIPS** clip.

23. Before you begin keyframing your effect, move your position indicator to the frame the Producer wants to remain in position in the Timeline.

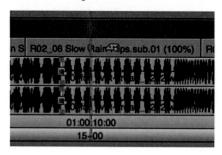

Figure 9.57 The position indicator located at the frame the Producer wants to remain in position in the Timeline.

24. Add a keyframe at the frame specified, and then click the **ANCHOR FRAME BUTTON**.

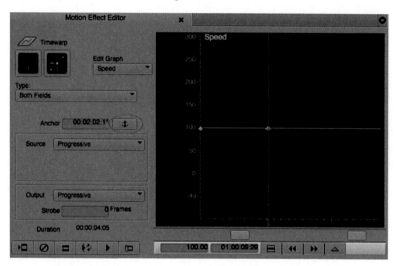

Figure 9.58 The Anchor Frame button in the Motion Effect Editor.

25. Continue keyframing the rest of your effect. The content around this frame will change, but the Anchor Frame will always remain in the same position in the Timeline.

26. Play through all the new changes and make any necessary adjustments to pacing using Trim mode.

27. Conclude the lesson by **BACKING UP** the **MC110_TN PARKOUR** project folder.

Tracking and Blurring Objects

There are many scenarios in which you may need to blur or somehow hide a portion of the video image. In this lesson, you will learn the tools to obscure elements in the video through blur and mosaic effects, plus Media Composer's built-in tracking tools that make it easy to keep the effect in place over the moving image.

Media: TN Parkour

Duration: 45 minutes

GOALS

- Understand stabilize techniques
- Blurring effects
- Hide jump cuts with Fluid Morph

Blurring Unwanted Objects

In any unscripted program, from news to documentaries to reality TV, you may need to obscure some portion of the image.

Around the world, standards and practices dictate that certain things are restricted from news and other programming broadcast over the public airwaves, including vulgarity, nudity, or offensive gestures. Corporate policies for the broadcast station or the company producing the program may further restrict the display of certain brands or logos deemed inappropriate, or whose appearance on products has not been paid for through advertising. Privacy, of course, is another important concern, be it to protect the identity of a sensational interview in a tell-all scandal or the more mundane scenarios of license plates or individuals in the background who didn't sign a model rights release. Blurring it is a commonly accepted way of obscuring these unwanted elements.

Media Composer has a number of built-in effects that can be used to blur, disguise or otherwise hide unwanted portions of the image. All are found in the Image category of the Effect Palette, as shown in Figure 10.1:

- Blur effect

- Paint effect

- Mosaic effect

- Scratch Removal effect

- Spot Color effect

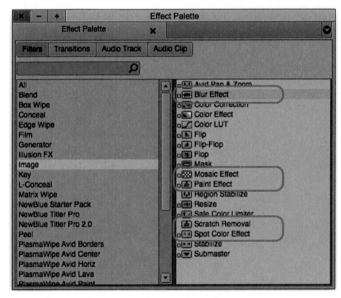

Each of these effects uses shapes to define the area in which the effect will appear. Because video is a medium of *moving* pictures, there is the added challenge of animating the effect to ensure that the shape stays over the object you want to blur. It obviously does no good if you only protect someone's identity for only a few frames.

Figure 10.1 Drawing tools in the Effect Editor.

There are two ways to animate the position of a Blur effect

- Keyframing

- Tracking

Keyframing you already know. You define the value of an effect parameter at one point in time – in this case, the position of a blur – and define a different value at a different point and the system animates the change from one to another. This works fine when the movement or change required is fairly consistent. For animating a blur over an object with complex movements, tracking is the preferred method.

Tracking can be used to match an object's movement automatically. Media Composer has an advanced tracker built-in that can track up to 8 individual points at a time. You can use the tracking points (aka, *trackers*) to track either multiple objects, or track a single object with complex movement. For example, one tracker may be enough to track an object if it is only moving up/down and left/right – e.g. a person walking by, left to right in the background of a static shot. If, however, that person is also moving toward or away from the camera, you may need two or more tracking points to accurately track them.

 Learn more about advanced tracking in the advanced Media Composer course, MC201 and MC210, Media Composer Professional Editing I and II.

Creating a Blur Effect

When you first apply the Blur effect, visually it does nothing to the image by default.

The Blur effect uses shapes to define the area of the frame in which the effect will appear. On the right-hand side of the Effect Editor are drawing tools, as shown in Figure 10.2, which include an Oval and Rectangle, plus additional tools. You may also notice that until the shape is created, the parameter sliders do not even appear in the Effect Editor.

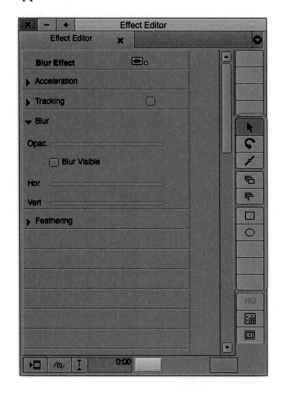

Selection Tool: Used for selecting and moving shapes.

Z Rot: Used to rotate a shape around its Z axis.

Reshape Tool: Allows you to add, subtract and modify the control points that define a selected shape.

Bring Forward: Moves a shape in front of others.

Send Backward: Moves a shape behind others.

Rect Tool: Used to create rectangles.

Oval Tool: Used to create ovals.

Figure 10.2 Drawing tools in the Effect Editor.

 We will refer to the Blur effect throughout this lesson, you can just as easily use the Mosaic effect if you prefer. The technique is the same for both.

If you are going to use tracking, the first step is often to track the area you want to affect before you even create the shape. You can open the Tracking Window by clicking its button on the side of the Effect Editor (see Figure 10.3).

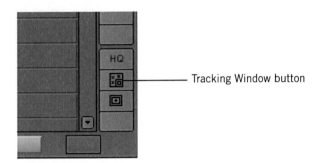

Tracking Window button

Figure 10.3 The Tracking Window button in the Effect Editor.

 Any effect that includes a tracker button in the Effect Editor can be tracked.

The Tracking Window opens and a single yellow tracker appears in the Effect Preview monitor, as shown in Figure 10.4. By default, the "Correlation Tracker" is active, which is exactly what you want to use for a track like this.

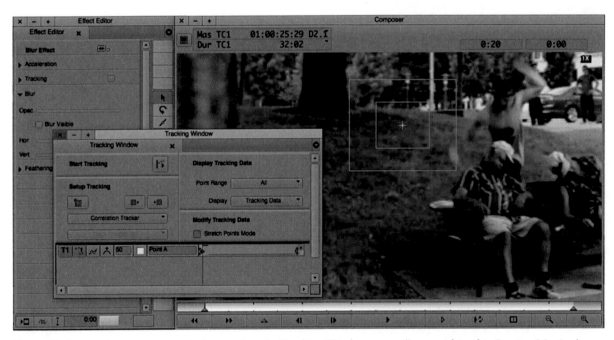

Figure 10.4 A tracker appears over the image when the Tracking Window opens. (Image enlarged in Preview Monitor).

The tracker is displayed in the Effect Preview monitor when the position indicator is parked on the first frame of the effect. It includes three onscreen controls (also visible above in Figure 10.4):

- **Search region:** The outer rectangle

- **Reference pattern:** The inner rectangle, defines the pixels that will be followed and tracked from frame to frame

- **Tracking point:** The mark/crosshair

The Correlation Tracker works by first taking a "snapshot" of the reference pattern (the inner rectangle). It then advances a single frame in the shot and searches the search region (the outer rectangle) for the reference pattern. When it finds it, it re-centers the tracking point on the target, records the location and then repeats the process.

Ideally, you initially position the reference pattern over a well-defined, high-contrast region of the image that remains onscreen and unobstructed for the duration of the shot. Perhaps surprisingly, you do not need to track the actual object you want to obscure. As long as the object you track moves the same way as your target, the tracking data will still be usable. For example, you may want to track someone's face, but their shirt may provide a better target with a more distinctive pattern.

In some cases, you may need to shrink or enlarge the reference pattern to focus on the region of interest. You can change the rectangular shape of the reference pattern using the scale handle in the upper-right of the rectangles, as shown in Figure 10.5.

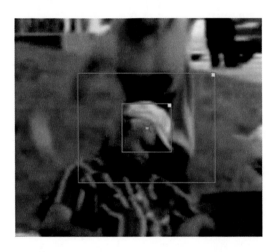

Figure 10.5 The Reference Pattern (inner box) has been resized to limit the search area to the gentleman's hat and face, excluding the background that will change during the track.

On fast-moving shots, it's very possible that the reference pattern you select will fall outside the outer yellow search rectangle as the frame advances. In that case, you would need to resize the outer search rectangle to increase the search area and try re-tracking.

 When using the Correlation Tracker, only one tracking data point is required if the camera is moving up, down, or side to side. If the camera is also rotating or zooming, then an additional tracking data point can be added using the Create New Tracker button.

When the tracking is complete, a yellow tracking motion path will appear in the Effect Preview monitor, which indicates how the reference pattern moved during the segment from frame to frame within the segment.

Of course, not every track completes perfectly. In some cases, the first point you choose may not be the best, and you may want to try a different point to get better results. You can rerun the tracking as many times as you like by placing the position indicator at the start of the Tracking Window Timeline, repositioning the tracking data point to a new location, and clicking Start track.

Once you have a good track, you can close the Tracking Window and return to the Effect Editor.

Selecting a drawing tool allows you to define the area in the Effect Preview monitor for the size of your Blur, Mosaic or other effect. Once you have drawn your shape, you then attach the tracker by selecting and enabling one of the trackers in the Effect Editor's Tracking group (see Figure 10.6).

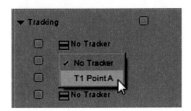

Figure 10.6 Selecting a tracker in the Effect Editor.

Once you assign the tracker, the shape then follows the tracker's motion path.

 If you use more than one tracker, you can select the tracker you want from the pop-up menus in the Tracking section of the Effect Editor. This is useful if you create multiple shapes and you want each shape to follow a different tracking path.

To use tracking with a Blur effect:

1. Apply the **BLUR** effect, and then enter **EFFECT MODE**.

2. Open the **TRACKING WINDOW**.

3. Drag the Tracking Window **POSITION BAR** to the start of the segment.

4. In the Effect Preview monitor, drag the **TRACKER** over a high-contrast, well-defined reference pattern.

5. Click the **START TRACKING** button.

6. If the track is good, continue. If the tracker wandered off its target, repeat steps 3-5 until you have a good track.

7. Close the Tracking Window.

8. Drag the **POSITION BAR** back to the first frame of the segment.

9. Select one of the **SHAPE** tools on the side of the Effect Editor.

10. Using the **RECT TOOL** or the **OVAL TOOL**, draw a **SHAPE** in the Effect Preview monitor, over the area you want affected.

11. Adjust the effect's **PARAMETERS** to get the look you want, including:

    a. **BLUR** group: **HORZ** and **VERT** to control the intensity of the blur and **OPAC.** to adjust the opacity of the blur

    b. **FEATHERING** group: **HORZ AND VERT** to soften the edges of the shape, and **BIAS** to control whether the feathering is applied to the inside or outside shape.

12. In the Tracking group in the Effect Editor, enable the first tracker, labeled **NO TRACKER**, and then click the corresponding Fast menu, and select **T1 POINT A**.

13. **PLAY** the effect to verify that the shape follows the object appropriately.

14. (Optional) If necessary, add keyframes to modify the shape over time, or its path in relationship to the track.

Exercise Break: Exercise 10.1
Pause here to practice what you've learned.

Review/Discussion Questions

1. True or False: When the Blur effect is applied to a segment, the blur is immediately visible.

2. When applying a Blur effect, how do you control where the blur affects the image?

3. Refer to the toolbar displayed to the right.

    a. Which button can be used to create a rectangle?

    b. Which is used to select and move shapes?

    c. Which button is used to reshape an existing shape?

    d. Which button opens the Tracking tool?

4. When using tracking with a Blur effect, how do you attach a tracker to the shape you created?

5. What characteristics should you look for when picking a tracking target?

6. What is the inner box in a tracker called? How is it used?

7. What is the outer box in a tracker called? How is it used?

8. How does Feathering affect the appearance of your shape?

Tracking and Blurring Objects

In this exercise, you will practice the techniques for tracking and blurring an object by blurring the faces of some bystanders in the TN Parkour footage.

Media Used: TN Parkour

Duration: 1 hour

GOALS

- Obscure an individual's face with the Blur effect

- Use tracking to ensure the Blur remains over the target throughout the shot

Exercise 10.1: Using Tracking with Effects

In this exercise, we will the apply the Blur effect to one of our clips in the Tennessee Parkour Montage and use tracking to keep the effect localized to the faces of two men whose identity the Producer needs you to obscure.

Media Used: Tennessee Parkour

Time: 1 hour

For this exercise, we will use the **MC110_TN PARKOUR** project.

1. Begin by opening the bin **STUDENT_LESSON SEQUENCES**.

2. Duplicate the sequence **10.1_TNPARKOUR MONTAGE_TRACKING** and move the duplicate sequence into the **TNPARKOUR_EXERCISE SEQUENCES** bin.

3. Load the duplicate **10.1_TNPARKOUR MONTAGE_TRACKING** into the Timeline.

    You will notice the Producer has left a marker in the sequence:

    "We don't have releases for these gentlemen sleeping on the bench. Can you blur their faces?"

Figure 10.7   The Producer's marker and note (in the sequence) indicating that they don't have releases for the men sleeping on the bench, can you blur their faces?

4. Play through the shot of the young man jumping over the sleeping men on the bench. Access what will be required to fulfill the Producer's request.

    You will need to apply a blur to each of the men's faces as well as track the camera movement of the shot so that the blur will stay on the men's faces as the camera moves.

5. Go to the **EFFECTS TAB** in the Project Window, select **IMAGE** from the left column, and grab the **BLUR EFFECT** from the right column.

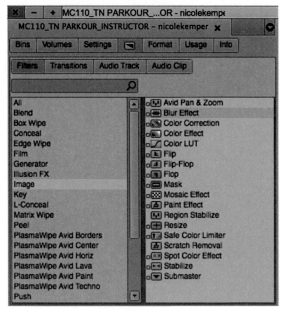

Figure 10.8   The Effects tab with the Image > Blur Effect selected.

6. **DRAG** the **BLUR EFFECT** onto the shot **R01_16 OVER SLEEPING BENCH.**

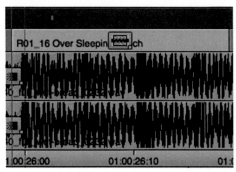

Figure 10.9   The Blur effect dragged onto the "R01_16 Over Sleeping Bench" clip.

First, we need to track the area you want to blur out. Let's start with the man sleeping on the left.

7. Park the **POSITION INDICATOR** over the shot **R01_16 OVER SLEEPING BENCH** in the Timeline and open it in the Effect Editor.

8.   Click the **TRACKING TOOL BUTTON** to open the Tracking window in the Effect Editor.

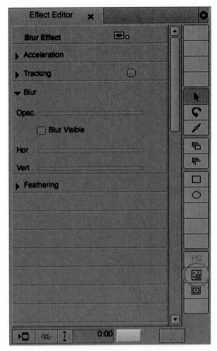

Figure 10.10 Click the Tracking Tool button in the Effect Editor.

9.   Be sure that the Position Bar in the Tracking Window Timeline is at the start of the segment.

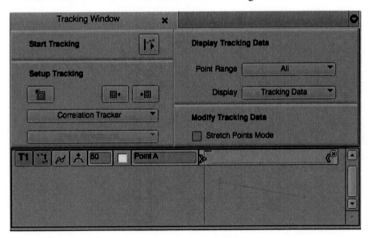

Figure 10.11 Be sure that the Position Bar in the Tracking Window Timeline is at the start of the segment.

10. Drag the tracker to the man's face that is sleeping on the left.

    Adjust the size and position of the tracker to a place on the man's face with enough contrast to provide the best reference point for tracking.

    Use the Zoom In feature in the Effect window to help you get the best look at the image.

Figure 10.12 The tracker on the man's face. Use the Zoom In feature to help you get the best look at the image.

11. Click the START TRACKING BUTTON in the Tracking window.

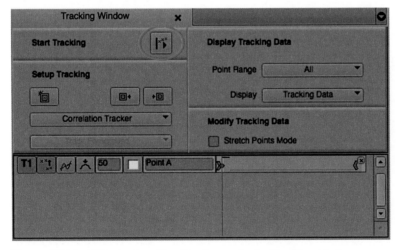

Figure 10.13 Click the Start Tracking button in the Tracking window.

Now that you have tracked the man's face, you can draw a shape around it to blur it out.

Figure 10.14 Tracking the man's face.

12. **DRAG** the **POSITION BAR** in the Tracking Window Timeline back to the first frame of the segment.

13. Click the **OVAL TOOL BUTTON** on the side of the Effect Editor.

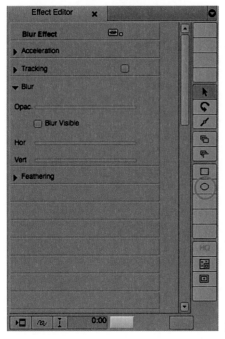

Figure 10.15 Click the Oval Tool button in the Effect Editor.

14. **DRAW** an oval over the man's face in the Effect Preview Monitor, adjusting to cover his face as accurately as possible.

Figure 10.16 An oval drawn over the man's face.

15. Make adjustments to the opacity and feathering of the blur as needed in the Effect Editor.

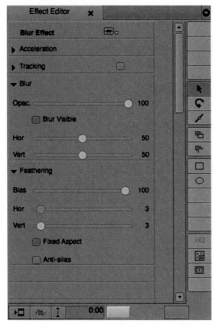

Figure 10.17 Making adjustments to the opacity and feathering in the Effect Editor.

Make sure you have the oval selected in the Effect Preview Monitor in order to adjust the parameters of the effect.

16. To add the tracking information to your blur, open the Tracking parameters in the Effect Editor. Make sure that your shape is selected, then enable the box next to the first Tracker.

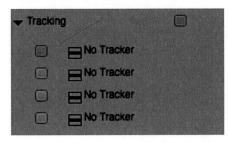

Figure 10.18 Enable the box next to the first tracker to add tracking information.

17. Change the Tracker from No Tracker to **T1 POINT A**.

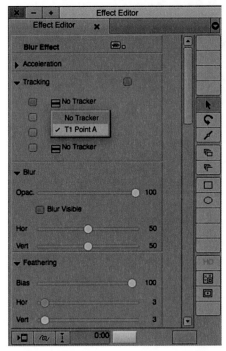

Figure 10.19 Selecting "T1 Point A" from the Tracking Info box.

18. Play through your effect to make sure everything is correct.

19. To blur the man's face on the right, click the CREATE NEW TRACKER BUTTON in the Tracking window. Also, DEACTIVATE the button labeled T1.

    This will prevent new tracking data from recording over the existing data.

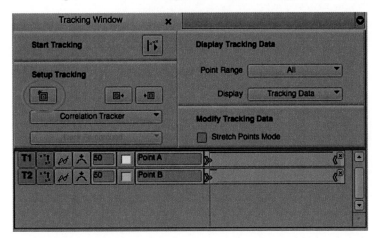

Figure 10.20 Click the "Create New Tracker" button in the Tracking Window.

20. Using your new Tracker, repeat steps 10-17 to add a blur to the second man's face.

Figure 10.21 The tracker on the second man's face.

21. Play through the effect to make sure everything is correct.

Figure 10.22 Following steps 10-17, a blur is added to the second man's face, play through the effect.

22. Conclude the lesson by saving your work, and then backing up the MC110_TN PARKOUR project folder.

Introduction to Multilayer Effects

So far, you've added effects to video clips on a single track of video. But that will only take you so far. Many effects require multiple tracks of video, with effects that combine, or **composite**, them together into a single image. In this lesson, you will learn how to start building multilayer effects in Media Composer.

Media Used: TN Parkour

Duration: 60 minutes

GOALS

- Understand multilayer effects
- Use the 3D PIP to create a split-screen
- Keyframe animations with advanced graphs
- Change interpolation methods to modify the style of animation

Creating a Split-Screen Effect

The use of split-screens is a common filmmaking technique, used across a wide variety of video programming. Split-screens can be found in reality TV and travel shows, documentaries and news magazines, music videos, commercials and feature films of almost every genre.

A split-screen effect, by definition, displays two or more video images on the screen at once. This requires layering the video clips over each other in the Timeline on multiple tracks. It is not enough to edit video onto a higher-level track, though. If you have ever put a cutaway shot on V2 (or above) you know that the higher-level clip will be seen *instead of* the lower clip. To blend the images together in Media Composer, you must use an effect.

The Picture-in-Picture (PIP) effect is commonly used to build split-screen effects like the one seen in Figure 11.1. PIP effects allow you to layer one clip over another and adjust the size, position, and opacity of the foreground clip.

Figure 11.1 A split screen effect shows two video clips on the screen simultaneously.

The Picture-in-Picture effect, found in the Blend category, is a simple 2D version of the effect, and perfectly useful for creating a split-screen. The more sophisticated 3D PIP can be found in the Xpress 3D Effect category of the Effect Palette. The 3D version, shown in Figure 11.2, is superior to the 2D version in that it adds Z-Rotation plus the convenience of enable buttons for the parameter groups.

Using the 3D PIP, you'll explore the basics of building multilayer effects and an advanced method of keyframing that is especially useful when animating the position of these effects.

Check out the article, "Art of the Split Screen" on the PremiumBeat.com blog for a look at the history of the split-screen in cinema, complete with video clips: http://www.premiumbeat.com/blog/split-screen-editing-and-composing/

Quick Review

The process of building multilayer effects can seem complicated at first, but you already have the core skills required to do so. These include:

- Adding and Patching Tracks

- Three-Point Editing

- Applying Effects to Multiple Segments

- Selectively Viewing Tracks

If you are not confident in your skills in these areas, now would be a good time to review them by turning to the Essential Tools section, toward the end of this lesson.

Applying the Effect

The 3D PIP is a segment effect, so you apply it by simply dragging it from the Xpress 3D category of the Effect Palette to the foreground segment (on V2 or higher).

When a 3D PIP effect is applied, it automatically resizes the clip by 50%, centering it in the frame. The parameters for the 3D PIP shown in Figure 11.2 provide 2D controls like crop and scale as well as 3D controls like position and rotation.

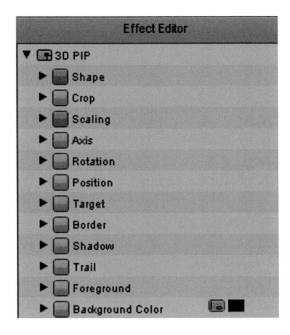

Figure 11.2 3D PIP parameters in Effect mode.

Avid calls the button next to each parameter group an "enable button." When activated, it enables the parameters of the effect. Its usefulness extends beyond the obvious function of turning on a parameter you want to use – as it is, the buttons come on by default when you adjust a parameter slider.

The real value of the enable buttons is in a.) being able to toggle the enable button on/off to momentarily bypass the effect of a single parameter – e.g. bypass the crop to get a quick look at the entire image again; and b.) being able to reset the values of an individual parameter group without having to remember the default values, and without having to recreate the effect.

To use the enable buttons:

1.   Click the ENABLE BUTTON to toggle the parameter group, and bypass the adjustment without resetting the values.

2.   ALT-CLICK (Windows) or OPTION-CLICK (Mac) on the enable button to reset the values of the parameter group

Adjusting the Parameters

The most used parameters of the 3D PIP are: Scale, Position, Rotation, and Crop.

To create a standard 2-up split-screen, as shown previously in Figure 11.1, the Scale must be set to at least 100% (so that each shot still fills the frame vertically without distortion, and then the Crop and Position parameters are used to control which portion of the image is visible, and its horizontal placement in the frame.

A less intuitive aspect of creating the split-screen is that *both shots* – the foreground *and the background* – must have a PIP applied. Applying a PIP to the background allows you to similarly adjust which portion of the image is seen, and its placement within the frame.

 To quickly reset the Scale parameter to 100%, Alt-click (Windows) or Option-click (Mac) the enable button.

The Position parameters can be set to values in X, Y and Z, with 0 being the center of the screen. Positive values represent positions up, to the left of center, and toward you. Negative values represent positions down, to the right of center and away from you, as shown on Figure 11.3.

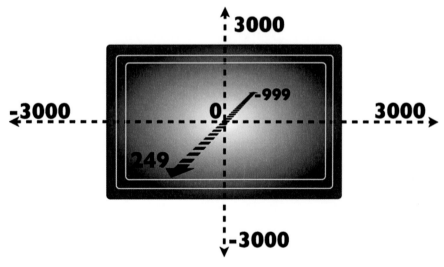

Figure 11.3 3D positioning coordinates.

The Rotation parameters can rotate an image on three axes: X, Y and Z. Although you can use the X, Y and Z rotation parameters, you can also enable the X, Y and Z onscreen controls, shown in Figure 11.4, to rotate an image directly in the Effect Preview monitor.

Figure 11.4 3D Rotation buttons in the Effect Editor.

Finally, the Border control can be useful for adding a visual boundary to divide the images. Depending on the similarity of the shots used in the split screen, and the intended effect, it may be desirable to add a dividing line.

The Border parameter applies a border to all four sides equally. With some creativity, the Border can be hacked to create individual lines. The white bar that divides the frame vertically in Figure 11.1, for example, was created using the border parameter on the right-hand panel. The shot is scaled to over 100% to force the other three sides of the border out of view.

Ordering the Layers

In the process of building any multilayer effect, you will need to decide the order in which elements appear. Which is in front of, or behind, the other? This is particularly true when you begin creating animations to fly/push/slide/move the elements into and out of view.

From your work in the MC101 course, you should already be familiar with the concept that elements on higher level tracks appear in front of objects on lower level tracks.

Think about how you have created a title or a cutaway shot, for example. A title is placed on a *track above* the background video so that it appears *in front of* the video. This logic follows through, even though you may have several elements in a multilayer effect. If the size and position of the PIPs causes them to overlap, the order in which they appear in the Timeline will control their relationships on screen, as shown in Figure 11.5.

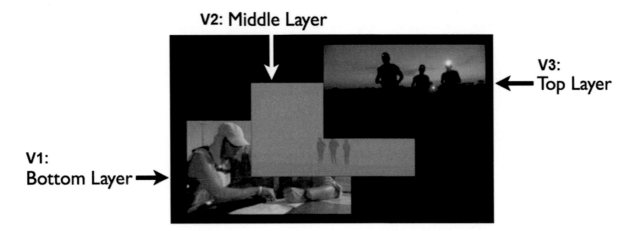

Figure 11.5 The Timeline layering determines the visual order.

Before you build the effect, take a moment to pre-visualize what it is you are setting out to create, which elements should appear on top, on the bottom, or somewhere in between. You can rearrange the order of overlapping PIPs, bringing a layer to the front or sending layers to the back using the Segment Lift/Overwrite tool from the Timeline Smart Palette. See Figure 11.6.

Figure 11.6 The Segment Lift/Overwrite tool.

To rearrange segments with the Segment Lift/Overwrite tool:

1.   Add an empty VIDEO TRACK above the clips you want to reorder, or simply drag a segment upwards, beyond the current top video track, and watch Media Composer magically create a new track for you.

2.   Activate the SEGMENT LIFT/OVERWRITE tool in the Smart Tool.

3.   Drag a lower SEGMENT up to the new empty layer you added, as shown in Figure 11.7.

4.   (Optional) To constrain the movement, do one of the following:

   •   Holding the Ctrl+Shift (Windows) or Control+Shift (Mac) keys while using the Segment Lift/Overwrite tool will limit the segment to snap only vertically in the Timeline.

   •   Hold the Ctrl (Windows) or Control (Mac) key to snap the head frame of the segment you are moving to the cut points, IN mark, or position indicator.

   •   Hold the Ctrl+Alt keys (Windows) or the Command+Option keys (Mac) to snap the tail frame of the segment you are moving to the cut points, OUT mark, or position indicator.

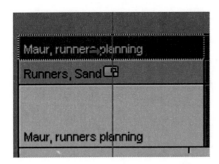

Figure 11.7 Moving the clip from one segment to another.

Exercise Break: Exercise 11.1
Pause here to practice what you've learned.

Using Advanced Keyframe Graphs

Standard keyframing under the Effect Preview window is convenient for simple animations but limited. In the Effect Editor, you have the tools to create complex animations using advanced keyframing.

Advanced keyframing enables you to set keyframes for each parameter independently, with just a few exceptions. Each keyframeable parameter is shown with a keyframe track, and can also further display an animation graph to help finesse the acceleration between keyframes.

To hide/display keyframe tracks:

1. Park on a transition or segment effect and enter **EFFECT MODE**.

2. Click the **SHOW/HIDE KEYFRAME GRAPHS** button (see Figure 11.8) to hide the keyframe tracks.

3. Click the **SHOW/HIDE KEYFRAME GRAPHS** button again to show the keyframe tracks.

Figure 11.8   Show/Hide Keyframe Graphs button.

To avoid confusion as you start adding keyframes, it is important to understand how the keyframes are displayed in the tracks. If you add a keyframe to an individual parameter – e.g. the X parameter, as shown in Figure 11.9 – not only will you see a keyframe on the X track, but you also see one on the track of the parent group, Scale, and another in the master track at the top. In short, every keyframe is "reflected up" to its parent track(s). This is a very useful display because it ensures that even if the view of a parameter group, subgroup, or the effect itself is collapsed, you'll always be able to see the location of a keyframe within the effect. Additionally, moving a keyframe in a Parameter Group track (e.g. Scaling), or the Master Effect track at the very top, will move all the keyframes at the same position that are below.

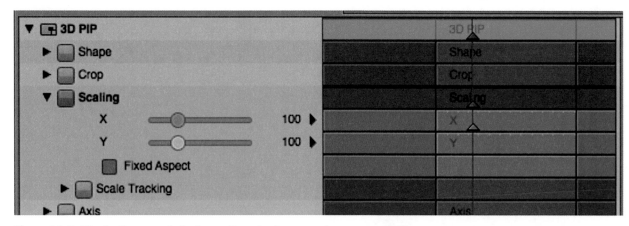

Figure 11.9 The keyframe tracks "reflect up" any keyframes to the parent track(s).

Adding Keyframes

Keyframes are set independently for each parameter. That being the case, many different results are possible when you click the Add Keyframe button. Before the keyframe can be added, you must determine how to add the keyframe. The following options are provided:

- **Add Keyframes to Active Parameter:** This adds keyframes only to the active, or selected, parameter. As only one parameter can be active at any given time, this option affects only a single parameter. A parameter group must be open and a parameter selected or no keyframe will be added.

- **Add Keyframes to Active Group:** This adds keyframes to all parameters in the active group. If a parameter is selected in a group, keyframes are added to all parameters within that group. A parameter group must be open and a parameter selected or no keyframes will be added.

- **Add Keyframes to Open Groups:** This adds keyframes to all parameters in all open parameter groups. At least one group must be open, or no keyframes will be added.

- **Add Keyframes to Enabled Groups:** This adds keyframes to all parameters in all enabled parameter groups. The groups can be either opened or closed. At least one parameter group must be enabled, or no keyframes will be added.

- **Add Keyframes to Open Graphs:** This adds keyframes to all parameters that have their keyframe graphs displayed. At least one keyframe graph must be open, or no keyframes will be added.

- **Add Keyframes to All Parameters:** This adds keyframes to every parameter in the effect. This is the default setting.

To select a keyframe addition option:

1. Right-click the **ADD KEYFRAME** button at the bottom of the Effect Editor, or in the open gray area of the Effect Editor window.

2. Choose the desired **OPTION** from the list at the bottom of the menu (see Figure 11.10).

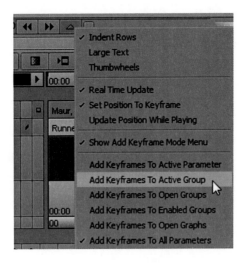

Figure 11.10 Add Keyframe options.

Removing Keyframes

While you are learning to use the Advanced Keyframe controls, the easiest way to start is to leave the setting on "Apply to All Parameters". Anytime you press the semicolor key, or click the Keyframe button, a keyframe will be added to all parameters, ensuring that you have a keyframe available for whichever parameter you plan to adjust at that location.

The disadvantage to this workflow, however, is that you can quickly be working with a cluttered view of the keyframe tracks, unable to see which keyframes actually change the animation and which ones don't. These useless keyframes that have no value change associated with them are called *redundant keyframes*, and Media Composer makes it easy to remove them.

To remove redundant keyframes:

■   Right-click on the master keyframe track at the top of the Effect Editor, and select REMOVE REDUNDANT KEYFRAMES.

To remove keyframes:

1.   Select the KEYFRAME(S) in the appropriate keyframe track for the parameter, group, or overall effect.

2.   (Optional) Shift+click to select MULTIPLE KEYFRAMES.

3.   Press the DELETE or BACKSPACE KEY on the keyboard; or, right-click in the Effect Editor window and choose DELETE KEYFRAMES from the pop-up menu, as shown in Figure 11.11.

Figure 11.11 Delete keyframe option in menu.

Right-clicking on a single parameter track (e.g. X Position) removes the selected keyframes on just that track. Right-clicking on a Parameter Group track (e.g. Scale) removes all the selected keyframes within that group. And, lastly, right-clicking in the Mater Effect track at the very top will remove all selected keyframes in the entire effect.

Using the Keyframe Graphs

In the keyframe tracks area, you can display an animation graph for each parameter, showing the acceleration change over time.

To display a parameter's keyframe graph:

■ Click the ARROW next to a keyframed parameter to display its keyframe graph, as shown in Figure 11.12.

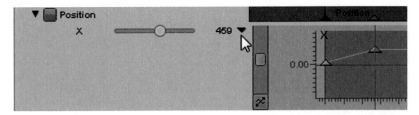

Figure 11.12   Click the disclosure triangle to display the keyframe graph.

To make it easier to work in the graph, you can resize it vertically using either the vertical slider or the Zoom to Curve Height button (see Figure 11.13.)

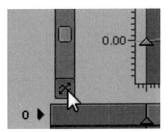

Figure 11.13   Keyframe graph resize controls.

 You can also resize a keyframe graph vertically by dragging between the graph and the keyframe track below the graph.

Keyframe Interpolation Options

As is the case with Timewarp effects (Lesson 9), Advanced Keyframes Effects support four methods of animation interpolation:

■ **Linear:** A linear keyframe creates a direct path between two keyframe values. Linear mean that the rate of change is continuous between the two keyframes, and there is no gradual acceleration ("ease-out") or deceleration ("ease-in") from one keyframe to another.

■ **Spline:** Spline creates a path with natural ease-in and ease-out at every keyframe. The amount of ease-in and ease-out is automatically calculated to create a smooth transition into and out of keyframes and cannot be adjusted.

■ **Bézier:** Bézier creates a path with natural ease-in and ease-out at every keyframe. Unlike spline interpolation, the shape of the animation curve can be adjusted on either side of the keyframe by manipulating the Bézier curve handles.

■ **Shelf:** Shelf holds a keyframe's value until the next keyframe. This interpolation causes the parameter to jump instantly from one value to another.

To switch the keyframe interpolation:

1. Right-click inside an open **KEYFRAME GRAPH**.

2. Choose a **KEYFRAME INTERPOLATION** method from the pop-up menu. (See Figure 11.14.)

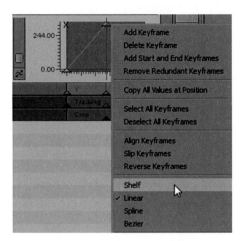

Figure 11.14 Keyframe interpolation.

 Many effects in Media Composer contain a Reverse Animation parameter that will swap the order of all keyframes within the effect. This is useful for setting up the exact opposite animation for two different layers.

Changing the Compositing Order of a Layer Mid-Animation

Earlier, we reviewed the fundamental concept that video segments on higher level tracks appear in front of ones on lower tracks.

It is not hard to imagine a scenario in which you may want one element to begin behind another one, but move so that it ends up in front. To accomplish this, use Add Edit to divide the first segment into two pieces. Leave one piece on a lower-level track, and move the other onto a higher level track, as shown in Figure 11.15.

Figure 11.15 Use Add Edit to divide and reorder layers, like "R05_21 Roof Flip."

The process of creating and fine-tuning the animation is easier if you work on it as a single animation within one effect, and then splitting it, rather than trying to create a consistent animation across two segments. So the key is to animate the movement first, then divide the segment and reorder the layers afterward. Media Composer remembers the original animation and automatically adds new keyframes with the necessary values to maintain the original animation.

Essential Tools

This section reviews essential tools and techniques used in building multilayer effects, many of which are familiar.

Adding and Patching Tracks

By their very nature, multilayered effects require you to know how to add additional video tracks and patch from the source video track to one of the layered video tracks.

To create a split-screen effect

1.   (Optional) Right-click anywhere in the TIMELINE and choose NEW > VIDEO TRACK from the menu.

2.   Edit the background clip into the sequence, if not already there.

3.   In the Timeline, click the V1 source track in the patching panel and drag it to the V2 sequence track, as shown in Figure 11.16, to patch the source to video track 2.

4.   Overwrite the foreground clip onto V2.

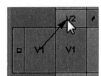

Figure 11.16 Patch source to sequence track V2.

Three-Point Editing

Three-point editing is one way to layer up the segments in the Timeline that will be combined into the multilayer effect, as seen in Figure 11.17.

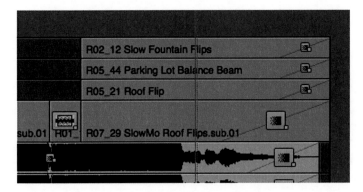

Figure 11.17 Use 3-point editing techniques to quickly layer up the segments to create the effect.

Commonly the foreground shots need to begin and/or end at the same moment as the background shot. Since the background is often edited to the sequence first, you can use it as a marking guide to quickly define the edit for the foreground element(s).

Use the following techniques to set marks based on a background segment:

1. To mark the same duration on the track above:

    a. Park over the background segment and, with the background track active, press the **T** KEY, or click **MARK CLIP** under the Record monitor.

    b. Change the track activation to select only the desired track.

2. **CTRL+CLICK** (Windows) or **COMMAND+CLICK** (Mac) to snap to the head frame of an existing segment and mark an IN.

3. **CTRL+ALT+CLICK** (Windows) or **COMMAND+OPTION+CLICK** (Mac) to snap to the tail frame of an existing segment and mark an OUT.

Adding Segment Effects

The 3D PIP is a segment effect found in the XPress 3D Effects category of the Effect Palette. To apply it to a segment in the Timeline, simply drag it from the Effect Palette to the desired segment.

To create a simple side-by-side split-screen effect like the one shown earlier, however, both segments in the stack – the background and foreground – would need to have a PIP effect applied. Applying the PIP to the background segment allows you to adjust its position horizontally within the frame

To apply the 3D PIP to multiple segments:

1. Using one of the Segment Mode arrows, **SHIFT-CLICK** each of the target segments

2. Double-click the effect in the Effect Palette.

    The effect is added to each of the segments.

    Remember, both the 2D and 3D PIPs will immediately resize the image to 50% when applied to a segment. If you apply PIPs to multiple segments, they will all be scaled to 50% and appear perfectly lined up, one behind the other as shown in Figure 11.18. Only the top layer is visible until you change your view or you modify the parameters in Effects Mode.

Figure 11.18 Multiple layers of PIPs, all scaled to 50%, but only the top layer is visible.

Selectively Viewing Tracks

As you work with multilayer effects, you will want to selectively view the segments on individual tracks, or certain combinations of segments. Use the following functions and shortcuts to view only those elements that you want to see at any point in the process.

Solo'ing a Track

Media Composer allows you to "solo" one video track, which displays the contents of the track in isolation. Any foreground elements in front of it, or background elements behind it, disappears. If the shot on V2, for example, doesn't fill the frame, it will be shown over a black background.

To toggle the solo on a video track:

■   Ctrl+click (Windows) or Command+click (Mac) on the Video Monitor button for the track you wish to solo.

When solo'd, the track monitor button turns green, as shown in Figure 11.19.

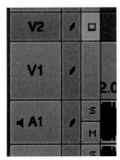

Figure 11.19 Solo a track to see it in isolation.

Muting a Clip

Another very useful function when working with a multilayer effect stack is the ability to *mute* a clip. When you mute the clip, you effectively remove it from the composite. The segment is still visible in the Timeline window, but the video is not visible in the Record monitor.

The mute function offers you a happy medium between the full composite and the isolation of the Solo function. When working with multilayer effects, it is not uncommon to want to see how just a couple elements work together. Using Mute Clip, you can remove the unwanted elements from your view, and focus on just those you are adjusting at the moment.

To mute a clip:

1.   Activate either of the SEGMENT MODE ARROWS found in the Smart Tool (e.g. red Lift/Overwrite).

2.   Select the SEGMENT(S) in the Timeline you wish to mute, holding SHIFT KEY to select more than one.

3.   Right-click a selected segment and choose MUTE CLIP from the menu.

     All selected segments will no longer be visible, and the segment will turn gray.

To unmute a clip:

■ Using the Segment Lift/Overwrite, first, select a segment(s) and then right-click on the muted clip(s) and select **UNMUTE CLIPS**.

 Any muted clips not only disappear from the composite view of the sequence, and will likewise be excluded from any outputs that are generated.

Slipping a Shot

As you learned in an earlier lesson, the Slip function is a type of dual-roller trim that allows you to change the contents of the shot, leaving the length of the segment and its position in the sequence unchanged.

To slip a shot in Trim mode:

1. In Source/Record mode, drag a **LASSO** around the entire segment from right to left

2. Use the **J-K-L KEYS**, the Trim keys, or drag the **TRIM ROLLERS** left to reveal an earlier portion of the shot or right to reveal a later portion of the shot.

   There is another way to slip a shot that is particularly useful when building split-screens and other multilayer effects. It allows you to slip the shot without entering Trim mode. Instead of using the 4-frame display to focus on the first and last frames, it allows you to focus on the location of a particular frame in the middle of a shot – perfect for matching action between two shots, or an action in the video to a cymbal crash in music.

To slip a shot in Source / Record mode:

1. Park the **POSITION INDICATOR** over the segment in the Timeline.

2. Activate *only* those tracks that you want to affect.

3. Press the **TRIM KEYS** on the keyboard (M, Comma, Period, Forward Slash)

   a. The outer keys, M and Forward Slash, will slip the shot by 8 frames (in a 24 fps project) or 10 frames (in a 30 fps project).

   b. The inner keys, Comma and Period, will slip the shot by 1 frame

   As you slip, you will see the visible frame in the Record monitor change as it passes under the playhead, but nothing will visibly change in the Timeline.

 Exercise Break: Exercise 11.2
Pause here to practice what you've learned.

Review/Discussion Questions

1. How is a 3D PIP effect different from other effects you've worked with so far, such as the Resize effect?

2. What key(s) must you hold down on the keyboard to make sure that when moving clip vertically, it does not shift its position in time?

3. If you add a keyframe to the Keyframe position bar underneath the Effect Preview Monitor, what parameters are keyframed?

4. What happens to the animation if you change the Keyframe interpolation from linear to spline?

Lesson 11 Keyboard Shortcuts

Key	Shortcut
Ctrl+Y (Windows)/Command+Y (Mac)	Adds a new video track
Ctrl+8 (Windows)/Command+8 (Mac)	Opens the Effect Palette

EXERCISE 11

Introduction to Multilayer Effects

Let's return to **TN Parkour** and use multilayer effects to add a bit of extra excitement to the closing shots of the sequence. You will be creating a multilayer split-screen with up to four shots.

Media Used: TN Parkour

Duration: 1 hour 45 minutes

GOALS

- Create a split-screen with the 3D PIP effect
- Animate a 3D PIP effect
- Use advanced keyframing to animate the effect
- Modify the timing and style of animation using the keyframe graphs

Exercise 11.1: Using Multilayer Effects

In this exercise, we will use multiple video tracks to add a split screen to the Tennessee Parkour montage.

Media Used: TN Parkour

Time: 45 minutes

For this exercise, we will use the **MC110_TN PARKOUR** project:

1. Begin by opening the bin **STUDENT_LESSON SEQUENCES**.

2. Duplicate the sequence **11.1_TNPARKOUR MONTAGE_MULTILAYER** and move the duplicate sequence into the **TNPARKOUR_EXERCISE SEQUENCES** bin.

3. Load the duplicate **11.1_TNPARKOUR MONTAGE_MULTILAYER** into the Timeline.

4. Choose **TOOLS >MARKER**.

    Read over the note the Producer has left for you regarding some additional effects that need to be added to the Tennessee Parkour Montage.

5. Read the note:

    "Create split screen image: two small boxes on the left and one long panel on the right. Choose any other three clips where someone does a flip or aerial trick. Crop and adjust the image so that we can see them flipping in all panels."

    The producer needs you to create 3 image panels in addition to the image that is currently playing in the Timeline. So, in the end, you'll have four images on screen at the same time. You will fill these panels with clips of people doing flips.

    For this task, we will use the "3D PIP" effect.

6. Start by adding three additional video tracks by choosing **TIMELINE > NEW > VIDEO TRACK** or clicking **CTRL+Y** (Windows) or **COMMAND+Y** (Mac).

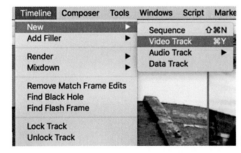

Figure 11.20 Solo a track to see it in isolation.

7. Park on the **R07_29 SLOWMO ROOF FLIPS** clip in the Timeline, which will be the bottom image in the split screen. Click the **T BUTTON** to mark and IN and OUT around the clip. Next, enable only the V2 track. All other tracks should be disabled.

8. Go through the footage in the **TNPARKOUR_FOOTAGE** bin and select three more clips that contain aerial flips.

9. OVERWRITE each of the new clips into the Timeline using the **B** KEY.

    When you're finished, you'll have four shots stacked-up, and they'll all be the same duration as the segment on V1.

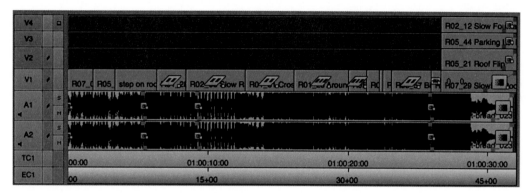

Figure 11.21 Solo a track to see it in isolation.

10. Return to the EFFECTS TAB in the Project window.

    Under the "Xpress 3D Effect" category in the left column, you'll see the "3D PIP," or Picture-in Picture effect.

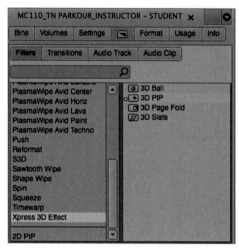

Figure 11.22 Xpress 3D Effect > 3D PIP effect selected on the Effect tab.

11. To add the PIP effect to the clips on tracks V2, V3, and V4 – select all three clips using the mouse to click and drag a lasso around them.

12. From the **EFFECTS TAB** in the Project window, double-click on the **3D PIP** effect.

    The PIP effect will be added to the clips on tracks V2, V3, and V4.

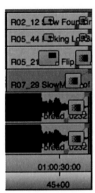

Figure 11.23 The PIP effect added to the clips on tracks V2, V3, and V4.

Without changing any of the parameters, what you'll see is the shot on V4 will appear as a smaller image with the video on the V1 track as the background.

Figure 11.24 The shot on V4 appears as a smaller image with the video on the V1 track as the background.

If you move the Video monitor (the small square icon currently next to the V4 track selector), down to the other tracks, you'll see that their images have been reduced in size as well. When you are finished examining the other tracks, be sure to place the Video monitor back onto track V4.

13. Open the **EFFECT EDITOR** to create the first panel. Start with the shot on track **V4**.

14. Mute the segments on the V2 and V3 tracks so you can deal cleanly with one panel at a time. To do this, use the **SHIFT KEY** to select the two shots, then right-click on them. From the menu, select **MUTE CLIPS**.

15. Using the Scaling, Position, and Crop parameters, create a small box of action in the upper left corner of the frame.

16. Add white border around the image until you have something like this:

Figure 11.25 Using the Scaling, Position, and Crop parameters, a small white box is created around the image.

Before you select V3 to start work on it, there may be a keyframe or two to delete. If you used direct manipulation in the Effect Preview monitor to scale and/or reposition the image, then Media Composer has automatically created one or more keyframes. The "Auto Keyframe" feature is always on. It's really helpful in many situations.

17. But in this case, DELETE any keyframes that were added.

18. Next, UNMUTE the segment on V3 (you can do this while in Effect mode) and create a panel that is below the first, as see in Figure 11.26.

19. From the Image category in the Effect Palette, get a RESIZE EFFECT and place it on the V1 segment. Use its Position parameters to adjust the placement of the image, so you can better show off the flip.

Figure 11.26 A panel is created that is below the first image, and an image showing off the flip.

20. Once you have all the panels created, play through the effect using the PLAY LOOP BUTTON in the Effect Editor.

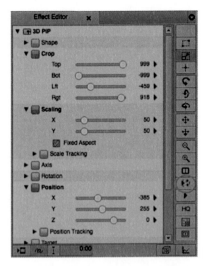

Figure 11.27 The Play Loop button in the Effect Editor.

21. Adjust the timing of each of the shots as needed by slipping either in Trim mode or directly in the Timeline using the TRIM KEYS.

 Figure 11.28 Trim keys.

*If you have any trouble playing back your multilayer effects in real time, try adjusting the playback resolution using the Video Quality menu as seen in Figure 11.29.

Figure 11.29 Use the Video Quality menu to adjust any playback resolution issues.

Exercise 11.2: Animating a PIP Effect

In this exercise, we will use keyframes to animate the PIP (Picture-in-Picture) effect we created in Exercise 11.1.

Media Used: Tennessee Parkour

Time: 1 hour

For this exercise, we will continue to use the **MC110_TN PARKOUR** project:

1. Begin by opening the bin **STUDENT_LESSON SEQUENCES**.

2. Duplicate the sequence **11.2_TNPARKOUR MONTAGE_ANIMATED PIP** and move the duplicate sequence into the **TNPARKOUR_EXERCISE SEQUENCES** bin.

3. Load the duplicate **11.2_TNPARKOUR MONTAGE_ANIMATED PIP** into the Timeline.

4. Choose **TOOLS > MARKERS**.

#		Marker Name	TC	End	Track	Part	Comment
0001	◉	Producer	01:00:27:06		V1		Fly in panel #1 from screen left
0002	◉	Producer	01:00:28:05		V1		Panel #2 comes up from the bottom and pushes Panel #1 into place. Panel #3 flies in from screen right.

Markers - 11.2_TNPARKOUR MONTAGE_ANIMATED PIP

Figure 11.30 The Markers window displaying markers and the Producer's notes.

The Producer has left you some notes detailing some animation that needs to be done on the split screen effect you created in the previous exercise.

Figure 11.31 A split screen displaying panels that the Producer has supplied notes about.

The Producer would like you to animate the PIP effect so that the panels fly in from off screen.

They want Panel #1 to animate on first, then be pushed into place by Panel #2 at the same time as Panel #3 animates onto screen from the right.

This sounds complicated, but it is easily done!

5. Start with the first note:

    "Fly in Panel #1 from screen left."

    In the last exercise you muted the clips by selecting them. This time, let's try another method. In the Track Control Panel each track has an Activate/Deactivate button that has the power symbol on it (see Figure 11.32).

6. Deactivate tracks V2 and V3.

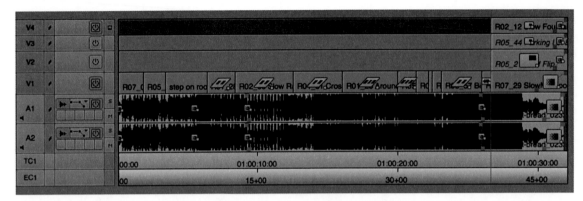

Figure 11.32 The Track Control Panel displaying the Activate/Deactivate button that has the power symbol on it.

7. Park your position indicator at the second Marker in the Timeline and open the 3D PIP on track V4 in the Effect Editor.

8. Add a keyframe at this position. This is where you want Panel #1 to end up at the end of the animation.

    Make sure the keyframe is being made for all parameters. You can check this by clicking the "Show Keyframe Graph" button in the Effect Editor.

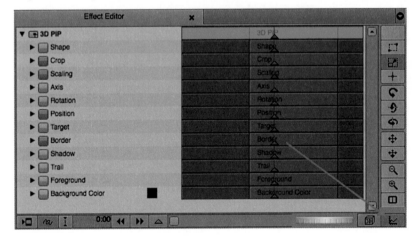

Figure 11.33 Click the Show Keyframe Graph button in the Effect Editor.

9. Move the position indicator to the first Marker in the Timeline and add a keyframe.

    This is where you want Panel #1 to hit when it first animates on.

10. To animate the panel, start by zooming out of the image in the Effects window so you can see more of the space off-screen.

Figure 11.34 Zooming out of the image in the Effects window so you can see more of the space off screen.

11. In the **EFFECT EDITOR**, use the **Y AXIS SLIDER** to move Panel #1 to the bottom left corner of the screen.

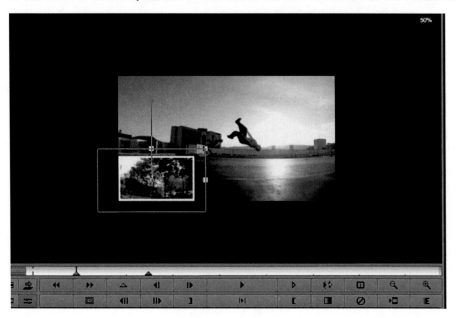

Figure 11.35 Using the "Y axis" slider in the Effect Editor to move Panel #1 to the bottom left corner of the screen.

12. Play through the animation using the **PLAY LOOP BUTTON** in the Effect Editor.

 Figure 11.36 Play Loop button.

13. Next, move the position indicator to the very beginning of the shot and add a keyframe.

This is where your panel will start off screen.

14. In the Effect Editor, use the **X AXIS SLIDER** to move Panel #1 off-screen left.

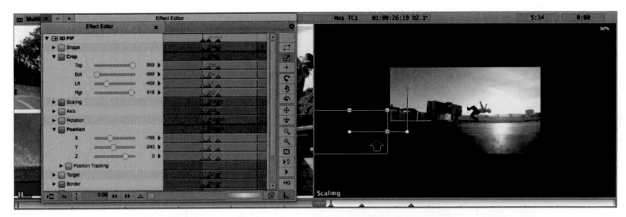

Figure 11.37 Using the "X axis" slider in the Effect Editor to move Panel #1 off screen left.

15. Play through the animation using the **PLAY LOOP BUTTON** in the Effect Editor.

 Figure 11.38 The Play Loop button.

Notice that the panel moves continuously from the second keyframe to the third keyframe.

Let's add an additional keyframe so that it holds its first position for a moment.

16. Park your position indicator between the 2nd and 3rd keyframe and add another keyframe.

17. Click on the 2nd keyframe so that it is active and copy its parameters using **CTRL+C** (Windows) or **COMMAND+C** (Mac).

Make sure all the parameters are active in the Effect Editor.

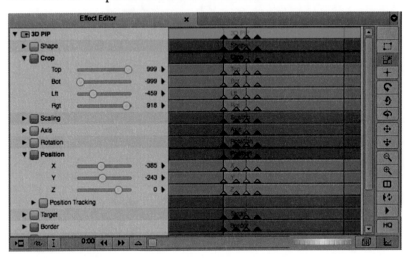

Figure 11.39 Make sure all the parameters are active in the Effect Editor.

18. Click on the next keyframe and paste the parameters by clicking CTRL+V (Windows) or COMMAND+V (Mac).

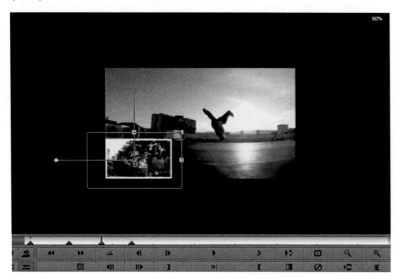

Figure 11.40 The parameters copied onto the keyframe.

19. Play through the animation using the PLAY LOOP BUTTON in the Effect Editor.

 Figure 11.41 Play Loop button.

Panel #1 should now animate on to its first position, hold its position at the 2nd and 3rd keyframes, and finally move into its final position at the 4th keyframe.

When you are happy with panel #1's animation, move on to animating the other two panels.

20. Animate Panel #2 so that it comes up from the bottom of the frame and appears to push Panel #1 into place in the top left of the frame.

21. Keyframe the animation for Panel #3 so that it moves in from off-screen right at the same time that Panel #2 is coming up from the bottom of the frame.

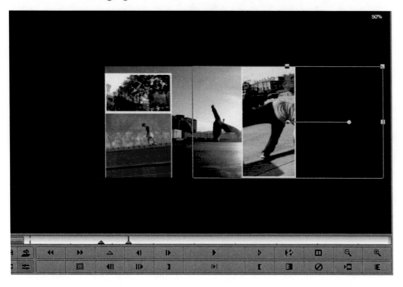

Figure 11.42 Keyframing the animation for Panel #3.

22. When you have animated all the panels into place, try out a few different types of Keyframe Interpolation (e.g. Shelf, etc.) and observe how the movement of your animation is affected.

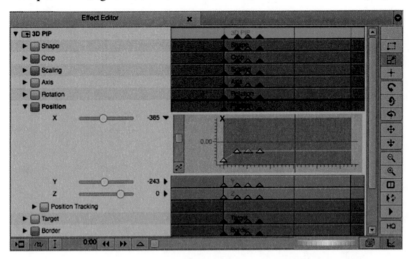

Figure 11.43 Using the Effect Editor to try a few different types of Keyframe Interpolation.

23. To change the type of Keyframe Interpolation, right-click inside the keyframe graph and choose one from the drop down menu.

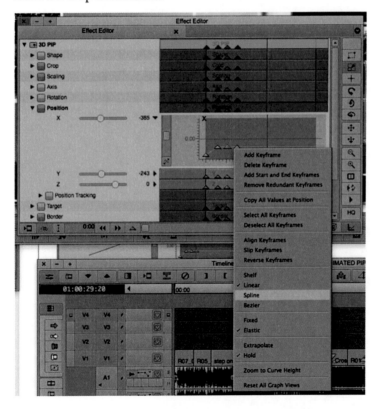

Figure 11.44 Right-click inside the keyframe graph and choose a Keyframe Interpolation (e.g. Spline) from the drop down menu.

24. Observe how the different interpolation methods affect the animation.

25. Conclude the lesson by saving and then backing up the project folder.

Nesting Multiple Effects

Until now, you've applied no more than one effect to a given clip. There are times, however, when more than one effect is required. For example, perhaps you want to apply a treatment to a shot and also blow it up. Media Composer allows you to do this by nesting effects.

Media: TN Parkour

Duration: 50 minutes

GOALS

- Apply more than one effect to a clip
- Change the order of nested effects

Nesting Effects

In the previous course, you learned that if you apply an effect to a segment that already has one; the new effect replaces the old, unless you hold a modifier key, in which case both effects appear on the segment.

This process in Media Composer is called *nesting*. At the most basic level, a nest contains multiple effects on a single video segment. Nests, however, can be much more complex, with multiple video layers all nested within a single clip.

In this lesson, we'll quickly review the simpler forms of nests, and then look at multilayer nests as a continuation of our discussion of multilayer effects.

Autonesting

If you need to apply more than one effect to a clip, the easiest approach is to use a technique known as *Autonesting*. This technique adds a new effect on top of an existing effect, such as a Resize on top of a Color Correction.

To Autonest one effect on top of another:

■ Hold down the ALT key (Windows) or OPTION key (Mac) and apply a SEGMENT EFFECT.

The Effect Editor shows the parameters for all nested effects on the segment, as shown in Figure 12.1. Use the disclosure triangles to open and manipulate the effect parameters of each effect.

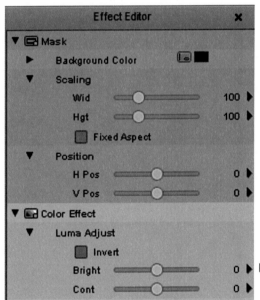

Figure 12.1 The Effect Editor with two effects displayed.

 If any of the effects in the nest are not the Advanced Keyframe type (e.g. Blur effect), then their parameters cannot be viewed in the Effect Editor. To modify these effects, you will need to select them directly while in Effect mode.

The bottom-most effect in the Effect Editor is at the bottom of the nest. All other effects are listed, traveling upward, in the order they are applied. The top effect in the Effect Editor is the same effect you see at the top level in the Timeline.

Displaying a Nest in the Timeline

There are two ways to display the nest in the Timeline: Simple Nesting view, or Expanded Nesting view.

Method One: Simple Nesting View

In this method, you travel down inside a nest, and you see only those segments from within the nest displayed in the Timeline. This is a very useful technique for complex effect nests because it gives you the full use of the Timeline window to view and edit the elements inside the nest.

To move down through each effect and back up to the top effect, you use the Step In/Step Out buttons (see Figure 12.2).

Figure 12.2 Step In/Step Out buttons.

To step into an effect nest:

1. Park on a CLIP that is nested with multiple effects.

2. Make sure it is the top-most active track.

3. Click the STEP IN button at the bottom of the Timeline.

    When you step into a nest, the Timeline view changes, and only the contents of the nest (that is, what's beneath the top effect) are visible, as shown in Figure 12.3.

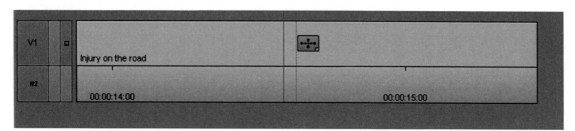

Figure 12.3 A nested effect's contents.

Viewing the nest in isolation is both the advantage and disadvantage of the Simple Nesting view. It can be a disadvantage if, for example, you want to time something to the music.

Method Two: Expanded Nesting View

The Expanded nesting view lets you see the sequence and the nest contents simultaneously. It also allows you to listen to audio and access all material in the sequence before and after the effect nest you are working with.

To expand an effect nest:

■   Double-click on the segment containing nested effects.

   The Timeline displays the tracks inside and outside the nest, with the tracks inside the nest appearing directly above the track that contains the nest, as shown in Figure 12.4. In this example, the Mask effect is on the surface of the nest, while the Color Effect is one layer deeper into the nest.

   You can continue to double-click deeper layers to reveal any additional effects on that segment until you reach the base layer of video.

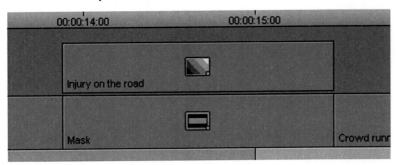

Figure 12.4 Expanded nesting view.

To collapse the nest:

■   Double-click the segment in the surface-level track – e.g. V1

Changing the Order of Nested Effects

Although it isn't the case for all effect combinations, there are times when the order of the effects in the nest is important. If the effects are in the wrong order, in some cases you'll get an undesirable result.

To reorder effects in a nest:

1.   Park on a CLIP that is nested with effects.

2.   In the Effect Editor, drag an EFFECT'S ICON to change its position in the nest. (See Figure 12.5.)

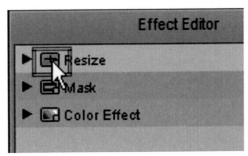

Figure 12.5 Reordering effect icons in Effect mode.

For the most part, effects that can be nested can also be reordered. There are some exceptions to this, and the system will display a dialog box explaining why when you encounter one.

Deciding When to Layer or Nest

As you've seen, both layering and nesting are useful and powerful. But how do you decide whether to layer or nest? Use the following guidelines to help you decide:

- Layer to composite video into a multilayer effect design. For example, three video tracks where each segment on the tracks has a Picture-in-Picture (PIP) effect applied, and three images can be seen at the same time.

- Nest to make a modification to a shot that already has an effect on it. An example would be adding a Color Effect to one shot in the three track PIP composite, so that you can make only that shot blue.

Another example would be to add a title within a PIP effect, so that they are both affected by the PIP. As the PIP performs the animation you designed, then the title would move right along with it. Media Composer treats the multiple tracks of video beneath the PIP ("inside the nest") as if they were just one shot.

Exercise Break: Exercise 12.1
Pause here to practice what you've learned.

Editing Inside a Nest

As you may recall from the previous lesson, whenever you add an effect to a clip, you create a nest, and you can step into that nest and apply additional effects. It is even possible to add video tracks within a nest and create self-contained effects. This can be extremely useful, as it allows you to do things such as add a title to the contents of a PIP and use the 3D PIP effect parameters to animate both the clip and the title.

Stepping inside some effects will show that the nest contains two tracks: an empty V1 and a V2 that contains the clip onto which the effect was applied (see Figure 12.6). That's because the 2D PIP and 3D PIP are compositing effects. In more technical terms, they are called "Two-Input," or "Two Stream" effects because the computer processes two video clips (streams of video) at the same time. Another example of a "Two Stream" effect is a dissolve.

Figure 12.6 Stepped in to a two-input effect.

Each video "input" is represented in the nest. The top track is the foreground input. It's the clip that has the effect applied. The empty bottom track represents the background and references the contents on the track (or tracks) beneath the effect (outside of the nest).

With compositing effects, you should always leave the V1 track inside the nest empty, as editing a clip into this track will replace the background.

Inside the nest, you have full editing capabilities, including the ability to create additional video tracks. Any additional video layers added inside are grouped with the original nested clip. If you rotate or reposition the top effect that created the nest, then all the contents within the nest are rotated and repositioned.

To add a clip inside a nest:

1. Move the POSITION INDICATOR over a two-input effect, like a PIP.

2. Click the STEP IN button.

3. Add a third VIDEO TRACK.

4. Load a CLIP into the Source monitor

5. Press the T key on the keyboard to mark the nest duration.

6. Use the Timeline Track Selector panel to PATCH the source to V3 in the sequence.

7. Check to make sure that track V2 in the sequence is DESELECTED.

8. Press the B KEY on the keyboard to overwrite the source clip onto V3.

9. Apply a 3D PIP EFFECT, KEY, TITLE, or some other multi-input effect to the new V3 segment so the background is viewable.

10. Click the STEP OUT button at the bottom of the Timeline to step out of the nest.

 Exercise Break: Exercise 12.2
Pause here to practice what you've learned.

Measuring Performance

As you build up multiple layers of video in the Timeline, you may reach the point at which the system is unable to process the entire composite in real time, even though each individual effect is a real-time effect. If it can't keep up, the system will "drop," or skip, frames.

You will probably notice if the system drops frames. It's clearly visible during playback and looks like the video stutters for a moment, or worse, it freezes for a second or two until the playhead moves past the stack of effects. You probably don't need any special indicator to tell you when frames are dropped. But how do you know when you're getting close to the break point?

Every time you play the Timeline, Media Composer is monitoring system performance. If it detects that the system is reaching its limits, it warns you using playback performance indicators. These display as a yellow, red, or blue bar on the timecode track and in the timecode ruler at the top of the Timeline.

 It may be necessary to adjust the Timeline zoom to see the performance bars.

Depending on the color, these bars show where the system either is being stressed or is dropping frames. Figure 12.7 shows an example of these performance bars.

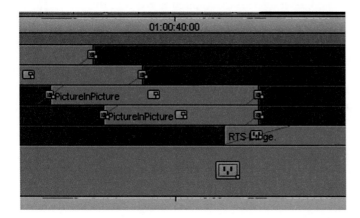

Figure 12.7
Timeline performance bars
above and below Timeline tracks.

- **Yellow bars:** These indicate areas that stressed the system—the CPU and GPU—during playback but did not cause it to drop frames.

- **Blue bars:** These indicate areas that stressed the hard drives on which the media is stored but did not cause it to drop frames. If these bars occur frequently, you may want to move your media to faster drives or change your drive configuration (for example, to a RAID 0 configuration).

- **Red bars:** These indicate areas that overtaxed the system during playback. In these areas, the system dropped frames in order to play through the effect composite. The effects in these areas must be rendered to prevent dropped frames next time you play the sequence.

Even if your system was able to play the sequence in its entirety at the current quality level, knowing that you stressed the system can help you decide, for example, if you need to render the Timeline before that important screening comes up.

If you stressed the system or dropped frames, you have two options: adjust the playback quality setting or render the effects.

Adjusting Playback Quality

Media Composer provides settings that enable you to adjust playback quality to squeeze more real-time performance out of your system. The concept is simple: It's easier and faster for the system to display a low-quality image—a sketch—of the final effects composite than it is to process and display the full-quality image. As an editor, it makes it easier to design complex effect composites if you don't have to stop and render until the very end.

Video Quality Menu

The Video Quality menu (see Figure 12.8) is located at the bottom of the Timeline. You use it to change the amount of processing that is done when playing back effects. Right-click the Video Quality button to display the Video Quality menu.

Figure 12.8 Video Quality menu.

The following video quality options are available:

- **Full Quality:** This option processes video at full quality with full-frame video that is not altered from the resolution which it was imported, consolidated, or transcoded. Although it provides the best-looking images, it can significantly stress the system. Media Composer displays a solid green icon when this option is enabled.

- **Draft Quality:** This option scales the frame by 50% in each direction (or 1/4 frame, which means 1/4 the data). This results in a slightly softer image but enables more effects to be processed in real time. This is the default quality setting. Media Composer displays an icon that is half yellow and half green when this option is enabled.

- **Best Performance:** This option reduces the processing even further by scaling the image by 75% in each direction (or 1/16 frame). This results in a very soft image but enables maximum real-time effects processing. Media Composer displays a solid yellow icon when this option is enabled.

 Depending on your video hardware configuration, you may also see a Full Quality, 10-bit option. This option also increases the bit depth of the video being sent to your video hardware from 8-bit to 10-bit.

To see the impact of changing the video playback quality:

1. Load an effects-heavy SEQUENCE into the Record monitor.

2. Right-click the VIDEO QUALITY button and select FULL QUALITY (green).

3. Play the SEQUENCE from beginning to end, taking note of the playback performance around the effect composites.

4. After playback is complete, look for any colored PERFORMANCE BARS in the timecode track.

5. Click the VIDEO QUALITY button to toggle it to BEST PERFORMANCE (yellow).

6. Play the SEQUENCE again from beginning to end. Take note of how the performance improves and the image quality is reduced.

Most of the time, lowering the playback quality can enable you to complete your effects design work without rendering. However, for playback at full quality, you will need to render. Like most things in Media Composer, there are a number of different render options and techniques. We'll explore these in the next section.

The Technical Side of Real-Time Effect Playback Limitations

Many different things can affect real-time performance. Some limitations cannot be changed without replacing your system, but others can be worked around by either changing the way you work or reconfiguring your system.

System Performance

Media Composer uses an effects processing architecture called Avid Component Processing Library (ACPL). With ACPL, Avid is less dependent on dedicated effects hardware, as it leverages both the CPU and the graphics card (GPU) for maximum processing power. The Avid system automatically selects the most efficient and highest performance combination of processing elements, whether via CPU or GPU. This results in 300% to 400% faster effects processing than previous versions of Media Composer.

Because effects processing depends on the power of the host rather than dedicated hardware, determining the elements of system performance is critical. Several of these factors are listed here.

CPU speed and configuration. This affects performance because the faster and more efficient the processor, the more rapidly it can process effects. Avid strongly recommends using multiprocessor systems for the best possible performance. The CPU has two primary responsibilities: decompressing media and compositing effects. Depending on the effect and your system configuration, the GPU may also be involved in effect compositing, which lets the CPU focus on other things.

RAM speed. This is critical because video is played out of a RAM buffer rather than directly off the drives. RAM speed is affected by both the physical speed of the memory and the configuration of that memory. For example, the fastest systems not only use high-speed RAM but also pair, or interleave, the RAM chips. This process, which is similar to drive striping, allows even greater RAM speed.

Overall system transfer speed. This affects the ability to move media around the system. Several areas affect performance, including the system bus speed, the speed of the GPU, the use of PCIe cards, and the number of lanes allowed for data transfer. In addition, the way the system is designed can affect transfer performance. It is impossible to determine these bottlenecks without extensive system testing. This is why Avid tests and qualifies computer systems for use with their systems. For a complete list of qualified systems, refer to the system specifications on the Media Composer product page: www.avid.com/products/media-composer/hardware-options.

Graphics card (GPU) performance. This affects effect processing because both the CPU and the GPU are used for compositing. This hybrid relationship dynamically sends effects to be processed by each, so it is very important that your system is equipped with a qualified graphics card.

Other running system processes. System processes such as a music player can take processing cycles away from Media Composer and negatively affect real-time playback performance. This is especially true of programs that are accessing the drives or moving large amounts of data across the system. For example, antivirus scanning checks files as they are accessed and will have some negative impact on playback performance. By the same token, rendering an animation in a 3D application in the background will have a dramatic negative impact, as rendering heavily tasks the entire system.

Hard Drive Performance

Your hard drive configuration and drive type can definitely affect performance. If the system is displaying lots of blue performance indicators, you may need to change the way your drives are configured on your system.

SCSI and SAS drives provide excellent performance on Avid editing systems. In addition, their performance can be enhanced by striping multiple drives together. Striping dramatically increases performance and increases the number of streams possible. For the very highest possible performance, you should four-way stripe SCSI drives across two SCSI buses.

Striping is a process where two or more drives are joined together by the system and treated as a single drive. By combining multiple drives, the system can read and write material much more quickly. Striping is available for all SCSI and Fibre drives. Some systems also support SATA drive striping.

- Serial ATA (SATA) drives vary in performance and do not approach the performance of SCSI drives, even when striped. SATA drives are available at various performance levels, and a common metric is the drive speed, usually measured in RPM. It is strongly recommended that you use drives that run at 7,200 RPM or greater.

- USB 2.0 and FireWire drives are essentially external SATA drives that connect by either a FireWire or USB 2.0 interface. Because of the limited speed of these connections, their performance usually is worse than internal SATA drives.

- USB 3.0, eSATA, and Thunderbolt drives are also essentially external SATA drives, but they connect via a much faster interface. These drives potentially can run as fast as internal drives, but the performance is highly dependent on the drive inside the case.

- Fibre channel drives provide a high level of performance but are rarely connected to a single workstation. Instead, these drives are typically attached to an Avid server, such as Nexis.

Rendering Effects

When you decide it's time to render, you'll also need to decide which effects to render. Depending on the situation, you may choose to render all the effects, such as for final output, or you may choose to render only certain effects, such as to review an effect composite at full quality for director or client approval.

When an effect composite or a clip with multiple nested effects is rendered, the render file always contains the combination of the effect being rendered, plus all tracks and effects that are below it. This is the basic tenet of all rendering in Media Composer and a key consideration in how you choose to render the sequence.

Rendering Individual Effects

Sometimes all you really need to render is one effect. The simplest way to render a single effect is to use the Render Effect button in the Timeline, shown in Figure 12.9.

Figure 12.9 The Render Effect button in the Timeline.

Although the Render Effect button does render a single effect, if and when multiple tracks are enabled, it also renders effects at the current position, on the active tracks. A Render Effect dialog box will open, allowing you to select the hard drive for the rendered file but also informing you of how many effects will be rendered.

 The Render Effect button can be mapped to your keyboard. It is available on the FX tab of the Command palette. Using it from the keyboard is the same as clicking the button in any window. The function will be determined by whichever window is active.

To render an individual effect in the Timeline:

1. Load a SEQUENCE with effects into the Record monitor.

2. Place the POSITION INDICATOR over an unrendered or real-time effect.

3. Enable the track(s) with effects you want to render.

4. Click the RENDER EFFECT button.

5. Select the DRIVE that will store the render files and click OK.

 You can immediately recognize when a clip has been rendered because the blue or green dot disappears from its effect icon. If the dot is still there, it hasn't been rendered yet.

Once an effect is rendered, it will remain rendered until you modify the effect. This includes moving the clips in a composite, since it changes the relationship of the frames that are being combined. The good news is that if you accidentally break the render, you can undo it. Media Composer will relink to the rendered file.

Rendering Multiple Effects with ExpertRender

After building a series of more complex effects, you may want to render the entire group while you take a break. This is easily done using IN and OUT marks to define the region.

 Use this technique to render the entire sequence before final output. Simply set your IN and OUT marks at the beginning and end of the sequence, respectively.

To render multiple effects:

1. Load a **SEQUENCE** with effects into the Record monitor.

2. Set an **IN** mark at the beginning of the sequence and an **OUT** mark at the end (or just around the area you want to render).

3. Right-click in the **TIMELINE** and select **RENDER > EXPERTRENDER IN/OUT**.

4. Select the **DRIVE** on which to store the render files and click **OK**.

 The effect source drive listed in the various drive selection menus isn't one particular drive. Rather, it will place the rendered file on the same drive as the original source media. If the effect is a transition, this refers to the media on the outgoing shot.

Partial Renders

You can interrupt lengthy render processes by pressing Ctrl+. (period) (Windows) or Command+. (period) (Mac). Media Composer will ask if you want to save the partial rendered files. Any segments that were partially rendered will display a render bar—a red line at the top of the segment—indicating the portion of the effect that still needs to be rendered. See Figure 12.10.

Figure 12.10 The red render bar shows that V1 is partially rendered.

Understanding ExpertRender

ExpertRender is a feature designed to save you time in the render process, while ensuring that your system is capable of playing back all the effects in your sequence in real time. Like any automatic process in which decisions are made for you, it will do a great job most of the time.

ExpertRender works either where the position indicator is parked or between IN and OUT points that define a range. Based on the system's playback performance, as indicated by the performance bars, ExpertRender determines what effects within the marked range need rendering by analyzing the effects using a couple of basic rules to determine which individual effects to render.

ExpertRender selects segments at the location of the position indicator, or between IN and OUT points using the following rules:

■ If and when video is stacked vertically (composites together), and the top most effect in the stack totally covers the effects below it, ExpertRender will render only the topmost effect (the render file it creates contains it, and every element below it).

■ Render any effect that isn't completely covered by another effect.

■ Render any non–real-time effects, unless completely covered by another effect that will be rendered. This includes nests that contain non–real-time effects.

■ If you have played back the sequence, or a portion of it, and a section or two caused dropped frames, and the red lines have appeared in the timecode track, ExpertRender will follow the rules above, and will provide a dialog box with the following choices:

  • "Render recommended ranges" – select this to render only the effects necessary for successful real-time effects preview.

  • "Render entire selection" – select this to render all the effects that ExpertRender chooses for rendering within your marked region.

Before the actual rendering happens the ExpertRender dialog box opens, as shown in Figure 12.11. By default, the Render Recommended Ranges option is selected. This will render any effect segment where frames were dropped during playback along with the effects just before that location. The segments chosen for rendering are highlighted, and a window shows the progress of the renders. When complete, the sequence can be played back in real time.

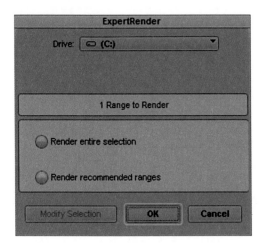

Figure 12.11
Select Render Recommended Ranges
to leverage your system's performance.

 In the ExpertRender dialog box, the Render Entire Selection option will apply the logic of ExpertRender without taking into account your system's performance capability. This will result in a very conservative render selection and depending on the situation, may only be slightly faster than rendering all effects in the sequence.

The logic of ExpertRender errs on the side of caution, taking a conservative approach to how many effects need to be rendered. If you are going to play a sequence directly to broadcast from the Timeline, or are screening a scene for the client, Media Composer assumes that you'd rather spend an extra minute rendering than have the system hiccup during playback. But let's be realistic, not every render is in a high-stakes playback situation. As a result, there are times that you may wish to change the selection of ExpertRender.

Improving ExpertRender

As mentioned, ExpertRender understands that if a segment is completely covered by a segment on a higher track that needs to be rendered, the lower effect can be skipped. But what if the lower track sticks out a little beyond the upper track, like the example shown in Figure 12.12? Most of the effect is covered by another effect, but ExpertRender will want to render the lower one completely.

| B-Roll 01 | ⊞ |
| Runners, Focus on Runner 1 | ⊞ |

Figure 12.12 ExpertRender would select both these effects for render.

Depending on how much the lower effect sticks out, you may be able to get away with rendering only the top effect. As usual, there is an easy way to override the automatic function.

To override the ExpertRender selection:

1. Load a SEQUENCE into the Record monitor

2. Mark an IN and an OUT point to encompass the effects.

3. Right-click on the TIMELINE and select EXPERTRENDER IN/OUT.

4. Click the MODIFY SELECTION button.

5. Shift-click any short SEGMENTS that might not need to be rendered.

6. Click the RENDER EFFECT button in the Timeline.

7. Select the DRIVE on which to create the rendered files and click OK.

 Another way to improve ExpertRender's selection is to use the Add Edit command to divide a segment so the portion that sticks out is rendered by itself.

If you change the ExpertRender selection, it's always a good idea to test playback of the sequence when the render is complete, just to be sure you are still able to play all the effect composites in real time.

Controlling Render Speed and Quality

If you're like most editors, your first inclination is always to want the best quality possible. This produces beautiful images, but it's also the slowest way to go.

During the edit process, you may find yourself building complex effects and simply need a quick view of how well all the animated elements work together. Once all effects are finished, you can re-render at a high quality before showing the director or client.

This approach is often the most efficient way to work with effects-heavy sequences. There are two keys to this workflow:

- Changing the render quality setting

- Clearing existing renders to be able to re-render

Changing the Render Setting

The render settings, found in the Settings pane of the Project window, have a number of options that control the quality of renders and image scaling, as well as the default render method used for motion effects. Opening the Render Setting dialog box reveals several drop-down menus, as shown in Figure 12.13. The top one, Image Interpolation, controls the algorithm used to process effects, thereby controlling both the quality and the time it takes to complete. Setting this menu to Draft (Nearest Neighbor) will cause all the effects to render as quickly as possible, but at a lower image quality.

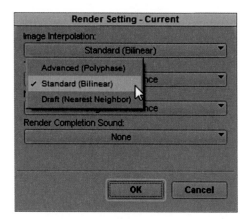

Figure 12.13
Use Draft (Nearest Neighbor) for "quick and dirty" renders.

To set the render quality for fast, draft-quality renders:

1. Open the **RENDER SETTING** dialog box from the Settings pane of the Project window.

2. Click the **IMAGE INTERPOLATION** menu.

3. Select **DRAFT (NEAREST NEIGHBOR)**, and then click **OK**.

    This is the ideal configuration when working on an effects-heavy sequence in which you will be doing numerous renders and want to minimize render time during the creative process. Before final output, you should re-render the effects at a higher quality setting.

To set the render quality for mastering-quality renders:

1. Open the **RENDER SETTING** dialog box from the Settings pane of the Project window.

2. Click the **IMAGE INTERPOLATION** menu.

3. Select **ADVANCED (POLYPHASE)**, and then click **OK**.

Clearing Renders

Once an effect is rendered, Media Composer won't automatically render it again. This is a convenient feature most of the time. For example, suppose you've rendered several effects in the sequence, and you want to render the rest of the effects before output. You could simply render the entire sequence; no time will be wasted re-rendering any effects already rendered.

However, in cases where you've rendered some effects at draft quality and you want to re-render at mastering quality, the default behavior won't do at all. Not to worry, you can easily get around it with the Clear Renders command, which breaks the link between an effect and its rendered file, leaving the effect again unrendered.

To open the Clear Renders dialog box, right-click the Timeline and choose Clear Renders at Position, as shown in Figure 12.14. The default settings will protect the render files of any motion effects as well as those of any plug-in effects not installed on your system—a.k.a. "unknown effects." (See Figure 12.15.)

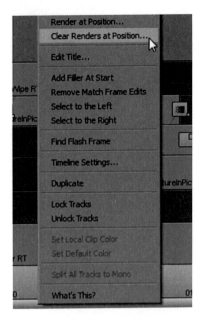

Figure 12.14
Open the Clear Renders dialog box using this menu command.

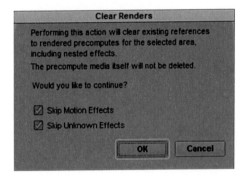

Figure 12.15 The Clear Renders dialog box.

 If you accidentally clear renders on an effect that you didn't mean to, press Ctrl+Z (Windows) or Command+Z (Mac) to undo the action. Media Composer will relink the rendered file to the effect.

To clear renders:

1. Load a SEQUENCE into the Record monitor.

2. Mark an IN point at the beginning of the sequence and an OUT point at the end.

3. Enable all TRACKS, then right-click in the TIMELINE and select CLEAR RENDERS IN/OUT.

4. Click OK. All effects within the selected area of the Timeline will now be unrendered, ready for you to render at a higher quality.

 Exercise Break: Exercise 12.3
Pause here to practice what you've learned.

Review/Discussion Questions

1. How do you add an effect to a clip in the Timeline on top of an existing effect?

2. What is that procedure in #1 called?

3. What are the two different methods you can use to view the effects inside of a nest?

4. What is an advantage of simple nesting view?

5. What is an advantage of expanded nesting view?

6. How do you change the order of effects within a nest?

7. What do the red, yellow and blue bars in the Timeline mean?

8. What does Clear Renders do?

Lesson 12 Keyboard Shortcuts

Key	Shortcut
Ctrl+8 (Windows)/Command+8 (Mac)	Opens the Effect Palette

Nesting and Order of Processing

In this exercise, you're going to look at how order of processing can affect effect results. You'll also learn how you can take advantage of this order of processing to get better results.

Media Used: TN Parkour

Duration: 90 minutes

GOALS

- Nest effects

- Step in and out of an effect

- Rearrange the order of nested effects

Exercise 12.1: Nesting Effects

In this exercise, we will use nesting to add multiple effects on a segment without altering the PIP effect we created in a previous exercise.

Media Used: Tennessee Parkour

Time: 30 minutes

For this exercise, we will use the **MC110_TN PARKOUR** project.

1. Begin by opening the bin **STUDENT_LESSON SEQUENCES**.

2. Duplicate the sequence **12.1_TNPARKOUR MONTAGE_NESTING** and move the duplicate sequence into the **TNPARKOUR_EXERCISE SEQUENCES** bin.

3. Load the duplicate **12.1_TNPARKOUR MONTAGE_NESTING** into the Timeline.

4. Choose **TOOLS > MARKERS**.

   Read over the notes the Producer has left for you regarding some additional changes that need to be made to the Tennessee Parkour Montage.

#		Marker Name	TC	End	Track	Part	Comment
0001	◉	Producer	01:00:27:14		V3		Panel #1 - this shot is too dark, let's up the brightness and contrast.
0002	◉	Producer	01:00:28:09		V3		Panel #2 - Zoom in 25%
0003	◉	Producer	01:00:28:28		V3		Panel #1 - Zoom in 15%

Figure 12.16 The Marker window displaying markers and notes from the Producer.

5. Start with the first note.

   The Producer believes the shot in Panel #1 is too dark and asks you to increase the brightness and contrast.

Figure 12.17 The Producer believes the shot in Panel #1 is too dark, you need to increase the brightness and contrast.

6. To nest a color effect on this shot, begin by navigating to the **EFFECTS TAB** in the Project Window.

7. From the Effects tab, select the **IMAGE** category from the left column.

8. From the right column, choose the **COLOR CORRECTION EFFECT** and hold down the **ALT** (Windows) or **OPTION** (Mac) key and **DRAG** the effect to the segment used in **PANEL #1**.

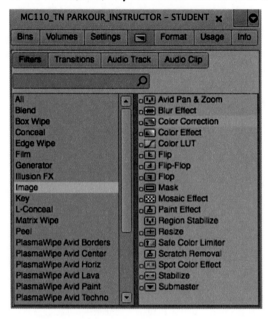

Figure 12.18   The Color Correction effect selected from the Effects tab.

This will nest the Color Correction effect on the segment.

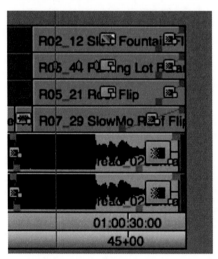

Figure 12.19   The Color Correction effect nested on the segment.

9. Open the segment in the Effect Editor.

10. Go to the following parameters in the Color Correction Effect: **HSL > CONTROLS > MASTER**, until you see the **BRIGHTNESS AND CONTRAST SLIDERS**.

11. Increase the **BRIGHTNESS** by **10** and the **CONTRAST** by **15**.

    You will notice that the other shots below the shot in Panel #1 (located in the V4 track) are also affected by the color effect as is the white box around the panel. This is not what we want.

12. To correct this, go back to the Effect Editor and drag the Color Correction effect below the Picture-In-Picture effect so that the PIP comes first in the order of the nest.

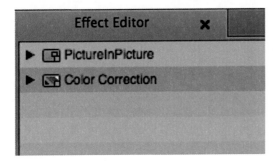

Figure 12.20   The Color Correction effect should be moved below the Picture-In-Picture effect so that the PIP comes first in the order of the nest.

This should correct the problem and only the footage inside Panel #1 should be impacted by the color effect.

13. Read the next note.

The Producer also needs you to resize the shot in Panel #1 by 15%.

14. First, step into the nest by double-clicking on the segment in the Timeline.

You will see that the first layer of the nest is the PIP, followed by the Color Correction.

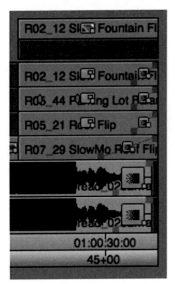

Figure 12.21   The first layer of the nest is the PIP, followed by the Color Correction.

15. Step further into the effect by double-clicking on the layer containing the Color Correction effect.

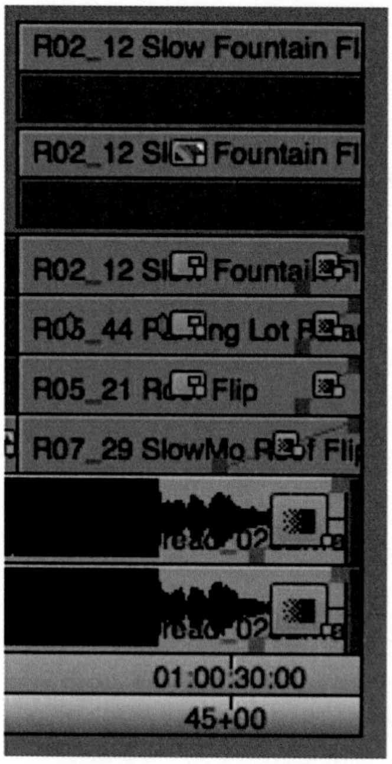

Figure 12.22 The layer containing the Color Correction effect.

16. From the **EFFECTS TAB** in the Project window, grab the **RESIZE EFFECT** and drag it on to the empty layer of the nest.

Figure 12.23 The Resize effect applied to the empty layer of the nest.

17. Open the segment in the Effect Editor and increase the **SCALE** of the shot to **115**.

18. Make sure **FIXED ASPECT** is **ENABLED**.

19. Adjust the **POSITION** of the shot within the panel accordingly.

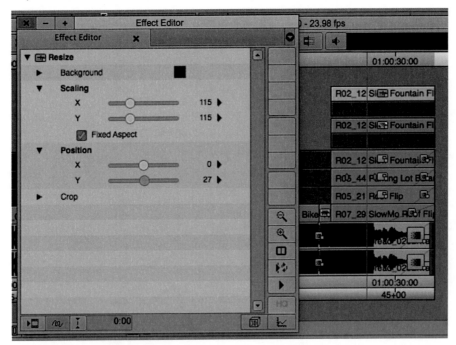

Figure 12.24 Adjusting the Position of the shot in the Effect Editor.

20. Collapse the nest by double-clicking on the bottommost layer with the PIP effect on it while in Source/Record mode.

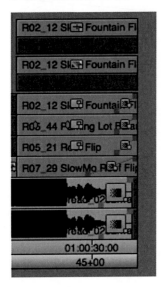

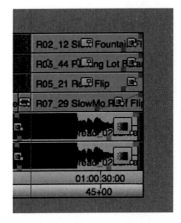

Figure 12.25 Before collapsing the nest.   Figure 12.26 After collapsing the nest.

Exercise 12.2: Editing within the Nest

In this exercise, we will use Simple Nesting View to swap out a shot without altering the PIP effect we created in a previous sequence.

Media Used: Tennessee Parkour

Time: 30 minutes

For this exercise, we will continue to use the **MC110_TN PARKOUR** project.

1. Begin by opening the bin **STUDENT_LESSON SEQUENCES**.

2. Duplicate the sequence **12.2_TNPARKOUR MONTAGE_NESTING REV** and move the duplicate sequence into the **TNPARKOUR_EXERCISE SEQUENCES** bin.

3. Load the duplicate **12.2_TNPARKOUR MONTAGE_NESTING REV** into the Timeline.

4. Choose **TOOLS > MARKERS**.

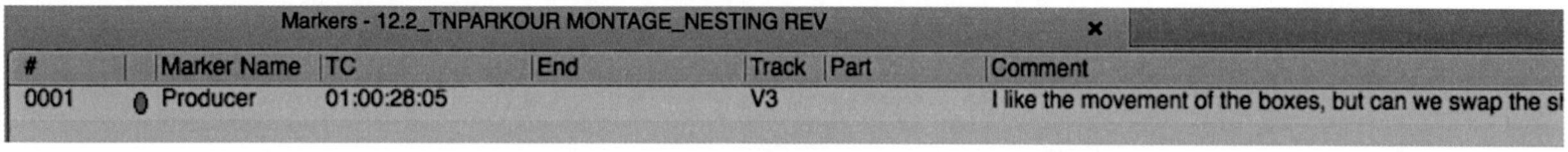

Markers - 12.2_TNPARKOUR MONTAGE_NESTING REV						✕	
#	Marker Name	TC	End	Track	Part	Comment	
0001	Producer	01:00:28:05		V3		I like the movement of the boxes, but can we swap the s	

Figure 12.27 The Marker window displaying markers and the Producer's notes.

Read over the note the Producer has left for you regarding an additional change that needs to be made to the Tennessee Parkour Montage:

"I like the movement of the boxes, but can we swap the shot in Panel #2 for shot "R02_01 Slow Bench Over Railing" - right when the guy with the purple shirt is flipping off the ledge."

5. Pull up the shot that the Producer is referring to, to find the shot, use **CTRL + F** (Windows) or **COMMAND + F** (Mac) to bring up the Finder window in Media Composer.

6. Type **SLOW BENCH** and click **FIND**.

7. Double-click the clip **R02_01 SLOW BENCH OVER RAILING** Master clip in the Finder window and it will load into the Source monitor.

8. In the Timeline, step into the nest on track V3 by ENABLING the **V3** track selector, parking the position indicator on the shot, and then clicking the **STEP IN BUTTON**.

▼ Figure 12.28 Step In button.

The video clip that is beneath the PIP effect will now appear in the Timeline.

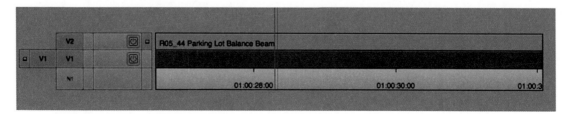

Figure 12.29 The video clip beneath the PIP appears in the Timeline.

9. Press the **T KEY** to mark an **IN** and **OUT** around the shot.

10. Next, turn off V1 and make sure that V2 is enabled.

11. In the **SOURCE MONITOR**, mark an **IN** point in the shot **R02_01 SLOW BENCH OVER RAILING** where the guy in the purple shirt is flipping over the ledge.

Figure 12.30 In the Source monitor, an IN mark is set where the guy in the purple shirt is flipping over the ledge.

12. **OVERWRITE** the shot into the Timeline using the **B KEY**.

13. Make sure your Overwrite is targeted only to the **V2** track in the nest.

14. Step out of the nest using the **STEP OUT BUTTON**.

    Figure 12.31 Step Out button.

15. Play through the change you made to verify that the shot has been replaced.

    Observe that although the shot was replaced, you still need to adjust the position of the image as well as the timing.

Figure 12.32 After playing through the changes you made, you still need to adjust the position of the image, as well as the timing.

16. Step into the nest again using the Step In button.

 Figure 12.33 Step In button.

17. From the **EFFECTS TAB** in the Project window, use the search box. Type in **RESIZE**. Click and grab the **RESIZE EFFECT** and drag it on to the video in the Timeline.

18. Step back out of the nest using the **STEP OUT BUTTON**.

 Figure 12.34 Step Out button.

19. Enter Effect mode and use the Position parameter of the Resize effect to adjust the position of the guy in the purple shirt in Panel #2.

Figure 12.35 Using the Position parameter of the Resize effect, adjust the position of the guy in the purple shirt in Panel #2.

20. To adjust the content of the shot, so that the guy in Panel #2 is flipping over the ledge just as the panel comes to rest in its position in the frame, use the Trim Keys on the keyboard to slip the shot without entering Trim mode.

 Figure 12.36 Trim Keys.

21. Make sure V1, V2, and V4 and the audio tracks are disabled so you do not accidently slip their content as well.

Figure 12.37 Playing through the effect.

22. Play through the effect until you are satisfied.

If your system is having any difficulty playing back the effect, try lowering the playback resolution of your sequence using the Video Quality Menu.

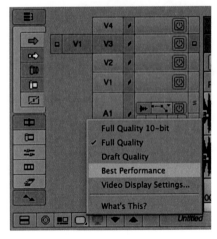

Figure 12.38 Choosing a different resolution from the Video Quality menu.

Exercise 12.3: Rendering Effects

In this exercise, we will use Expert Render to improve the playback performance of our multilayer effect.

Media Used: Tennessee Parkour

Time: 30 minutes

For this exercise, we will continue to use the **MC110_TN PARKOUR** project:

1. Begin by opening the bin **STUDENT_LESSON SEQUENCES**.

2. Duplicate the sequence **12.3_TNPARKOUR MONTAGE_RENDER** and move the duplicate sequence into the **TNPARKOUR_EXERCISE SEQUENCES** bin.

3. Load the duplicate **12.3_TNPARKOUR MONTAGE_RENDER** into the Timeline.

4. Besides lowering the playback resolution using the Video Quality Menu, we can also render our multilayer effect to improve playback performance.

5. Go to the multilayer effect that we have been working with at 01:00:26:19 and park your position indicator anywhere on the stack of effects.

6. Make sure all tracks are enabled.

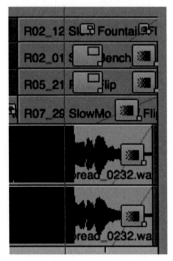

Figure 12.39 Parking your position indicator anywhere on the stack of effects to render our effects..

7. Choose TIMELINE > RENDER > EXPERTRENDER AT POSITION.

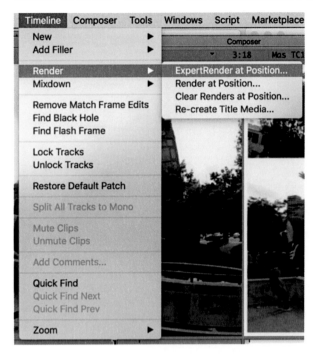

Figure 12.40 Choosing "ExpertRender at Position" from the Timeline > Render menu.

8. When the ExpertRender window appears, make sure the render is targeted to the correct hard drive and click **OK**.

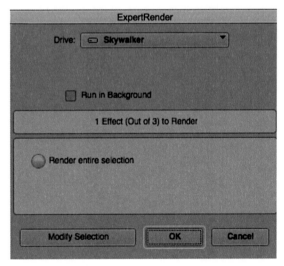

Figure 12.41 ExpertRender window with the correct hard drive selected.

ExpertRender will choose to render only the segments necessary to create all the effects, in this case, the topmost effect on V4.

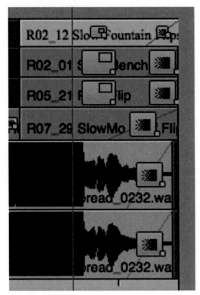

Figure 12.42 The topmost effect on V4 is rendered.

9.   When the render is complete, play back your effect to make sure it runs smoothly.

10. Conclude the lesson by saving your work.

Creating ChromaKey Effects

Let's say you're making a film and you need a shot of someone on the moon or of your star actor hanging from a burning building. You can get those shots if you know how to create composites and, to start with, how to "key."

Media Used: "Godiva Medium" Shot

Duration: 60 minutes

GOALS

- Learn the different types of keys
- Explore the SpectraMatte
- Crop out garbage
- View the Matte channel

Different Keying Types

In generic terms, **keying** means to create transparency in a foreground image and combine it with a background image to create one composite image. To create a composite, you select a portion of the foreground that will be transparent. The transparent portion is called the **Matte channel** (see Figure 13.1).

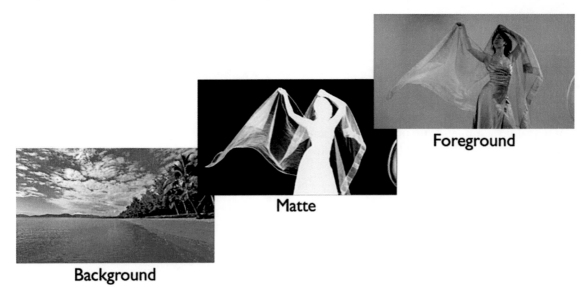

Foreground

Matte

Background

Figure 13.1 Background, Matte channel, and foreground.

There are three primary tools used to generate a matte in Media Composer.

- **Rotoscoping tools:** Rotoscoping tools require you to manually draw or paint the matte frame by frame over the portion of the image you wish to keep. Media Composer includes a sophisticated intraframe effects including AniMatte and Paint Effect, as well as cropping parameters, which can be used to rotoscope mattes.

- **Keying effects:** Using one of the keying effects, the matte is procedurally generated by Media Composer based on color or luminance.

- **Matte keys:** A matte key uses a separate grayscale image to create the transparency. Although a title is a form of matte key, the actual Matte Key effect is typically applied to imported grayscale images or automatically applied when you import QuickTime with Alpha channels.

  Alpha channels are mattes that are incorporated into the actual media file. Typically generated by motion graphics, visual effects, or 3D animation software, the Alpha channel is a fourth channel of the image, the first three being the red, green, and blue channels.

In this lesson, you'll look more closely at the keying tools in conjunction with cropping to create a composite. Then we'll touch upon importing a QuickTime file with Alpha to create a matte key.

 The terms mask and matte are often incorrectly used interchangeably. A matte is a grayscale image used to identify transparency in an RGB image. A mask is the application of a matte. For example, you *mask* out the boom microphone using a matte.

Exploring the SpectraMatte

Successful keying depends on planning. The foreground should be shot in a manner that helps generate the matte. The most common way is to isolate it against an evenly lit, solid-color background, typically a blue or green screen. Media Composer includes a number of different keyers, located in the Effect Palette's Key category. The best keyer for blue or green screen is the SpectraMatte effect. SpectraMatte not only provides a better quality key compared to the RGB keyer effect, it also makes it easy to fine-tune your keys and to solve problems such as shadows and color spill.

When setting up the tracks for a green- or blue-screen composite, the foreground subject should always be placed on a track directly above the background segment.

When working in Effect mode it is common to use just a single monitor (the Effect Preview Monitor). However, with SpectraMatte, you will want to have a Dual Monitor setup. If the Composer window is not already in that configuration, then right-click and from the menu choose "Show Dual Monitor."

To apply the SpectraMatte:

1. Edit the blue screen or green screen SEGMENT on the track above the background segment.

2. From the KEY category of the Effect Palette, apply the SPECTRAMATTE effect to the foreground image.

    SpectraMatte will immediately key out blue colors in the shot. If there are any, this can make for some interesting results.

3. Enter Effect mode, and click the BYPASS CHECKBOX at the top of the Effect Editor.

4. Place the cursor pointer over the COLOR PREVIEW DISPLAY.

    The pointer will change to an eyedropper icon.

5. Click the COLOR PREVIEW DISPLAY one time (clicking two times will open the OS color picker).See Figure 13.2.

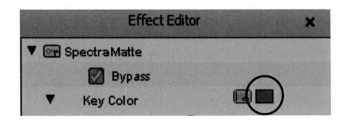

Figure 13.2 Click the Color Preview Display to display the eyedropper.

6. Move the EYEDROPPER to the Effect Preview monitor and click the mouse button on the blue screen or green screen, close to the subject.

    When you click the mouse, the system samples the background color and immediately creates the transparency channel based on the effect's default parameters.

7. Deselect BYPASS to see the results.

    SpectraMatte is an excellent keyer and can produce dramatic results just with the initial sample, but to produce a truly professional quality effect, you will need to further refine the key. Before you dive into adjusting the parameters, there are two things to do first that will make the job of keying much easier: 1.) View the matte channel; 2.) Use a garbage matte.

Viewing the Matte Channel

To get the matte perfect (or as close as possible), you need to be able to view it.

When using SpectraMatte with a dual monitor set-up, the left monitor is the "Effect Analysis monitor," and the right monitor is the Effect Preview monitor (as usual).

The grayscale Matte channel can be displayed in the Effect Analysis monitor, while the composite is shown in the Effect Preview monitor. Alternatively, you can leave the SpectraGraph displayed in the Effect Analysis monitor and display the Alpha channel in the Record monitor. An advantage of displaying the Alpha channel in the Effect Preview monitor is that you can use the Enlarge and Reduce buttons to zoom into the image for critical analysis of the matte.

To view the Matte channel, do one of the following:

- In the Matte Analysis section of the Effect Editor, click the Show Alpha checkbox.

- In the Matte Analysis section, choose ALPHA IN SOURCE MONITOR from the SPECTRAGRAPH SOURCE MONITOR menu (see Figure 13.3).

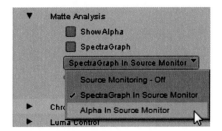

Figure 13.3

Choose Alpha in Source Monitor to display the Matte channel in the Source monitor.

The white areas of the matte represent the opaque parts of the foreground image. The black areas represent the transparent parts. Your goal should be to create a solid white foreground and a solid black background without any specks in either area.

To help control the amount of gray or black specks in the foreground, the Inner Softness and Outer Softness parameters determine how narrow or broad the falloff is between the keyed-out color and the foreground, and often make the biggest impact on semi-transparent areas of the image. These are often subtle changes and it is much easier to see the effects of these adjustments while looking at the matte.

For critical viewing of the image, it can help to zoom in and pan around on the image.

- To zoom in, click the Enlarge button, or alternatively Ctrl+click (Windows) or Command+click (Mac) on the Alpha image in the Effect Preview monitor.

- To zoom out, click the Reduce button, or alternatively Ctrl+Shift+click (Windows) or Command+Shift+click (Mac).

- To pan the zoomed image, hold Ctrl+Alt+drag (Windows) or Command+Option+drag (Mac) the image.

 When analyzing the matte, be sure to scrub through the clip and look at how it changes with the movement in the shot.

Cropping Out Garbage

In many blue- or green-screen shots, large portions of the shot are just green screen, and the subject never crosses over them. Sometimes the green screen is just a small screen behind the talent, or other times there is rigging or other set equipment visible around the edges of the shot, as shown in Figure 13.4. Whatever it is, this "garbage" should be removed.

Figure 13.4 Crop out any visible set rigging, and other unwanted portions of the image to make the job of keying easier.

You can simplify the keying task with a garbage matte, effectively ignoring unwanted portions of the frame. A *garbage matte* allows you to focus on removing the key color screen that is immediately around the subject rather than having to key out the entire green screen.

How a garbage matte is created varies from drawing complex spline shapes to simply cropping the image as tightly as possible without cutting off any of the subject. Media Composer includes a separate rotoscoping tools called the Paint Effect and AniMatte, but also includes cropping built directly into the SpectraMatte for simpler tasks. Whatever method you use, mask out the garbage early in the keying process so you don't waste time trying to perfect an area that is easily masked out.

 Learn more about using the Paint Effect and Animatte effect to create advanced composites in Media Composer by taking the MC201 and MC210 courses, Media Composer Professional Editing I and II.

So, with the garbage masked out and the Alpha channel displayed for analysis, you're ready to start refining the key.

Adjusting the SpectraMatte

When you open a SpectraMatte effect in the Effect Editor, the Source monitor converts to a special Effect Analysis monitor. By default, it shows the SpectraGraph screen (see Figure 13.5), a color wheel–style swatch that represents the color space within which the SpectraMatte effect works. The darkened wedge in the SpectraGraph screen shows the range of color used to generate the matte.

Figure 13.5 The SpectraGraph screen provides visual feedback on the color range being keyed.

The center point of the swatch is neutral gray. Similar to a color wheel, the various hues are displayed in circular fashion around the swatch, and saturation is displayed increasing from the center out. The wedge that shows the color range selection gets wider at the perimeter of the color swatch, keying out a relatively broad range of highly saturated colors from the chosen key color. Because green screens and blue screens should be well-lit, highly saturated colors, and because those colors rarely exist in nature, the kinds of color values that should always require keying out will appear at the perimeter of the swatch. That's in a perfect world, however. Often, you'll have poorly lit green or blue screens, so the wedge also provides very precise control over low-saturation color values and hue color values. These colors fall on the borderline between those you want to key out and those you want to retain. These are the kinds of color values that you often need to blend or fine-tune—for example, to improve the edges of the foreground subject.

Refining the Alpha Matte

To start refining the matte, start in the Chroma Control group and work your way down. As you adjust each parameter, keep one eye on the Alpha channel to whether an adjustment is improving or damaging the matte. Finding the best value is a bit like manually focusing a camera. You only know the best value for a given parameter by going too far in one direction or another and then settling on the value that produces the best results.

The SpectraGraph screen lets you clearly see the relationship between the current result of the key, represented by the black wedge, and the color values in your image. Superimposed on the color swatch is a vectorscope-style display that shows the distribution of color values in the foreground image.

As shown in Figure 13.6, there is typically a concentration of either green or blue color values that represent the background screen color you want to key out, along with the distribution of other color values from the foreground subject that you want to retain.

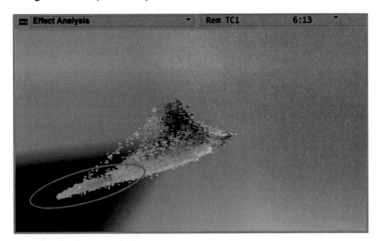

Figure 13.6 Foreground distribution of colors.

Picking the key color sets the position of the wedge around the color swatch, then Tolerance, Key Sat Line, and Key Saturation define its size, shape and position. As you adjust the parameter values, the SpectraGraph changes dynamically to show you how that's impacting the image. Use this in conjunction with viewing the alpha matte to guide you as you refine the key.

The Chroma Tolerance parameter defines the width or spread of the wedge (see Figure 13.7). Too narrow and you will see portions of the background reappear in the alpha. Too wide, and portions of the foreground element will start to become transparent.

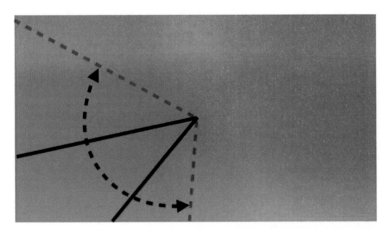

Figure 13.7 The Tolerance parameter adjusts the range of hues included in the key.

The saturation value set by the Key Saturation parameter defines the location of the center point of the wedge. You can shift the entire wedge away from the center of the swatch by increasing the Key Saturation value as shown in Figure 13.8.

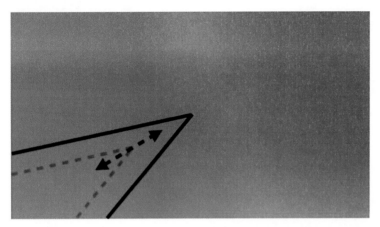

Figure 13.8 Key Saturation shifts the center point of the wedge.

Between the Tolerance and Key Saturation parameters is the Key Sat Line, which determines the minimum saturation level for the key color range (see Figure 13.9). Raising the value "cuts off" the point of the wedge. As the value goes up, more unsaturated colors will be excluded from the key, and kept in the image. Use Key Sat Line to fine-tune the threshold at which the key removes low-saturation parts of the image.

Depending on the particular values of the image you are using, Adjusting Key Sat Line may or may not improve it.

 Raising the Key Sat Line value can sometimes produce a halo effect around hair, excluding the unsaturated greens at the ends of and between the hairs of your talent.

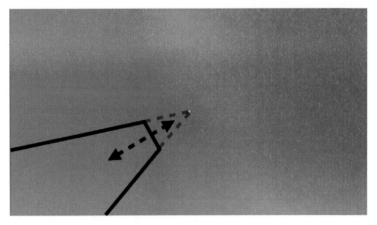

Figure 13.9 The clipping point for unsaturated colors is set by the Key Sat Line parameter.

The other secondary parameters control how the key color wedge is refined. Inner Softness and Outer Softness offer subtle control over semi-transparent areas near the edge of the key wedge. Although the changes are visible in the SpectraGraph, their impact is easier to evaluate by looking at the Alpha Matte.

Continue to adjust the Chroma parameters until you achieve a solid black and white Matte channel, then you should move on to focus on the edges of the foreground.

Refining the Edges of the Matte

The edges are often the most difficult area of keying. Okay, not often—always! That being the case, it gets special attention in the Matte Processing section of the Effect Editor. The Matte Processing controls, shown in Figure 13.10, let you blur, shrink (Erode), or expand (Dilate) the edges of the Matte channel to make the matte fit better around your subject.

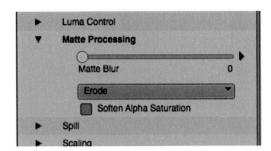

Figure 13.10 Use the Matte Processing controls to refine the edges of your foreground image.

Dealing with Spill

Spill is any tinting of areas on the foreground toward the backing screen color. Light reflects off the blue or green screen and "spills" onto the foreground subject. Spill suppression replaces the spill color with another color outside of the defined spill suppression zone (see Figure 13.11).

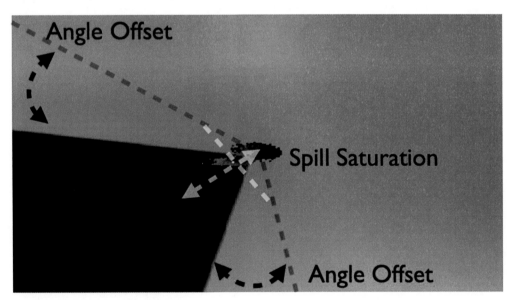

Figure 13.11 Spill suppression zone.

You can change the spread of the spill correction using the Spill Angle Offset parameter. Larger adjustments usually result in too much color correction of the foreground image, but subtle adjustments can neutralize the green spill without adding too much magenta.

Saturation determines the threshold for where spill suppression begins. The lower the number, the more key colors with less saturation are included in the suppression. The higher the number, the closer the spill saturation matches the Key Saturation value. If the Key Saturation value is 0, then this slider has very little effect.

These fundamental areas of adjustments can be used to produce high-quality composites on almost any green or blue screen. There are times when matte edges may need more work and your garbage matte may need a more refined shape, but the fundamentals remain the same. You can learn how to handle more complicated keying scenarios in the course *MC201: Media Composer Professional Editing I.*

Exercise Break: Exercise 13.1
Pause here to practice what you've learned.

Review/Discussion Questions

1. The transparent channel in a clip is called which of the following?

    a. The green screen

    b. Luminance

    c. A matte

2. True or False: The SpectraMatte effect provides a better key than the RGB keyer effect, and it also makes it easier to fine-tune your keys.

3. If you have a background clip on track V2, what track should your green screen clip be edited onto?

4. What do the L and R parameters stand for in the Crop Parameter group of the SpectraMatte?

5. True or False: The purpose of a garbage mask is to remove all of the green or blue screen from the foreground.

6. What is the Alpha in Source Monitor menu selection used for?

Creating Keying and Matte Composites

In this exercise, you will use the SpectraMatte effect to key out a green screen and replace it with a new background.

Media Used: "Godiva Medium" Shot

Duration: 30 minutes

GOAL

■ Create a composite using the SpectraMatte effect

Exercise 13.1: Keying Out a Green Screen Using SpectraMatte

In this exercise we will use the SpectraMatte effect to key out a green screen and replace it with a new background.

The foreground clip of the model is provided courtesy of Hollywood Camera Work. Visit their website to download free, high-quality green screen plates to practice keying, matchmoving, compositing, tracking, and much more.

http://www.hollywoodcamerawork.com/greenscreenplates.html

 All green screen plates available from HollywoodCamera.com are image sequence files. Refer to "Importing Image Sequences" in Lesson 2 to review how to convert images sequences to video clips on import.

For this exercise, we will use the **MC110_EFFECTS** project.

1.   Begin by launching Media Composer and loading the **MC110_EFFECTS** project.

2.   Open the **STUDENT_LESSON SEQUENCES** bin.

3.   Duplicate the sequence **13.1_SPECTRA MATTE** and drag the duplicate into the **EFFECTS_EXERCISE SEQUENCES** bin.

4.   Load the duplicated **13.1_SPECTRA MATTE** sequence into the Timeline.

5.   Play through the sequence.

     You will see that what you have is a clip of an actress that has been filmed in front of a green screen.

6.   We will use the SpectraMatte effect to key out the green screen so we can replace what is behind the actress with a background of our choosing.

Figure 13.12 Green screen behind the actress.

7.   Start by creating a new video track. **CLICK CTRL+Y** (Windows) or **COMMAND+Y** (Mac).

8.   Move the green screen footage to the **V2** track.

9. Link to or import the high-resolution image.

    For the purposes of this demonstration, we are using a still image of the beach. Using a stock video clip will create a more realistic composite. You will find the still image in this location: Supplemental Media > For SpectraMatte_Exercise 13.1 > Holloways_beach_1920x1080.jpg.

Figure 13.13 The background beach image: Holloways_beach_1920x1080.jpg.

10. Import your image to the **GODIVA_GREEN SCREEN** bin.

11. Overwrite your image onto the **V1** track below the green screen footage.

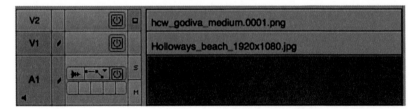

Figure 13.14 The "Holloways_beach_1920x1080.jpg" footage overwritten onto the V1 track.

12. From the Key category of the Effects Palette, drag the **SPECTRAMATTE EFFECT** onto the segment **HCW_GODIVA_MEDIUM.0001.PNG** on the **V2** track in the Timeline.

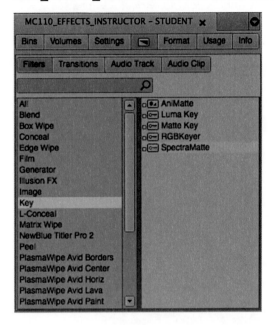

Figure 13.15 The SpectraMatte effect selected in the Effects tab > Key category.

13. The image immediately changes as the SpectraMatte keys out her blue dress.

Figure 13.16 The image immediately changes as the SpectraMatte keys out her blue dress.

14. Open the **SPECTRAMATTE EFFECT** in the **EFFECT EDITOR** and click the **BYPASS CHECKBOX**.

15. Click the Color Preview Display next to Key Color.

The mouse icon changes to an eye dropper.

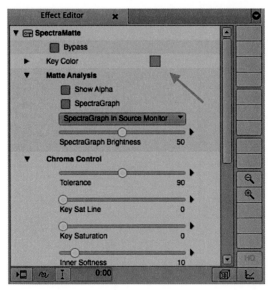

Figure 13.17 The Color Preview Display in the Effect Editor.

16. Using the **EYEDROPPER**, click the green screen in the **EFFECT PREVIEW MONITOR**, choosing a point close to the model.

17. Deselect (uncheck) the **BYPASS** option.

When your green screen is first keyed out, it should look like this:

Figure 13.18 When your green screen is first keyed out.

Not bad for fully automatic, but you can do better. To start, you need to get a critical look at the matte.

18. Click the drop-down menu in the MATTE ANALYSIS PARAMETER GROUP, and select ALPHA IN SOURCE MONITOR.

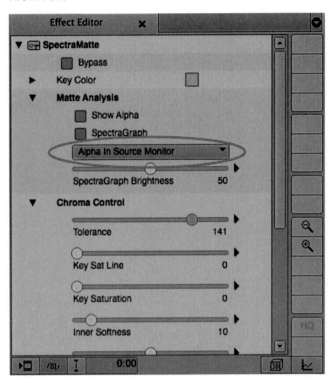

Figure 13.19 The "Alpha in Source Monitor" option in the Effect Editor.

The Spectragraph in the Source monitor will change to display the matte.

Figure 13.20 The Spectragraph in the Source monitor changes to display the matte.

The first problem is the fan, visible on the right side of the frame. Let's take care of that.

19. Scroll down in the EFFECT EDITOR to the CROP PARAMETER GROUP, and then click the disclosure triangle to open the group.

20. Drag the **R PARAMETER SLIDER** to the left until the fan disappears, as shown in Figure 13.21.

Figure 13.21 Drag the R parameter slider to the left until the fan disappears.

Nice job. Now, on to the matte.

21. Scrub through the clip, looking at how the key affects the composite image and the matte.

    In particular, look for problem areas in the matte – pinholes or grey "shadows" in the white areas, white noise in the black areas, especially near the edges of the frame where the green screen maybe isn't evenly lit.

    Look closely at your subject's hair. How clean and refined does it look? Have you lost the fine detail or is there a green halo around it? Are there any areas of the image that have green tones or reflections that shouldn't? (For example, the actress's drape still has a lot of green in it.)

    These will be the areas to improve, and the same things to watch out for as you adjust the effect parameters. Take any parameter too far in one direction or another, and you will often find that you can introduce problems, rather than fix them. As you work, remember the analogy of focusing a lens – keep working a parameter back and forth until you find the sweet spot.

22. Increase the **TOLERANCE** parameter to remove the remaining green in the sheer drape the actress is holding.

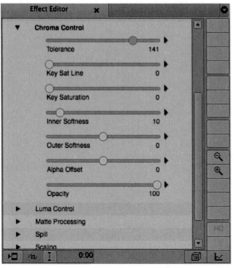

Figure 13.22 Increase the Tolerance parameter in the Effect Editor.

The result is definitely improved, but in certain frames there are areas of the drape that become fully transparent. It should never fully disappear, so we need to fix this.

Figure 13.23 In certain frames there are areas of the drape that become fully transparent.

23. Adjust the **INNER SOFTNESS** and **OUTER SOFTNESS** parameters to restore the transparent areas of the sheer drape.

24. Finally, experiment with the **MATTE PROCESSING CONTROLS** to see how **BLUR**, **ERODE** and **DILATE** can improve (or degrade) the edges

25. (Optional) Enlarge the composite image in the Effect Preview monitor for a closer view of the actress's hair, and scrub through the shot again. Refine the Matte Processing parameters as needed.

Nice work! You have pulled a very effective key.

Animated Titles & Graphics

As you move toward the completion of a sequence, you might need to display titles over the video or add text slates or other graphical elements. The NewBlue Titler Pro enables you to create and add these elements easily, but it goes beyond basic titles by letting you easily create 3D title animation.

Media Used: MC110_EFFECTS

Duration: 45 minutes

GOALS

- Begin titles in NewBlue Titler Pro
- Format and position titles
- Modify title properties
- Use the template library
- Animate objects in a scene
- Save titles to a bin
- Edit an existing title
- Link to an animated logo with alpha channel

Creating Titles with NewBlue Titler Pro

NewBlue® Titler Pro is now available as an addition to the titling capabilities of your Avid editing system. This new Titler is available in all project types.

In higher than HD projects (UHD/2K/4K), the legacy Title Tool and the Marquee Title Tool are not supported. An error message appears if you try and open either title tool in a UHD/2K/4K project. For these formats, titles will be created using the NewBlue Titler.

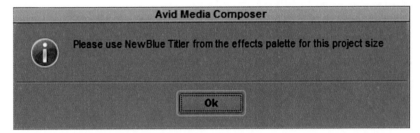

Figure 14.1 This error message appears if you try and open either title tool in a UHD/2K/4K project.

NewBlue Titler Overview

The NewBlue Titler is an effect, not a separate tool. You will find it in the Effects Palette, under the NEWBLUE TITLER PRO video effects category. This effect is applied to filler in your video track, or can be dropped on a piece of video you place in the Timeline.

Overview steps to use the NewBlue Titler Pro:

1. Apply the effect to a segment in your Timeline.

2. If the NewBlue Titler interface does not open automatically, then open the EFFECT EDITOR.

3. Open the plug-in by clicking on TITLER PRO > LAUNCH USER INTERFACE.

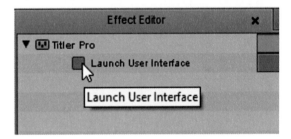

Figure 14.2 Launching the NewBlue Titler from the Effect Editor.

4. Create the title.

5. CLOSE the Titler tool.

    Titles do not appear in the bin, they are effects in the Timeline. They can be shared and copied by dragging the effect icon from the Effect Editor into a bin.

At this time, there is no way to conform an Avid Title Tool title created in an SD or HD project into UHD/2K/4K titles. Titles from SD and HD will be brought into your larger than HD projects at the smaller media sizes of SD or HD, as they were originally created. They will simply be blown up to fill the larger frame; they will not be recreated at the larger size.

Creating a Title

To create a title with the NewBlue Titler Pro:

1. Begin by applying the NewBlue Titler to a shot or to a filler segment in your Timeline, open the Effect Editor and click on the **LAUNCH USER INTERFACE** button.

2. When the NewBlue Title Tool opens, a paragraph of text will be present. Click where it says **ENTER TEXT** and **TYPE** in your new title text.

3. (Option) To add additional text, click the **NEW PARAGRAPH** button to create other paragraphs (text fields) if they are required.

Figure 14.3 To add additional text, click the New Paragraph button.

4. At the top of the interface are all the familiar text formatting controls – font, size and other formatting options. With the block of text selected, make adjustments as desired.

Figure 14.4 At the top of the interface are all the familiar text formatting controls.

5. Click the STYLES button to display a tab full of presets. With your Paragraph text field selected (no need to highlight the actual text), mouse over the presets to see a preview of the styles that can be applied to your selected text. When you find one that you like, simply double-click on the preset to apply it to the text.

Figure 14.5 The Styles button displays a tab full of presets.

6. The ATTRIBUTES TAB contains sliders you can use to adjust the text paragraph: position, rotation, scale as well as opacity and justification, make adjustments where needed.

Figure 14.6 The Attributes tab contains sliders you can use to adjust the text paragraph.

7. To create a Drop Shadow, choose the **ATTRIBUTES TAB** and click the **STYLE BUTTON**. You will find a button labeled **+2D**, click here to add a 2D effect. You can choose to add a Shadow, Border, or to modify the font Face.

Figure 14.7 Choose the Attributes Tab and click the Style button to create a drop shadow.

8. Close NewBlue Titler by clicking on the window's close button.

    Your title is now in the sequence and ready for real time playback since it's a green dot effect.

 To learn more about using NewBlue Titler Pro within Avid Media Composer, check out their tutorial videos on the NewBlueFX YouTube Channel: https://www.youtube.com/watch?v=mwcqq8gazuk.

 Exercise Break: Exercise 14.1
Pause here to practice what you've learned.

AMA Linking to Real-Time Moving Matte Keys

As an editor, you are responsible for combining different elements from various sources. Many of those elements will come from motion graphics software, 3D animation tools, or visual effects systems. Those applications output their own mattes either embedded in the file or as a separate grayscale image. Not all file formats support embedded Alpha, however. Table 8.1 summarizes the recommended formats.

Table 14.1 Recommended File Formats

Format	Extension	Alpha Support	Comments
Photoshop	.psd	Yes	RGB images, flat or layered, are supported.
			CMYK images and files with more than four channels are not supported.
			Blending modes, Layer Styles, and Smart Filters are ignored.
PNG	.png	Yes	Graphics should not be web interlaced or compressed.
QuickTime	.mov	Some	ProRes 4444 and Animation codecs are recommended.

QuickTime files typically use one of two codecs with embedded Alpha channels. The older, slower codec is the Animation codec. The newer, more efficient codec is ProRes4444. The ProRes files are much smaller in size than Animation files—often 10× smaller or more. If you are using QuickTime, there are only a few scenarios where you should use the Animation codec.

When you install Media Composer, a QuickTime AMA plug-in also gets installed, providing AMA support for any QuickTime movie that uses an Apple-supported codec. This allows both Animation and ProRes files to be AMA-linked into Media Composer on either a Mac or Windows. ProRes however, can be created only on a Mac, so you may find Windows-based motion graphic artists and 3D animators who can only deliver QuickTime with an embedded Alpha channel using the Animation codec.

When you bring in the QuickTime file either through AMA linking or importing, the Matte Key effect will play back in real time.

To import a QuickTime file with Alpha:

1. Configure the Import Settings dialog box's IMAGE SIZE ADJUSTMENT, COLOR LEVELS and ALPHA CHANNEL options for the file you are importing.

2. Choose IMPORT from the FILE menu.

3. Select the VIDEO RESOLUTION based on the other media you are using.

4. Select the drive that will store the media files that are created.

5. Select the FILE in the window and click OK.

 When you import a file with Alpha, two media files are created. The fill media is created at the resolution set in the Media Creation settings or at what is chosen in the import window. The Alpha is imported as uncompressed.

Files that you AMA link to may also require Alpha Channel settings to be configured correctly. You can access them in two ways:

■ Project Window > Settings > Link > Link Options tab.

■ When using the Source Browser, click the gear icon next to the Link radio button > Link Options tab.

To AMA link to a QuickTime file with Alpha:

1. Open the SOURCE BROWSER from the Tools menu, and then activate its LINK RADIO BUTTON.

2. Click the GEAR ICON next to the Link option. In the LINK OPTIONS PANE configure the ALPHA CHANNEL setting as needed.

3. Navigate to the file(s) you want to link to. Select them, and then choose a TARGET BIN from the menu.

4. Click the LINK BUTTON in the bottom right corner of the Source Browser.

    The Alpha channel is automatically detected. After the linking is complete, the bin displays a matte key icon for the file, as shown in Figure 14.8.

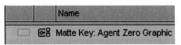

Figure 14.8 Linked Matte Key icon in bin.

    The matte key clips are always edited on the track above your background track(s). The background track(s) under the matte key clip will show through where the Alpha channel indicates transparency. You can step into the clip and see the components. The black and white matte is on V3, while the foreground element is on V2.

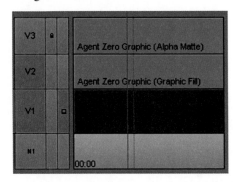

Figure 14.9 Stepping into the imported matte key clip.

Configuring Settings for QuickTime with Alpha

The Import settings must be configured correctly regardless of whether you are using the Import Settings dialog box or the link for QuickTime files with Alpha. There are two critical options located on the Image tab in the Import Settings dialog box that affect QuickTime with Alpha.

■ File Pixel to Video Mapping

■ Alpha Channel options

When you capture an image or a movie, you create a media file that is then displayed on a computer screen in the RGB color space. The most common form of RGB is 8-bit RGB, which gives you 256 discrete levels of color per color channel. So, for example, in 8-bit RGB, values range from 0, which is considered black, all the way up to 255, which is considered white. Every color is some combination of red, green, and blue, each with a discrete value from 0 to 255.

TV screens don't work in quite the same way. When you import an RGB image into Media Composer, it needs to be remapped to a range specified by a TV standards committee known as ITU-R BT.601 (ITU-R BT.709 for HD), often called 601/709. The result of this is that in 601/709, black is set at a value of 16 for R, G, and B, and white is set to 235. Everything in between is adjusted accordingly. If you don't convert RGB images with a range of 0–255 to 601/709 with a range of 16–235, your whites come in too hot and your blacks will be crushed.

With that remapping in mind, Media Composer includes video mapping options in the Import Settings dialog box, as shown in Figure 14.10.

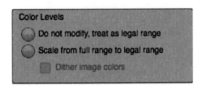

Figure 14.10 Video mapping options.

Depending on how your file is created you have three options:

- **Scale from full range to legal range:** You use this setting when you have created graphics in an RGB color space (sometimes called Unmanaged). Images and movie files are remapped from 0–255 to 16–235.

- **Do not modify, treat as legal range:** You use this setting when you have created graphics in a 601/709 color space (sometimes called Managed). Images and movie files are not remapped. They are assumed to have blacks set to 16 and whites set to 235.

- **Dither image colors check box:** This does not change the color levels but instead adds a bit of noise to randomize the levels. This can help remove banding that is sometimes apparent with graphics created in 8-bit with a gradient of some kind. (Note that real-world images never have artificial gradients, so you will not need to use this setting with photographs.)

The video mapping options handle the fill for the imported/linked movie file, but there are also settings to help with the Alpha or Matte channel. As you recall from the SpectraMatte, when an image is keyed, it is the Matte channel that dictates what is visible/opaque and what is transparent.

When Media Composer links to a graphic or movie file with embedded Alpha, black represents the opaque areas in an image and white represents the transparent areas (yes, opposite of the SpectraMatte key you looked at earlier). This is the way the film industry worked in the old days of optical effects on film. It is also the way Media Composer works. But almost all graphics and 3D animation software generates embedded Alpha with white representing opaque areas and black representing transparent areas—in other words, opposite what Media Composer expects.

Luckily for us all, the Alpha Channel section of the Import Settings dialog box, shown in Figure 14.11, can handle the Alpha no matter which way it was created. In most cases, the Alpha channel will need to be inverted (as far as Media Composer is concerned) and you'll need to select the Invert on Import button. (This is the default setting.)

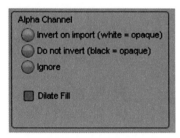

Figure 14.11 Alpha Channel options.

Lastly, and without going too deep, Alpha channels can be created in two ways: straight or pre-multiplied. Media Composer only supports straight Alpha channels. When you import a pre-multiplied Alpha channel, you often end up with a noticeable black halo or outline around the graphic as shown in Figure 14.12.

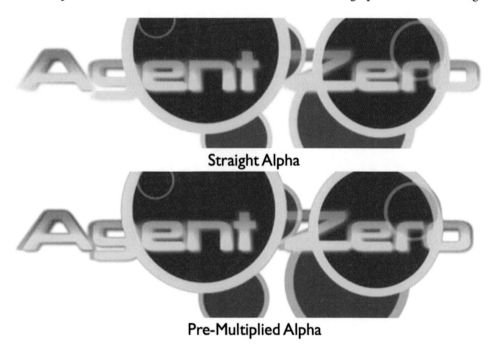

Figure 14.12 Straight versus pre-multiplied Alpha channels.

Really, the mathematical differences of how these two Alpha channel types are created are insignificant. Most applications provide the option to output Alpha channels either way. As the editor, you need to know that straight, not pre-multiplied, is the way Media Composer wants it and conveys that important information to any still and/or motion graphics artist you're working with.

Exercise Break: Exercise 14.2
Pause here to practice what you've learned.

Review/Discussion Questions

1. How do you open NewBlue Titler Pro?

2. In which tab would you modify the font?

3. In which tab are the controls for adding a drop shadow?

4. True or False: Titles created with NewBlue Titler Pro must be rendered before they can be played in the Media Composer Timeline.

5. What is the alpha channel?

6. Which two Link settings affect the appearance of a QuickTime logo animation with alpha?

7. True or False: Pre-multiplied alpha channels are preferred for use in Media Composer.

Creating Animated Titles

In this exercise, you'll create an animation for the opening title of the **Agent Zero** movie.

Media Used: MC110_EFFECTS

Time: 1 hour 30 minutes

GOALS

- Create and edit a static title with NewBlue Titler Pro
- Animate a title with NewBlue Titler Pro

Exercise 14.1: Adding Titles Using NewBlue Titler Pro

In this exercise we will use NewBlue Titler Pro to add and edit a basic title into the "Ah San Francisco" Project.

Media Used: MC110_EFFECTS

Time: 45 minutes

For this exercise, we will use the **MC110_EFFECTS** project.

1. Begin by launching Media Composer and loading the **MC110_EFFECTS** project.

2. Open the **STUDENT_LESSON SEQUENCES** bin.

3. Duplicate the sequence **14.1_AH SAN FRAN_NB TITLER** and drag the duplicate into the **EFFECTS_EXERCISE SEQUENCES** bin.

4. Load the duplicated **14.1_AH SAN FRAN_NB TITLER** sequence into the Timeline.

5. Choose TOOLS > MARKERS and read the marker the Producer has left you regarding the title that needs to be added to AH SAN FRANCISCO.

#		Marker Name	TC	End	Track	Part	Comment
0001		Producer	01:00:00:20		V1		Please add the title "San Francisco, California" to the lower left corner. Have it fade in and then fade out.

Figure 14.13 The Marker window displaying markers and the Producer's notes.

6. "Please add the title 'San Francisco, California' to the lower left corner. Have it fade in and then fade out."

    The Producer wants you to add this title only to the first shot, **A030_C011_09099G**.

7. Start by adding a second video track using **CTRL+Y** (Windows) or **COMMAND+Y** (Mac), then move the Video monitor from V1 to V2..

8. Create an Add Edit at 01:00:03:13 on the V2 track using the Add Edit (insert Add Edit button) button.

9. Go to the **EFFECTS PALETTE** in the Project window.

10. In the left column, select **NEWBLUE TITLER PRO**, grab the Titler Pro effect from the right column, and drag it into the Timeline.

Figure 14.14 The Titler Pro effect dragged to the Timeline.

The NewBlue Titler Pro design interface will immediately pop up in a new window.

Figure 14.15 The NewBlue Titler Pro interface.

11. Type your text, SAN FRANCISCO, CALIFORNIA into the text box.

Figure 14.16 The text "San Francisco, California" added in the text box of the NewBlue Titler interface.

12. Adjust the variables of your text to make the following aesthetic changes:

    - Change the font to "Copperplate"

    - Left justify the text

    - Reduce the size of the word "California" using the Font Size entry box or pull down menu at the top of the NewBlue Titler window.

    - Move the text to the bottom left of the screen, within the Title Safe area.

Figure 14.17 Additional changes made to the text of your title.

13. Now add the fade in.

    In the Design window, choose LIBRARY > TRANSITIONS > ANIMATIONS > FADE IN.

    Drag the LINEAR FADE to the front of your title in the Timeline located in the Design window.

Figure 14.18 Drag the Linear fade to the front of your title in the Timeline located in the Design window.

14. Using your mouse, shorten the fade until it is 15 frames.

Figure 14.19 Shortening the fade until it is 15 frames.

15. Zoom into the Timeline in the Designer window for greater precision.

Figure 14.20 Zoom into the Timeline.

16. Repeat steps 12 and 13 to add a fade out to the tail of the title.

    Even though the effect is in the folder labeled "Fade In," when you drop that effect at the tail end of the title in the Timeline, it becomes a Fade Out.

Figure 14.21 Adding a Fade In and Fade Out title to the end.

17. Play through the effect in the Design window to make sure you are satisfied with the result.

18. **EXIT** the NewBlue Titler Design window.

19. Play through your title in the Media Composer Timeline to make sure you have what the Producer has asked for.

20. If you need to make any changes, open the title in the Effect Editor and click LAUNCH USER INTERFACE.

This will reopen the NewBlue Titler Design window.

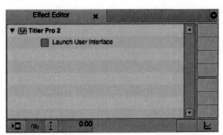

Figure 14.22 Launching the NewBlue Titler Pro from the Effect Editor.

Exercise 14.2: Animating Titles with NewBlue Titler Pro

In this exercise we will promote temporary titles created by the Avid Title Tool to NewBlue Titler Pro and create a simple animation.

Media Used: MC110_EFFECTS

Time: 45 minutes

For this exercise, we will continue to use the **MC110_EFFECTS** project.

1. Begin by launching Media Composer and loading the **MC110_EFFECTS** project.

2. Open the **STUDENT_LESSON SEQUENCES** bin.

3. Duplicate the sequence **14.2_AH SAN FRAN_NB TITLER_REV** and drag the duplicate into the **EFFECTS_EXERCISE SEQUENCES** bin.

4. Load the duplicated **14.2_AH SAN FRAN_NB TITLER_REV** sequence into the Timeline.

5. Choose TOOLS > MARKERS and read the markers the Producer has left you regarding the title that needs to be edited in AH SAN FRANCISCO.

#		Marker Name	TC	End	Track	Part	Comment
0001		Producer	01:00:08:09		V1		Animate in: "Dust" from frame left and "of the feet" from frame right to meet in the middle and slight push forward. 15 frame fade out.
0002		Producer	01:00:14:24		V1		Animate in "And DUST" from frame right and "of the wheels" from frame left -meet in the middle and slight push forward. 15 frame fad
0003		Producer	01:00:22:18		V1		Fade title in. Slight push forward. Animate off just as the camera moves to skyward with "Wagons" flying off screen and the top and "
0004		Producer	01:00:27:01		V1		Animate up from bottom and slight push forward. Fade out as music drops out.

Figure 14.23 The Markers window displaying markers and the Producer's notes.

The temporary titles that were created in the Avid Title Tool need to be replaced with permanent titles, created in NewBlue Titler Pro that match the style of the "San Francisco, California" title effect we created in the last exercise.

Some simple animation also needs to be added.

Let's begin by replacing the first temporary title with a NewBlue Titler Pro title effect.

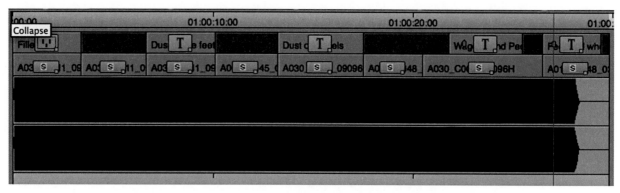

Figure 14.24 Temporary titles created with the Avid Title Tool in the Timeline.

6. If your temporary titles are offline, you can recreate them. Mark an **IN** and an **OUT** around the titles, then make sure that the **V2** Track Selector is enabled.

7. Choose **CLIP > RE-CREATE TITLE MEDIA.**

   Avid's traditional Title Tool will open automatically as the title media is recreated.

Figure 14.25 Selecting to recreate title media.

8. Go to the first title that the producer wanted you to animate.

9. **ADD** another video track (**V3**). Create **ADD EDITS** on V3 that isolate a section of Filler that is exactly the same duration as the temp title on V2.

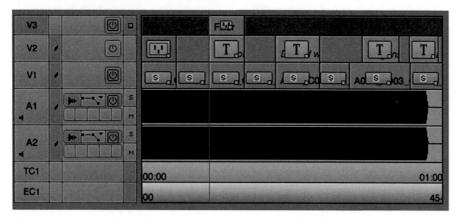

Figure 14.26 Adding another video track, and creating Add Edits on V3 that isolate a section of Filler that is exactly the same duration as the temp title on V2.

10. Next, go the **EFFECT PALETTE** and locate the **NEWBLUE TITLER PRO CATEGORY**.

11. Place the **TITLER PRO EFFECT** onto track **V3**, above the temp title. Make a note of the temp titl's text and the text's layout.

12. Next, use the RED LIFT/OVERWRITE SEGMENT arrow to move the title on V3 onto V2, which will overwrite the temp title.

    If you forgot what the temp title said, it was "And DUST" on the first line, and "of the wheels" on the second.

13. In the EFFECT EDITOR, click LAUNCH USER INTERFACE.

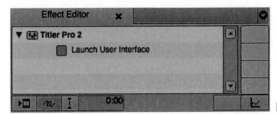

Figure 14.27 Launching the Titler Pro in the Effect Editor.

14. Begin by adjusting the variables of your text so that they match the design of the graphic we created in the previous exercise.

    Play around with the size of the text to get a more dynamic look.

Figure 14.28 Playing around with the size of the text to get a more dynamic look.

15. Because you will be animating the word **DUST** separately from the phrase "of the feet," you need to separate these into two separate text containers, which NewBlue refers to as paragraphs.

16. Right-click anywhere in the image area and choose **ADD PARAGRAPH**. Next, copy/paste "of the feet" into the new text box.

17. **REMOVE** it from the text box containing **DUST**.

Figure 14.29 Separating "Dust" and "of the Feet" into two text boxes.

18. Select the paragraph containing the word **DUST**. In the **ATTRIBUTES TAB**, click the **OBJECT BUTTON** and enable the **TURN ON KEYFRAMING** box located under the text box parameters.

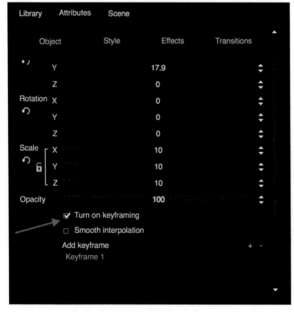

Figure 14.30 Select the "Turn-on keyframing" option.

This will automatically create a keyframe at the beginning of the paragraph.

A new checkbox appears, labeled "Smooth Interpolation." Also, right below the new checkbox is the small "+" Add Keyframe section which includes "+" and "-" buttons.

19. Move the red POSITION INDICATOR in the Timeline of the Design window to the point at which you would like the word DUST to have finished animating on.

Try about 1 second in.

Figure 14.31 The position indicator is at the point where you would like the word DUST to have finished the animation.

20. Make another KEYFRAME here, using the small "+" BUTTON next to the box displaying all of your current keyframes.

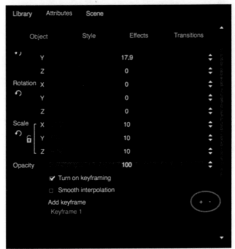

Figure 14.32 Use the "+" button to add another keyframe.

This will create a new keyframe where the red position indicator is located.

Figure 14.33 Another keyframe added where the position indicator was parked.

21. In the box displaying your keyframes, click on the first keyframe and adjust your parameters so that the word **DUST** begins off frame left.

    You can do this by either dragging the paragraph text container, or by using the X Position slider control.

Figure 14.34 Adjusting the keyframe parameters so that the word DUST begins off frame left.

22. Play through the animation and make sure you are satisfied.

23. **CREATE** a third **KEYFRAME** at the end of the clip and adjust the **Z POSITION** to **65**.

Figure 14.35 Add a third keyframe and adjust the Z position to 65.

This will create the slight "push forward" the producer wants the text to make.

24. Play through the animation and see how it feels.

25. Enable the **SMOOTH INTERPOLATION** checkbox, and play through it again.

26. If you are happy with the way it looks, repeat steps 12-18 to animate the phrase OF THE FEET – so that it animates in from offscreen right and meets **DUST** at its position in the middle.

Add the same push forward.

Figure 14.36 Animating the phrase "of the feet," so that it animates in from offscreen right and meets **DUST** at its position in the middle.

27. In the Design window, choose LIBRARY > TRANSITIONS > ANIMATIONS >FADE IN and add a 15 FRAME LINEAR FADE OUT to both paragraphs.

Figure 14.37 Adding a 15 frame linear fade out to both paragraphs.

28. Play through the animation one more time to make sure you are happy with it before closing the NewBlue Titler Design window.

29. **CLOSE** the window and you will immediately be taken back to Media Composer.

30. Once you are back in Media Composer, play through the animation again.

    If everything looks good, keep moving through the rest of the Producer's notes until each of the titles have been redesigned and animated in NewBlue Titler Pro.

    You can turn off the temp titles by muting the V2 track.

31. When you have added all the new titles and everything looks good, **DELETE** the **V2** track, removing the temporary titles.

 You may find you will be able to time the fade out of the last title with the music more efficiently by using the **Quick Transition Tool** in Media Composer.

Figure 14.38 Once you are back in Media Composer, play through the animation again.

32. Conclude the lesson by saving your work.

Packaging and Export

When you have completed the edit, the program will typically go through a final approval prior to output. Once approved, a finished master sequence will be prepared and then output to meet delivery specifications. In this lesson, you will learn the process and the tools required to complete it.

Media: Anesthesia

Duration: 60 minutes

GOALS

- Understand the review process
- Use Full Screen Playback and the Timecode window for in-suite reviews
- Learn to provide good critical feedback
- Mix down video and audio tracks
- Create bars and tone
- Set the start timecode
- Add timecode burn-in

Understanding the Review Process

There are two things that can be said definitively about the review process. First, every project gets reviewed. Whether by a director, a producer, the client before public exhibition or the viewer after release, your work will be judged by others. It is always preferable, then, to have your work reviewed while you can still improve it.

Second, no two review sessions will be exactly alike, and no two reviewers will look at the work with the same perspective, goals, or opinions. There will be reviewers whose direction you must take and others whose opinions you should evaluate but may choose to disregard. Generally speaking, in a film, it is the director who gets to dictate changes. The film is his or her vision, he or she has the most at stake personally, and it is his or her decision to use you as the editor. In other programming, it is often the producer who is creatively responsible and is therefore the authority on the project. If you are working as an independent producer and editor, you are responsible to your client, whose opinions you may be able to guide but must ultimately follow. Regardless of a person's authority, however, it will be wise for you to really listen to the opinion of others. A good idea can come from almost anyone, and it is best to try it out (time permitting) before you argue or discount an idea.

"Review" is not a singular event. In many productions, there is a review early in the edit to approve the structure and tone of the piece, followed by others to approve the piece as it develops, and to confirm the final version.

 If you are even unsure of how well a sequence or particular edit is working, have someone else come watch the video. Even if they are not a trained video professional, just having a fresh set of eyes in the room will make you see it differently too. Try it!

A review session may be conducted live and in-person. Or, it may be that video files are sent to the stakeholders on physical media (DVD, flash drive, etc.) or, commonly, posted online for review. There are numerous online services offering a variety of features, from simple but secure FTP sites to simple video sharing sites like YouTube or Vimeo, to full-featured services like Wipter, Screenlight, Kollaborate, Remark, Frame.IO, and more. These services offer more advanced tools to gather feedback including drawing tools to markup the video frames directly, tag frames (or regions of the video) with markers and comments, plus the ability to see each other's comments and reply directly. The best ones even provide a way to export that feedback back into Media Composer as frame-accurate markers on the sequence.

For live screenings and review sessions, it is common to have multiple stakeholders in the room. First, the program is screened by playing it start to finish with no interruptions. Each reviewer takes notes of things he or she wants to discuss or change, using timecode for reference. When the sequence finishes playing, there is typically a discussion period during which each reviewer's notes are discussed. The editor will jump back to the approximate timecode location corresponding to each note (and if needed, add a marker and comment). Afterward, it is then up to you to prioritize and complete the requested changes.

Regardless of the workflow, the end goal is the same: get feedback from the stakeholders on how you can improve the video.

 It is important that you do not stop playback during a screening. Stopping playback would interrupt the experience and alter the reviewers' perception of the duration and pace of the film.

Tools for Review

Media Composer includes several features that can be used to facilitate the review process.

Adding Timecode Burn-In

It is common practice to prepare sequences for review with timecode burn-in. This is an overlay of timecode, and possibly other information, that can be referenced by the producer when making notes. You may also hear it referred to as a "window burn" or "window dub" because the timecode appears in a small black window. Adding timecode burn-in is especially common when the sequence will be viewed separately, such as posting it to an FTP or video-sharing site (e.g. Vimeo) that does not have built-in timecode references.

When outputting to tape, the tape deck that is recording the video creates the timecode burn-in. However, in today's world of file-based output, you can apply a real-time effect to create the timecode overlay: Avid's Timecode RT effect. This customizable effect allows you to add timecode displays or text annotations that update in real time. Usually, you apply the effect to an empty video track above all other tracks. You can then monitor or unmonitor the track to display (or not display) the timecode and text information as necessary.

The Timecode RT effect allows you to display up to four customizable pieces of timecode and/or information at once. There are several drop-down menus that will allow you to customize the information and the appearance of each of the burn-in displays.

To apply the Timecode RT effect:

1. Press **CTRL+Y** (Windows) or **COMMAND+Y** (Mac) or choose **TIMELINE MENU > NEW > VIDEO TRACK** to create a video track above the rest in the sequence, and move the video monitor to the new top track.

2. From the **GENERATOR** category of the Effect Palette, drag the **TIMECODE BURN-IN EFFECT** to the new video track you just created.

   A small timecode burn-in window appears over the image in the bottom, center of the Record monitor.

3. Open the **EFFECT EDITOR**.

   With the Effect Editor open, as shown in Figure 15.1, you will see that the effect can include up to four different displays, plus a Notes Track display. Pink crosshairs appear over the Effect Preview monitor marking the placement of each.

4. Click the disclosure triangle to open the **APPEARANCE** group under Display 1.

5. Drag the **FONT PIXEL SIZE THUMBWHEEL** to the right to **ENLARGE** the timecode numbers over the image.

6. To adjust the position of the burn-in window, click the cross-hairs at the corner of the burn-in window and drag to the desired position.

7. (Optional) Enable any additional displays you desire, and adjust the parameters accordingly. For example, you may use another to display the Source Timecode, and a third to display the Source Clip Name, or the name of the sequence.

Figure 15.1 The Timecode burn-in offers up to four displays, plus a Notes Track.

 You can restrict the region the timecode burn-in to just a portion of the sequence by using the Add Edit command to cut the filler track.

Creating a Watermark

The Notes Track of the Timecode Burn-In effect can be used to create a text watermark on the image. A watermark clearly labels the video for its intended purpose, such as "For Review Only," "Not for Distribution," or "Delta Airlines." See Figure 15.2 below.

To create a watermark:

1. Apply and configure the Timecode Burn-in effect, as described above. Alternatively, if you do not want to see timecode, disable the Display 1 parameter group by clicking the highlighted box next to Display 1.

2. Click the box to enable the **NOTES TRACK**, and click the disclosure triangle to open the Parameter group.

3. In the text field, type the text of the watermark.

    The text will appear in a burn-in window with the same formatting as the timecode burn-ins. You need to modify the Appearance parameters to turn it into a watermark.

4. Open the **APPEARANCE GROUP** under Notes Track.

5. Set the **BACKGROUND OPACITY** to **0**.

6. Set the **TEXT OPACITY** to the desired value (0.2 – 0.5 is generally good).

7. Adjust the TEXT SIZE and POSITION, as desired.

Figure 15.2 Use the Notes Track to create a watermark to indicate restricted use of the video.

Using the Timecode Window

For a live review session, it may be preferred to not display the timecode over the image. The Timecode Window is a dedicated, free-floating window that displays multiple lines of timecode and other tracking data. What most distinguishes it from the displays at the top of the Composer window is that you can make it BIG. (See Figure 15.3.)

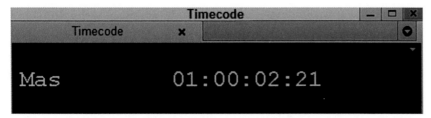

Figure 15.3 The Timecode window provides a large, free-floating timecode display, perfect for seeing at a distance.

To open the Timecode window:

■ Choose TOOLS > TIMECODE WINDOW.

The Timecode window opens with a small font size, designed for use with editing. Hidden within each display in the Timecode window are hidden menus used to access and display the settings.

To modify the Timecode window's display:

1. Click on a DISPLAY LINE in the Timecode window.

2. Select an OPTION in the cascading windows.

   The menus in the Timecode Display include options to change font size, add lines of data, and select from various types of data relating to either the sequence or the source of the segment under the position indicator. See Figure 15.4.

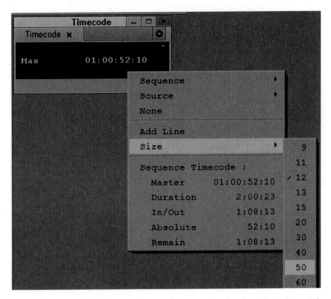

Figure 15.4 The Timecode window can be displayed with a wide range of font sizes—small sizes useful for editing, and larger ones useful for screening.

 For conducting a review session, pick a point size of 40 or more.

Using Full Screen Playback

The Full Screen Playback option allows you to view your video on a full-screen monitor. This option is not available when connected to I/O hardware such as Avid DnX-IO or one from Avid's third-party partners. It is assumed that you will use this hardware to output to a client monitor instead.

If you have hardware attached, but still wish to use Full Screen Playback, you can temporarily disable the hardware connection by clicking the HW/SW Toggle button in the Timeline, shown in Figure 15.5. It appears on the interface to the right of the Timeline audio meters.

Figure 15.5
The HW/SW toggle. The red circle with a slash indicates the HW is currently inactive.

To activate full screen playback:

■ Select COMPOSER > FULL SCREEN PLAYBACK. Alternatively, press SHIFT+CTRL+F (Windows) or SHIFT+COMMAND+F (Mac).

To deactivate full screen playback:

■ Click anywhere in the MONITOR or press SHIFT+CTRL+F (Windows) or SHIFT+COMMAND+F (Mac).

Full Screen Playback will work on either monitor in a two-monitor setup.

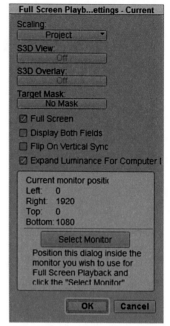

To choose the monitor for Full Screen Playback:

1. Activate the PROJECT window and click the SETTINGS BUTTON to display the settings list.

2. Double-click the FULL SCREEN PLAYBACK setting to open it.

   The window is shown in Figure 15.6. The default settings are suitable for most users.

3. Drag the SETTING WINDOW to the desired monitor.

4. Click the SELECT MONITOR button.

5. Click OK.

Figure 15.6 The Full Screen Playback settings.

 If your footage looks slightly washed out during full-screen playback, select the Expand Luminance for Computer Displays check box.

Tips for Reviewing Sequences

Here are some basic things to look for when reviewing your work or the work of others. The questions may vary depending on the type of production and at what stage of the edit the review is taking place.

- Do the shot selection and pace of editing work to support the story?

- Do the edits seem appropriate and effective according to the style of the program?

- Do any of the edits or shots seem out of place or distracting?

- Are there distracting or inappropriate items in the background—such as production equipment, an unacceptable logo on a shirt, etc.—that need to be removed or fixed?

- Are there noticeable flaws in either the picture or the sound?

- Do audio and video stay in sync?

- Do the music and sound effects support the emotion of the scene?

- Are there problems with continuity?

Exercise Break: Exercise 15.1
Pause here to practice what you've learned.

Preparing for Output

Prior to having your sequence reviewed by the stakeholders in your project, there are a number of things you can do to package the sequence and prepare it technically for output. The output process is detail-oriented, and it requires careful attention to ensure that you meet the requirements.

Most broadcasters have specific requirements for the material that precedes a program on the tape. These requirements are detailed in the delivery specifications.

Understanding Delivery Specifications

A delivery specification is the list of technical requirements that a video must meet in order to be accepted. It typically includes file format, codec, frame dimensions, frame rate, data rate, etc.

There are delivery specifications for every distribution channel, including broadcast, cable and network television, cinema distribution, and of course Web-based distribution. The distribution spec will vary from one network to another. For example, National Geographic is different from Discovery, which is different from PBS. (The PBS delivery specification, called the Red Book, is so specific that I have heard many editors say, "If you can deliver to the Red Book, you can deliver to anybody.") Even if you are planning to just post the video to YouTube, Vimeo, or your own website, there are video and audio specifications to ensure that your program looks its best.

When it comes to delivery specs, never assume. Always check. Delivery specifications are freely available online, so there really is no good excuse for delivering the wrong format. It is certainly not worth missing a deadline or even the added stress of needing to generate a second output under pressure.

To check out the PBS Red Book specs for yourself, go to
www.pbs.org/producing/red-book/

Packaging a Sequence

If delivering for broadcast on videotape, the delivery requirements will include a detailed list of additional elements that need to precede the program start. These include varying durations of bars and tone, a slate, perhaps a separate countdown timer, etc. For a review by the stakeholders in your project, it may be beneficial to prepare your sequence with these elements as well as adding burn-in timecode.

Adding Bars, Tone and Countdown

You can add a segment of bars and tone, followed by a countdown, to the front of your sequence. To do this, you must prepare these elements in advance by importing the necessary elements.

Avid provides a variety of color bars and test patterns for importing and editing into your sequence. For more information, see "Importing Color Bars and Other Test Patterns" in the Media Composer Help. You can find these files here:

- **Windows:** drive:\Program Files\Avid\Avid Media Composer\SupportingFiles\Test_Patterns

- **Mac:** Macintosh HD/Applications/Avid Media Composer/SupportingFiles/Test_Patterns

You can find many free countdowns on the Internet for use in your sequences. Search for "Video Countdowns" or "SMTPE Countdown" in your browser.

You can create your own tone media as a master clip for editing directly into sequences.

To create tone media:

1. Open a BIN.

2. Select TOOLS > AUDIO TOOL.

3. Click the PH (PEAK HOLD) menu in the Audio Tool and select CREATE TONE MEDIA.

4. Set the appropriate calibration tone parameters for the project. You can also use the default output tone of **–20 DB** (digital scale) with a 1,000 Hz signal.

 A value of 0 generates random noise. A value of –777 generates a tone sweep.

5. Select the number of tracks of tone you want to create (up to 64 tracks).

6. Click the MENUS and select a TARGET BIN for the tone master clip and a TARGET DRIVE for the tone media file.

7. Click OK.

    Media Composer creates the media file and a master clip appears in the target bin. The default name reflects the options you selected. You can rename the clip by typing a new name.

 The Meter Menu button in the Timeline meters can also be used to create tone media.

Adding Filler at the Start of the Sequence

It is common to need to add filler at the head of the sequence as a "pad" before the program starts, or to comply with delivery specifications.

To add filler at the start of a sequence:

1. Select TIMELINE MENU > ADD FILLER > AT START.

2. Alternatively, right-click in the TIMELINE and select ADD FILLER > AT START.

    By default, Media Composer adds 30 seconds of filler to the head of the sequence. You can change this in the Timeline Settings > Edit tab. The master timecode of the sequence is backtimed by the same amount. For example, if the sequence began at 01:00:00:00, it will begin at 00:59:30:00 after adding filler.

Changing the Start Timecode

It is standard within the industry that your program must begin on an hour, though regionally the hour designated may vary. For example, in the United States, programs typically begin exactly at 01;00;00;00. In some European countries, programs must begin at 10:00:00:00.

To meet this requirement, you may need to adjust the start timecode for you sequence. If you have elements that precede the program start, you will need to subtract the appropriate amount of time. For a program start of 01;00;00;00, with one minute of material preceding the program, the sequence needs to begin at 00;59;00;00. Although Add Filler at Start changes the start timecode of the sequence, you may find that there are situations in which you still need to change it manually.

You may have noticed that the timecodes above were written in different formats. The use of semicolons versus colons when specifying timecode is an indication of the timecode format, drop-frame versus non-drop-frame timecode, respectively, as defined by the SMPTE specification. In Media Composer, the same holds true.

To change the Start TC of a sequence in the bin:

1.   Open the BIN and select the TEXT view.

2.   Click on the START TC for the sequence.

3.   Enter the new VALUE.

      You need to type only the first colon (non-drop-frame timecode) or semicolon (drop-frame timecode). For example, type **01:000000** for 01:00:00:00.

Technical Preparations

Prior to performing the export, there are steps you can take to prepare the sequence to ensure consistent quality with the fastest, most headache-free output process. The following checklist is a set of recommendations for preparing your sequence:

- Make sure all media for the sequence is online. You can double-check this by checking Clip Color > Offline in the Timeline Fast menu. This is enabled by default.

- If you want to archive the source sequence before making any alterations, duplicate the sequence, place the duplicate in another bin, and prepare the duplicate for export. The original sequence is unaffected.

- Consider rendering all effects in advance. Although any unrendered effects are rendered on export (except for an OMFI or AAF export), rendering effects in advance saves time during the export process.

- Always render fast-saved titles before using OMFI or AAF to export a sequence or before creating an EDL from the sequence.

- If your sequence contains numerous video tracks, consider mixing down the tracks in advance for faster export unless you need to preserve the multiple-track information.

- If your sequence contains numerous audio tracks with various audio effects and level adjustments, consider mixing down the tracks in advance for faster export unless you need to preserve the multiple-track information.

- If your sequence contains audio clips with different sample rates, use the Change Sample Rate dialog box to ensure that all the clips have the same sample rate. (Right-click on your sequence in the bin and choose Change Sample Rate to open this dialog box.)

- Check and adjust all pan and audio levels in advance. All current pan and level settings in the sequence are carried to the exported media.

Mixing Down Video

A common practice before exporting is to use video mixdown to flatten a sequence. Mixdowns lets you combine several tracks into a new master clip. You can use video mixdown after you finish building your sequence and want to make it into one piece (for example, a standard opening to a program).

Video mixdown is useful when you want to:

■   Finalize a complex sequence before consolidating, exporting, or transferring.

■   Create a complex sequence you need to use repeatedly.

■   Retime an entire sequence using a motion effect.

   Video mixdown "flattens" or "merges" the selected track and all tracks under it. If you want to perform a video mixdown of only one track, select the track for solo monitoring by Ctrl-clicking (Windows) or Command-clicking (Mac) the Record Track Monitor button.

To perform a video mixdown:

1.   Select the RECORD TRACK MONITOR button in the Track Selector panel for the highest track you want to include in the video mixdown. This should include titles and other graphics that may be on higher level tracks.

2.   Mark an IN point and an OUT point around the area to mix down.

3.   Select TIMELINE MENU > MIXDOWN > VIDEO.

The Video Mixdown dialog box, shown in Figure 15.7, opens.

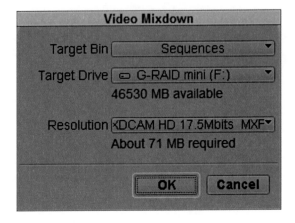

Figure 15.7 The Video Mixdown dialog box.

4.   Select a TARGET BIN, TARGET DRIVE, and RESOLUTION for storing the new master clip, and then click OK.

A progress indicator appears. When the video mixdown finishes, a new clip appears in the bin along with the sequence, and a new media file is created on the target drive.

You cannot generate an edit decision list (EDL) for a sequence that contains a video mixdown. (EDLs are common in film workflows, and sometimes used to transfer sequence information between applications.) To work around this, you can either remove the video mixdown or maintain a version of the sequence that does not contain a video mixdown.

Mixing Down Audio

When you work with multiple audio tracks while editing your material, you might need to mix down the final audio to the number of tracks supported by your output format. For example, if you are outputting to tape, the deck may support four channels of audio; if you are outputting to a stereo QuickTime file, there will be two channels.

If you are doing a file export, the system will create the mix as part of the export process. Doing a mixdown before you export gives you the opportunity to verify that everything sounds just as good in the final version, prior to output.

When you mix down audio, your Avid editing application inserts the mixdown audio in the next available track in the Timeline by default. You can override the default target track by selecting another one in the Audio Mixdown dialog box, shown in Figure 15.8.

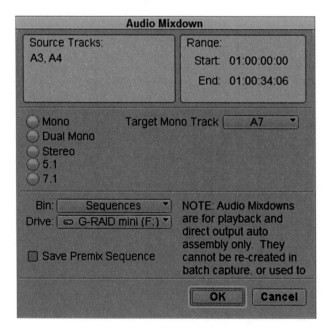

Figure 15.8 The Audio Mixdown dialog box.

To mix down several edited audio tracks to one or two audio tracks:

1. Load a SEQUENCE into the Record monitor.

2. Click the TRACK buttons in the Track Selector panel to select the audio tracks you want to mix down.

3. Mark an IN point and an OUT point at the start and end of the material you want to mix down.

    If you do not mark the section of audio you want to mix down, the system mixes down all of the selected audio tracks.

4. Select TIMELINE MENU > MIXDOWN > AUDIO > TO SEQUENCE.

    The Audio Mixdown dialog box opens. The Source Tracks area lists the source audio tracks and the Range area lists the start and end timecodes for the section of audio you have selected to mix down.

5. Select MONO, STEREO, 5.1, or 7.1 and select the target TRACK to which you want to mix down the audio.

    A mono mixdown goes to the next available mono track in the Timeline and a stereo or surround-sound mixdown goes to the next available stereo or surround-sound track. If there are no appropriate tracks in the Timeline, the mixdown operation creates them.

6. Select a DRIVE and a BIN.

    The drive is the media drive where the system stores the media files from the mixed-down audio.

7. Select SAVE PREMIX SEQUENCE if you want to save the sequence before mixing down the audio.

8. Click OK.

    Media Composer mixes down the audio, displays the new master clip in the bin, and edits the mixdown clip into the sequence.

Media Composer includes a feature to perform multiple different audio mixdowns simultaneously. You can learn more about this and other professional mixing techniques in the next course MC201: Media Composer Professional Editing I.

Exercise Break: Exercise 15.2
Pause here to practice what you've learned.

Exporting a File

There are several ways to get a finished program out of Media Composer. If you want to output a file, you can perform an Export; use Send To templates to automate the export process; create and write a file directly to a device, such as an XDCAM disc, P2 card; or use AMA to export a specialized AS-11 bundle. If you want to output to tape, you will need to attach input/output hardware and use the Digital Cut tool.

The most common output method is to simply export a file.

From your work in the MC101 course, you should be familiar with exporting a file, so we will only review it quickly.

Media Composer includes a number of export templates that are useful for a variety of common workflows. These make the export process very simple and straightforward.

To export a sequence using an export template:

1. Select the finished SEQUENCE in the bin, then select FILE MENU > OUTPUT > EXPORT TO FILE.

2. Alternatively, you can load the finished sequence and then right-click on the Record monitor and choose EXPORT.

    The Export As dialog box opens.

3. Navigate to the FOLDER DIRECTORY in which you wish to save the exported file.

4. If necessary, rename the FILE.

5. Click the EXPORT SETTING menu and select the desired setting from the list, as shown in Figure 15.9.

6. Click the SAVE button to begin the export.

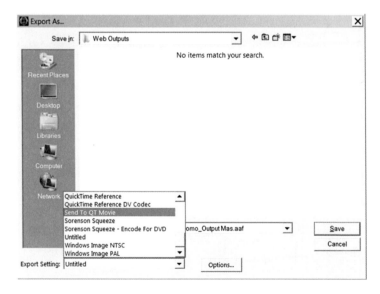

Figure 15.9
The Export As dialog box.

The Export Settings Dialog Box

All settings for controlling the type and attributes of the exported file are accessed through the Export Settings dialog box. The settings displayed in the dialog box will change based on what is selected in the Export As menu. The settings and controls shown in Figure 15.10 appear because the Export As menu is set to QuickTime Movie. If a different setting were selected, the options would be different.

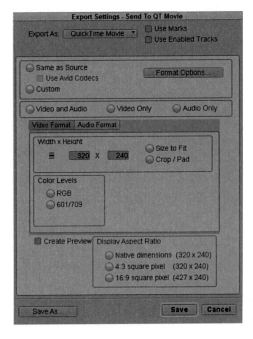

Figure 15.10
The Export Settings dialog box offers a wide range of controls over the export format.

Before you start using them, take a moment to familiarize yourself with the following controls:

■ **Export As menu:** This is used to change the type of export—i.e., AAF, QuickTime Reference, Graphic, etc.

■ **Use Marks/Use Enabled Tracks check boxes:** When enabled, these check boxes limit the exported file to the area within edit marks placed on the sequence and to active tracks, respectively. When these are disabled, the entire sequence is exported.

■ **Same as Source/Custom option buttons:** Same as Source encodes the exported file in the current media format. Custom allows you to click the Format Options button to change additional settings such as the codec, frame rate, data rate, etc.

■ **Video and Audio/Video Only/Audio Only option buttons:** These are self-explanatory.

■ **Video Format/Audio Format tabs:** These tabs contain additional settings for the frame size.

■ **Frame Size Presets menu:** This menu, signified by an icon, opens a list of common frame sizes.

■ **Color Levels area:** Select RGB for viewing on computers and mobile devices or 601/709 for television broadcast.

■ **Save As button:** This button allows you to save the current settings as a new preset.

Take a moment to look at a few of the other export settings, too.

Using the Send To Export Templates

The Send To feature is the quickest and simplest way to perform most common export tasks. Send To enables you to send sequences or master clips from your Avid editing system to other applications, automating your workflow.

The Send To option provides you with a choice of several pre-defined templates to streamline your workflow. These templates are set to default parameters, customized for the specific workflow. In many instances you can choose to automatically launch the application to which you are sending your clip or sequence.

To use the predefined templates:

1. Select a SEQUENCE in a bin.

2. Choose FILE > SEND TO.

3. Select the desired SEND TO option:

    - Send To DigiDelivery

    - Send To Digidesign Pro Tools

    - Send to DVD Authoring

    - Send to DVD One Step

    - Send to Sorenson Squeeze

    - Send To Avid DS

4. Click SET and choose a destination FOLDER for the exported files.

5. Click OK.

    The file is exported to the selected destination.

 For more details about individual Send To options, see the corresponding Help topic (for example, "Exporting Using Send to DVD Authoring").

Customizing a Send To Template

Delivering your program will be faster and more consistent if you create custom templates that match the delivery specifications for your most common distribution channels. Customizing a Send To template is very similar to customizing the export settings, which you did earlier in this course. In fact, it leverages the same settings dialog boxes (see Figure 15.11). The advantage of a Send To template over a straight export is that a Send To template can perform multiple exports with one template. An example is that you may be required to deliver a high-quality master plus a compressed version for the Web. A Send To template would allow you to do that in a single step.

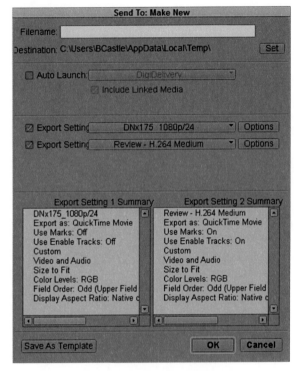

Figure 15.11
A Send To dialog box, for creating a new Send To template using custom export settings.

To customize a Send-To template:

1. Select the SEQUENCE in the bin.

2. Choose FILE > OUTPUT > SEND TO > MAKE NEW.

3. Do one of the following:

   • Click the Export Setting menu and choose an existing export setting.

   • Click the Options button to define a new setting; then configure the Export Options as needed

4. Optionally, enable the check box for the second export setting.

5. Repeat step 3 for the second export setting.

6. Optionally, select the AUTO LAUNCH check box and choose the desired APPLICATION from the list.

7. If the application is not listed, select ADD ITEM in the menu, as shown in Figure 15.12. Then select the application of choice from the OS window that opens.

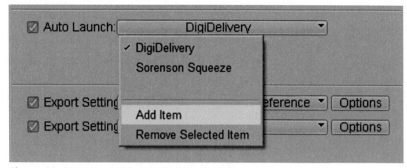

Figure 15.12 Select Add Item from the menu.

8. Optionally, choose INCLUDE LINKED MEDIA to include any AMA-linked media files.

9. Click SAVE AS TEMPLATE.

Technique: Faster, Better Compression

It is easier to be the best at one thing than to be the best at everything. The same is true for software. When it comes to compressing your video, you will get the best-looking video files in the fastest time if you use dedicated compression software such as Sorenson Squeeze.

The most efficient workflow for outputting a file for encoding with compression software is to use a QuickTime Reference file. A QuickTime Reference file is an empty container file that holds no media of its own. Instead, as the name implies, it references the original media files used by Media Composer.

The advantage of this workflow is that it is extremely fast to export the QuickTime Reference file. The video is not recompressed for handoff to the compression software, so it looks better. And, because another application is doing the compression, you are free to keep working in Media Composer.

A QuickTime Reference setting is included in the Export Settings list and can be used for a standard export or as part of a Send To template.

Warning: Because QuickTime Reference files contain no media, they must be used on the same system. You cannot send this file to someone on a different computer.

Exporting XDCAM Media

Sony XDCAM has become an industry-standard media format. Many of the top broadcasters around the world have adopted it as the format of choice for end-to-end workflows.

Media Composer supports XDCAM as a native format, meaning that from acquisition to output, it does not need to convert the media essence to another format. It can also capture, import, render, and export media using XDCAM codecs. Media Composer also includes dedicated output options for writing media back to an XDCAM disk or for exporting an XDCAM-formatted file.

The system will allow you to export a clip, subclip, or sequence directly to an XDCAM disk. You cannot export individual titles, effects, group clips, or rendered effects. The export mixes down the sequence and creates an XDCAM clip.

If you have been using AMA to read a disk, disable volume mounting in the AMA setting and restart the application prior to export.

To export to XDCAM disc:

1. Connect your **XDCAM** DEVICE and select the appropriate MODE corresponding to the video format.

2. Select the SEQUENCE or CLIPS to export

3. Choose FILE MENU > OUTPUT > EXPORT TO DEVICE > XDCAM or, right-click on a selected CLIP in a bin and choose OUTPUT > EXPORT TO DEVICE > XDCAM.

    The XDCAM Export Settings dialog box opens.

4. Optionally, select USE MARKS or USE ENABLED TRACKS if you want the current setup in the Timeline to be reflected in the output. To export the entire sequence, deselect these options.

5. Select an **XDCAM** DISK from the TARGET **XDCAM** DISK menu. (More than one deck may be connected.)

    Clips will be created with the number of audio tracks existing on the disk. For instance, an Avid clip with two audio tracks may result in a clip with four audio tracks on the disk.

6. Select a VIDEO FORMAT:

    *   **For SD projects:** Select DV-25, IMX30, IMX40, or IMX50. For SD, a disk cannot have mixed formats. For example, a disk that contains IMX40 material can only have IMX40 media added to it (unless you reformat the disk).

    *   **For HD projects:** Select XDCAM-50, XDCAM-35, XDCAM-25, or XDCAM-17. For HD, a single disk can have clips with mixed bit rates (17.5, 25, and 35 Mbits). Additionally, a sequence that is being exported to an HD XDCAM disk can have mixed bit rates.

7. Select a SAMPLE BIT DEPTH. Choose 16 or 24 bits. (For HD projects, select 16 bits.)

8. Click **OK**.

    Sony applies its own file-naming convention. Exported clips are given a new sequential name of C*xxxx*.mxf—for example, C0019.mxf. A progress bar appears, displaying the new Sony XDCAM sequential clip name. The sequence or clip is exported. You can check that the item has been successfully exported by using the Sony browsing software.

In a broadcast facility with a file-based XDCAM workflow, the editors need to export XDCAM files that are transferred to playout servers. This is done through the standard Export or Send To options, using a specific XDCAM setting.

To export an XDCAM file:

1. Select the ITEM in the bin.

2. Choose FILE MENU > OUTPUT > EXPORT TO DEVICE > XDCAM.

    If you have a sequence loaded in the Record monitor, the sequence exports when you select Export to Device. You can also right-click the clip or sequence in a bin and select Export to Device.

    The XDCAM Export Settings dialog box opens.

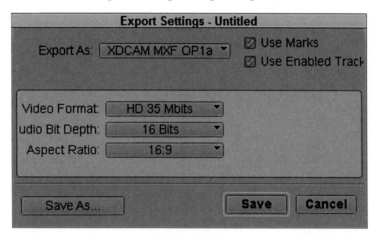

Figure 15.13 The Export Settings dialog box reveals a simplified group of settings.

3. (Option) Select Use Marks.

    The current IN and OUT points in the selected clip or sequence determine starting and ending frames for the export.

4. (Option) Select Use Selected Tracks.

    The system uses tracks that are enabled in the timeline. To export all the tracks in the sequence, deselect this option.

5. Select an XDCAM disk from the Target XDCAM Disk list.

    If the target XDCAM disk you are exporting to already has other clips on it, you are only allowed to export a clip with the same number of audio tracks. For example, if the target XDCAM disk has a clip with 4-tracks of audio, you cannot export a new XDCAM clip with 2 tracks. You either have to reformat the disk and wipe it clean or add two dummy tracks to your 2-track sequence before you export.

6.   Select a video format:

- For SD projects, select DV-25, IMX30, IMX40, or IMX50.
  For SD, a disk cannot have mixed formats. For example, a disk that contains IMX40 material can only have IMX40 media added to it, unless you reformat the disk.

- For HD projects, select XDCAM-50, XDCAM-35, XDCAM-25, or XDCAM-17.
  For HD, a single disk can have clips with mixed bit rates (17.5, 25, and 35 Mbits). Additionally, a sequence that is being exported to an HD XDCAM disk can have mixed bit rates, as well. If you use the Sony PDW HD1500 or the Sony PDW 1500 XDCAM device, export of up to 8 tracks of audio is supported for the MPEG IMX and XDCAM HD 50 Mbits formats. For other formats or devices that do not support 8 tracks, the system mixes down to audio tracks 1 and 2 during export.

7.   Select a Bit Depth: 16 or 24 bits.

For HD projects, select 16 bits. XDCAM HD devices are not capable of handling 24 bits, except for the Sony PDW HD1500 device, which is capable of handling 24 bits.

8.   Click OK.

Sony applies its own file-naming convention. All exported clips are given a new sequential name of Cxxxx.mxf, for example, C0019.mxf.

A progress bar appears displaying the new Sony XDCAM sequential clip name. The sequence exports

Exercise Break: Exercise 15.3
Pause here to practice what you've learned.

Review/Discussion Questions

1. Name two tools that can be helpful for live review sessions.

2. What are two things you might look for when critically reviewing a sequence?

3. How does the Timecode window differ from other timecode displays in the interface?

4. What might be one reason Full Screen Playback is grayed out in the menu?

    a. The system is configured to output through hardware.

    b. It is not supported in the current project type.

    c. Timecode burn-in has been added to the sequence.

    d. All of the above.

5. True or False: A video mixdown flattens the sequence but does not create new media.

6. What is a video mixdown used for?

7. What is an audio mixdown used for?

8. What is the difference between using a Send To template and using Export?

9. What is the difference between a QuickTime movie and a QuickTime reference?

10. How do you create color bars and reference tone?

    a. Apply the Test Patterns effect to a top track of filler.

    b. Choose Test Patterns from the Meter menu in the Timeline.

    c. Choose Clip > Generator > Bars and Tone.

    d. Generate tone media using the Audio Tool and import the test pattern file.

Output and Review

This is it. The final steps to culminate the hard work you have put into editing your project. In this exercise, you will package a sequence with additional elements, flatten the sequence for output, and then output it using a custom Send To template. In contrast to the creative work of editing, this is both technical and detail-oriented.

Media Used: Anesthesia

Duration: 1 hour 45 minutes

GOALS

- Mix down video and audio tracks
- Create bars and tone
- Set the start timecode
- Add timecode burn-in

Exercise 15.1: Preparing a Screener Copy of "Anesthesia"

It is common to add a timecode burn-in when outputting cuts of a project for review. In this exercise, we will use the Timecode Burn-In effect to customize a timecode overlay and watermark on the short film, Anesthesia.

Media Used: Anesthesia

Time: 30 minutes

For this exercise, we will use the **MC110_ANESTHESIA** project.

1.   Begin by opening the bin **STUDENT_LESSON SEQUENCES**.

2.   Duplicate the sequence **15.1_ANESTHESIA_FOR REVIEW** and move the duplicate sequence into the **ANESTHESIA_EXERCISE SEQUENCES** bin.

3.   Load the duplicate **15.1_ANESTHESIA_FOR REVIEW** into the Timeline.

     This sequence is a final cut containing all the edits and changes we have made to the film "Anesthesia" up to this point.

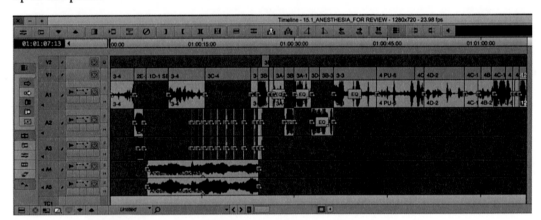

Figure 15.14   The final cut sequence containing all the edits and changes we have made to the film "Anesthesia" up to this point.

4.   In the **15.1_ANESTHESIA_FOR REVIEW** sequence, create a new video track (V3) using CTRL+Y (Windows) or COMMAND+Y (Mac).

5.   Go to the Project window and navigate to the EFFECTS TAB.

6. Use the search box to look for "Burn," to quickly locate the Timecode Burn-In effect (stored in the Generators category).

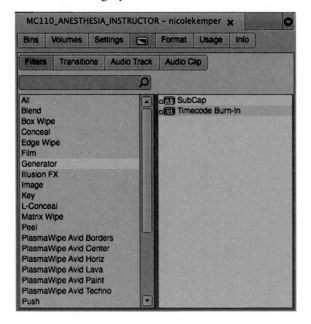

Figure 15.15 The Timecode Burn-In effect in the Effects tab > Generator category.

7. From the right column in the Effects tab, click the TIMECODE BURN-IN EFFECT and DRAG it to the uppermost V3 TRACK.

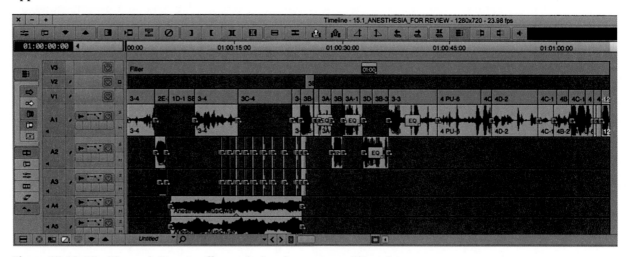

Figure 15.16 The Timecode Burn-in effect applied to the uppermost V3 track.

8. Scrub through your Timeline.

    You will see that there is now a timecode overlay on your sequence.

    In a previous exercise we used a prebuilt, template timecode burn-in effect. Now we will go into the Effect Editor and customize the effect to suit the needs of our production.

9. Begin by opening the effect in the EFFECT EDITOR.

10. Under "Display 1":

- Alter the appearance and position of the timecode overlay.

- Increase the font size to 50.

- Adjust the position so that the timecode overlay appears in the bottom-left side of the screen.

Figure 15.17 The timecode overlay appears in the bottom-left side of the screen.

Be sure to turn on the Title Safe grid when positioning your overlay. You can turn this feature on by clicking the Grid button in the Effect Editor.

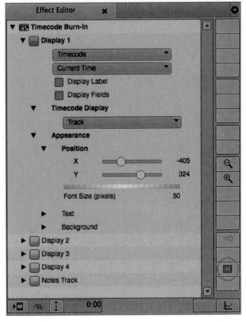

Figure 15.18 The Grid button in the Effect Editor.

11. To add the watermark, click the box next to **NOTES TRACK**.

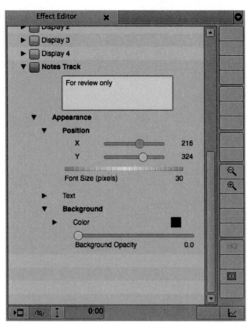

Figure 15.19 The box next to Notes Track is selected.

12. Open the parameters and make the following adjustments:

    • Type the text: "For review only"

    • Reduce the background opacity to 0.

    • Position the watermark in the bottom right corner of the screen, within title safe boundaries.

Figure 15.20 The new parameters are applied to the timecode overlay.

At this point, your cut is ready for review.

To conduct a live review of "15.1_ANESTHESIA_FOR REVIEW" using software only, proceed with the following steps:

13. First, open the **FULL SCREEN PLAYBACK** settings.

14. Configure the SETTING to use the preferred monitor. If using two monitors, it is recommended that you use the bin monitor.

15. Close the SETTING.

16. To review the sequence, choose COMPOSER > FULL SCREEN PLAYBACK.

17. If using an external client monitor, open the TIMECODE window and configure it so that it has point size of **50** or above.

18. Add an additional line to the Timecode window to display the SOURCE CLIP NAME.

19. Conclude the exercise by reviewing the sequence with a classmate and saving your work.

Exercise 15.2: Preparing "Anesthesia" for Output

In this exercise, we will prepare the final cut of the film "Anesthesia" for output as though we were delivering it for broadcast television. We will add bars, tone, and an identification slate in accordance with industry standard broadcast specifications:

Timecode	Duration	Information
00:59:00:00	00:00:10:00	10 seconds of black
00:58:30:00	00:00:60:00	60 seconds of SMPTE bars and tone
00:59:30:00	00:00:10:00	10 seconds of black
00:59:40:00	00:00:05:00	5 seconds of slate
00:59:58:00	00:00:02:00	2 seconds of black (The remaining time before the start of the program can be used for a countdown, if requested by the network. If so, you would leave a minimum of 2 seconds of filler (black) before Program Start. More than that is fine, too.)
01:00:00:00		First frame of Picture/Program (EFOP)

Media Used: Anesthesia

Time: 45 minutes

For this exercise, we will continue to use the **MC110_ANESTHESIA** project.

1. Begin by opening the bin **STUDENT_LESSON SEQUENCES**.

2. Duplicate the sequence **15.2_ANESTHESIA_OUTPUT** and move the duplicate sequence into the **ANESTHESIA_OUTPUT** bin.

3. Add today's date on the end of the duplicate sequence name **15.2_ANESTHESIA_OUTPUT**.

   Use only numbers in the naming convention mmddyy. For example, if today it is June 24, 2016 – your sequence should be called "15.2_ANESTHESIA_OUTPUT_062416".

   In a real world situation, adding the date will help you to keep track of multiple versions or revisions to the final sequence.

4. Right click in the Timeline and select TIMELINE SETTINGS.

5. In the Timeline Settings window, click on the EDIT TAB.

6. In the START FILLER DURATION entry box, you will customize the duration to 1 minute and 30 seconds. To do this, TYPE in **00013000**. When you have correctly completed the change, press **OK**.

7. Right-click in the Timeline and from the menu, select ADD FILLER > AT START.

   Media Composer will add the 1 minute, 30 seconds you specified, and backtime automatically for you. Your sequence still begins at 01:00:00:00, exactly as it should.

8. Now create a new bin to store the assets we need to add to your output sequence. Click CTRL+N (Windows) or COMMAND+N (Mac).

   Name the new bin "ANESTHESIA_OUTPUT ASSETS."

   Import your color bars.

9. In the **ANESTHESIA_OUTPUT ASSETS** bin, right click and choose INPUT > IMPORT MEDIA.

10. In the Import window, navigate to:

    Windows: Program Files\Avid\Avid Media Composer\SupportingFiles\Test_Patterns\HD 720\SMPTE_Bars.tif

    or

    Mac: Applications/Avid Media Composer/SupportingFiles/Test_Patterns/HD 720/SMPTE_Bars.tif

    Before you import the Color Bars:

    • Set the Resolution to 1:1.

    • Select the drive to store the media file that is created.

    • And very importantly, you must ensure their accuracy by doing the following: Click the Options button. This will open the Import Settings .In the Import Settings window, the following are the correct settings to import Avid's SMPTE Color Bars correctly:

       a. Image Size Adjustment: Image sized for current format.

       b. Color Levels: Do not modify, treat as legal range.

       c. Alpha Channel: this file does not have an Alpha channel, so you do not have to worry about changing this.

       d. File Import Duration: 60 seconds.

11. Click **OK** to close the Import Settings Window.

    You can now import your Color Bars.

    Your color bars will now be imported into the bin.

12. Create your SMPTE tone. Open your Audio Tool using the key command CTRL+1 (Windows) or COMMAND+1 (Mac) or choose TOOLS >AUDIO TOOL.

13. Click the **PH button** and choose **Create Tone Media** from the drop-down menu.

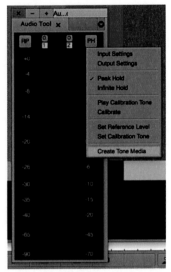

Figure 15.21 Selecting Create Tone Media from the Audio Tool PH menu.

14. In the pop-up window, set the length of the tone media to 60 seconds, choose 2 as the number of tracks to create, and set your target bin to **ANESTHESIA_OUTPUT ASSETS**.

The gain of your tone should be set to -20db.

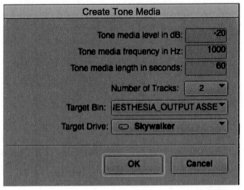

Figure 15.22 The parameters you should set in the Create Tone Media dialog.

15. Finally, using your Title Tool, create a slate with the following information:

- MC110 Version 8 Curriculum
- "Anesthesia" Final Cut
- Edited by Your Name
- TRT: 01:07:12
- Today's Date

 "TRT" means total running time.

16. Save your slate to the **ANESTHESIA_OUTPUT ASSETS** bin.

17. Load the **Color Bars** into the Source monitor and **Overwrite** them starting at the very beginning of the sequence.

18. Load the 1K tone you created into the Source monitor. Overwrite it exactly in sync with the Color Bars.

    Be sure to disable V1, so you don't overwrite your Color Bars.

19. Add your slate. Load your slate into the Source monitor and mark an **IN**.

20. Type **+04:23** and press Enter. Mark an **OUT**.

    When you check your Center Duration display, you'll see that you have correctly marked 5 seconds of the slate.

21. In the Timeline, go to **00:59:40:00** and mark and **IN**.

22. Overwrite the slate into the sequence.

23. Check to make sure everything is working properly and that all the sequence assets are starting at the appropriate timecodes.

    If everything looks good, you are now ready to export the final cut of Anesthesia!

Exercise 15.3: Outputting "Anesthesia"

In this exercise, we will perform a quick audio mixdown and output a digital file of the film "Anesthesia".

Media Used: Anesthesia

Time: 30 minutes

A best practice when outputting a sequence is to mix down both audio and video tracks. This flattens the sequence into a single file for each track

1. The exercise assumes you are proceeding from where the previous exercise left off. If you have taken a break, reopen the project **MC110_ANESTHESIA**.

2. In the **ANESTHESIA_OUTPUT** bin, duplicate the sequence **15.2_ANESTHESIA_OUTPUT** and rename it **15.3_ANESTHESIA_EXPORT**.

3. Load the **15.3_ANESTHESIA_EXPORT** sequence into Timeline.

4. Move the **POSITION INDICATOR** to the first frame of the program (at 01:00:00:00) and mark an **IN**.

5. Press the **END** key to jump to the end of the sequence, and mark an **OUT**.

6. Select tracks **A1–A5** and deselect **V1** and **V2**.

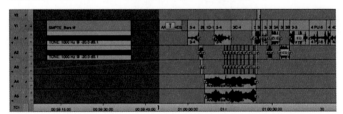

Figure 15.23 Selected tracks A1–A5 and deselected V1 and V2.

7. Choose TIMELINE > MIXDOWN > AUDIO > TO SEQUENCE.

8. Using the controls, configure the following Audio Mixdown settings, as shown in Figure 15.30:

    • **Dual Mono:** Selected

    • **Bin:** ANESTHESIA_OUTPUT ASSETS

    • **Drive:** Your media drive

    • **Save Premix Sequence:** Selected

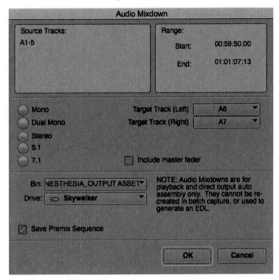

Figure 15.24 The Audio Mixdown settings you should have configured.

9. Click **OK** to begin the mixdown process.

    When the mixdown is finished, the mixdown audio appears on new A6 and A7 tracks, as shown in Image 15.19, and two new items appear in the Output bin:

    • A duplicate sequence called "15.3_ANESTHESIA_EXPORT.premix.01". This is the sequence before the mixdown.

    • A new master clip with the suffix "15.3_ANESTHESIA_EXPORT,Audio Mixdown,1" This is the flattened audio in a single Master clip.

Figure 15.25 The sequence in the Timeline after the mixdown.

10. Load the sequence, **15.3_ANESTHESIA_EXPORT** from the **ANESTHESIA_OUTPUT** bin.

11. In the **15.3_ANESTHESIA_EXPORT** sequence, move the **POSITION INDICATOR** to the first frame of the program (at 01:00:00:00) and mark an **IN**.

12. Press the **END** key to jump to the end of the sequence, and mark an **OUT**.

13. **SELECT** the **A1-A5** tracks and deselect all others.

14. Remove the old audio using the **Z (LIFT) KEY**.

15. Using the red **LIFT/OVERWRITE SEGMENT TOOL**, drag the mixdown audio tracks on A6 and A7 up to A1 and A2.

16. Hold down the **SHIFT+CTRL** (Windows) or **SHIFT+COMMAND** (Mac) key to keep the tracks from moving out of place.

17. Next, select the **V1** and **V2** tracks and deselect all others.

    All sequence video material is now selected.

18. Choose **TIMELINE > MIXDOWN > VIDEO**.

19. Select the **OUTPUT** bin, your **MEDIA DRIVE**, and **DNxHD 115**.

20. Click **OK** to start the mixdown.

    This process is longer than the audio mixdown. Any video material that isn't already at the target resolution will be converted. The result is a single master clip in the Output bin with the suffix "15.3_ANESTHESIA_EXPORT,Video Mixdown,1."

    Load the video mixdown **MASTER CLIP** into the Source monitor.

21. With the sequence still marked as before, press the **B** key to overwrite the video onto V1.

    You will now have one continuous track of video, and two continuous tracks of audio.

22. Scrub through the sequence and makes sure everything looks okay.

    If everything looks and sounds good, proceed with the export.

23. Press the **G** KEY to ensure that there are no marks in the Timeline.

24. Make sure all your video and audio tracks are enabled.

25. Choose **SELECT FILE > OUTPUT > SEND-TO > MAKE NEW**.

    The Send To dialog box opens.

26. Click the **SET** button located at the top right to determine the save location, for the QuickTime file you'll create.

27. A Browse window opens. For the purposes of this class, select **DESKTOP** and then click **OPEN**.

28. Enable the checkbox for **EXPORT SETTINGS 1**. Then from the menu, choose **SEND TO QT MOVIE**.

    This opens the Export Settings window.

29. In the top-right, deselect (uncheck) all of the selections.

    The codec of your master file will depend on the specifications provided by the client you are delivering to, but, for the purposes of this exercise, you will use the H.264 codec.

30. Enable the **CUSTOM RADIO BUTTON**. Then select the **FORMAT OPTIONS BUTTON** that has appeared on the right.

    The QuickTime window opens.

31. Set the following settings:

- Settings button:

  a. Compression Type should be H.264.

  b. Set the compressor Quality to Medium

  c. Set the Encoding to Faster Encode (Single Pass)

- Size: Current

- Sound: Make sure the Sound checkbox is enabled

- Prepare for Internet Streaming: This checkbox can be left enabled all the time, and the selection set to Fast Start.

Figure 15.26 The QuickTime Settings dialog.

32. After all the QuickTime settings have been set, click **OK**.

33. In Avid's Export Settings window, select **VIDEO AND AUDIO**, if it's not selected already.

34. From the Width x Height Fast menu, select 1920 x 1080.

35. In the Color Levels section, **KEEP AS LEGAL RANGE**, which is for broadcast.

36. Click **SAVE AS** and name the template **BROADCAST H.264 MEDIUM QUALITY**.

Figure 15.27 The Save Export Settings dialog with the newly named template.

37. Click **OK** to close the Export Settings window.

    The Send To dialog box appears again.

38. Click **OK** and your file will begin exporting to the desktop.

39. Once your file is finished exporting, check it to make sure it is complete and conclude the lesson by saving your work.

Managing Project Media

Working effectively on any editing system requires familiarity with certain technical concepts. These concepts form the foundation of everything that happens in an editing system. In this lesson, we will focus on those related to media management. Understanding them will enable you to make informed decisions throughout the project—from production and acquisition to editing, finishing, output, and delivery.

The first part of this lesson is a technical primer, really. It appears at the end of the book instead of the beginning because a certain degree of familiarity with the tools and terminology is required to discuss these concepts in context. This lesson will provide you with enough information to deepen your understanding of many of the concepts taught in this book. It should also help you recognize topics with which you're unfamiliar and that merit deeper study if you are planning on a career in TV, film, or video production.

Media Used: TN PARKOUR

Duration: 60 minutes

GOALS

- Locate media files associated with a clip
- Use the Media Tool to identify and delete project media
- Consolidate and Transcode clips and sequences

Managing Your Media

Avid is famous for its robust media management. It uses a simple system that keeps the user from directly interacting with the media files. Instead, you are given simple, powerful tools to manage your media through Avid. If you are used to directly interacting with your media files, this can feel restrictive. You will soon come to appreciate the freedom you have to focus on the creative process of editing.

All media files created by Media Composer through capture, import, render, and so on go to the same place, shown in Figure 16.1: *media drive*\Avid MediaFiles\MXF\1.

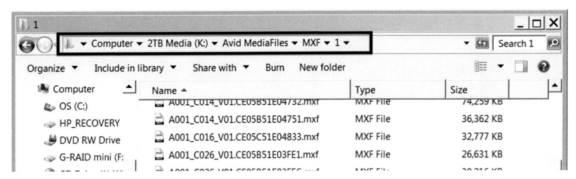

Figure 16.1 All Avid media files are organized together in the same location.

Media Composer puts all the files it creates from all projects into the same folder (indicated with a 1) until it reaches the limit: 5,000 files. Then it starts a folder labeled "2", and so on. Besides the MXF media files, each folder has two database files: *msmFMID.pmr* and *msmMMOB.mdb*. (See Figure 16.2.) Media Composer uses the database files to track each file's metadata and all the metadata links that relate to those media files.

FK-1102.WAAU4.CEU5C51EU4891.mxf	MXF File	15,561 KB
Hatun_RuA01.51EDA881.50CA70.mxf	MXF File	569 KB
msmFMID.pmr	PMR File	27 KB
msmMMOB.mdb	MDB File	1,333 KB
ssV01 CF05R989 511851F04149.mxf	MXF File	323,151 KB

Figure 16.2 The two Avid database files catalog the media in the folder.

You have no direct control over which file goes into which folder, nor can you separate the files by project. Again, some may find this frustrating at first. You may want to double-click a media file to see which clip it is. Or, you may want to grab all the clips from one project and organize them into a folder. From Media Composer's viewpoint, you're working backward. Instead of going to the files, use the tools provided in Media Composer to bring the files to you, letting you manage your media more efficiently.

Identifying a Media File

You may remember from the last course, you can easily identify the media file linked to a master clip in the bin.

To identify a media file:

■ Select the file in the bin, and then choose FILE MENU > REVEAL FILE.

An OS window will open, with the linked file(s) selected. If working on a Windows-based system, and more than one file is linked to the clip, the system will show you the first file. When you reactivate Media Composer, a dialog window will prompt you to view the next.

Using the Media Tool

You manage your media with the Media Tool. It allows you to see the media files on all mounted hard drives in a display that is similar to your bin. You can use the Media Tool to view and delete the available media files. The Media Tool also allows you to track down all media files used in a particular project or sequence.

To identify all the media associated with a project:

1. Open the PROJECT whose media you want to see.

2. Choose TOOLS MENU > MEDIA TOOL.

    The Media Tool Display dialog box opens, as shown in Figure 16.3. Here you can select the drives, projects, and media file types you want to see.

    Precomputes are how Media Compose refers to render files, and are identified by type.

    Generally there is no need to select Media Files for display. Displaying them is equivalent to looking at the files at the OS level and is typically used only to troubleshoot a problem with the assistance of Avid technical support staff.

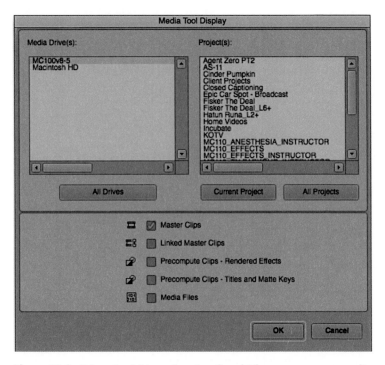

Figure 16.3: Select the drives and project for which you want to see media.

3. Click the ALL DRIVES button; then click the CURRENT PROJECT button.

4. Ensure that the MASTER CLIPS check box is checked, then click OK. The Media Tool opens, displaying the online master clips associated with this project, as shown in Figure 16.3.

 Media files are associated with the project in which they are created. Master clips borrowed from another project will only show up in the original project in which they were created.

Media Composer creates its media using the MXF OP-atom format, which means that it creates a separate file for every track of media in the master clip. When you choose to view the master clips, Media Composer presents associated V1, A1, and A2 files together as a master clip for convenient viewing.

Name	Tracks	Start	End	Duration	Mark IN	Mark OUT
Woman on Wall.new.01	V1 A1-2	00:00:00:00	00:00:20:22	20:22		
Woman on Wall	V1 A1-2	00:00:00:00	00:00:20:22	20:22		
Timelapse Group Working Hospital.new.02	V1 A1-2	12:17:21:11	12:17:30:15	9:04		
Timelapse Group Working Hospital.new.01	V1 A1-2	12:17:21:11	12:17:30:15	9:04		
TimeLapse Clouds Over Mountain.new.01	V1 A1-2	13:20:12:04	13:20:30:07	18:03		
TimeLapse Clouds Over Mountain	V1 A1-2	13:20:12:04	13:20:30:07	18:03	13:20:13:15	13:20:15:07
Tilt Up Control Panel.new.02	V1 A1-2	15:19:13:17	15:19:36:02	22:09		
Tilt Up Control Panel.new.01	V1 A1-2	15:19:13:17	15:19:36:02	22:09		
STE-012.old.01	A1-2	00:00:00:00	00:29:31:18	29:31:18		
STE-012	A1-2	00:00:00:00	00:29:31:18	29:31:18		
STE-006.old.01	A1-2	00:00:00:00	00:22:15:05	22:15:05		
STE-006	A1-2	00:00:00:00	00:22:15:05	22:15:05		
Sliding Solar Panel.new.01	V1 A1-2	00:00:00:00	00:00:24:20	24:20		
Packing Solar Panel_WS.new.01	V1 A1-2	10:15:11:08	10:15:37:11	26:03		
Packing Solar Panel_WS	V1 A1-2	10:15:11:08	10:15:37:11	26:03	10:15:20:18	10:15:37:11
Packing Solar Panel_CU	V1 A1-2	10:14:01:16	10:14:19:10	17:18	10:14:04:11	10:14:07:11
Packing Solar Panel_CU	V1 A1-2	10:14:01:16	10:14:19:10	17:18	10:14:07:05	10:14:08:15
MVI_3512.new.01	V1 A1-2	00:00:00:00	00:00:27:03	27:03		
MS Teaching about Electrical Box.new.02	V1 A1-2	15:10:34:13	15:11:02:08	27:19		

Figure 16.4 The Media Tool looks and functions much like a bin.

The Media Tool looks and functions very much like a bin, making it immediately familiar. It provides the same database functionality as a bin, including the ability to sort, sift, display column headings, and view clips in Frame, Text, or Script view.

Restoring Master Clips to a Bin

You can drag master clips from the Media Tool into bins. Although not a common task, it is useful in a couple ways.

First, suppose you accidentally deleted master clips and their associated media files, but have the media files saved on a backup media drive. You could restore those clips to the bin using the Media Tool. Mount the backup drive, use the Media Tool to look at all media from the current project on that drive, and drag the clips back to a bin. To move the media from the backup drive to the media drives holding the rest of the project, you could use the Consolidate/Transcode tool, discussed later in this lesson.

The other way this is quite useful is when you want to copy or convert all of the media for a project without going through all the bins. You can easily set up the Media Tool to identify all master clips from a given project, drag all those clips to a new bin, and then copy or convert those, again using the Consolidate/Transcode tool.

Deleting Media Files

One of the primary uses of the Media Tool is for deletion. Unlike when you delete from a bin, deleting from the Media Tool will only delete media from the drive, not master clips or other bin-level metadata. The most common type of file to delete is a render file, or as Media Composer calls it, a *precompute*.

Deleting Render Files

Render files are created when you render an effect, obviously, but also when you create titles, freeze frames and motion effects, or when you import a matte key. While any of these *can be* recreated, it may be an inconvenience to do so. Media Composer v8.6 includes separate designations for the different types of render files in the Media Tool Display to make it easier to display only those types of precomputes you may wish to delete.

Going a step further, you can also identify the render files that are not in use by any of the current sequences. The Fast menu in the Bin and the Media Tool alike contain a command to select only unreferenced clips, as shown in Figure 16.5 Render files without an active link to a sequence are considered unreferenced.

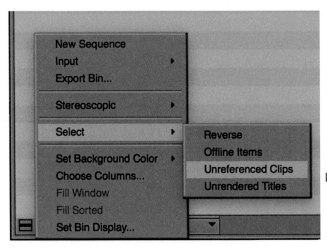

Figure 16.5 The Select > Unreferenced Clips command helps identify unused media that may be ready for deletion.

To delete unused render media using the Media Tool:

1.   Open the **MEDIA TOOL**.

2.   In the Set Media Display window, select the following:

     a.   The **DRIVE(S)** on which to view media

     b.   The **CURRENT PROJECT BUTTON**

     c.   The **CHECKBOX** for **PRECOMPUTE CLIPS – RENDERED EFFECTS**.

3.   Click **OK**.

     The Media Tool opens, displaying the clips.

4.   Open the **BIN(S)** containing any sequences for which you want to *keep* the render files.
     This is a critical step. The system does not track links to items in closed bins.

5. In the Media Tool, select the FAST MENU > SELECT > UNREFERENCED CLIPS.
   An alert message appears, informing you that the system will only take into account links to items in open bins, as shown in Figure 16.6.

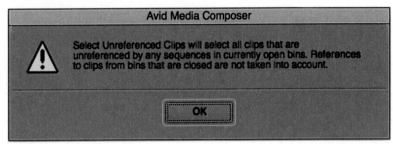

Figure 16.6 The alert message explains why it is so important to open the sequence bin first.

6. Click **OK**, and the unreferenced clips are selected for you.

7. Press **BACKSPACE** or **DELETE**.

   The deletion dialog box opens, as shown in Figure 16.7.

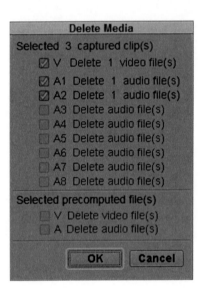

Figure 16.7
The Delete Media dialog box from the Media Tool lets you delete individual media files, which correspond to each track in the master clip.

8. Select (or deselect) the track-specific files to delete, and then click **OK**.

   Another confirmation dialog box opens, asking for final confirmation, as shown in Figure 16.8.

9. Click the **DELETE** button to delete the files.

Figure 16.8 A second dialog box asks you to confirm that you are doubly-sure that you want to delete the files.

Media deletion is permanent. You cannot Undo. Exercise caution whenever you delete media.

Deleting Unused Project Media

On larger projects, the Media Tool is sometimes used to delete media mid-project that will not be used in the final sequence.

A feature-length documentary film, for example, could easily have more than 20 hours of footage captured. Let's say the initial rough cut is 2.5 hours long, and after screening it with the director, it is decided that you got all the best stuff in. The final film will be drawn only from what is in that 2.5-hour sequence. That means so you could safely delete the other 17.5 hours of footage from your drives. In the optional Exercise 16.3, you can go through the steps to perform a task similar to this.

The same workflow described above could be used to delete unused media files. Let's review the key points.

To delete unused media files:

1. Open the MEDIA TOOL to display all the MASTER CLIPS from the CURRENT PROJECT on ALL DRIVES.

2. Open all the BIN(S) that contain sequences for which you wish to *keep the media* online.

3. In the Media Tool, select the FAST MENU > SELECT > UNREFERENCED CLIPS.

4. (Optional) Take a deep breath.

5. Delete the media.

Concluding a Project

Knowing how to properly wrap up a project is important to your long-term success. One of the tasks is to delete all project media from the media drives regularly used for editing. If not done properly, "orphaned" files—media from old projects for which you no longer have master clips in bins—are left behind, collecting on the drives like detritus at the bottom of an unused pool.

Deleting media, though, is just the final step. Prior to deleting the media, all project assets need to be archived in some way. Typically, this means preserving the original media sources, graphics files and fonts, saving a copy of the project folder, and copying all sequence media to another drive that can be stored long-term. (Copying the sequence media to another drive would be done using Consolidate, covered later in this lesson.) Once those tasks are complete, you can safely delete all project media, confident that you could restore the project at a later date if needed.

To delete all project media:

1. Verify that all archive tasks have been completed.

2. Disconnect the archive drive, if still attached.

    This is an important safety step to ensure you don't accidentally delete the archive.

3. Open the MEDIA TOOL.

4. Click the ALL DRIVES and CURRENT PROJECT buttons.

5. Select **MASTER CLIPS** and both **PRECOMPUTE CHECKBOXES**. Then click **OK**.

   The Media Tool opens, displaying the project media.

6. Press Ctrl+A (Windows) or Command+A (Mac) to select all items.

7. Press Backspace or Delete.

8. Select all available tracks in the Delete Media dialog box and click OK.

9. Click OK again to confirm the deletion.

 Exercise Break: Exercise 16.1
Pause here to practice what you've learned.

Understanding Consolidate and Transcode

Consolidate is an important media-management tool. When you consolidate, the system finds the media files associated with (linked to) the selected master clips and copies that media to a target drive that you specify. In the case of subclips or sequences it will copy only the portion of the file associated with the clip. Then, it will either keep or delete the original files, depending on your direction.

No doubt you can think of at least a couple scenarios in which you would want to simply copy the media. If, however, you copy a clip and choose to delete the original, the result is that you have **moved** the media from one drive to another. Obviously, this is equally valuable at other times.

Use Consolidate to do the following:

■ Move media files from one drive to another.

■ Copy media files from many disks onto one disk.

■ Clear excess media by consolidating subclips.

■ Clear excess media by consolidating a sequence.

Transcode is a special type of consolidating that simultaneously converts the resolution of your clips and/or sequence during the copy operation. Unlike Consolidate, it will not delete the original media when finished.

Use Transcode to:

■ Capture at high res and transcode to low-res media (e.g. for offline editing).

■ Downconvert from HD to SD media (e.g. for offline editing or delivery).

■ Upconvert SD clips in a mixed SD-HD sequence.

■ Prepare to output a sequence with mixed SD-originated and HD material.

■ Convert from MPEG LongGOP (HDV) to HD for more efficient editing.

■ Homogenize sequences with media of mixed frame rates before output.

■ Perform general clip-conversion tasks such as removing 2:3 pulldown from 29.97i sources (to generate 23.976 sources) or generating NTSC material from a PAL source.

Both Consolidate and Transcode can be used with AMA mixed media. In fact, it is generally recommended that you consolidate or transcode AMA linked media at the earliest opportune moment in the workflow for maximum performance. Of the two, Consolidate is faster, but only works on MXF formats. Transcode can convert any linked file. Processing time varies.

Using Consolidate

Using Consolidate is quite simple. The harder part is mentally keeping straight where your files are and where you want them to go. Start with a bin view that shows the drive on which the media currently resides. You may even want to sketch a quick diagram to better visualize it, as shown in Figure 16.9.

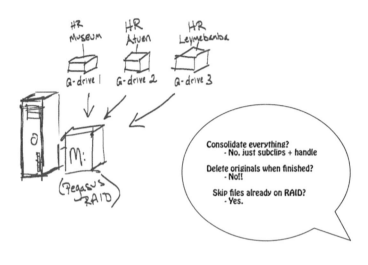

Figure 16.9

If consolidating subclips containing footage on multiple drives, which options should you choose? A sketch can help.

To consolidate clips:

1.   Open a BIN and select the master clips whose media files you want to consolidate.

2.   Choose CLIP > CONSOLIDATE/TRANSCODE.

     The Consolidate/Transcode dialog box opens.

3.   Select the CONSOLIDATE option button in the upper-left corner, as shown in Figure 16.10.

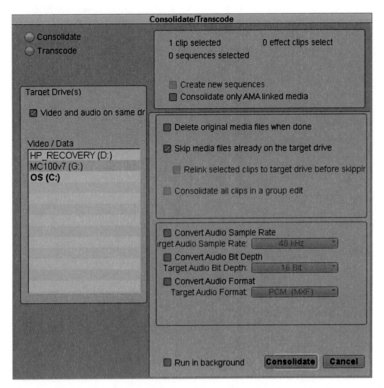

Figure 16.10 Choose Consolidate or Transcode using the option button in the top-left corner.

4.   Choose video and/or audio target DRIVES. This determines the destination for your consolidated media.

5.   Choose options for handling the media:

     • Choose to delete the original media files when done to "move" the media or to eliminate the excess from the originals.

     • Choose to skip media files already on the drive if some media already exists there and you don't want redundant copies.

     • If you select the Skip Media Files Already on the Target Drive option and you previously copied some of the media files to the target drive, select Relink Selected Clips to Target Drive Before Skipping.

6.   Optionally, convert the audio by choosing any of the AUDIO CONVERSION options.

7.   Click CONSOLIDATE.

   When you consolidate subclips or sequences, new master clips are created with a new duration, based on that of the subclip or the segment in the sequence (plus the Handle duration you dictated).

If you did not choose to delete the original media files when finished, you will have two sets of media files for the clips in your bin. To ensure that you can differentiate the copies, Media Composer will create a duplicate set of master clips. When you click Consolidate, Media Composer will ask you to choose which set the original media files to link to. (See Figure 16.11.) The master clips pointing to the other drive are given a .old or .new extension.

Figure 16.11
Choose which drive to link your masters clips to, and by extension how you want the "other" clips labeled.

Basically, this is a question of which drive you want Media Composer to be looking at for those media files. If you choose to link the original master clips to the new media files, the others are called "old." If you choose to keep the original master clips linked to the original media files, the others are called "new." In the sketch example, you should pick the Target Drive option because you would want Media Composer to be looking at your Pegasus RAID for that media. As a result, the master clips associated with the original media files on the G drives would be appended with the .old extension.

Using Transcode

While the Transcode and Consolidate processes have some similarities, transcoding is really designed for changing your resolution or frame rate while you copy media. Also, it does not offer the option to delete media upon completion of the Transcode operation.

Perhaps the most common need you will have for transcoding is to convert AMA linked media to native Avid MXF for better performance, such as with H.264-encoded QuickTime movies from a DSLR. For this, simply choose the target resolution and drive. If those clips are already edited into a sequence, you can efficiently convert only the AMA linked media in the sequence by enabling the Transcode Only AMA Linked Media check box, as shown in Figure 16.12.

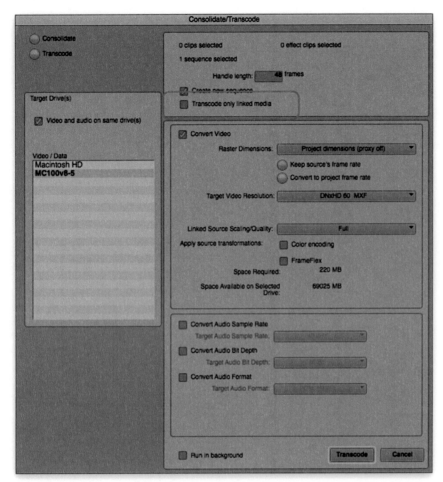

Figure 16.12
If transcoding a sequence, you can restrict the operation to convert only the AMA linked media by enabling the Transcode Only AMA Linked Media check box.

With transcoding, you can change clips of any edit rate, including clips that you have edited into a sequence, to any resolution available within your current project. You might need to transcode mixed-rate material as part of common workflows like offline/online conversion or creation of a QuickTime reference movie. By default the radio button is set to CONVERT TO PROJECT FRAME RATE, as shown in Figure 16.12.

To transcode clips:

1. Decide on the TARGET RESOLUTION.

2. If your target format is different from the current project format, choose the TARGET FORMAT in the FORMAT tab of the Project window. For HD projects, also choose a RASTER TYPE setting.

3. In a bin, select the CLIPS or SEQUENCE that you want to transcode.

4. Choose CLIP > CONSOLIDATE/TRANSCODE.

5. Select TRANSCODE in the upper-left corner of the window.

6. Choose video and/or audio TARGET DRIVES.

    This determines the destination for your transcoded media.

7. (Optional) Choose TRANSCODE ONLY AMA LINKED MEDIA to restrict which clips are converted.

8. Click the TARGET VIDEO RESOLUTION pop-up menu and select a VIDEO RESOLUTION.

9. (Optional) Click the radio button to CONVERT TO PROJECT FRAMERATE.

    Be aware, however, that converting a clip(s) to a different frame rate will preclude the ability to later relink back to that original file (s).

10. Choose the appropriate AUDIO CONVERSION options for the target media.

11. Click the TRANSCODE button in the lower-right corner.

    When the transcode is finished, new master clips will appear in the bin, named .transcoded.**n**.

 The drive whose name is bold is the drive with the most available space. It may or may not be the drive you want to use, however. This is true in all dialog boxes in Media Composer that show a list of drives.

Background Processing

Consolidate and Transcode can both be run as background processes. A small check box at the bottom of the Consolidate/Transcode dialog box enables you to specify that the job should run in the background, as shown in Figure 16.13. This lets you continue editing while the media is being copied or converted.

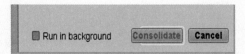

Figure 16.13 To be able to continue working while a Consolidate or Transcode job runs in the background, select Run in Background.

As a background process, it will take longer to copy or convert the files. If you continue editing, the system will allocate its resources to editing tasks first; anything left over goes to background processes. The advantage is that your editing experience is not degraded as a result.

It is recommended that you have a minimum of 16 GB ram to use this feature, so it is disabled by default. If you have less, it may not work properly.

When using background processing, the master clips (metadata only) are created immediately, and are offline until the media process has finished. Then they are automatically relinked to the new media files.

 Exercise Break: Exercise 16.2 and 16.3
Pause here to practice what you've learned.

Review/Discussion Questions

1. Which function can be used to find the media for a clip?

    a. Match Frame

    b. Find Bin

    c. Find

    d. Reveal File

2. What can you use to see render files?

    a. Clear Renders command

    b. Effect Editor

    c. Smart Tool

    d. Media Tool

3. Name the media database files.

4. Which function can be used to convert the format of a media file?

    a. Consolidate

    b. Link to Media Files

    c. Reveal File

    d. Transcode

5. Why is it important to open a sequence bin before you identify unreferenced clips?

6. True or False. If you accidentally delete an important media file, you can use Undo to restore the file.

Media Management

Understanding media management and being able to perform it reliably is a critical skill for long-term success. It can also help differentiate you in a meaningful way from your competition when going for a job. Like anything, the more you do it, the more comfortable you will become. This exercise will help you build familiarity with the tools, giving you the opportunity to perform some common media-management tasks.

Media Used: TN PARKOUR

Duration: 40 minutes

GOALS

- Locate media files associated with a clip
- Use the Media Tool to identify and delete project media
- Consolidate or transcode AMA-linked media to Avid-native MXF

Exercise 16.1: Deleting Render Files Using the Media Tool

In this exercise, we will demonstrate how to delete render files from a particular project using the Media Tool.

Media Used: Tennessee Parkour

Time: 15 minutes

For this exercise, we will use the **MC110_TN PARKOUR** project.

1. Begin by opening the bin **MC110_TN PARKOUR** project.

2. Choose **TOOLS > MEDIA TOOL**.

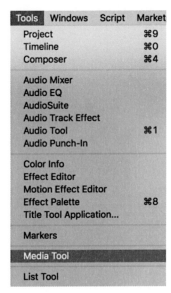

Figure 16.14 The Media Tool option on the Tools menu.

3. In the Media Tool Display window, select **ALL DRIVES**.

4. Select **CURRENT PROJECT**.

5. Check the box next to PRECOMPUTE CLIPS – RENDERED EFFECTS.

    Be sure only this box is checked.

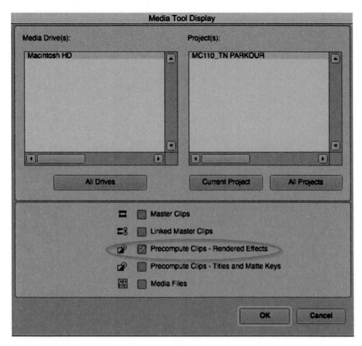

Figure 16.15 The "Precompute Clips – Rendered Effects" option from the Media Tool Display dialog.

6. Click **OK** to open a list of rendered effects in the Media Tool.

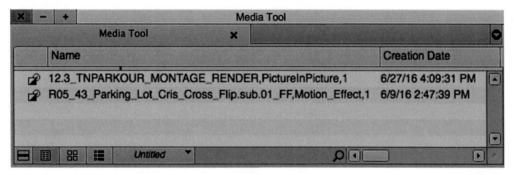

Figure 16.16 The rendered effects displayed in the Media Tool.

7. At this point, you can continue with the deletion of render files, with the permission of your instructor, or you can back out of the Media Tool and conclude the exercise.

    Although the Media Tool is very useful for media management, deletion of files from the Media Tool is permanent-so proceed with care!

Exercise 16.2: Consolidating Media from the "TN Parkour" Project

In this exercise, we will demonstrate how to consolidate (copy) media from one drive to another, using the Tennessee Parkour Project as an example.

Media Used: Tennessee Parkour

Time: 15 minutes (plus consolidation time)

For this exercise, we will use the **MC110_TN PARKOUR** project.

1. Begin by opening the bin **STUDENT_LESSON SEQUENCES**.

2. Duplicate the sequence **16.2_TNPARKOUR MONTAGE_FINAL** and move the duplicate sequence into the **TNPARKOUR_EXERCISE SEQUENCES** bin.

3. Select the **16.2_TNPARKOUR MONTAGE_FINAL** sequence in the **TNPARKOUR_EXERCISE SEQUENCES** bin.

4. Choose **CLIP > CONSOLIDATE/TRANSCODE** or right-click on the sequence and choose **CONSOLIDATE/TRANSCODE** from the drop-down menu.

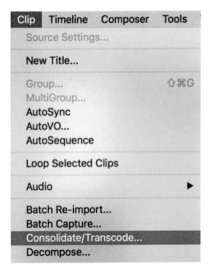

Figure 16.17 The Consolidate/Transcode option from the Clip menu.

This will open the Consolidate/Transcode dialog.

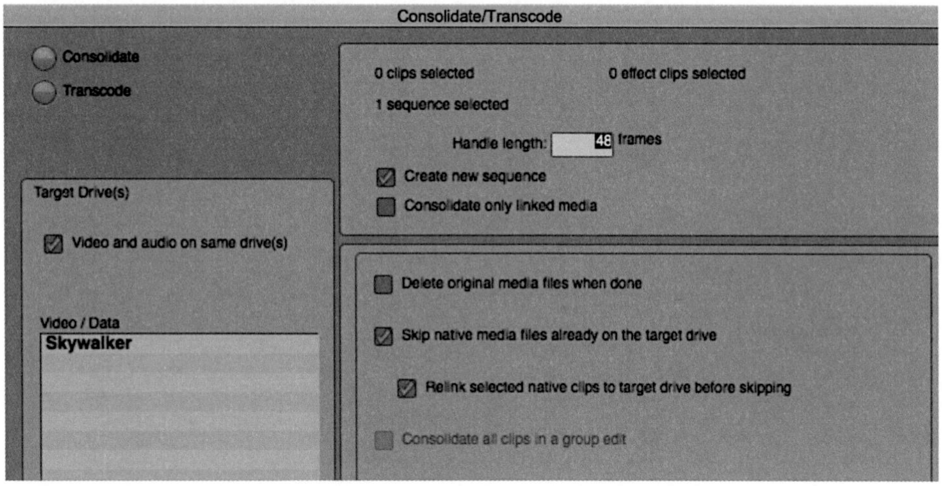

Figure 16.18 The Consolidate/Transcode dialog.

5. In the Consolidate/Transcode dialog, choose the following:

    a. Make sure "Consolidate" is the selected operation in the upper left corner

    b. Select the hard drive you wish to consolidate to from the list of available drives

6. From here you have several other options, most notably:

    a. You can choose to create a new sequence that points to the consolidated media or redirect the "16.2_TNPARKOUR MONTAGE_FINAL" sequence to the copied media on the new drive. Creating a new sequence is the safest option.

    b. You can choose to delete the media files on the current drive once they have been copied to the new drive. Do this only if you're at the end of a project and wasn't to clear drive space, as well as maintain a playable sequence.

    c. You can convert all the audio files in the project to the same audio specs.

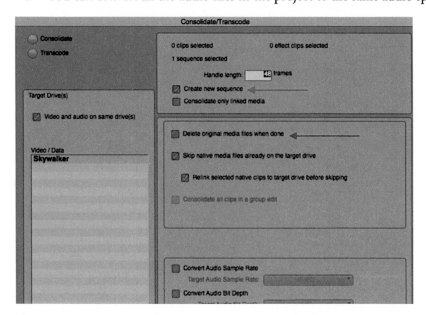

Figure 16.19 Options you should choose in the Consolidate/Transcode dialog.

7. Once you are satisfied with your selections, you can stop at this point and back out of the Consolidate/Transcode window, or you can proceed with the consolidation if directed by your instructor.

Exercise 16.3: Delete Unused Project Media Files

As projects grow, so does the likelihood of having unused media. Even in today's world of cheap hard drives, storage space is not limitless. Especially if you are working high-performance media drives, you may wish to remove unused media from those drives to free up space for other projects. In this exercise, you will go through the steps to identify unused media.

 Media deletion is permanent. If completing this course at a school, do not delete any media unless so directed by your classroom instructor.

Media Used: TN Parkour

Duration: 10 minutes

1. Open the PROJECT.

2. Choose TOOLS MENU > MEDIA TOOL.

3. Select ALL DRIVES.

4. Select CURRENT PROJECT.

5. Select MASTER CLIPS and both PRECOMPUTES checkboxes.

6. Click OK to open the Media Tool.

   The Media Tool displays all media for this project. You are going to delete any clip(s) not being referenced by the final sequence, but first, you need to find out which is which.

7. Without closing the Media Tool, open the bin TNPARKOUR_EXERCISE SEQUENCES.

8. In the MEDIA TOOL, select the FAST MENU > SELECT > UNREFERENCED CLIPS.

   A dialog box appears, explaining how the function works. As you see, this function selects any clips that aren't being referenced by any sequences in an open bin. At the moment, that means it will only highlight a clip if it is not referenced by **any** sequence in the TNPARKOUR_EXERCISE SEQUENCES bin.

Figure 16.20 The dialog box that appears to confirm your selection in the Media Tool Unreferenced Clips.

9. Click OK.

Stop here unless directed by your instructor to continue.

Index

Volume Automation mode, 197
volume, level display and slider, 186

W

watching raw footage, 22-23
watermark, adding, 408-409, 433
waveforms, for syncing audio, 66-69
workflow, overview, 4

X–Z

XDCAM media format, 424-426
    export to disc, 424-425
    export to file, 425-426
Yellow Ripple Trim, about, 152